The Confederate Congress

WILFRED BUCK YEARNS

THE CONFEDERATE CONGRESS

THE UNIVERSITY OF GEORGIA PRESS

DEDICATED TO MY PARENTS

Paperback edition, 2010
© 1960 by the University of Georgia Press
Athens, Georgia 30602
www.ugapress.org
All rights reserved
Printed digitally in the United States of America

The Library of Congress has cataloged the hardcover edition of this book as follows:
Library of Congress Cataloging-in-Publication Data

Yearns, W. Buck (Wilfred Buck).
The Confederate Congress.
293 p. 25 cm.
Includes bibliography.
1. Confederate States of America. 2. Congress. 3. Confederate States of America—
Politics and government. I. Title.
E487 .Y4
973.713   60-9897

Paperback ISBN-13: 978-0-8203-3476-9
ISBN-10: 0-8203-3476-6

CONTENTS

	Preface	vii
I	Secession and Confederation	1
II	Life at the Confederate Capitals	11
III	Trial and Error Government	22
IV	Congressional Elections	42
V	Mobilization of Manpower	60
VI	Conscription Under Attack	74
VII	More Men!	86
VIII	Of Officers and Men	102
IX	Economic Organization	116
X	The Conduct of the War	140
XI	The Writ of Habeas Corpus	150
XII	Foreign Affairs	161
XIII	The Peace Movement	171
XIV	Financing the War	184
XV	The Loyal Opposition	218
	Appendix: *Biographical Notes on Confederate Congressmen*	236
	Notes	245
	Bibliography	270
	Index	280

PREFACE

THE TASK OF DESCRIBING THE WORK OF THE CONFEDERATE CONGRESS can be approached only in the light of the peculiar circumstances of war. During wartime the value of a single source of responsibility has given the American president a special predominance over the other branches of government. His powers as commander-in-chief are great; he epitomizes the war effort, and the people, whether they like or dislike his policies, recognize his leadership. On the other hand, Congress is a deliberative body designed to reflect varying interests. Its laws are ordinarily compromises, and when compromise is impossible important matters are delayed, abandoned, or ignored. But during a war, when survival issues face the government in quick succession, indecision seems weakness and inaction seems almost treasonable. If Congress passes an unpopular administration measure, it shares the responsibility of that measure with the president; if Congress rejects an administration measure, it is considered uncooperative; if Congress proposes alternatives to the president's suggestions, it is considered discordant. Consequently a wartime American Congress has difficulty distinguishing itself.

The Confederate Congress was no exception to this wartime legislative predicament, for all considerations in the Confederacy were secondary to winning the war. At first Congress and President Jefferson Davis were in essential agreement on how to win the war and, save for minor exceptions, the administration's program was obediently enacted. This program demanded few sacrifices from Southern people and was generally acceptable to them. The last half of the war saw this harmony change somewhat. The increased pace of war forced the administration's program to be more demanding; people then became restless and Congress began voicing their discontent by asserting itself in law-making. Generally Congress only modified the administration's measures, but on occasion it either substituted its own ideas or refused to act at all. Whatever it did, Congress was unable to make a good reputation for itself. Supporters of the Davis administration censured Congress for its occasional independence; critics of the administration urged Congress to assert itself more often. Congress's reputation stems from the fact that it consistently pursued neither of these courses. While originating few major policies, it probably meddled too much with those of the administration. In all that it did, however, Congress gave the impression of a devoted body hard at work.

My research carried me into each of the Confederate states, as well as into the Library of Congress, the National Archives, and the New York Public Library. Everywhere that I went the assistance rendered me was as gracious as it was competent. I express particular appreciation to Dr. Fletcher M. Green of the University of North Carolina for the help that he gave me so unsparingly.

WILFRED BUCK YEARNS

Wake Forest College
Winston-Salem, N. C.

SECESSION AND CONFEDERATION

THE MEETING OF THE CONFEDERATE CONGRESS ON FEBRUARY 4, 1861, was the climax of a long sequence of events. Secession, which had finally occurred earlier in the winter, seemed to most Southerners the logical result of a series of sectional contests in each of which the South had been compelled to retreat. During the last half of the 1850s events had become critical. The struggle over Kansas was proof enough to the South that the North intended to confine slavery to its existing realm and ultimately to abolish it. Until this time two national party organizations had helped bind the nation together, but the decrepit Whig party fell apart over the Kansas issue, while the Democrats barely managed to hang together. In 1856 the election of the Democrat James Buchanan gratified the South, and two days after his inauguration the Supreme Court handed down the Dred Scott decision. Since the decision ruled that Congress could not bar slavery from any territory, to the South the slavery issue seemed settled. The North, however, denied the permanency of this ruling, and Southerners began to believe that not even the Constitution could guarantee their rights within the Union. In 1859 John Brown, the leading anti-slavery zealot in Kansas, came eastward to liberate the slaves. Federal troops easily broke up his raid on Harper's Ferry, Virginia, and on December 2 he was executed. But Southerners misjudged Northern sympathies and were inclined to feel that Horace Greeley expressed the majority opinion when he wrote that "the noblest manhood in America swings off the gallows of a felon."[1]

Sectional antagonism was aggravated by the upsurge of the Republican party. While this party favored a curb on the extension of slavery, not its abolition, Southerners seldom distinguished between the two ideas and believed that a strong sectional party with an anti-slavery basis was the ultimate threat to their civilization. This threat was intensified by the Republican nomination in 1860 of Abraham Lincoln for the presidency. Though Lincoln himself was no abolitionist, his public utterances so obscured his political aims toward slavery or hit so directly at its moral and social evils that the South despised him.

For this reason Southerners, fearing danger not only to slavery but also to the way of life associated with it, rejected the possibility of a Republican administration. Northern industry and Southern agriculture were developing a rivalry which manifested itself in national legislation on most economic matters. With their staple crop economy naturally dependent on an industrial system, Southerners began to recognize themselves as colonists economically dependent on an aggressive business world. As the economic imbalance between the sections increased, the colonists might expect continued diminution of profit.

In their extremity Southerners considered separate state secession always a potential, even though undesirable, refuge from the politically intolerable. They venerated the nation they had helped to win and the Constitution they had helped to write, but they would not submit to the perversion of both. Secession was a clear-cut solution in which they had implicit faith. Slavery would then be untroubled and the new government would rest on acceptable principles. They were confident that they could dictate terms of secession by threatening to withhold cotton from Northern mills.

In April of 1860 the Democrats held their national convention at Charleston, South Carolina. After heated sessions the platform committee submitted majority and minority reports. The "Yancey platform" insisted that the federal government protect slavery in the territories and that the party pledge itself to uphold the Dred Scott decision. The supporters of Stephen A. Douglas, fearing alienation of Northern Democrats, countered with a platform of territorial determination of slavery. When the convention adopted the Douglas program, a majority of the delegations of the lower South walked out in protest; the disrupted convention, unable to choose a candidate, adjourned to meet at Baltimore. When a similar walk-out occurred at the Baltimore meeting, those remaining nominated Douglas and Herschel V. Johnson of Georgia. The Southern bolters then held their own convention and nominated John C. Breckinridge of Kentucky and Joseph Lane of Oregon, with a strictly Southern platform.

One other party entered the lists at this time. The Constitutional Union party, composed mostly of old Southern Whigs and of

Secession and Confederation 3

such elements of the Know-Nothing party as were unwilling to unite with the Republicans, convened at Baltimore and adopted a middle-of-the-road course. They appealed to a distraught country on the sole issues of maintaining the Constitution, the Union, and the laws. They nominated the conservative candidates John Bell of Tennessee and Edward Everett of Massachusetts.

In the four-sided contest that followed, each candidate maintained devotion to the Union; however, the final choice made was probably the one most likely to disrupt it. When the votes were cast on November 6, Lincoln had 180 electoral votes, Breckinridge 72, Bell 39, and Douglas 12. Breckinridge carried the entire lower South plus Delaware, Maryland, and North Carolina. Bell carried Tennessee, Kentucky, and Virginia. In ten of the Southern states Lincoln received not a single popular vote.

The vote for Breckinridge, neither an immediate secessionist nor a complete adherent to Southern principles, did not necessarily indicate the precise strength of secessionism. Moreover, his opponents, all of whom opposed secession, together received 120,000 more votes in the slave states than he. Nevertheless the vote implied that a majority in the lower South considered Lincoln's election provocation for secession. It is also true that the Bell and Breckinridge votes were anti-Lincoln votes, votes to avoid secession by defeating Lincoln, and thus revealed Southern willingness to consider secession should Lincoln be elected.

Radical Southerners now opened their secession guns with full force. Unionists complained that they did not present the issue fairly to the popular mind,[2] but to a people already conditioned to possible secession Lincoln's election itself was sufficient catalyst. Congressman Reuben Davis promised that, if the people of Mississippi submitted to Lincoln, he would leave Washington five days before the inauguration, that his eyes "might never behold the degradation of the South."[3] Lawrence M. Keitt of South Carolina vowed that Lincoln would *"never* receive the homage of Southern gentlemen."[4] Robert Toombs asked the Georgia legislature for the sword or "as God lives, I will take it myself!"[5] A little later his scholarly friend Thomas R. R. Cobb declared simply that "We can make better terms out of the Union than in it."[6] Most influential was the address of a number of Southern congressmen to their constituents that "All hope of relief in the Union" was gone and that "the sole and primary aim of each slaveholding State ought to be its speedy and absolute separation from an unnatural and hostile Union."[7]

Some Southerners denounced this "impatient, overbearing, dictatorial and intolerant" attitude.[8] They believed secession as yet unwarranted, and Alexander H. Stephens, the leading Southern unionist, told the Georgia legislature that the election of no one man could outweigh the benefits of union. They pointed out that Lincoln lacked unanimous support in the North, that he represented only one branch of the federal government, and that the Democrats would probably win Congress and be able to neutralize his authority. Furthermore they maintained that there was no reason to believe that a Republican administration would reject further efforts at compromise. These Southern unionists admitted the theoretical right of secession, but urged that the South await an overt act by the Lincoln government. Secession would mean war, to be avoided if at all possible.

Meanwhile the chain reaction to Lincoln's election was already under way. Alabama and South Carolina had promised conventions to consider secession in the event of a Republican victory and the other lower South states had been almost as specific. When the election results were known the South Carolina General Assembly ordered a convention for December 17 to consider secession, and within a short time the Gulf states followed suit.

The selection of delegates to these conventions crystallized a new political alignment that was to be of importance in Confederate politics. Those favoring immediate and separate state action were variously known as "secessionists," "straight-outs," "Southern rights men," and "Democrats." They argued that delay and indecision would dampen public enthusiasm, while positive action would unite the lower South and persuade doubtful states to follow. Many wanted the border states to remain temporarily in the United States to serve as buffer areas; they could join the others when the initial problems of reorganization had been solved. Needless to say, they considered separate state action only for withdrawal; for the future they visualized a Southern union.

The "cooperationist" or "conservative" group held a hodgepodge of opinions on when and how to secede. Some, like the South Carolina National Democrats, talked much of cooperative secession with other states, but were actually working to preserve the union. Others were convinced unionists compelled to work under a more respectable banner. Most cooperationists were merely cautious secessionists. They contended that separate state action would result in a group of isolated and vulnerable states. Some, though uninterested in further compromise, sought to

Secession and Confederation 5

strengthen their course by joint action, even with only two or three other states, but the majority wished all the cotton states and preferably all slave states to act together. Usually they proposed a national convention to give the Northern states a last chance to concede all Southern demands.

Even as late as January, 1861, every state had its embarrassing group of unionists. These "submissionists" contended that secession would solve nothing, and a hopeless minority of them known as "Ultras" were unwilling to secede under any circumstance. Unionists were so generally despised, even to the extent of having vigilante committees organized against them, that in the secession conventions they usually posed as cooperationists.

As it worked out, cooperation was being achieved even before the conventions assembled. During the late fall of 1860 the states had been informally exchanging commissioners to determine a joint course of action. On December 17 Governor Christopher Gist assured the South Carolina convention that several other states were merely awaiting its leadership. The situation, however, was too uncertain for most cooperationists, who sought in the conventions to restrain their impetuous associates. The general procedure in these conventions was the submission of a resolution proposing immediate secession, quickly countered by a cooperationist substitute proposing a final ultimatum to the North and further guarantees that, in the event of its rejection, secession would be accomplished collectively. The final vote, however, was close only in the Alabama convention, and with defeat certain many cooperationists voted for secession to avoid appearing divided on resistance to Republican rule. By the end of January, 1861, the seven states of the lower South had left the union.

During this critical interim, one assurance stood out with remarkable clarity: the states, when and if they seceded, would form a Southern union. Leaders both publicly and in correspondence presupposed such an immediate regrouping, and in early December, 1860, several congressmen in Washington advised their constituents that "the honor, safety, and independence of the Southern people are to be found only in a Southern Confederacy."[9] By now the states were exchanging commissioners to bolster each other's courage with assurances of union; generally the secession ordinances mentioned a "Southern Confederacy" or a "Union of slave states." Indeed secession when it actually occurred was considered no more a disunionist movement than a demonstration that the lower South was finally united.

After adopting an ordinance of secession the South Carolina convention realized that it was now separate from the South as well as from the North and felt compelled to continue its leadership. On December 31 it assigned commissioners to each slave state holding a convention, invited their cooperation in the formation of a Southern Confederacy, and briefly proposed a plan of union. The seceding states should meet in convention before March 4 at the latest, with each state entitled to one vote and represented by a delegation equal to its former congressional membership. They should organize a "Provisional Government" based on the Federal Constitution, which would last until a new constitution could be written and a "Permanent Government" established. It then took the first step by electing eight South Carolina deputies to the proposed convention.[10] The impact of this action was soon felt in other states and swept many cooperationists into the secessionist ranks.

South Carolina had devised this invitation cleverly, particularly by offering the old Constitution as the basis for the new government. Conservatives were thus persuaded that no radical experiments in government would be attempted, and their response was gratifying. To the various conventions the South Carolina plan seemed a "complete scheme of confederation, capable of being speedily put into operation."[11] Even border states, admittedly distrustful of cotton state radicalism, might also be expected to secede when confronted with a "Southern Confederacy, with the Federal Constitution slightly altered to suit an entirely slaveholding community."[12]

According to the South Carolina plan the Confederacy was to be formed no later than the date of Lincoln's inauguration. Though President James Buchanan would never attempt to block secession, the incoming administration might be more aggressive. Safety demanded that the new president be confronted with a successfully operating government, not a weak scattering of helpless states. The Southern senators in Washington proposed February 15 as being early enough to organize and late enough to let Louisiana and Texas participate. Meanwhile they themselves could remain in Washington until March 4 to block any Republican tricks to give the incoming president emergency powers.[13] South Carolina contemplated naming the date February 15 and the place Montgomery, Alabama, but decided, for fear of arousing antagonism, to leave these details to others.[14]

Both the time and place of the Southern convention seem to

have been determined by the South Carolina commissioners, who, before leaving Charleston, had agreed among themselves to suggest February 4 and Montgomery. They did their work well, appearing before state conventions to read the South Carolina secession ordinance and to invite cooperation in the proposed new nation. Alabama accepted their suggestions on time and place, and on January 11, 1861, extended an invitation to all slave states to meet the people of Alabama in convention on February 4.[15] Meanwhile the other commissioners had promised their respective hosts a forthcoming invitation from Alabama. Several conventions, therefore, solemnly considered an Alabama invitation before it was actually extended.

South Carolina also set the pattern for electing delegations to Montgomery. All the conventions except that of Florida elected two delegates at large and one from each congressional district, a majority of the votes cast being necessary for election. Florida's convention gave up after two ballots and assigned the task of selecting delegates to Governor John Milton,[16] recalling, perhaps, an earlier John Milton's success with a convention of fallen angels. There was no popular election of a member to the Provisional Congress, and vacancies were filled either by state conventions or by legislatures, or, if both were in adjournment, by the president of the convention subject to future approval.

A few cooperationists maintained — with some validity — that the conventions should have called for popular elections. But an election before February 4 would have been impossible, and the vast majority agreed with William R. Smith that "the great importance . . . of having a common government to manage their federal and foreign affairs in the emergency now pressing upon them, outweighed . . . the considerations which suggested delay."[17] Legally the conventions were the people embodied and actually they represented with accuracy the mind of the people. Arguments to the contrary were mainly delaying tactics. The Alabama cooperationists made a last effort to exclude prominent secessionists from Montgomery by proposing that members of the convention and of the legislature be declared ineligible for election, but the proposal was defeated by a narrow vote.[18]

The most significant feature of the Montgomery convention personnel was its moderation, and the ordinarily pessimistic Alexander H. Stephens found "more conservatism . . . in Congress than I expected to see. . . ."[19] This healthy condition was attributable as much to the good judgment of the secessionists in selecting delegates as to the strength of their opposition. Most secessionists hoped to attract the border states and even part of the northwest United States and could offer no better self-recommendation than to share the task of organizing with their past opponents. Appeasing the cooperationists and the unionists was also desirable. During the early days of the Confederacy unity was a paramount consideration, and, as Professor William E. Dodd stated, the "universal acceptance of states' rights as a political truism made the realization of the scheme easy."[20] Even unionists accepted this truth and its concomitant, the right, if not the advisability, of secession. Since most Southerners agreed on the nature of the new union, there was little risk here. Finally many secessionists were wary of the radical leadership offered by some Southern hotheads. There had been some opposition even to electing Robert Barnwell Rhett of South Carolina to his own state convention because he was "so damned impracticable, that I am afraid he will kick up hell in the Convention. . . ."[21] William L. Yancey of Alabama was denied a seat at Montgomery by his state convention, a most unwilling sacrifice to the vigorous Alabama cooperationists.

This "maudlin disposition to conciliate the union men"[22] had one salutary effect: the new nation started on its precarious journey in relative harmony. Even Toombs and Stephens, representing opposite poles of opinion, established a temporary *"enteinte cordial"* [sic] which left the Georgia radicals "in a minority in our own delegation."[23] Stephens himself had accepted nomination to Montgomery to "do all I can to prevent mischief"[24] and at least during the first weeks showed some enthusiasm. Howell Cobb, a Georgia fire-eater whose "fat, pussy, round-faced" appearance belied his intensity of spirit, wrote that "everything is going on well and will end well."[25] He admitted that while there was "much diversity of opinion," there was "a general good feeling and disposition to unite and harmonize on whatever may be found the best policy."[26] James T. Harrison of Mississippi also reported that they were "all in good spirits & firm in the faith" even to the extent of accepting "the bloody issue of war . . . to secure our independence."[27]

The radical secessionists in turn suspected this accord, being particularly fearful that some delegates desired the accomplished fact of secession only to engineer a favorable reconstruction with the North. They witnessed with alarm the occasional references to their "rash and hasty action," the absence of several leading secessionists, and the presence of so many moderates. Rhett, who

...... *Secession and Confederation* 9

saw in the use of a provisional congress a delay that might lead to reconstruction, wanted to go swiftly into a permanent government. Thomas R. R. Cobb confided to his wife that some of the Alabama delegates were "not only re-constructionists but absolutely union men," and later added Jefferson Davis to his list.[28] Actually these worries were groundless for no one at Montgomery gave any indication of desiring reconstruction. Howell Cobb undoubtedly expressed the unanimous opinion by writing that "Such is the fixed & unalterable purpose" of the convention that "the first allusion has not been made to" reconstruction.[29]

Of the fifty delegates to Montgomery, the secessionists outnumbered the cooperationists and the unionists by slightly more than a three-to-two ratio, with Alabama and Mississippi having the only secessionist minorities. The Democratic majority was somewhat less, since Alabama and Louisiana had Whig majorities and Georgia was divided.[30] Thus the actuality of secession had little effect on the selection of delegates. Neither Whigs nor cooperationists were slighted for their earlier conservatism and the state conventions usually selected delegates whose sympathies were in accord with the district they represented.

As a whole the Provisional Congress represented a higher type of leadership than either of the subsequent congresses. Over half of the original membership had been members of their secession conventions, elections to which had eliminated many purely local politicians. The men prominent in 1861 had generally been long associated with major political parties and were not chosen, as later happened, to voice local complaints. Finally, when congressmen under the Permanent Constitution were forbidden to hold army commissions, some like Toombs, Keitt, and the Cobbs chose the more exciting field service.

Thirty-six members of the Provisional Congress had attended college and some were graduates of recognized professional schools. Forty-two were licensed lawyers, having studied at college or under private supervision; several, however, were not practicing attorneys. Colin J. McRae of Alabama was a prominent commission merchant, William Porcher Miles of South Carolina a college professor of mathematics, Thomas Fearn of Alabama a doctor, and James B. Owen of Florida a Baptist preacher. Seventeen were planters and two were editors. Christopher G. Memminger, born in Württemberg, Germany, was the only foreign-born member. Several had taught school while studying law, Jackson Morton was a leading Florida lumberman, and John H. Reagan had been and generally exhibited the manners of a Texas overseer. The average age of the members was 47, with Fearn at 72 the oldest and Josiah A. P. Campbell of Mississippi at 31 the youngest. Only the Georgia and the South Carolina delegations contained a majority of native sons; not a single member of the Florida, Alabama, or Texas delegation was born within the state he represented. Thirty-four had had previous legislative experience, twenty-four having served in the United States Congress. Charles M. Conrad of Louisiana had been secretary of war under President Millard Fillmore, and John Tyler had been the tenth president of the United States.

LIFE AT THE CONFEDERATE CAPITALS

WHEN THE DELEGATES AND THEIR FAMILIES BEGAN DRIFTING INTO Montgomery a few days before the convention they found a pleasant and provincial city located on a high bluff adjoining the Alabama River. Though small, the city was second in size and importance to Mobile and could boast of a number of iron foundries, mills, warehouses, and factories located on its outskirts. Communication was adequately handled by the Montgomery and West Point Railroad and by the Alabama River, which was navigable for some distance above the town. Most of the homes, fairly well centered in the town, were comfortable frame buildings with large gardens attached.

At the end of a long street up the city's hill and only a few minutes' walk from the business district stood the old state Capitol where the Provisional Congress met. It was a plain, quadrangular structure with Grecian pillars on its south front and broad flights of steps leading to its side porticoes. From a distance it appeared stately and imposing as it dominated the lesser buildings around it, but a closer look revealed an unkempt lawn and a general coating of tobacco juice, the customary plight of state houses then and now. The Alabama House of Representatives lent Congress its quarters during the stay in Montgomery. This was a large chamber with a gallery running half way around it which, together with the space directly beneath, accommodated curious visitors who when permitted flocked into the sessions of Congress. The downstairs visitors' area was separated from the congressmen's chairs only by a light, low screen, which did little to impede conversation when debate became dull. During the first few weeks the Montgomery ladies kept two tables in the hall covered with meat, fruit, and bread for the refreshment of members and visitors, but they discontinued this courtesy when the place became famous around town as a source of a good, free meal.

The people of Montgomery were eager to please their illustrious visitors and made every effort to offset the deficiencies of a small town. Governor Andrew B. Moore had the congressmen's hotel rooms provided with refreshments and stationery, and the townspeople conducted themselves with "every manifestation of respect."[1] The firing of the guns on Capitol Hill reverberated daily, and at night the streets rang with complimentary serenades beneath the windows of important officials and with their patriotic responses. After a few weeks Montgomery began to have "a real Washingtonian appearance."[2] Many congressmen and their families knew each other from United States days and kept the hotel lobbies filled with the same kind of talk and the same brand of cigar smoke. Lobbyists soon began to pressure congressmen at every hour of the day. A Montgomery joke was that lobbyists differed from congressmen only in that they chewed their cigars rather than smoked them. The first weeks were filled with rounds of receptions, dinners, plays, salons, and other entertainment, with the experienced ex-Washington crowd leading the way, and only the notoriously crude congressmen being snubbed. The president of the Alabama and Florida Railroad invited all of Congress to visit Pensacola and about twenty-five members accepted. Arriving about midnight, they were unable to find lodging and so spent the night in the train as best they could. The next day they were in poor humor for sight-seeing in the sultry weather, and the trip was a fiasco.

Montgomery was never able to compensate for its smallness and after the first enthusiastic weeks congressmen and particularly their wives began to be more and more conscious of personal discomforts. The city had but two hotels, and only the Exchange, at that time in the hands of a Northern firm, provided first-rate accommodations. It was a favorite headquarters for politicians and was crowded so much beyond its capacity that it soon became "horrible in its filth and astounding in its bills."[3] Several congressmen lodged in private homes, but even these were limited, for William Russell Smith found it so "impossible to get respectable or comfortable quarters" in a private home that he preferred to stay at the Exchange even though his roommate Robert Jemison snored "like a steam-boat."[4] The central Alabama weather distressed border state representatives, particularly those rotund like Robert M. T. Hunter of Virginia, while mosquitoes and flies plagued up-country people by their number, size, and appetite.

Meanwhile Congress and the President were contemplating

moving the capital for better reasons. So far the Confederacy had been the work of the cotton states and the administration properly decided to flatter the border states. Since Virginia, as the greatest producer of war materiel and food, could be expected to receive the brunt of the Northern attacks, Richmond won over the bids of several other cities from all sections. Montgomery merchants, who appreciated the free-spending outsiders, protested any suggestion of a move, and the Alabama legislature even offered to establish a federal district like the District of Columbia if the permanent seat of government remained in Alabama.[5] But only the Alabama delegation favored Montgomery. As the *Charleston Mercury* put it, "no thriving village in Texas would receive fewer votes than Montgomery."[6]

On April 27 the Virginia legislature invited Congress to make Richmond the new seat of the government. A month later Congress ordered the next session to convene there on July 20, authorized a small committee to make suitable arrangements, and appropriated $40,000 for the expenses of moving.[7] The removal was uneventful despite General Winfield Scott's oath, announced with pride by the Richmond papers, to prevent it, though the ladies now dreaded the added distance to Richmond on the closely packed and cinder-ridden trains. Some congressmen never accepted Richmond as the best location and at intervals for the next four years insisted that the capital be located in a more protected locality. Much later the pressure of Northern armies around Richmond became so great that Congress on May 27, 1864, authorized President Davis to designate whenever he saw fit any other place as the seat of the government.[8] It adjourned on March 18, 1865, and was no part of the refugee Confederate government that abandoned Richmond shortly thereafter.

At Richmond the Provisional Congress met in the State House, designed from a French model by Thomas Jefferson, in a room especially prepared for it. The room itself was pleasant and airy, about twelve by twenty-five yards in size, with the speaker's chair in the center opposite the room's entrance. The walls, however, were bare, the chairs uncushioned, and the desks "slashed with pocket-knives. . . ."[9] When the body was in open session visitors sat in small galleries at each end, and members sitting under them always complained about not hearing well there. A large stove in the rotunda provided inadequate heat, and chilly members sometimes kept their hats on for warmth.

When Congress became bicameral the House retained these

quarters and the Senate was left to shift for itself. Its regular place was on the third floor in a plain, dingy room, made by combining the adjutant general's room with an adjoining one. It was cramped and drafty, with only a rail to separate senators from spectators, and was so unsatisfactory that whenever the Virginia state senate was not in session the Confederate Senate moved downstairs into its chamber just across the rotunda from that of the House.

After a year in Richmond congressmen and members of departments were as hard pressed as ever for living accommodations. The standing committees engaged rooms or suites of rooms around the city, but unless they could get them in public buildings "the Shylocks of Richmond" overcharged them unmercifully. When James Lyons of Virginia suggested that Governor John Letcher build a room in the portico of the Capitol for the additional accommodation of the House, Letcher, with a Virginian's sense of proportion, answered that the addition would "mar the exterior of the building." Instead he offered his own office as a room for the speaker of the House and promised to provide more light and fewer drafts by re-arranging the doors in the House chamber.[10] In desperation the House assigned its Committee on Public Buildings to investigate renting or buying the Richmond Exchange Hotel. The Committee reported that the building would easily accommodate all of Congress and its committees, but Congress thought $24,000 rent or $175,000 for the purchase too high and by a close vote dropped the matter.[11]

While Congress often lacked admirers, it usually had attentive audiences, particularly during the first weeks of each session. In Montgomery spectators were especially enthusiastic, and "all Montgomery . . . flocked to Capitol Hill in holiday attire."[12] Ladies wore their best garb while visiting the galleries and provoked a continuous shuffling about by the men, particularly in Richmond where only rude timber seats were available, in their polite efforts to avoid crowding the ladies or treading on their skirts. The younger women enjoyed "ogling" the members of Congress during debate and plainly disconcerted some rural members who could hardly keep their wits about them. Miss Nelly Nisbet once threw handsome young Francis Bartow a bouquet, which Thomas R. R. Cobb, thinking it intended for him, intercepted. On learning differently, Cobb gallantly handed it over to his fellow Georgian. A Mrs. Fitzpatrick carried her attentions even further and, after sitting with Congress during the inauguration of President Davis, poked him "in the back with her parasol that

...... *Life at the Confederate Capitals* *15*

he might turn and speak to her."[13] Generally, however, the galleries behaved acceptably and neither house ever had to clear them for misconduct.

The most unusual outside participation occurred late in 1864 when a handsome lady called George Vest of Missouri into the lobby and without explanation began to belabor him with a cowhide whip. She then took the speaker's stand and stated that Vest had traduced her character and caused her husband to leave her by saying that she had been "on intimate and criminal terms" with Vest.[14] Vest retorted that she was probably "ration crazy" and denied any knowledge of her, and messengers were sent flying to newspapers asking them not to report the incident.[15]

Congress was not always able to resist a crowded gallery and at times feasted visitors with oratorical viands. There might be "windy dissertations on the color of the flag," on the prospects of the new nation, "on the establishment of a patent office," or "bearing on no special point. . . ."[15] Senator William L. Yancey of Alabama was the most renowned speaker in either house. Representative Francis B. Sexton of Texas, who once slipped across the hallway to hear him, reported a typical Yancey performance as "very interesting" and "one of the most withering pieces of sarcasm I ever heard."[17] In March, 1861, Mrs. James B. Chesnut wrote that all members had now "spoken in the Congress to their own perfect satisfaction," and were paying more heed to their jobs.[18]

Some of the older members imagined "that they [had] a prescriptive right to occupy the floor" and would sometimes speak "twice or thrice each day."[19] Henry S. Foote of Tennessee, a bald and pugnacious little man with an experienced impromptu delivery, was by far the worst offender in this respect, and tried everybody with his "many bills and stump speech preambles."[20] At times his colleagues lost patience with the tiresome Mr. Foote. On February 13, 1863, he was as usual trying to steer debate into one of his favorite channels when Augustus H. Kenan of Georgia accused him of being out of order. Foote replied excitedly that he was not to be lectured by the member from Georgia, whereupon Kenan threatened to "take the responsibility of teaching him manners or *anything else at any time.*" At the speaker's insistence both huffily came to order without blows.[21] Another incident involved Judge Edmund S. Dargan, an eccentric Alabaman known on the streets of Richmond for his "soliloquies" with himself and in Congress for his habit of addressing the speaker as "Mr. Cher-man." During debate Foote indiscreetly called Dargan a "d—d rascal," whereupon Dargan attacked Foote with a bowie knife. Several members threw Dargan to the floor and disarmed him, while Foote stirred the galleries into laughter by striking a pose and shouting, "I defy the steel of the assassin!"[22] Foote had two recorded fights outside Congress, one in a committee room with Thomas B. Hanly of Missouri, who pounded him severely, and one with a fellow Tennesseean, William G. Swan, who cut Foote's head with an umbrella and whom Foote probably would have shot had not Edward S. Pollard, editor of the *Richmond Examiner,* interfered.

The only Senate altercation seems to have been the one between Yancey and Benjamin H. Hill of Georgia. Hill accused Yancey of trying to disrupt the Confederacy, upon which Yancey scornfully berated Hill as an imitator and an imbecile. Hill angrily threw a glass inkstand at Yancey, grazing his skull. When Yancey calmly ignored this attack from the rear, Hill picked up a chair and rushed at Yancey, but was stopped and disarmed.

Generally Congress steered its heroics into better channels. On May 6, 1861, it officially declared war against the United States and authorized the President "to use the whole land and naval force . . . to meet the war thus commenced. . . ."[23] A year later the body pledged "unalterable determination . . . never, on any terms" to rejoin the United States or to slacken resistance to their aggression.[24] Its most thunderous pronouncement appeared in an address to the people on January 22, 1864, condemning the North and the Republican party, restating Confederate war aims, and asking the people for "life or fortune" if necessary.[25] Some members believed that frequent observations of days of fasting and prayer would induce God to *"intervene* & appear for our deliverance,"[26] but Congress and the President proclaimed such days only rarely.

The war strongly colored the outside activities of congressmen. In addition to the inevitable requests for civilian jobs, they received endless pleas for changes in army status. Enlisted men wished to be transferred to another company, to be stationed nearer home, to be assigned to less dangerous or arduous duties, or to be discharged because of illness or wounds. Officers asked for such favors as a transfer to the Quartermaster or the Commissary Departments, a post as a recruiting officer, a judge advocacy in a military court, or simply a promotion. Francis B. Sexton "Worked for a soldier till 11 A.M.,"[27] and most congressmen were as energetic. James T. Harrison handled his patronage correspondence during the afternoon sessions and stated that as they had no individual desks several other members were "writing away as hard as they can at the same table. . . ."[28] The departments usually respected the awarding of patronage with a consistent courtesy, and department letter books often bear such phrases as "you will call at the Department at your earliest convenience as he [the Postmaster General] wishes to consult you before filling the vacancy."[29]

After the First Battle of Manassas Richmond became a receiving depot for wounded soldiers, and the army hurriedly began to expand its hospital facilities in the city to accommodate them. Congress appropriated $5,000 to aid the work and appointed a committee of one from each state to cooperate with the city officials. These committeemen contacted citizens in Richmond from their respective states and set up a rough organization. Each state group worked independently of the others, but followed, in an amateurish way, about the same practices. The groups had varying degrees of success, depending mainly on their size. Some of their duties and services included providing regular visitors for their soldiers, organizing state "Relief and Hospital" associations, setting up soldier homes, assigning ministers to these homes and to the hospitals, securing cemetery lots for the deceased, enrolling ladies for certain nursing duties, and helping parents and wives find loved ones. Other congressmen helped wherever they could and the newspapers complimented some for their work. Thomas R. R. Cobb from time to time visited every wounded Georgian in the city. The Toombses entertained soldiers frequently and once had sixty or seventy "Wilkes Co. fellows" to dinner. William L. Yancey sold a favorite gift horse for $170.25 and donated the money to the hospitals, and Eli M. Bruce of Kentucky donated $1,000 to his state's Relief Society. John Perkins worked so diligently in the soldiers' behalf that the Louisiana legislature complimented his "ceaseless and untiring efforts."[30]

In May, 1863, all of Congress, together with other officials in the city, organized themselves into a volunteer company captained by William E. Simms of Kentucky and placed themselves at the call of the government. Their sole contribution to the war effort occurred on Dahlgren's raid near Richmond, when their particular assignment was to mount guard around the capital. On another occasion they were disgracefully routed when the Surgeon General proposed to vaccinate all the members and had no volunteers.

During their recess most congressmen served in other capacities. Some made speaking tours, stumping one or more states in behalf of the war. Those martially inclined enlisted as volunteer aides in the service of a general officer who was usually a personal friend. Texan Louis T. Wigfall, before his personal break with President Davis, was the latter's "sort of aid-de-camp" and enjoyed nothing more than galloping around with his pants stuck in his boots. Alexander R. Boteler of Virginia became an unofficial envoy with the special assignment of carrying messages between Generals Lee and Jackson. Many, however, preferred to stay in Richmond and try to direct as much attention as possible to their states' defense needs.

When not at work congressmen liked to idle around the streets and in front of public buildings. A large number usually concentrated near the War Department eager for news, though some awaited it in the offices of Department friends who kept good whisky. Hunter sometimes promenaded with different Cabinet officers and caused bystanders to speculate at what weighty decisions were in the making. "Speculators, contractors, government clerks, middle-men," and lobbyists were "as thick about the Capitol as vultures," and stayed busy "button-holeing every member they knew."[31] A few congressmen took law cases during sessions, while E. M. Bruce shocked everyone by investing in the Erlanger loan, which Congress had debated in strict secrecy. He hoped to dispose of his cotton to France at a fabulous profit, but when the House questioned his ethics he claimed to have revoked his contract. The House, after "a dozen furious speeches," then declared the subject closed.[32]

Living conditions in Richmond were at first much superior to those in Montgomery. Most congressmen brought their wives for the first sessions and usually stayed at one of the four better hotels, the American, the Ballard House, the Exchange, or the Spotswood. The city soon became thoroughly congested, however, and hotels began to pack even the parlors and halls with beds and to serve wretched meals. As a result private boarding homes sprang up on every block to accommodate the overflow. Since wives usually found these places as dull as the hotels were unbearable, most of them eventually stopped accompanying their husbands to Richmond. Some of the homes far excelled any hotel facility and became noted for their cuisine. Sexton thought that the meals at Miss Yarborough's were "good – but no dessert,"[33] and even the demanding Wigfall complimented the "good wood fires & plenty to eat" at Mrs. Winn's.[34] The choice lodging was at the home of Senator Thomas J. Semmes of Louisiana, who lived in a rented house opposite the executive mansion. Mrs. Semmes was good to her husband's friends, and graciously boarded Alexander Stephens, Augustus H. Garland of Arkansas, and Edward Sparrow of Louisiana. Toward the end of the war each of them paid her $900 a month, but as the expense of running the Semmes home by that time was about $25,000 a month the charge was only nominal.[35]

Hardly had the congressmen become settled when inflation began to drain their pocketbooks. Food prices were particularly exorbitant and in mid-1862 the *Richmond Enquirer* reported that the cost of living had increased over 1000%. A contemporary witticism was that "You take your money to market in the market basket, and bring home what you buy in your pocketbook."[36] In December, 1863, Clement C. Clay of Alabama was paying $75 a month "for room rent & attendance of servants" and $40 for coal and gas; he was forced to borrow $500 at 12% to get him through the session.[37] At the same time restaurants charged $10 for an ordinary dinner and hotel rooms were about $30 a day for half of a double room. Two unidentified congressmen struck against these prices and hired a Negro to do their marketing and to cook for them. When they ascertained that their first breakfast cost $14 they frugally abandoned the experiment and returned to their former boarding house.[38]

It is small wonder that the members awaited with open pleasure the end of the session when they could return home to a more attractive existence. Those from the border states and the West found that by 1863 trips home were always hazardous and often impossible. Once in the last of 1864 Sexton spent thirty-three tedious days in traveling from Texas to Richmond.

Richmond society was large and sophisticated enough to absorb the influx of congressmen without blinking, and quickly weeded out those not precisely *comme il faut*. The snubbing of undesirables was usually a matter of individual selection, though some delegations took on a group personality. Thomas J. Withers of South Carolina was most irascible and besides was "an avowed infidel" who had *"refused to kiss the Bible"* at President Davis's inauguration;[39] nevertheless he was politically and socially prominent at home and apparently the best Richmond circles enjoyed his biting wit. The Kentucky delegation was a model of decorum, and Mrs. Chesnut avowed that nowhere else could she find such nice men for a tea party.[40] Except for Wigfall, the Texas members were considered rough and conceited and frequented less exclusive groups. The Missourians were so uninhibited that their escapades reverberated back across the Mississippi to worry Governor Thomas Reynolds. Several drank excessively. Thomas A. Harris broke his leg in a gambling house so badly that he could not run for reelection in 1863. John B. Clark treated Cabinet officials with crude familiarity, once climbing through a window into Secretary of War George W. Randolph's room for a talk; he drank heavily until the "high price of liquor and fear for his health . . . improved his habits"; and the gossip was that he tried to steal Albert Pike's mistress.[41]

There were a few homes in Richmond of commanding prestige to which an invitation was a signal honor. Mrs. Robert G. Stanard had the nearest thing to a salon. She chose the most brilliant and brainiest but not necessarily the most important people, and entertained almost daily. James Lyons, an old school Virginian, resided in his home, Laburnum, about a mile outside the city and received only the cream of society. Guests probably enjoyed the Semmes hospitality more. Mrs. Semmes, lively and quick-witted, catered principally to the Confederate officialdom, and her food, mostly brought from Louisiana, made invitations particularly desirable. The gay, bohemian set flocked around the home of General James Chesnut and his vivacious wife. Her dinners were often thin and impromptu, but the conversation was excellent and the gossip choice. President Davis usually included a few congressmen at his evening affairs, showing no preference or exclusion; at his small breakfasts he entertained only personal friends or political supporters. He must have had difficulty receiving some of the latter gracefully. James Phelan of Mississippi, ordinarily a quick-witted and beguiling Irishman, once lectured General Robert E. Lee over breakfast and even planned a campaign for him, at which presumption Lee was said to have merely smiled blandly with only an occasional "mild sneer."[42]

None of the Richmond papers esteemed Congress very highly and there were several quarrels over the publishing of debates. Whenever a paper reported information taken from debates that Congress felt should have been confidential, the former maintained that any secret so poorly kept as to get into a reporter's hands was no secret at all. Congress several times discussed outlawing further publication of debate, but never took such action. While James T. Leach of North Carolina was unique in wishing to hang all editors "by their neck until they were DEAD, DEAD, DEAD!",[43] several others took offense at journalistic indiscretions. On January 7, 1864, the *Examiner* charged that an unnamed member took a $3,000 bribe to get three Jews passports to the North. When the House investigated the article Editor John M. Daniel apologized and explained that it had been published accidentally and against his express order.⁴⁴ In March, 1863, a Senate committee decided that an *Enquirer* article was couched in offensive and indecent language and the Senate excluded the paper's reporter for the remainder of the session.⁴⁵ The *Enquirer* insisted that its reporter was only summarizing the debates and presenting his opinion about them, but the next day was forced to print its farewell poem.⁴⁶

> Farewell to the Senate, that reverend body
> That grasps in its big paw the fate of the land;
> That discusses the strength of a treaty, or toddy;
> Where an army shall move — a reporter shall stand!
>   . . . .
> After asking a man to a seat on your floor,
> You abuse him, then give him no chance to be heard,
> Don't object, if he says, as he backs out the door,
> "We reverence no goat for his long and grey beard."

III

TRIAL AND ERROR GOVERNMENT

THE FIRST PRESSING TASK ON THE AGENDA AT MONTGOMERY WAS TO revive the routine operations of national government. Since old procedures would apply in most instances, there was a hearty disposition to continue them whenever possible. Opinion, however, was solidly in favor of a trial-and-error period to test the old Constitution under different conditions. There was also the possibility of trouble with the United States, and a provisional government was accepted because there was not time enough to form a permanent organization.[1] South Carolina had suggested that the provisional government last not more than two years, to be followed by a permanent government under a revised constitution, and the other states agreed with slight reservations. Georgia won the point that the temporary government should last no longer than twelve months. Mississippi insisted that the Permanent Constitution be written by a convention of the states, and her plan was given token compliance when the Provisional Congress, as it was called from the beginning, from February 28 to March 11 daily resolved itself into a convention to consider a permanent constitution.

But establishing the new nation required more than tinkering with a constitution. Officials had to be selected, agencies established, policies determined, defenses prepared, and the like, none of which was self-operative. Haste was particularly urgent, for Southerners feared that the North would stiffen its spine under Lincoln and find the Confederacy helplessly floundering. One discouraged delegate stated the problem in this fashion:[2]

With no Treasury at command, no machinery of government to raise & collect money, no national existence where credit can be pledged to get money & if it existed no credit upon which to raise it, no com-

. . . . . . Trial and Error Government 23

merce to pay duties, no custom house system to give commerce a start, no navy to protect it & no merchant marine with which to carry it on, no army to hold the ports on our seaboard, no postal arrangements for conducting intelligence & all these wants in the face of an apparently determined policy on the part of the old government to act quickly in seizing & closing our ports & cutting off our mail facilities I feel really like I was called on to build a great edifice in a short time without any tools or materials to work with.

These circumstances persuaded the majority that an immediate law-making body was mandatory. The delegations had been instructed to organize a provisional government and to write a constitution for the future permanent government, but beyond this their duty was less clear. Normally they would have written the constitution, ordered elections for a president and a congress, and adjourned; abnormal circumstances, however, brought delegates to Montgomery already fully determined to grant the convention legislative powers. The favored plan was the "Georgia project," whereby they would elect a president, assume all legislative powers, and thus become, without election, the Congress of the new government. On the second day Thomas R. R. Cobb proposed that a committee of 12 draw up a provisional constitution which would accept "this Congress as the legislative branch" of the Confederacy.[3] Strict state righters condemned this apostasy, but were unable to instruct the committee to order new elections. Two days later it reported a constitution under which "All legislative powers herein granted shall be vested in this Congress . . . until otherwise ordained."[4]

This presumption irked some of the state conventions. Mississippi had assumed a new election for a bicameral congress and had already elected its congressmen and senators; Florida had already announced beforehand that she would not consider such action binding.[5] Therefore their delegations at Montgomery felt bound to contest the action of Congress. Nevertheless when outvoted they acquiesced and later explained to their state conventions that necessity had forced them to waive their instructions. The Floridians maintained that for "a body of men . . . from distant sections of the country . . . to agree in a few days to a constitution . . . would have been wonderful, if not miraculous. The exigencies of the times admitted of but little if any delay."[6] Alexander M. Clayton of Mississippi told of "creditable information" that President Buchanan planned an immediate attack on Fort Sumter which had rendered their instructions impractical.[7]

Some conservatives back home could not swallow this boldfaced interpretation of the instruction to form a provisional government. Their newspapers maintained that the secessionists in Congress wanted to entrench themselves lest the people, now recovering from their secession hysteria, oust them in another election. It was rumored in Georgia and Alabama — and with some truth — that the secessionists feared an election for this reason, but undoubtedly a referendum would have sanctioned secession. However irregular the Congress's metamorphosis may have been, the Southern people probably would have accepted any action taken by their leaders.

The Alabama invitation had proposed that the Provisional Constitution follow closely that of the United States and every delegation had such instructions. There were practical as well as emotional reasons for the proposal. They were obsessed with the need for speed and harmony, and the use of a familiar model would simplify the transition. In addition, the thought of coming under a strange constitution written without their assistance might alarm the border states. These factors, combined with the Southern aptitude for parliamentary tactics, enabled Congress to write its first constitution in record time. Christopher G. Memminger, who was chairman of the Committee of 12, had come to Montgomery with a prepared draft for a new constitution, and on February 7 the committee reported to Congress proper. After one full day's discussion the delegates around midnight on February 8 unanimously ratified the Provisional Constitution, which Stephens gloated was "the Constitution of the United States, with such changes as are necessary to meet the exigencies of the times."[8]

The Provisional Constitution was no mere interim makeshift; it represented a serious effort to incorporate Southern state rights principles into organic law. The preamble omitted the "general welfare" clause, which had been used to add implied powers to the United States Constitution, and it referred pointedly to the "Sovereign and Independent States." States were permitted to have peacetime armies and navies, but could not wage war with a foreign power unless invaded. Congress became something of a throwback to the Philadelphia Convention of 1787. It consisted of one chamber representing the states, with a quorum being a majority of the delegations regardless of the number of congressmen present. Each state could fill its vacancies as it wished. The word "United" was omitted from the title, and "The Republic of Washington" rejected as a substitute, in preference to "Confederate," which one delegate said "truly expresses our present condition."⁹

The Provisional Constitution made a number of changes designed to improve the administration of government. Stephens and Toombs hoped to imitate the English cabinet form of government by requiring the president to select his cabinet from Congress. The Constitution failed to make this mandatory, but left the way open both for it and for congressmen to serve in the army by omitting the United States ban on plural office-holding. It attempted an economy by forbidding Congress to appropriate any money, other than for its own expenses, except at the specific request of the president, and by allowing him to veto any one or more items from appropriation bills. The authorization of an export tax indicated that Congress expected to derive a large share of its income from an export duty on cotton and tobacco.

Unlike the United States Constitution, which left to Congress the organization of inferior federal courts, the Provisional Constitution organized each state as a single federal judicial district, with the district courts, until otherwise provided by Congress, having the same jurisdiction as they did in the United States. No one of the United States had contained fewer than two districts and this economy proved most awkward when Congress began organizing the district courts in the large states. The error was corrected by the only amendment made to either constitution when Congress on May 21, 1861, was given the right to determine judicial districts as it saw fit.¹⁰ The Provisional Constitution provided for a Supreme Court to be constituted of all the district judges. This was a temporary arrangement, for a high court composed of judges of the next lower level of courts had been previously tried by many states without success. Judicial power was extended to all cases of law and equity arising under the laws of the United States, the purpose being to continue judicial procedure under way before secession.

The desire for haste forced Congress almost to ignore matters which had been under fire for a half century. For instance, only South Carolina favored an absolute ban on a protective tariff, and only she wished to continue the African slave trade. The fugitive-slave paragraph of the United States Constitution was actually weakened by shifting to the governor of the state to which the slave fled the responsibility either of returning him or compensating the owner for his loss.

It had been hoped that a full complement of slave states might write the Permanent Constitution, but the border states continued to waver and on February 9 Congress appointed another committee of two from each state to establish the "final form & boundaries of a Southern Confederacy."[11] For over two weeks the committee worked nightly from seven o'clock to ten and sometimes later, and finally reported on February 26. Thereafter Congress, acting in convention, devoted most of its working hours until March 11 to the meticulous overhauling of the report.

This period was filled with clashes of basic ideas. The radical state rights group was determined to complete the break with the philosophy of the United States Constitution, while the conservatives now felt free to combat experiments and innovations. Since the committee had been almost evenly divided between the two points of view, most problems were returned to Congress without the benefit of strong committee opinion. The result was that rivalry was keen and argument interminable. Stephens wrote his brother Linton that he was "in an agony" lest "some serious mischief" be done to the old Constitution and told of "some very bad passions and purposes" at work. He added that a divided state "saved us several times upon points almost vital."[12] During the discussion, Georgia and Alabama, and to some extent Mississippi, states with strong cooperationist elements, most often supported conservative doctrines. Florida and South Carolina voted consistently for a radical departure from the previous balance between the states and the central government. Sometimes debate became picayune — as when Thomas R. R. Cobb attempted to prohibit Sunday work for government employees — but generally the convention focused its attention on fundamentals.

The completed document was a mixture of rigid adherence to tradition, a desire to write a truly Southern constitution, and further recognition of practical flaws in previous ones. The long controversy on the nature of the union was now settled: the theory that the central government possessed inherent powers was abolished; it was only an agent of the states. The preamble designated the Confederacy as a "permanent federal government" with each state "acting in its sovereign and independent character. . . ." It was inevitable that the powers of the central government were now "delegated" rather than "granted," an unnecessarily explicit provision, since they would have been so interpreted regardless.

The rights and duties of Congress occupied the greatest attention, while the power of the dollar was manifested in the fact that most changes here related to fiscal matters. Georgia and Louisiana

...... *Trial and Error Government* 27

favored a protective tariff, but the majority decided that no import duties could be laid "to promote or foster any branch of industry. . . ."[13] Export duties were permissible by a two-thirds vote of both houses, though Louisiana again fought unsuccessfully for a guarantee that none of her products would be discriminated against. Financing local projects was discouraged by denying Congress the power to appropriate money "for any internal improvement intended to facilitate commerce" except certain navigational aids. To avoid a drain on the treasury, the Post Office Department was required to be self-supporting after March 1, 1863. A final precaution was taken by requiring Congress to set up a special court to handle claims against the Confederate government.

The presidency under the United States had generally been less inimical to the South than the legislative branch and changes here were mainly to remedy long-recognized procedural flaws. The Constitution continued the president's right to veto parts of appropriation bills and discouraged log-rolling by requiring a two-thirds vote of both houses for appropriations not requested by an executive department. Congress tried to formulate a way to elect the president without parties, conventions, or campaigns, but the idea of election by state legislatures or by Congress was deemed too conservative and the United States plan was adopted.[14] The appointment powers of the president were curtailed. He was forbidden to give recess appointments to nominees previously rejected by the Senate. He could remove cabinet members and diplomats at will, but had to explain to the Senate the dismissal of other executive officers. The Constitution now left to Congress the decision of whether its members could serve in the president's cabinet. This well-nigh worthless concession left department heads still responsible to the president, and the separation of powers unchanged.

Most of the changes in article III were designed to clarify the jurisdiction of federal over state courts. The United States and the Provisional Constitutions extended federal jurisdiction over controversies between citizens of different states, but in March, 1861, the radicals succeeded in striking out this clause. They made their most daring raid by proposing to remove the Supreme Court's appellate jurisdiction from any case that had been decided by a state court, and only a divided Florida delegation foiled them.[15] The same group proposed several other reductions of federal authority, but the good judgment of their ancestors and their fellows prevented further successes. Finally Congress struck from article

III the assignment of judicial powers to all cases of law and equity. Though the distinction between the law and the equity sides of the federal court was not abolished, the guarantee of legal rights and equitable remedies was left to Congress. The omission was in the interest of state rights, since it made it possible to correlate the operation of the federal courts with that of the state courts in Louisiana and Texas where the Roman concept of a single jurisdiction prevailed.[16]

South Carolina and Florida in particular, with scattered assistance from other delegations, insisted on re-evaluating the entire issue of slaves and slavery. Both constitutions banned the foreign slave trade except from the slaveholding states of the United States, and Congress could even make this ban complete if doing so would persuade any of the border states to join the Confederacy. South Carolina maintained, without success, that the matter was one of congressional policy rather than a constitutional principle. To induce other states to secede, Congress retained the federal ratio which allowed each state, for the purpose of representation, to count three-fifths of its Negroes in its total population. The duty of returning fugitive slaves was removed from the state governors and restored to the federal government. Citizens with their slaves were guaranteed the unimpaired right of transit through or sojourn in every state and territory, and both Congress and the territorial legislatures must support slavery in the territories. Several attempts were made to deny the admission of nonslaveholding states, and Rhett proposed to expel any state that abolished slavery. The majority decided not to hamper the possibilities for the growth of the Confederacy and defeated all such restrictions.

The hastily written Provisional Constitution had been silent on the matter of the admission of new states; a month later Congress appeared uneasy at the thought of leaving their control to the implied powers of the central government. It specifically permitted the acquisition of new territory, provided express authority for territorial courts, and permitted the admission of new states by a vote of two-thirds of both houses of Congress.

The procedural rights of the states were increased in two other ways. Any federal officer "resident and acting solely within the limits of any state" could be impeached by a two-thirds vote of that state's legislature. This privilege was never used though it was often discussed in relation to conscript and impressment officers. The state's role in the amending procedure was enlarged by reducing the participation of Congress and simplifying the initiatory action. If three state conventions agreed upon one or more amendments they could compel Congress to summon a convention of all the states to consider them, approval by two-thirds of the states being necessary for ratification.

In view of its emphasis on state rights, the Permanent Constitution surprisingly retained numerous limitations on the states and loopholes for an aggressive central government. This open-mindedness was of course based on the confidence that Southerners would never pervert their handiwork as the North had done. The prohibitions on the states almost duplicated those in the United States Constitution, and state officers were under oath to support the Constitution. The preamble dubbed the Confederacy a "permanent federal government"; the expandable "necessary and proper" clause was retained with heroic disregard of the fact that it had been a storehouse of implied powers; and the Constitution was still the "supreme law of the land," enforceable against contrary provisions in the state constitutions. All these went uncontested during debate! Three members tried to include the specific recognition of the right of secession, but others believed that its inclusion would discredit the claim that the right had been inherent under the old government.

The secession conventions had requested that this Constitution be referred to them for ratification. On March 12, Howell Cobb, president of the constitutional convention, forwarded the unanimously approved document to them with the advice that its differences from the United States Constitution "had been suggested by the experiences of the past," and "are intended to guard against the evils and dangers which led to the dissolution of the late Union."[17] Several congressmen hurried home to plead its case, but despite some grumblings, usually against its conservative nature, all conventions approved the document by large majorities. The only awkwardness was that no convention referred it back to the people, their reason being that any hesitancy in ratification would belie the claim of unanimity and the conventions were more dependable than the electorate. Many unionists and cooperationists, however, contended that former dangers no longer existed, and William R. Smith warned the Alabama convention that soon the people would ask, "In what, of all these things, have we been consulted?"[18]

Only in South Carolina was ratification more than a formality. Its convention felt that the new Constitution, though excellent, had dangerous defects; so, despite the "able and cunning arguments"[19] in its behalf by the South Carolina congressmen, the convention accepted it with reservations. On April 5 the convention resolved that as soon as the Confederacy was "securely established and in peaceful operation," South Carolina should demand a convention of the states to consider amendments to: (1) base representation and direct taxation on the total white and Negro population; (2) withdraw the right of Congress to borrow money on the credit of the Confederate states; (3) change the prohibition on slave importation from an organic compulsion to a congressional choice; (4) require the unanimous consent of all states for the admission of non-slaveholding states; and (5) limit import duties to 15%.[20] These points had been raised by South Carolinians during the writing of the Constitution; as they had been once defeated in debate they were later ignored by Congress, and the Permanent Constitution went unamended.

The next important task was to select a president and a vice-president. Many feared that an impromptu vote would reveal distressing political and personal differences; so Congress postponed the balloting a day to permit opportunity for backstage maneuvering. By this time several contenders for the presidency had emerged. Robert Toombs, the most consistent adherent of state rights of the Georgia Triumvirate, felt a vested right to the honor, while his friendliness and his reputation as a statesman more than offset his occasional intemperance in language and drink. "Little Alec" Stephens wanted it badly, but was personally and politically handicapped. He was eccentric and conceited, though withal rather shy. His unionism in 1860 and his rumored reconstructionism weakened him in the lower South where mention of his election to Congress had created "general and very unpleasant surprise."[21] Howell Cobb possessed a gentle and pleasing personality and was much admired for his work as Secretary of the Treasury under President Buchanan. He had been, however, a leading unionist in 1850 and an inconsistent Democrat, and these drawbacks, combined with his dread of the responsibility, had practically eliminated him by election time.

However much they deserved recognition, the radicals fared badly in the contest. Rhett and Yancey thought themselves logical candidates, but their colleagues disliked their principles and believed them too single-minded for good leadership. Yancey's own state had partly repudiated him by denying him a seat at Montgomery; Rhett indeed was there and much in evidence as he tried

...... *Trial and Error Government* 31

to take charge of affairs, but his candidacy did not even command the support of his own delegation. Congress was also determined not to endanger its courtship of the border states. Commissioners from Virginia "expressed much alarm at the idea" that Yancey might become president,[22] and this alone was enough to rule him out.

From the beginning the cards were stacked in favor of Jefferson Davis of Mississippi. His personal wish was to have chief command of the army, in which desire the Mississippi delegation supported him. But though the Mississippians were "wax in his hands," they would hardly ignore the favorable attitude toward his presidency, and for several days before the election were rumored to be backing his candidacy.[23] There was no denying his general popularity. During the Mexican War he had become the "Hero of Buena Vista," and had afterward been an outstanding Secretary of War under Franklin Pierce. Southern conservatives respected his disapproval of secession during most of the 1850s and even after the election of Lincoln. Secessionists remembered that he had been one of their leaders for a short time in 1851, and his retiring speech before the United States Senate was one of the most dramatic in senate history. Recently in the public eye because of his split with Stephen A. Douglas, for the moment he seemed the established leader in the Democratic party of the lower South.

Here again the desire for unanimity was evident, for there was little jockeying behind the scenes and "no effort made to put forward any man...."[24] Congress feared an impasse if electioneering was open and hoped that one man would secure a quick majority. The night before election the delegations of Florida, Alabama, Mississippi, and Louisiana met separately to canvass the field. It seems clear that from the beginning Mississippi and Florida supported Davis and that by February 8 Alabama had left Toombs for Davis when convinced that the border states preferred the latter.[25] These three states were certain Davis votes and one more would bring the remainder into line.

The *coup de grâce* to Toombs's hopes came from Georgia. A quick survey by some Georgians that night showed that Louisiana considered Toombs too radical, despite assurances by his friends to the contrary, and that they preferred Howell Cobb.[26] On learning this, Cobb, both to extricate himself and to spite Toombs, "announced his wish that Davis should be unanimously elected";[27] this announcement seems to have decided Louisiana for Davis. About this time South Carolina had wandered to the same conclusion, after being at first undecided between Cobb, Davis, and Toombs. Rhett did not call a caucus; so the delegates visited with each other far into the night discussing the candidates. Barnwell, working vigorously for Davis, seems to have convinced Rhett that he alone opposed Davis, while James Chesnut used the same tactics successfully on Judge Withers.[28]

When the Georgians met the next morning Stephens proposed to give Toombs the "complimentary vote" of Georgia. Toombs agreed to accept it if "cordially offered,"[29] but at that moment another Cobb entered the scene. Thomas R. R. Cobb disliked both Toombs and his politics and, moreover, was indignant about the latter's baiting of Howell over past politics.[30] To forestall even the nomination of Toombs he reported hearing that the other states were pledged to Davis and said that other nominations would bring politics into the open. Martin J. Crawford hurriedly verified the information and Toombs thereupon forbade the presentation of his name.[31]

Since the presidency had been denied Georgia the general agreement was that she could name the vice-president. The delegation nominated Stephens only after three leading secessionists had stalked out of the caucus room to avoid creating a scene, and the convention accepted him unanimously.[32] This selection was designed to "conciliate the union men,"[33] and the secessionists swallowed this "bitter pill" despite the implausibility of selecting as a leader of a revolution "a person known to be opposed to it."[34]

Most of the other work of Congress during this formative period was devoted to routine tasks. United States policies were continued whenever possible, though some of them were never satisfactorily adapted. Congress reduced its routine work tremendously by continuing until it "altered or repealed" all the laws of the United States not inconsistent with the Confederate Constitution.[35] It was never able, however, to define precisely which of these laws should continue in force. On March 12 it appointed a committee to select and digest these laws and recommend any changes needed.[36] For about six weeks the committee tediously mulled through statutes, court decisions, digests, and other works and eventually reported the job so "delicate and difficult" that it could not accurately say what still applied and what did not. It suggested that all its reference volumes be left in the committee rooms at the Madison House accessible to congressmen. Congress agreed and these rooms served as the Confederate Library of Congress.[37] In the spring of 1863 a digest of the military and naval laws of the

...... *Trial and Error Government* *33*

Confederacy was considered, but since the House and the Senate disagreed over what to include, nothing resulted.

The Provisional Congress ordered that at the end of each session the secretaries of Congress should assemble all the laws and resolutions passed at that session and turn them over to the Superintendent of the Bureau of Public Printing. He must contract with a publishing concern, order 3,000 copies prepared, and see that the printing measured up to certain specifications.[38] In Montgomery, Reid and Shorter, and in Richmond, Richard M. Smith, printer of the *Enquirer,* contracted to do this work. At first the printers received 25¢ per copy, but by 1864 this figure was so far out of line with other prices that Congress authorized the Superintendent to make the best contracts he could.[39] Several hundred copies were sent to courts, departments, governors, bureaus, and the like, and the remainder were held subject to the order of Congress.

Congress intended for the session laws to appear promptly after each adjournment. The acts of the first two sessions were brought out on schedule, but in Richmond publication always lagged. On its last day the Provisional Congress tried to catch up by letting the public printer bring out in one volume all session laws, both constitutions, and the Indian treaties.[40] Thereafter it resumed session publication and for the next two years the printers were fairly prompt. The government collapsed too soon after the adjournment of the last session of Congress for the printing of its acts and resolutions, and it was not until 1941 that they were collected and published.

Some laws needed immediate publication, and the attorney general was instructed to select those during each session and insert them in one newspaper at each state capital. The advertisements were to run weekly for one month, but in February, 1862, the number of insertions was cut to two. A year later it was restored to four a month and, because paper was so scarce that all newspapers except the *Richmond Enquirer* were down to one sheet, the attorney general was permitted to publish them in any three papers available in each state.[41] Compensation for this service was originally $1.50 per statute page; in February, 1862, it was raised to $2.00, where it remained.[42]

Congress also ordered its journals prepared and published in the same way. After a year no journals had been published and Congress turned them over to its president Howell Cobb. It instructed Cobb to have prepared two copies of the journals of the

Provisional Congress and of the constitutional convention, to check them for correctness, then to seal and deposit the copies with the attorney general and the originals with the secretary of state. All were to be preserved with seals unbroken until Congress ordered their publication.[43]

Congress hoped for speedy publication, particularly since the journals of the convention would present a "noble record" and relieve "many apprehensions."[44] But by the time Cobb had arranged for their copying, part of the records had disappeared, having been rushed out of Richmond along with other government documents at the threat of McClellan's peninsula campaign. Cobb had chosen Major John C. Whitner, a disabled commissary officer, for the work, and Whitner spent much of the next two years copying the journals on hand and searching for the missing sections. By late 1864 he had located them all, but Congress, then engaged in more pressing matters, dropped the whole program. Despite this discouragement Whitner completed his assignment, apparently without pay, and turned the finished job over to Cobb just in time for it to be presented to the United States army of occupation.[45]

The Permanent Congress hoped to secure full reporting and publication of its proceedings. In April, 1863, the Senate appointed a committee to investigate the matter, and from June to September it interviewed shorthand experts about making verbatim reports of the sessions. The next January the committee confessed that it had been unable to make satisfactory arrangements with any reporters and so was dismissed.[46] Soon afterward a House committee worked with a portion of the Senate Committee on Printing to investigate applications, but their offer of $20 per congressional day or $4,000 per year proved too small to attract any applicants. John Perkins estimated that satisfactory reporting would cost about $150 a day and suggested that the Bureau of Public Printing could do the job properly and much more cheaply.[47] This ended the matter for both houses and it remained for the United States forty years later to print all the journals of the Confederate Congress.

On the first day of Congress Stephens felt that "the crowd generally seemed green and not to know how to proceed," and graciously set them straight by proposing a committee to report rules of procedure.[48] When the committee visited him that night he presented them with a set mainly culled from the United

States House and Senate rules, which Congress adopted the next day. These rules had only one significant difference from those of the United States. Under the latter the "previous question," if sustained by a majority, stopped all debate and brought the house to a vote, first on the pending amendments and then on the first proposition. Stephens substituted for this "the question." Here any member could request the sense of the body immediately by calling for a vote on the pending question at that stage of the discussion. This enabled the house to secure a vote on any matter without halting debate on the original question.[49] These rules were adopted by the Permanent Congress with two significant revisions. The Senate rules specified that all matters relating to foreign affairs or public defense be considered in secret session. The House rules ordered that appropriation bills be considered only in Committee of the Whole.[50]

The only troublesome rules related to secret sessions. Secrecy was intended to allow freer debate and a greater use of confidential information, though it was commented that the removal of the gallery would expedite legislation just as much by preventing "buncombe speeches and windy harangues."[51] The Provisional Congress allowed any two members to resolve the body into secrecy without further vote, and did so much of its work, whether confidential or not, in secrecy that the eager public grumbled at being excluded from everything interesting. Both houses of the Permanent Congress continued this rule and by 1863 anti-Davis newspapers were saying that secrecy was being used to conceal the administration's ineptitude and malfeasance. According to the *Charleston Mercury* the information that leaked out was so distorted by rumor that it injured confidence in the government; the people, it later claimed, were losing their rights in secret sessions without knowing it.[52]

By the middle of 1862 groups in both houses sought earnestly to reduce the frequency of secret sessions. In August the Senate changed its rules to allow a resumption of open session by majority vote, but through senatorial courtesy requests for secrecy were usually respected. Other senators from time to time sought to require the approval of one-fifth of those present to invoke secrecy, but never succeeded. House opposition was more successful, for in August, 1862, the rules were altered to require a majority approval.[53] Charles H. Smith, the Tennessee humorist, who described these sessions as "the closest communion ever established in a well-watered country,"[54] apparently exaggerated their effectiveness, for news seemed to leak out from them within not more than a day.

T. R. R. Cobb, who hoped that his associates would "take no pay and set an example of patriotism," confessed that only a few individuals in Congress measured up to his expectations.[55] Congress originally set its compensation at $8 a day during session and 10¢ a mile traveling expenses.[56] A year later the Senate Committee on Finance recommended an annual salary on the grounds that a fixed sum would prevent long sessions and added expenses. After much haggling, to the disgust of the newspapers, which seemed always determined to starve the members, Congress agreed to a figure of $2,760 a year and 20¢ a mile for each session.[57] This pay, hardly munificent at the time, soon became hopelessly inadequate and congressmen complained that their pay allowed them neither adequate dignity nor food. A number of wealthy members decried this lack of patriotism, but despite public scorn Congress in December, 1864, and again in March, 1865, granted itself pay and mileage boosts of 50% and then 100%.[58]

On February 21, 1861, Congress established the several executive departments by virtually duplicating the United States laws pertaining to them. The only major change was in the Post Office Department. By 1860 the United States postal service had an annual deficit of almost two million dollars, which Southerners considered merely a subsidy to businessmen who used the mails so much. The Constitution, therefore, ordered the Department to be self-sustaining after March 1, 1863. James H. Reagan, at first hesitant to head the Department lest he be "martyred" on the experiment, accepted the appointment enthusiastically when promised congressional support.[59] Congress gave the Department a monopoly of the mail and express facilities, raised postage rates, and abolished the franking privilege with certain exceptions. It authorized Reagan to pare postal routes to a minimum, re-negotiate mail contracts with the railroads, and discontinue or curtail the service at his discretion.[60]

Postmaster Reagan found it impossible to operate in the black and give good service at the same time. Small communities suffered from the reduction of postal routes, but Congress refused most requests for new ones. The Department always lacked manpower. Sometimes its employees were forced into state militia organizations, and on October 11, 1862, Congress ended the blanket exemption from army service of all mail carriers.[61] Upon

...... *Trial and Error Government* *37*

Reagan's protests for mercy one contractor for each route was exempted. Reagan thereupon argued that the number drafted was too small to warrant disrupting the "proper and speedy transmission of intelligence,"[62] but Congress, inured to such departmental pleas, remained obdurate. The railroads soon began complaining about their low compensation for carrying the mail; often bids by route agents for mail contracts were "so extravagant and unreasonable" that those particular routes were simply dropped.[63] Reagan and Congress consistently disagreed, however, only on the franking privilege. Congress had early abolished it, with only a few exceptions, but as his difficulties increased Reagan protested the carrying free of any mail. Congress never complied and threatened at every session to allow the franking of newspapers to soldiers.

The failure of Congress to establish a Supreme Court is an interesting chapter in the history of the Southern state rights controversy. The Provisional Constitution set up a Supreme Court "constituted of all the District Judges," who should sit "at such times and places as the Congress shall appoint."[64] It was soon evident that Western judges would have difficulty making the long trek to Richmond for its sessions; moreover the judges realized that they might be charged with bargaining with each other for the support of their district court decisions. On July 31, 1861, Congress wisely suspended the Supreme Court until it could be organized under the Permanent Constitution, which left the composition up to Congress.[65]

President Davis, aware of the cohesive force of a strong judiciary, on February 25, 1862, asked Congress for the Court "in accordance with the mandate of the Constitution."[66] Within the next six weeks Representative Miles and Senator Semmes proposed similar bills, providing for a Supreme Court with a chief justice and three associate justices. After long postponements both houses unceremoniously dropped the matter without bringing it to a vote, and Georgia Senator Benjamin H. Hill's warning that a government without a Supreme Court would be "a lame and limping affair"[67] fell on deaf ears.

By 1863 more senators had become convinced of the evils of equal and conflicting judicial authorities, and on January 19 Hill introduced a bill much like Semmes's the year before. Discussion this time was vigorous and thorough; tempers flared, ink wells were hurled, personal spite cropped out,[68] and administration politics broke into the open.[69] The climax occurred when Clay proposed to strike from the Judiciary Act of March 16, 1861, sections 45 and 46, which conferred upon the Supreme Court appellate jurisdiction over the highest state courts.[70] These sections resembled the United States Judiciary Act of 1789 and were remarkably broad when considered in the light of Southern events in 1861.

The Senate nationalists attacked Clay's amendment on the grounds that appellate jurisdiction would stabilize the nation by guaranteeing that the laws of Congress would be enforced; that in the Confederacy there could be no such misinterpretation of the Constitution that permitted the "usurpations" typifying the history of the United States Court. The majority rejected this "poisonous" doctrine so reminiscent of John Marshall. Clay contended that the disputed sections placed the state courts so much "within the power of the courts of the Confederate States" that the Constitution would become only an instrument "to favor the consolidation of the government."[71] Yancey warned that this very principle "more than any other thing" had disrupted the United States and was intended to "chain" the states "to the ear of the government."[72]

These fireworks reveal the principal reason why the Confederacy had no Supreme Court. All but four senators desired one, but only six could accept the principle of appellate jurisdiction involved.[73] Only the adoption of Clay's enfeebling amendment allowed the bill to pass at all. The House Committee on the Judiciary valiantly recommended the Senate bill with sections 45 and 46 reinserted, but when this principle of appellate jurisdiction proved distasteful to the House majority as well the entire matter was dropped.

The absence of a Supreme Court, plus the fact that the district courts had no appellate jurisdiction over state courts either, about finished the prestige and usefulness of the federal court system. The Confederate government usually prosecuted its cases in the state courts in the knowledge that their decisions would be more respected than those of the district courts. The Judiciary Act further embarrassed the district courts by requiring them to abide by state laws and state court practices; in cases of equity the aid of the district courts could not be invoked where "plain, adequate remedy may be had at laws."[74] The Permanent Constitution furthermore removed from the jurisdiction of the district courts most cases involving claims by ordering Congress to establish a separate court of claims. Congress debated the matter often, but never complied, and the work of the claims court was handled by the executive departments, the district courts, and the Board of Sequestration which the Provisional Congress established.[75]

By 1863 communication with the Trans-Mississippi Department had become so difficult that the Richmond government was losing touch with it. Governor Reynolds of Missouri wrote that their being largely ignored was a real cause of dissatisfaction there, particularly in regard to postal and treasury matters; he proposed a Department that would be virtually autonomous within the Confederacy.[76] Secretary of War James A. Seddon agreed with Reynolds and in November suggested that the West be made self-sufficient militarily and administratively.[77] Davis passed the idea on to Congress which during 1864 and 1865 set up the program much as Seddon and Davis had advised. It gave special attention to matters relating to the treasury, the post office, and the army, usually delegating to the commanding general there almost the same authority that the President exercised in the East.

Most of the lower South delegates had arrived in Montgomery convinced that the addition of other states would strengthen the Confederacy. A few, like Tyler, Wigfall, and Toombs, favored welcoming any new state, but most believed that free states would bring an economy inimical to things Southern. Some even opposed the admission of other slave states. They foresaw that border state congressmen might represent districts useless to the Confederate war effort, but would advocate extreme measures to recapture their states. They believed that at best the border states would make milk-and-water allies, and at worst would dominate the less populous lower South and conceivably would be early reconstructionists.

Until April, 1861, the border states were torn between two loyalties, but Lincoln's call for 75,000 volunteers to quell the rebellion ended their wavering. The Confederate Congress hurried commissioners to them, and Stephens intimated to Virginia that she would be represented in Davis's Cabinet.[78] A Virginia convention was already in session and on April 17 voted, 88 to 55, to secede. In quick order North Carolina, Tennessee, and Arkansas called conventions which followed suit by overwhelming majorities. In Missouri secessionist Governor Claibourne Jackson summoned an extra session of the legislature. Only Southern sympathizers attended and the state seceded on October 28. Kentucky secessionists held a convention on October 30 and declared the state independent. When these states applied for admission into the Confederacy, Congress received them on equal terms and granted them representation equal to their United States representation.

Each of these conventions except that of Tennessee elected its delegations to the Provisional Congress. The Tennessee ordinance called for an election of congressmen simultaneously with the United States elections scheduled for that year. On the first Thursday in August the unionists and Confederates went together to the polls and elected congressmen, who went to Washington or to Richmond as they chose. The victors in the four Eastern districts took their seats in the United States Congress; their Confederate opponents in the first and second districts acknowledged defeat and declined seats in the Southern Congress.[79]

In the spring of 1861 Arizona territory was almost unanimously Southern and disunionist, and on March 16 a convention of citizens at La Mesilla seceded and declared for attachment to the Confederacy. The president of the convention sent copies of its resolution to Congress, but war had just been declared and Congress shunted Arizona's petition off to the Committee on Territories.[80] Meanwhile a handful of Arizonians had met in August at Tucson and selected Granville H. Oury as delegate to Congress with instructions to hasten the admission of Arizona. Oury went to Richmond at once, but Davis ignored him and Congress waited until December before asking him to appear before it in behalf of Arizona. Finally on January 18, 1862, Congress, after carefully scrutinizing the details of territorial organization, formally organized the territory of Arizona and admitted Oury as its non-voting delegate.[81]

The Southwest Indians were at first sympathetic with the Confederacy. Many owned slaves and before 1860 the tribes had had more contact with the South through the government personnel sent to work with them. Also they were probably too close to Arkansas and Texas to dare siding against them. During the spring and summer of 1861 the Choctaws, Chickasaws, Seminoles, Creeks, and Cherokees held tribal conventions, declared themselves free nations, and appointed commissioners to treat with the Confederacy. There were numerous smaller and less civilized tribes occupying the same territory and they followed the action of their stronger neighbors. Meanwhile Congress had created a Bureau of Indian Affairs and assumed a protectorate over the Indians. President Davis then appointed Albert Pike as Commissioner of Indian Affairs who proceeded west to deal with them.

Pike made three kinds of treaties with the tribes. Those with the five civilized tribes treated them as equal nations. For "so long as grass shall grow and water run" they were guaranteed a number of rights covering their political and territorial autonomy. They were allowed a non-voting delegate in Congress and the Confederacy assumed all debts owed by the United States to the tribes. In return they promised a number of volunteer companies of mounted men. The second class of Indians — Osages, Senecas, Shawnees, and Quapaws — received clothes and industrial aids and in return promised some military aid. The Comanches and ten other tribes and bands were so backward that the Confederacy asked only that they behave themselves. In return it promised them rations in addition to what it promised the second class.[82]

IV

CONGRESSIONAL ELECTIONS

POLITICS DURING THE CONFEDERACY TOOK A SURPRISINGLY BRIEF vacation considering the original emphasis on harmony. Even absorption in nation-making could not dampen interest in elections, campaigning, and political maneuvering. On May 21, 1861, the Provisional Congress ordered elections to be held for representatives to the First Congress on the first Wednesday in November, 1861. They were to be conducted under the constitutions and laws of the several states, which continued most of their former procedures and requirements. Congress, which had the constitutional right to make or alter state election regulations, specified that in the absence of other provisions the old United States election laws would apply.[1] Each state was allowed its former United States representation, and as new states were admitted Congress specified the size of their delegations.

Under the Provisional Constitution members of Congress were able to hold other federal office, and many succumbed to the lure of battle and spent much of their time in the field both in and out of session. The Permanent Constitution, however, forbade plural federal office-holding and forced congressmen to choose where to serve. When men like Francis Bartow, the Cobb brothers, James Patton Anderson, James Chesnut, and others chose the military service, Congress was severely criticized for expelling "nearly all it had of worth and talent. . . ."[2]

Of the eleven Confederate states in November, 1861, Virginia, North Carolina, Alabama, Florida, and Tennessee had provisions for absentee voting by their soldiers. Each qualified soldier, wherever he might be, could cast a ballot at his army camp for his home district congressman. The camp commander was to appoint officers to supervise the voting and was to forward the returns to the designated state officials. South Carolina and Georgia soon

...... *Congressional Elections* *43*

passed similar laws, while Arkansas and Mississippi did so after the second congressional elections in 1863. Congress finally authorized the soldiers of Louisiana and Missouri to vote in their camps, leaving Texas and Kentucky without specific provisions for soldier voting.[3] Some camp officers neglected this civilian function, and in 1862 and 1863 several states authorized their soldiers, in case of such negligence, to assemble and vote on their own initiative.

The occupation of parts or all of several states by the enemy raised the question of refugee voting. Virginia, South Carolina, and Georgia allowed their refugees to gather on a prescribed day, vote, and send their ballots to the state government for checking and tabulation. Louisiana, Arkansas, Missouri, Tennessee, and Kentucky were almost totally occupied in 1863, with their citizens scattered far and wide. In order to obtain a vote large enough to be significant their governments, or Congress at their inaction, provided for election to the Second Congress by a general ticket. Under this plan a qualified voter could vote for one candidate from each district in his state, with the person getting the highest number of votes for a district being commissioned as its representative. General elections had the advantage of selecting men with state-wide reputations; hence such elections were disliked by politicians who felt that their popularity was local. Election in faraway Arizona followed the former United States plan. Congress, except for setting their date, left Indian elections up to the tribes.

Elections to the First Congress went off quietly. The people were apparently engrossed in military matters and did not consider a regular political campaign desirable.[4] Newspapers generally told their readers that it was election day and that the tickets offered good and true men. Presumably there were no differences of opinion in the South, and every election involved merely a choice of men.[5]

Candidates in all states used fairly uniform practices in placing themselves before the public. Usually they stated that they would not campaign because of army duties or because the time was not appropriate. Some placed brief notices of their candidacy in local papers. Others inserted somewhat longer "cards," which pledged "strict adherence to the letter and spirit of the Constitution," "commercial independence of the Confederate States," "purity of the elective franchise," "a vigorous prosecution of the war," and other platitudes. Those candidates able to do so boasted of being "state rights" candidates; those unable simply dodged their pre-war loyalties and pledged full support to the Confederate government.

Some candidates were nominated by public meetings. Newspapers carried accounts of "spontaneous" and "non-partisan" nomination meetings, obviously most carefully arranged by friends of the candidate. Generally when a paper reported in any detail such a gathering it supported the candidate and hailed with delight the choice made. The other papers usually said nothing against him, but pointed out that the meeting could only bind those who participated in it. Though Governor Joseph E. Brown advised against it, a number of Georgia districts held bi-partisan conventions in September to nominate candidates. Out in Texas an attempt by the Democrats to hold a state convention failed through lack of interest.

Once the candidate was before the people, he turned his campaign over to his friends.[6] They acted with restraint, and evidence of their work is scanty. If a candidate wished to make a speaking tour, his friends arranged one that would carry him into each county of his district. The tour took place about three or four weeks before election time and seldom provided for more than a dozen speeches. John Goode of Virginia told how his supporters heckled the candidates speaking against him. "They [his opponents] addressed the people throughout the district, and after they had all spoken . . . some friend of mine would arise in the audience and say 'Gentlemen, you must remember that Mr. Goode is also a candidate. . . . He cannot be here to-day because he is down at the front with the other boys in the army.' "[7]

In only a few instances was the election of 1861 more than humdrum. In Virginia banker William H. McFarland dared contest the re-election of ex-President John Tyler and was accused of threatening his debtors with foreclosure unless they supported him.[8] Politics in the fifth district of North Carolina was always bitter and Archibald Arrington and Josiah Turner withheld few punches; on Saturday, October 12, at Laws' Store, Wake County, they almost caused a riot by a joint debate.[9] Mississippi had more than its share of excitement. Ethelbert Barksdale published an itinerary of thirty-six speaking engagements, the longest found in any newspaper, and announced that opposing candidates were invited to attend.[10] John J. McRae was one of the few candidates who included army camps in his tour. Henry Chambers of Cohoma forced Colonel W. A. Lake into a duel with rifles at fifty paces and killed him.[11] Texas was so solidly Democrat that most districts saw electioneering only by rival Democrats, with the result depending entirely on personal popularity. The closest contest in Arkansas was in the southeastern district, where Augustus H. Garland defeated the candidate of the Johnson machine by a plurality of 32.[12]

Purely local problems or issues influenced several district races. Clement C. Clay and John P. Ralls of Alabama were accused of land speculation.[13] John W. Lewis of Georgia was supposed to have left the Georgia State Railroad in deplorable shape when he resigned as superintendent to enter the campaign.[14] Since provisional congressman from the Virginia second district lived in Richmond, the people of Norfolk felt that their candidate should be accepted in 1861.[15] In Florida F. R. Cotton based his claim to office on the virtue of being a small farmer,[16] and in Tennessee William G. Swan boasted of being "the poor man's friend."[17] A mass meeting at Friar's Point, Mississippi, pledged its support to Henry Chambers because he had worked for stay laws when in the legislature, whereas Josiah Turner in North Carolina claimed that they were unconstitutional.[18] Several Western candidates pledged that if elected they would provide better frontier protection from the Indians.

The outcome of the first congressional elections depended chiefly on the relatively meaningless factor of former politics. Unionists, secessionists, Whigs, and Democrats had possessed good organizations during the winter of 1860-1861 and, practical men all, continued them into the Confederacy. Any candidate associated with an organization could hope for success; now that everyone was a loyal Confederate even former unionists could expect to be successful in districts which had once supported them.

Many insisted that political parties and issues no longer existed. In a sense this was true, for old party names were avoided lest they imply political division. It was inevitable, however, that old ties should continue, and newspapers soon began to report that party affiliations of the preceding fall had not been forgotten.[19] These parties, however, bore little resemblance to their pre-war namesakes. They had no issues, no visible organization, no intersectional ties, and no difference in loyalty to Southern principles. They can be described only in terms of the voters' inclination to support men whom they had supported before the war, and of politicians who saw no reason to reject any vehicle that might win them success. There is no evidence that the people thought otherwise. They continued to vote for about the same men without much thought of why they did so.

The secessionists, their cause justified and their escutcheon unblemished, tried to make attitude toward secession a test of loyalty. The only "true" men, they claimed that those who were most zealous for the war ought to conduct it.[20] The *Richmond Enquirer* supported James Lyons because he "was its advocate when to avow secession principles found more frowns than smiles."[21] William Lander and several other North Carolina candidates were even condemned for not bolting the Charleston convention of 1860.[22]

The accusation of "unionism" was entirely a political ruse, not a sincere imputation of distrust, and was intended merely to swing a few votes to the secession candidate whose principles had triumphed. The strategy was generally ineffective in former conservative districts, which considered even unionists not unbearable. Secessionists from such districts could well remark that the "best claim to distinction under the existing regime seems to be either to have opposed secession or have done nothing for it."[23] In Alabama Hugh Lawson Clay feared that the voters were going to reject their obligations to the ones who induced the secession movement.[24] The secessionist *Wilmington Journal* predicted that "a certain set of politicians" noted only for their "tardy and reluctant movements" might defeat the men with "deeper and more patriotic insight. . . ."[25] To some extent the old Democrat-Whig rivalry fitted into the matter of loyalty to the Confederacy. In North Carolina and Alabama the unionist-Whig and the secessionist-Democrat line-up had been close; so in these states candidates who had been both Democrat and secessionist sought even more strenuously to convince their hearers of their higher loyalty to Confederate principles.

The program of the Davis administration, while not a leading factor, occasionally figured in the 1861 election. The Confederacy in 1861 was popular and opposition to government policies was seldom expressed. Nevertheless, there were random signs of discontent. It was directed against such matters as the failure of the government to buy the entire cotton crop of 1861, the removal of the capital from Montgomery, and some of the President's appointments. It expressed itself in demands for free trade, for smaller government salaries, and for "cheap government." All the criticism was voiced quietly and without any real antagonism or desire for a new administration. It probably signified little more than that provisions were becoming scarce and extravagantly high, money was hard to get, and people were just beginning to feel the effects of the war.²⁶

The Permanent Constitution required that the Confederate senators be elected by their state legislatures. There was almost no senatorial campaigning, though the voting reveals that votes were frequently swapped. The usual practice in the United States had been for the legislatures to divide the senatorships between the two major sections, and nearly everyone expected this to continue. Newspapers warned that party politics could easily burst out again and urged the majority to share the senatorships with minority parties as well as sections.

The desire for political harmony caused most legislators to follow this rule. With the exception of Kentucky, every state in which the Whigs and the Democrats had been closely matched in 1860 selected a Whig and a Democratic senator. The Tennessee legislature even "set a good example of fraternity" by nominating "none but old Democrats" and selecting one of them, then choosing an "old Whig, or Bell man" in the same way.²⁷ Bell had run poorly in the 1860 election in half the Southern states and these states chose only Democratic senators.²⁸ More easily followed was the traditional geographic division, from which only North Carolina deviated. Most legislatures naturally contained some irreconcilables opposed to any division. When unsuccessful, they sometimes tried — and in North Carolina succeeded — to split the opposition by supporting a candidate only moderately acceptable to his party or section.

The legislatures usually sent their ablest available men to the Senate. R. M. T. Hunter of Virginia resigned his secretaryship of state and was elected senator on the first ballot.²⁹ Yancey of Alabama, then Confederate commissioner to England, sent word of his willingness to serve and was immediately elected. The Texas legislature offered Wigfall either a brigadier-generalship or a Senate post; he chose the latter and was duly honored. In Arkansas Robert W. Johnson, head of the "Johnson family machine," was able to secure his own election. The growing opposition to his organization, however, which had dominated state politics for a generation, prevented it from sweeping the race and Dr. Charles B. Mitchel, previously unaffiliated with the Johnsons, won the other seat. The North Carolina Whig party, dominant in the East, settled on George Davis; meanwhile the Western votes were divided between two leading secessionist Democrats, William W. Avery and Thomas L. Clingman, with William T. Dortch, an Eastern Democrat, running a poor third. A number of conservatives then gave their support to Dortch, who had been a late secessionist. Since neither Avery nor Clingman would give way, their divided vote permitted Dortch's election to the other seat.

The Georgia race was particularly interesting in that it involved the temperamental Robert Toombs. The legislature selected Hill on the first ballot and five ballots later chose Toombs as the second senator. Toombs, who had recently left Davis's Cabinet in a huff, knew that without a show of overwhelming support from Georgia he would be at a disadvantage in the Senate. But this treatment sent him on a rampage, and he notified Governor Brown that "the manner in which the legislature thought proper to confer this trust" relieved him of any obligation to accept it.[30] Brown then appointed John W. Lewis to serve until the legislature met again. In November, 1862, it selected Herschel V. Johnson mainly on the basis of his support of the recent conscription law.

This first general election went off quietly and without undue trouble.[31] Most of Missouri and Kentucky were under United States control and their secession governments in flight. Their governors appointed two senators and ordered elections for representatives by soldier and refugee vote. Balloting everywhere was light, as is usual when issues are absent. The army vote was particularly scant and was influential only in districts occupied by the enemy. In most states the government had few enemies except those who differed with it on principle, and Davis's early efforts to dodge trouble with the states had been very gratifying. Most provisional congressmen who sought re-election succeeded and those who declined were usually replaced by men of similar political tendencies and antecedents. It was well known that the Provisional Congress had been primarily a register of Davis's decrees, and the success of its congressmen implied a satisfaction with the President and his program. Although about a third of those chosen became administration opponents, they were not necessarily elected on this basis. As Confederate policies became more positive, and accordingly more objectionable, with the progress of the war, only then did one man after another add his name to the original anti-administration list.

The election results reveal that even at the height of Confederate enthusiasm the political hatchet had not been buried, for old preferences persisted. Democratic districts of 1860 returned approximately four times as many Democrats in 1861 as they did Whigs; districts that were Whig in 1860 fared only about half as well in 1861. In Mississippi, South Carolina, and Texas, where the Democrats had been strongly secessionist, they made almost a clean sweep. The Whigs had not been opposed to secession in 1861, but their leanings from it, slightly stronger than those of the Democrats, operated against them. There was no alteration of the Whig grouping over the Confederacy, and the only variations from its 1860 standing were occasional losses scattered over the nation.

A similar correlation existed on the matter of secession. Four-fifths of the secessionist districts elected former secessionists, while the blow to conservative prestige caused former conservative districts to return as many secessionists as conservatives. Here too the results only made clear the continuing nature of political organization, showing that the secessionists, somewhat more respectable early in the war, were consequently more successful at that time in Confederate politics.

When the second general election for congressmen occurred in the middle of 1863, politics had reverted to type. The major issue now, for issues there were indeed, had become the Davis administration. By this time the government's policies had not only become definite but were expansive in response to growing needs. They now touched the everyday life of each class and group, and people had too often come to judge administration policies by the condition of their pocketbooks or bills of fare, or by their draft status. This attitude of the people does not imply that they wished the war effort impaired; it simply means that some people wanted the impossibility of a war for independence that did not bear heavily upon them. Such an attitude was neither traitorous, anti-Confederate, nor contradictory: war weariness was upon the nation.

Candidates running on an anti-administration platform were in full cry. They generally based their campaign on the one or two government policies especially opprobrious in their own districts. Usually they failed to offer any clear substitute for policies they denigrated. When they commanded a known majority in a district, they arraigned the government severely on almost everything and proposed alternatives which might generously be called inadequate substitutes. Mixed with rodomontade was the familiar state rights ingredient which gave much criticism a respectable flavor. All of the strong war measures were condemned as evidence of centralized despotism which was abusing the states.

President Davis always maintained that he would never ask for peace and that if the North offered it he would insist on complete Southern independence. While everyone agreed with the latter principle, many felt that the North desired peace and that Davis's stubborn refusal to attempt negotiations was unrealistic. Several candidates for the Second Congress demanded that the government offer peace on the basis of independence. Contrariwise, the *Richmond Enquirer* said that the defeat of James Lyons would be "immediately misinterpreted by the Yankee newspapers as a return to Unionism. . . ."[32] In North Carolina William W. Holden headed a faction which condemned the incumbent delegation for not initiating a peace movement and in his paper, the *Raleigh Standard,* backed a number of candidates who favored peace by separate state action. In Georgia and Alabama this issue was important in over half the districts contested. The peace movement was an excellent index of dissatisfaction and during the campaign was always accompanied by several other issues.

The conscription and the exemption laws had rapidly developed into leading political issues. Many people felt that they injured state and local defenses and were an unwarranted centralizing force. Some elections turned on this issue almost alone, particularly along the Atlantic seaboard where conscription was heavy and therefore unpopular. This "horror of conscription" made itself felt even across the Mississippi, where Waldo P. Johnson of Missouri was severely criticized for being an effective conscript officer.[33] Some congressmen up for re-election felt compelled, in the face of the unpopularity of conscription, to deny falsely ever having supported it. Since congressional proceedings on the subject had usually been secret, opponents could only allege, but seldom prove, any mendacity. Those who posed as the poor man's candidate attacked overseer exemption as class legislation; administration defenders, who argued that overseers were necessary to agricultural production, found stubborn resistance from the plain folk, who claimed that it "made a broad and degrading line of distinction between . . . the silken son of pleasure and the hardy son of the soil."[34]

By 1863 Confederate financial demands upon the people were becoming increasingly exorbitant. Spiraling prices kept the na-

Congressional Elections 51

tion in an economic whirl and those hard-pressed criticized the government for stupidity, short-sightedness, mismanagement, or all three. Congressmen sympathetic to the fiscal program either pointed out its few successes or excused it as the best possible under the circumstances.[35] Opposition candidates claimed that Congress had permitted inflation by neglecting to start early funding schemes, that the government should have used cotton as a basis for its currency, and that the tax system oppressed those with small incomes. Some declared that impressment of produce and taxation in kind were ill-concealed confiscation and advocated that both be abolished. Cotton producers wanted the government to buy the entire crop at high prices, an issue on which several candidates were defeated. Some coastal districts felt that their commerce had suffered because their congressmen had not obtained for their seaports the status of "port of entry." A few still demanded free trade.

Another major issue was the suspension of the writ of habeas corpus. Thousands of able-bodied men were dodging military service, and the local police were sometimes unable to cope with bands of deserters roaming the countryside. State judges often released prisoners held under Confederate authority, and Chief Justice Richmond M. Pearson of North Carolina granted writs to almost everyone who applied. To prevent such abuses Congress on several occasions allowed the President to suspend the writ. Although he used the privilege sparingly, many violently resented such Lincolnesque usurpation. North Carolina, Georgia, and Alabama in particular defended the prerogatives of their judges to issue these writs, and in Georgia the acts of Congress on the matter were generally disregarded. Several candidates used this issue as the example *par excellence* of the breakdown of state rights.

Other phases of the administration program figured in the 1863 elections only a little less closely. People from districts near armies complained that impressment agents collected too heavily from them. Trans-Mississippi citizens wanted better protection from Yankees and Indians. Exposed districts all over the Confederacy wished their defenses strengthened by more fortifications and breastworks. Most candidates threw lures to the soldier vote. Over fifty of them had served in the army and assured the soldiers that they had special insight into army needs. Their promises included better rations, tobacco allotments, homesteads in the territories, and, above all, pay increases.

The defenders of the government's program reproduced the same arguments that the Davis administration had used for the previous two years. They harped on the principle that cooperation and self-sacrifice were necessary for success; that criticism of the government by "traitors and demagogues" would demoralize public sentiment and weaken the cause[36]; and that the Confederate government weak or strong, wise or unwise, was the only means of salvation.[37] They seldom lacked courage except in defending conscription. Pro-administration men up for reelection had a particularly delicate problem here, for most of them had voted against extending conscription on at least one occasion. Some more bold than others pledged 100% support to the administration, though the promise required extraordinary valor in districts still within Confederate lines. Most simply expressed "implicit faith" in President Davis, while reserving the right to oppose any separate part of his program. For instance in Virginia the liveliest issue was the impressment of army supplies, in North Carolina it was peace negotiation, and in Georgia it was conscription. In these states an administration supporter generally voted against the particular measure most disliked by the people and upheld the remainder of its policies. Most pro-administration candidates announced or implied that critics of the Davis program were wishing for the moon and offering no solution for reaching it.[38]

Even in 1863 the old Whig and Democratic organizations continued to be politically influential, and private correspondences reveal that the candidates depended on this carry-over. In Virginia the friends of Alexander H. H. Stuart warned him that "rabid democrats" would oppose him;[39] Allen T. Davidson of North Carolina feared the strength of "stinking democracy."[40] The *Montgomery Mail* bemoaned the fact that in Alabama the "pressing necessities" of war had "not been able to quench the old party spirit," and that the "same old Whig party" had preserved its organization.[41] Except for North Carolina and Alabama there was little relationship between these parties and their attitude toward the Davis administration. In these two states Democracy had been closely associated with secession, and now that Confederate policies were generally unpopular in them the Whigs rode high.

The question of whether a man had been a secessionist or a unionist had become more significant in the face of Confederate military reverses. In some disaffected areas candidates boasted of not having been a "Destructive" in 1861. In most of the districts, however, they withheld such assertions lest they appear to express dissatisfaction with the Confederacy itself. It was best to accept the fact that the voters knew one's position on secession and hope that they would consider it an asset. Only James T. Leach of North Carolina denied the right of secession,[42] and in no district was it a political issue. Former unionists sometimes received support from reconstructionists and were forced to use every precaution to avoid their contagion.

Secessionists continued to maintain that opponents to the establishment of the Confederacy should not be rewarded by a place in its government, for only "true" men could legislate properly.[43] They believed that a "staunch old Secession Wheelhorse" would make the best congressman, that the voters should weed out conservatives so that the original secessionists could "reassert their proud position by conducting the revolution to its happy destination."[44] Though it is doubtful whether the strategy was effective in any unionist district, secessionists occasionally represented "every body who is not of their number as a reconstructionist."[45]

With this fuel available, the second congressional elections proceeded furiously in most states. Congress did not set a specific election date, and from June until November the Confederacy was rocked by a series of political explosions. Occasionally a newspaper timidly urged moderation, but usually the press set the pace for bellicosity. Candidates spoke freely and often, and at times so many members were home campaigning that the House could hardly manage a quorum. Congressional candidates for occupied districts concentrated on the soldier vote, and Governor Reynolds of Missouri accused John B. Clark of posting friends around the balloting places.[46] Speeches before army groups were particularly optimistic, for it would hardly do to disparage the government in the presence of men fighting for it.

Elections in Virginia were relatively quiet. Despite the fact that a number of Virginia representatives to the Second Congress had berated Davis personally during the campaign, only four representatives became administration opponents. This contrast with the other Atlantic coast states was due to two factors: congressmen from western Virginia were elected largely by the soldier vote which was always strongly pro-administration; eastern Virginia was the center of the war effort and was reconciled to extreme measures. In 1862 Senator William B. Preston, a western Whig, died of heart trouble. The Democrats then dominated the legislature and could have named either John B. Floyd or Charles B. Russell to replace him. These men, however, were personal enemies and opposed each other so stubbornly that after much maneuvering and bargaining some of the western Democrats swung their support to Allen T. Caperton, a western Whig, and elected him on the twentieth ballot.

Every North Carolina district was hotly contested, with the administration supporters thoroughly on the defensive. The conservatives, with victory assured, uniformly represented the government as a military despotism, and were at odds only over the peace issue. The followers of Governor Zebulon B. Vance desired negotiations, but refused to countenance separate state action; Vance himself maintained that though his state was already ruined it was not yet dishonored, and denounced the "croaking Submission party" most vehemently.[47] Those behind editor Holden were even more violently anti-administration and, in addition, seemed to desire peace by separate state action. Of the state's ten congressmen, eight were new men in the Second Congress, and all became administration opponents. So strongly was the Democratic party in North Carolina associated with secession and the administration that only one Democrat was elected and he by a majority of only sixteen;[48] so unpopular was the conduct of the war that no original secessionist was elected.

In 1862 George Davis, a secession Democrat who had faithfully supported President Davis, was defeated for re-election by William A. Graham, a union Whig. Early in 1864, with only two months of his term remaining, Davis resigned to become Confederate attorney-general and Vance appointed Edwin G. Reade, a union Whig, to serve his unexpired term. In his two months at Richmond Reade proved an implacable administration foe, and at home gave hearty "aid and comfort . . . to the Holdenites. . . ."[49] In 1864 he contested the seat of Senator Dortch, who had drawn a four-year term. Reade's reconstructionism was unpalatable to the Vance men, who combined with the secessionists to elect Thomas S. Ashe, a union Whig who as a representative in the First Congress had opposed the Davis program on everything except peace matters. The Confederacy ended before Ashe's term began, and Dortch remained the lone North Carolinian in the Second Congress to support the President.

The South Carolina election was deceptively quiet, for the administration supporters were too few in most districts to make much of a showing. The state, however, exercised better judgment in handling discontent than did her northern or southern neighbor. Obstructionists of the Rhett type were usually defeated by candidates who disagreed with the administration but were willing to tolerate it until the war was over. Rhett was beaten again by Louis M. Ayer, who declared that to elect Rhett would be to war on the Confederacy.[50] Four of its six congressmen became administration opponents, but none ran on a peace platform and only William W. Boyce sponsored the peace movement that developed.

Florida's population was small and so widely dispersed that the Confederate laws were poorly enforced in her borders. Her main grievance was that because of government inattention to her coastal defenses she had lost her major ports. Florida's rather negative role in the war caused the elections to be quiet and its two representatives were divided on the Davis administration.

When the Georgians made their appearance in the Second Congress some congressmen looked upon them with suspicion, for this Georgia delegation represented a thorough reversal from its predecessors. Only one Georgian in the First Congress had consistently opposed the administration; six of these sought reelection, all were defeated, and eight of the new representatives were anti-Davis. This switch can be explained by examining the state's position in 1863. By then she had experienced so little direct contact with the enemy, that she was deprived of the political unity that invasion brings. This condition permitted the full enforcement of Confederate laws and nowhere were the conscription and the impressment laws more effectively applied. Governor Brown fumed and fulminated against them, and his machinations to impede their operation set a pattern of discontent for other Georgians.

In Alabama the administration program, particularly the peace issue, dominated every district race. The Democrats were thoroughly discredited and the *Montgomery Advertiser* stated that "when a disaster or two" befell the Confederacy the Whigs "sneaked forth" and ran obscure candidates for Congress with no record that could be assailed by the more loyal Confederates already in Congress.[51] Four of the victors became administration opponents and were rumored reconstructionists. In 1861 John P. Ralls defeated Williamson R. R. Cobb in the third district; in 1863 Cobb decisively swept Ralls from office. Cobb was a confessed reconstructionist and Congress unanimously expelled him.[52]

In the fourth district Marcus H. Cruikshank, an obscure editor and a suspect reconstructionist, defeated the incumbent Jabez L. M. Curry "on account of his identification with the Government. . . ."[53]

Senator Yancey died in 1863 and in August the Alabama legislature replaced him with Robert Jemison. Jemison had been a unionist Whig and continued in a quieter fashion Yancey's policies. Early in 1863 the Alabama malcontents commenced plotting to unseat Senator Clay, who had drawn a two-year term. In November the legislature replaced him with Richard W. Walker, a unionist Whig. Clay blamed his defeat on having opposed the increase of soldier pay, but detached observers more accurately placed it on his personal and legislative support of President Davis.

Because a large part of Mississippi was under federal control by mid-1863, campaigning was slight. The delegates elected resembled those of the First Congress in that they were largely secessionist and entirely Democratic. Most voters condoned the radical measures desired by the President and the delegation contained only two administration opponents. James Phelan sought re-election to the Senate, but the Democratic vote was so divided that John W. C. Watson, a union Whig, was elected on the thirty-eighth ballot.

The presence of the enemy in several Louisiana districts forced Governor Henry W. Allen to order elections by a general ticket, but even then the vote was small. Those seeking re-election were successful; Henry Marshall of the fifth district, the only Louisianian in the First Congress opposing the administration, refused to run and was replaced by Colonel Benjamin L. Hodge. John Perkins, who had always teetered on the brink, finally took the plunge and in the Second Congress was the only anti-Davis Louisianian.

By 1863 Texas was in a poor frame of mind. Military commanders were rigorously enforcing the Confederate laws there, and the rapid movement of armies across the state added further annoyance. Texans felt that their soldiers were being sent across the Mississippi and sacrificed by an administration of Easterners. Senator Wigfall "complained of nobody" and "stiffled his jalousies [sic]"[54] in an effort to soothe the discontent, but half the new delegation opposed the administration.

Arkansas made little change in her representation. Grandison

Congressional Elections 57

Royston declined re-election and Rufus K. Garland succeeded him. Most of the state was under federal occupation, and the soldier vote, which usually returned the incumbent, determined every election. Thomas B. Hanly had opposed the Davis policies in the First Congress, but in the Second he favored do-or-die measures. R. K. Garland became the only administration opponent from Arkansas in the Second Congress; the others bombarded Davis with advice and requests but generally backed his program.

Robert W. Johnson's term as Arkansas senator expired after two years and the legislature re-elected him in November, 1862. The Democratic party had been supreme in 1860 and their supremacy, combined with the tight organization backing Johnson, gave him the nod over his Whig rival Augustus H. Garland. Dr. Mitchel died in 1864 and Governor Henry M. Rector appointed Garland, who had served in the House for three years, to his unfinished senatorship.

Missouri was completely in federal hands by mid-1863. In July Governor Reynolds, then at Marshall, Texas, ordered a registry of Missouri voters "sojourning within our lines," but had only two registrees.[55] Several months later Congress, at Reynolds's request, placed the Missouri elections for May 2, 1864. Reynolds then advertised them widely and at the appointed date about 8,000 Missourians, most of them from east of the Mississippi, met at nearby camps to vote for a general ticket. Since little campaigning was possible, the election depended on the opinion of the administration and on the earlier reputations of the candidates. It was unique, however, in that, because of the notorious misbehavior of the previous delegation in Richmond, several new candidates announced a "sobriety & morality platform" in their brief electioneering.[56] Reynolds moved every stone to secure a more sober and pro-administration delegation and was completely successful at least in the latter aim.

The Missouri legislature was unable to meet after 1862 and Reynolds filled senatorial vacancies when they occurred. Robert L. Y. Peyton died and Reynolds replaced him in November, 1863, with Waldo P. Johnson, a unionist Democrat and an avowed friend of the Davis regime. John B. Clark had annoyed the President by his personal conduct and his talk of a counter revolution, and at the end of Clark's two-year term Reynolds appointed L. M. Lewis, a Methodist preacher and an early secessionist. Lewis, however, preferred army life, and for the last months of Congress Reynolds promoted George G. Vest from the House to the Senate.

On May 23, 1863, Governor Isham Harris of Tennessee called a convention to meet on June 17 at Winchester for the purpose of nominating a congressional ticket. The convention was hardly representative of the state, for two-thirds of its members were from counties within federal lines and most of the others were army officers. Nevertheless it nominated a full ticket and ordered an election for August 4. With a full election impossible because of the enemy occupation of much of eastern Tennessee, the nominees from the eastern districts were elected mainly by the army vote and the whole state's vote was exceptionally small. Only Henry S. Foote became an administration opponent.

The Kentucky provisional government, then at Macon, Georgia, called an election for February 10, 1864, and submitted a general ticket to its soldiers and refugee citizens. Most of the ticket was composed of army officers, and the only anti-Davis man elected was Humphrey Marshall.

The results of the second congressional elections proved that the trials then besetting the Confederacy had cost the 1861 aggressives some of their popularity. The voters still tended to select congressmen according to past political affiliations, but by 1863 the Whigs and the conservatives had regained slightly more districts than they had lost in 1861. In 1861 the Democrats in Congress outnumbered the Whigs by two to one, while the secessionists slightly exceeded that ratio over their opponents. In 1863 both majorities had been reduced to about a five-to-four margin. War-weariness had somewhat dimmed the halo of the Democrats and the secessionists, and the electorate returned to its traditional voting patterns.

The election of 1863 cannot be considered a vote of lack of confidence in President Davis for the nation as a whole. Out of 106 districts 24 had sent anti-administration men to the First Congress. In the Second this number rose to 41, while the opposition in the Senate increased from 11 to 12. In the First Congress opposition was most noticeable in North and South Carolina; no other state had a majority in opposition and Missouri had none at all. The Second Congress found Georgia thoroughly in line with the Carolinas, and Alabama, Florida, and Texas only slightly less antagonistic. These states, with 43 districts, could claim 32 of the 41 opposition representatives. In the other 63

...... *Congressional Elections* 59

districts of the Confederacy the administration opposition decreased from 12 to 9. Only the nearly solid support from occupied districts enabled President Davis to maintain a majority in Congress until the last days of the nation.

MOBILIZATION OF MANPOWER

SECESSIONIST LEADERS HAD CONFIDENTLY ASSURED THE PEOPLE THAT severance from the United States would be peaceable and uncontested. Nevertheless they recognized the need for an army, both as a precautionary measure and as a concomitant of national existence, and after outlining the preliminary framework of government Congress turned its attention to national defenses. The military tradition of the South had always been strong, and each state that joined the Confederacy had a well-organized militia of several thousand men. In his inaugural address President Davis advised Congress to use these militia as the basis for its army.[1]

On February 28 Congress authorized Davis to take control of all military operations in the Confederacy. It then set up the "Provisional Army" as the instrument for such control by allowing him to receive into the Confederate service for not less than twelve months whatever militia the states might offer or which might volunteer with the consent of their state. At that time there was considerable feeling against building up a large army, and on March 6 Congress limited the number of twelve-month volunteers to 100,000 from the militia army and naval forces. As a partial compensation the same law allowed the President to receive other troops or militia for a period not exceeding six months. To avoid conflict with the states, the President could receive men only in the units in which they volunteered and must allow them to be officered under the laws of their respective states. His only control over their organization was that he could form the smaller into larger units and, with the approval of Congress, appoint their general officers.[2] Except for the short enlistment this law was a precise enactment of Davis's requests. He had wanted three-year terms, but the Military Committee assured him that Congress would agree to no longer than one year.[3]

The attack on Fort Sumter required an about-face on army policies, and Davis hastily called a special session of Congress for April 20. He informed Congress that he was planning to hold in readiness for instant action the 100,000 volunteers and promised to ask for more if needed.[4] Congress, however, was in no dallying mood and set about clearing away the obstacles to a wartime army, namely, dependence on state consent for volunteering, short term enlistments, and a limit of 100,000 soldiers. As the law stood the President could not accept single volunteers or independent companies, while emergencies might demand larger armies or special services at a moment's notice. Augustus R. Wright of Georgia admitted that Davis conceivably might show "want . . . of a proper discretion" in accumulating these men, but that Congress should be willing to trust him with this power.[5] The advocates of long term enlistments contended that states' defenses would not be weakened because their regular militia would not be affected.

On May 8 and 11 Congress made important changes in its volunteer army. These changes allowed the President to accept for the duration and without the delay of state consent any company, battalion, or regiment which offered itself. He could group them into larger corps and appoint all field and staff officers; the enlisted men were to choose their company officers. The new laws removed all restrictions on numbers accepted.[6] These acts clearly weakened the hold over its enlisted citizens by the state, which retained control over its militia volunteers but which had no jurisdiction over companies raised and equipped independently. They also permitted the use of volunteers from states which had not yet seceded. On May 16 Congress voted each enlisted man a $10 bounty which was primarily designed to pay the recruit's transportation to camp.[7]

The First Battle of Manassas startled the United States into realizing that it had a war on its hands, for which it now began all-out preparations. Davis reported that the United States was preparing an invasion with a half-million men, and advised Congress to prepare for war "on a scale more gigantic" than had heretofore been expected.[8] Congress was in full agreement and, with some dissent, accepted the Military Committee's figure of an army of 400,000 men. The act of August 8 authorized the President to receive this number of militia volunteers with enlistment terms of from one to three years.[9]

The response to this law was overwhelming. In their enthusiasm more militia and independent volunteers came forward than either the individual states or the Confederate government could arm and equip. The result was that by the summer the War Department was usually accepting only three-year volunteers or twelve-month militia who could arm themselves. State governors badgered the Department frightfully to receive all their volunteers, but for several months Davis accepted only a few thousand from each state and left over 200,000 idling in camp at state expense. The President was choosy for reasons other than lack of equipment. He considered an army of several hundred thousand men unnecessary, and there was already talk about the threat of a military despotism. In addition several states offered "skeleton" regiments, composed of a full contingent of officers and a few enlisted men. Davis thus was left with the problem of filling the regiments out and at the same time was deprived of many officer appointments. The major reason for this wholesale rejection policy was Davis's distrust of short enlistments. The events of early April foretold anything but peaceful secession, and he foresaw the possibility that twelve-month volunteers would not re-enlist the following spring.[10]

Congress meanwhile was experimenting with other troop-raising methods. On August 8 it authorized the President to commission a number of select individuals to raise and command volunteer units of men who were or had been residents of the border slave states. Three weeks later it let Davis establish recruiting stations at which these border state volunteers could be enrolled and cared for until they were numerous enough to be received under the Acts of May 8 and 11.[11] At the suggestion of almost any high official, Congress readily granted the President the right to admit units of sappers and bombardiers, artillerymen, seamen, marines, and even one regiment of Zouaves. On August 21 it authorized him to accept for local defense and for special service in advanced positions an unspecified number of volunteers.[12] This act was intended to be applied infrequently, and Congress had made it unusually generous. As local defense became more necessary Davis's frequent use of the law caused numerous quarrels between the states and the Confederate government.[13]

Toward the end of 1861, military zeal, which had been unsurpassed at first, had begun to wane slightly. Davis had been unable to get enough three-year enlistments and over half of his veteran army was composed of twelve-month volunteers. There was thus the possibility that in the spring of 1862 half the army would vanish. Even if they could be immediately replaced, Secretary

Mobilization of Manpower 63

Judah P. Benjamin explained that making men into effective soldiers was difficult and expensive and warned that the army would be critically weakened if the present men, "inured to hardship, recovered from camp disease, [and] steadied by discipline" were lost. To induce them to re-enlist he proposed a "liberal bounty" and a "moderate furlough."[14] Congress complied as ordered and on December 11 offered a $50 bounty and a 60-day furlough to those who would enlist or re-enlist for a total of three years or the duration. It also let the men reorganize into companies, battalions, and regiments with the right of choosing their company and field officers.[15] This deprived Davis of some of his appointing power, but he felt more than compensated by the hope of a more stable army.

Though the purpose of the law was commendable, it was fashioned to please rather than strengthen the army. While it influenced few to re-enlist, the law inconvenienced and disorganized the army. Furloughed soldiers crowded the railroads almost to the breaking point. Since most officers were now elected, ambitious soldiers canvassed discontented men in established regiments, at times "filled the men with liquor and demoralized them,"[16] and on being elected, caused a large turn-over in officer personnel. These men, often with little ability, weakened the effectiveness of many commands and disconcerted everyone with their struggle to retain their positions. The complete reorganization that was permitted caused a general shifting of companies and regiments, which tended to unstabilize the entire Provisional Army.

During December and January Congress passed other weak measures to lure men into re-enlistment. On December 19 it authorized the Secretary of War to adopt measures for recruiting three-year enlistees, and a month later it allowed company commanders to detail officers and privates to recruit individual volunteers to fill their ranks.[17] Neither law was effective, for the Secretary was given no new means of recruiting, and, as for the second law, experience soon revealed that prospective soldiers preferred to form their own companies. A law of January 22, 1862, allowed the President to accept volunteers singly as well as in organized units, but this practice did not even offer the new soldier the camaraderie of belonging to one's own unit. Another act the following day let the President "call on" the states for three-year volunteers rather than "accept" those offered.[18] This Act made raising troops the patriotic duty of the states themselves and met with some success. By the end of the Provisional Congress, this continuous overhauling by Congress to meet the changing military scene had rendered the volunteer army system as complicated as it was uncertain.

As early as December, 1861, conscription was referred to seriously, its advocates urging two fundamental reasons for adopting it. According to the Secretary of War the terms of 148 regiments would end within thirty days and a majority of these would not re-enlist. Some element of compulsion was required to keep them in the army. In the second place, many felt that the less populated South could no longer maintain the North's rate of volunteering and must resort to some supplementary method of raising troops. Conscription, resting on the familiar Anglo-Saxon principle that every man between 16 and 60 must defend his country, gained increasing favor with both the press and the military.

Meanwhile the First Congress, though receptive to the idea of conscription, refused to take the initiative. During the emergency of war the body was unsure of its position and preferred to leave the advisability of conscription to executive judgment. Outright opponents of conscription tried to commit Congress inextricably to volunteering by proposing its extension, but the majority refused to be rushed. Davis himself was strangely tardy in suggesting conscription to Congress. Both R. E. Lee and Thomas J. Jackson were known to favor it (Jackson having even practiced it occasionally in Virginia), but Davis, who ordinarily valued their advice highly, delayed the issue for two months. On February 26, 1862, he informed Congress that short enlistments and furloughs, to which he had steadily objected since the commencement of the war, had disorganized the army, but added that the difficulties had now come substantially to an end.[19] Some representatives, who believed that the Provisional Congress had granted Davis everything he requested, rebelled at these "aspersions" and requested an explanation. Davis replied that he had favored an increase of 300,000 men "in the field," but still failed to suggest an alternative method of procuring them.[20] Possibly he was giving the newspapers time to accustom the people to the idea; again he may have been awaiting word from General Lee, who at the time was preparing a conscription bill.

On March 29 Davis finally asked for the conscription of all men between 18 and 35 and some simple, direct method for their enrollment and organization, "repealing all of the legislation heretofore enacted which would conflict with the system proposed."[21] Meanwhile Lee had reviewed the matter with Major

...... *Mobilization of Manpower* *65*

Charles Marshall and the latter had drafted a conscription bill. Lee then remitted it to Davis, who approved the principle and had Secretary Benjamin put the bill into formal shape. It was then introduced into the Senate on April 1 by Louis T. Wigfall, one of the few state rights leaders originally supporting conscription.

Wigfall keynoted the debate when he condemned volunteering as a "broken reed" and urged Congress to "Cease this child's play." He reproduced Falstaff's challenge to let anyone "spit in his face and call him a horse" if conscription were not constitutional.[22] Congress by this time had decided to sacrifice principle to practicality. A majority in both houses undoubtedly believed that they had no power except through the intervention of the states to force citizens into the Confederate army;[23] but by their docility they showed an equal conviction to yield to the recommendations of more expert authorities. The House considered establishing a joint committee of the House and Senate to prepare a conscription bill, but everyone was so anxious to complete the distasteful job that the Senate bill was the only one considered by Congress. The single test vote in either house was on South Carolina Senator James L. Orr's amendment to substitute a policy of requisitions upon the states, and this was easily defeated. Opponents in both houses saw the futility of contesting the law in principle and simply tried to retain some control for the states. They failed to require the consent of each state for its citizens to be drafted or to secure the exemption of all state militia. They succeeded, however, in giving the conscripts the right to elect their own officers and to be assigned to companies from their home states; they also gained the right of company and field officers to be elected by their own state laws. Approximately one-third of each house opposed conscription on the final vote, with two-thirds of the opposition coming from the four Atlantic seaboard states above Florida.[24]

The law of April 16 authorized the President to conscript for a term of three years or the duration all white men between the ages of 18 and 35 who were not legally exempt. Those already in service and qualifying under the act were to continue serving for three years from the date of their enlistment. Companies, battalions, and regiments might reorganize by electing all officers whom they as volunteers had had the right to elect heretofore. Men raised under the act were to be assigned, if they preferred, to companies from their own state now in the Confederate service. Anyone wishing to volunteer before being drafted could do so and gain the additional privilege of entering service in a new company of his own selection. Avoiding the law was made relatively easy by allowing men, by their own arrangement, to hire as substitutes any able-bodied men not subject to the law.[25]

The adoption of conscription made two important changes in the method of raising the army: to a large extent it dispensed with the instrumentality of the states, and, though it still allowed volunteering, it made compulsion the main principle. Most men now knew what the government expected of them under the law. One effect was that it stopped volunteering in state organizations and the reporting to camps of instruction, since all who did so were classed as conscripts. Not wishing to bear the odium of being so classified, thousands in 1862 and 1863 went directly into the regular service. The resulting increase, combined with the retention of those who otherwise would have been released, was largely responsible for the trained army with which Lee executed his first great campaign of the Seven Days' Battles around Richmond. Notwithstanding the friction that the system provoked, conscription worked better than one might have expected and no doubt enabled the Confederacy to prolong the war.

Few people were neutral about conscription. The patriotic objected to its implications, while would-be civilians resented compulsory army service. Men who were exempt or who could hire substitutes were noncommittal, but those who had neither position nor wealth loudly denounced it as class legislation. It was favored by those who had already volunteered and who wished others to share their glory and their discomforts. Four groups of people probably suffered from conscription: those rightfully exempt but constantly annoyed by enrolling officers; those soon to be liable to service who were not allowed to volunteer in organizations of their own choice; "deadheads" or malcontents who deserved and received no sympathy; and genuine unionists.

A majority of the press supported conscription now that it was an accomplished fact. They accepted it as a proper exercise of the war-making powers of Congress, and their reasoning closely followed that of the Selective Draft Law Cases of 1919. It was a "military necessity," and the *Richmond Enquirer* claimed that "Whatever is necessary, *must be done;* whatever is advantageous ... *must be adopted.*"[26] Volunteering had "played out," had only "filled the army with old men and boys,"[27] and could never provide an adequate army because it "leaves fighting to the most patriotic."[28] Conscription would shorten the war by giving the Confederacy a larger army and by removing "demagoguism" from the system of military commissions.[29] The *Wilmington Daily Journal* believed that it would get many men from districts where there was little stigma against slackers.[30] A most persuasive argument was that it operated equally on all people and classes, and put the "press on, boys!" shirkers on the same fighting terms as the most patriotic.[31]

A strong minority of the press opposed conscription. The *Yorkville Enquirer* dubbed it a confession of political death and felt that the enemy would consider it a desperation measure.[32] The *Raleigh Standard* believed it to be unconstitutional, for the state and the Confederate government had contracted to dismiss the twelve-month volunteers at the end of their stated service.[33] Most of them defended volunteering on the grounds that "No demand the President has yet made on a State Government for troops but has been met to the full extent."[34] Other objections were that conscripts would be poor fighters, that the states would be stripped of their defenders, that a draft would create a huge military machine amenable to no civil power, that it would result in cruelty of officers to their men, and that its moral effect would be bad.

While debating conscription Congress had also considered exemptions from military service. The maintenance of the home front forced Congress to distinguish between essential and nonessential jobs. The solution would have been easier had government and business been content with the aged, the infirm, and the very young, but no less than the military they desired men with energy and ability. It was up to Congress to strike a balance between workers and fighters. At first it indulged the home front, and many able-bodied men held seemingly non-essential jobs. Later when it tried to match the increasing United States forces Congress seemed determined to enroll everyone.

On April 14 Senator Yancey introduced a bill exempting certain persons from military service, which passed the Senate almost in its original form. The only significant House amendment was one adding to the exemption list "all persons who now are . . . exempted by the laws of the respective States."[35] A conference committee hurriedly met to discuss this controversial point, but on the last day of the session reported its complete failure to reach an agreement. The House thereupon withdrew its amendment and the bill became law on April 21.

This first exemption law was over-generous and established the familiar system of "class exemptions," which conferred blanket freedom from military service upon men in certain occupations. It exempted all physically unfit, judicial and executive officers and their clerks in the state and the Confederate governments, members of Congress and of the state legislatures, most men employed in communication and transportation, preachers, several classes of iron workers, printers, educators, employees of institutions for the indigent and the helpless, all textile workers designated by the Secretary of War, and most apothecaries.[36]

During the summer of 1862 the government and its generals soon found that the first experiments in compulsory military service had been shortsighted. The Northern forces grew steadily, and since the Confederacy hoped to take the offensive, larger armies were mandatory. Most national leaders soon became convinced that conscription should be extended to men of forty-five, and one by one the newspapers accepted this figure and seared it upon the public consciousness. In his message of August 18 President Davis advised Congress that the increasing Northern armies "may render it necessary hereafter to extend the provisions of the conscript law so as to embrace persons between the ages of 35 and 45 years."[37]

The House was eager to begin discussion and the following day Foote of Tennessee, a consistent opponent of conscription, got in the first blow by proposing that Congress raise 250,000 additional men through requisitions upon the states. He explained that, when the administration insisted that the fate of the nation was at stake, he and many others had swallowed their objections to the first conscription law. Now that the danger no longer existed he wanted the matter thoroughly and openly examined.[38] The administration accepted the challenge and conscription was debated until everyone was tired of the discussion.

Debate in the House was long and repetitious, though usually temperate. Foote, in a two-hour speech which Otho R. Singleton of Mississippi claimed to have heard the preceding April, sarcastically declared that, while President Davis was a "sage" whose name would be "gloriously inscribed in history," he was in error in claiming overwhelming support for the first law. Many representatives had "painfully voted for it, upon the ground of necessity."[39] Burgess S. Gaither of North Carolina admitted being one of them, and added that in voting for conscription the first time he had had no idea that it would become a permanent policy.[40] A half-dozen speakers defended anew the volunteer system, and

William N. H. Smith of North Carolina suggested asking the states to organize reserve armies and hold them in readiness for call by the Confederate government. Milledge L. Bonham of South Carolina cited the President's admission that more troops were not immediately needed; his associate, Boyce, urged that the Confederacy husband its manpower for the long war ahead by continuing its defensive strategy with small armies.[41]

There was criticism both of the first draft law and its manner of execution. William W. Clark of Georgia considered it "fraught with tyranny and injustice," and Caleb C. Herbert of Texas shocked his listeners by threatening another Texas secession if conscription was continued. Lucien J. Dupré of Louisiana used his own figures to prove that the system had left his state defenseless and had contributed directly to the fall of New Orleans. A telling argument was that the first law had not filled up the existing regiments as intended; that men waited until just before their enrollment and then volunteered in regiments of their own choosing. Eastern congressmen claimed that conscription had been poorly applied in the border states and that, since Congress was pledged to redeem these states, their manpower should be used. These critics did not demand that the first draft law be repealed; they recognized its accomplishments and only tried to block its extension.

The supporters of conscription had the advantage of defending an accomplished fact. They took care to appear confident during debate and left oratory to the other side. They believed that volunteering had failed, that the law of April 16 had saved the country, and that people were generally satisfied with conscription. Congress had recognized its constitutionality by passing the first law, though Thomas J. Foster of Alabama embarrassed his friends by offering to burn the Constitution if it "stood between him and his country's freedom. . . ." Advocates denied that a permanent draft policy would lead to military despotism. The House Military Committee explained that it only wished to fill up the regiments now in the field, and Chairman Miles predicted that the proposed extension would quickly end the war.

On September 1 Miles reported a committee bill to fill up "existing companies, squadrons, battalions, and regiments, and to increase the Provisional Army." The bill authorized the President to call into service for the duration all non-exempt men between 35 and 45. To aid its passage it contained an important procedural feature which provided that the President should first requisition from the state governors all or part of the men in this age group. Not until a governor had refused this call could the President order the men in that state enrolled according to the procedure in the first conscription law.[42] This feature, which was designed to avoid arousing the question of state sovereignty,[43] made the bill less decisive than the law of April 16 in that it appeared to recognize the state as a co-equal army-raising power.

Nevertheless a strong group of state righters tried vigorously to place with the states even more control in raising the troops. Bonham started the counterattack by proposing to let the President ask the states for not more than 300,000 three-year volunteers between the ages of 35 and 45; Gaither would at least let him extend conscription to these ages in a state that failed or refused to raise its quota. The administration forces, however, believed that the committee bill made enough concessions to the states. They staved off Bonham's bill and several like it, let the opposition talk itself out, and on September 17 showed their full strength by passing the committee bill almost unchanged by a vote of 49 to 39.[44]

Meanwhile the Senate was working on the same matter. Most senators had approved the first conscription law, and Wigfall now kept his hotel neighbors awake with loud arguments for extension.[45] For about two weeks the Senate perused various ways to supplement the first draft law, but Phelan finally protested so vigorously against frittering away time on half-way measures that on September 2 the Military Committee reported a bill merely extending conscription to men of 45. Both House and Senate committee bills required that all men raised be used to fill up their state's volunteer units, but the Senate let new companies be formed with the surplus. Yancey responded with a substitute essentially like the House bill, but the majority abruptly brushed it aside and rushed its bill through by a vote of 20 to 2.[46]

When both houses proved adamant a conference committee was appointed which adopted the Senate measure with one modification. To make the law more palatable it added the provision that the President, if he so desired, could call for those between the age of thirty-five and any other age less than forty-five.[47] Despite Foote's warning that the bill might cause civil war it became law on September 27. This new draft law cautiously refrained from depriving the states of more control of their manpower. It continued to channel conscripts into their state's regiments, permitted the President to suspend the law wherever it was impractical to apply it, and let him receive troops under any previous law of Congress.[48] There was nothing in it, except the implied establishment of conscription as a permanent policy, that created new hostility, and Congress had wisely refused to tamper with a system that was becoming familiar, if not popular.

Congress faced a less clear-cut problem when it re-examined the question of military exemptions. Since nearly every item in an exemption law is class legislation, the lines must be drawn with the greatest care. The hasty, inexact law of April 21 patently needed clarification and improvement. The greatest clamor arose from men who considered their occupation unexpendable. Religious sectarians, overseers, students, and many others flooded Congress with petitions for exemption. The War Department had included some classes — tanners, millers, and salters — in the spirit of the law and Congress had to review their exemption. Planters in particular considered themselves indispensable and during the spring of 1862 launched a vigorous campaign for blanket exemption.

On August 26 the Senate Committee on Military Affairs, after a number of conferences with the Secretary of War, introduced a bill expanding and clarifying the first exemption law. For three weeks the bill was before the Senate almost daily and the smoothness of its passage almost ruined it. Nearly every senator sponsored one or more classes, most of which were log-rolled onto the exemption list. Only professions or occupations known to be refuges for draft-dodgers received less than gentle treatment. Teaching, tanning, and preaching had become amazingly popular since the first exemption law, and the Senate required service in these occupations for two or more years for exemption.[49] A similar problem arose in regard to government employees. President Davis's order that personnel be selected from those not subject to military duty did not prevent his department heads from seeking special favors from Congress. Each pleaded that his department required none but the ablest men and asked that all his workers be exempt.[50] Congress, however, was exceptionally chary with this type of exemption, generally leaving the departments with no alternative but to comply with the President's directive.

The most interesting part of the discussion occurred over Dortch's proposal to draft all justices of the peace. At this point Wigfall provided strict state righters with the motto, "Perish the

Republic, but call not upon us to commit perjury."[51] Others, denying the right of Congress to incapacitate a state government, argued that the ability to force the humble justice of the peace into the army implied the same rights over all other state officers. Yancey warned that signs were "not lacking that the war power is quietly usurping the powers of both State and Federal Governments."[52] The administration forces replied that the war gave the government the right to take state officers as well as other citizens. Phelan assured everyone that the government would never abuse its powers "by laying hands on the executive officers of the States," but even though it did the offices and the government would remain and could survive until the war ended.[53]

The question of exempting overseers was controversial on another plane. Semmes of Louisiana led a movement to exempt one overseer on each plantation using Negro labor exclusively and on which there was no responsible white man. This practice was doubly criticized on the grounds that its basic principle was undemocratic and that Semmes had worded his amendment so that it could be interpreted to exempt most of the planters. When it was voted upon, the border state senators aligned with a few others representing non-planting elements and restricted the exemption to one person, whether owner or overseer, on each place only if the state law required a resident white man at all times.[54]

Most House amendments to the Senate bill were intended to clarify or to add other class exemptions. The only important contribution in principle was to limit the occupational profit of exemptees to 75% of the cost of production. A conference committee sustained the House amendments and the bill was signed on October 11.

The new law exempted the judicial and executive officers of the state and Confederate governments, but excluded those state officers declared by law liable to militia duty. It exempted all Confederate and state clerks holding office and all state volunteer troops raised for public defense and in active service. Most public utilities, pacifist religious sects, skilled artisans, managerial personnel, and laborers in essential occupations were exempt provided their net profits remained below 75%. Either the owner or an overseer was exempt for every plantation containing twenty or more slaves, or, in the event of a state law, any plantation on which it required a white man. The President could exempt such other persons as he saw fit. These exemptions were to continue only while the persons involved were actively engaged in their privileged occupations.[55] Thus by the fall of 1862 Congress had established a coordination of the military and the home fronts that was expected to last until the end of the war.

VI

CONSCRIPTION UNDER ATTACK

Though its early efforts to enlist and distribute the nation's available manpower seemed satisfactory, Congress was quickly obliged to a never-ending adjustment, exploring new avenues for raising troops and attending to existing laws. This adjustment was seldom easy, for domestic and foreign politics presented serious obstacles; but the fact that the principles of conscription and exemption were now firmly established provided at least the general direction for their solution. President Davis, who was quite willing to suggest policy in minute detail, continued to supply leadership and Congress seldom lacked for departmental advice.

On August 12, 1862, Secretary of War Randolph reported that the war had dislocated many men whom he was having difficulty enrolling. Some, refugees from occupied districts, had not set up permanent residence elsewhere; others were merely dodging about from one place to another to avoid military duty. He requested the power to enroll eligible men wherever they might be found.[1] Although no one defended shirkers, congressmen from affected districts believed that most refugees were busy seeking residence for their families and would be unjustly humiliated at being rushed into the army. The majority, however, felt that to ignore them would be to exempt most border state men, and the law of October 8, 1862, ordered them enrolled wherever found, and subject to the provisions of law as if fully enrolled in their home county.[2]

In October Congress passed two laws designed to reach beyond the arms of the Bureau of Conscription. In outlying areas where conscription was inapplicable a number of battalions and regiments had been organized which included some men of draft age. If the government enrolled these latter the services of the remainder would be lost; hence on October 11 Congress authorized the President to accept these units as originally composed provided they had been formed before October 1. Two days later Congress permitted men over forty-five or otherwise exempt to form small local defense units and become part of the regular army, with the exception that they would receive no pay or allowance.[3] Since the law, however, did not guarantee that these men would be used only within their state, few joined such units.

In the middle of April, 1862, Congress decided to add irregular bodies of troops to the army. Representative William Smith of Virginia proposed a band of "partisan rangers" to operate within enemy lines and to be paid $5 for each enemy killed.[4] The Military Committee preferred to keep them more subject to army behavior and proposed a substitute which passed both houses. The substitute plan authorized the President to commission officers to form bands of partisan rangers, but was completely silent as to their duties. Congress believed that the value of the scheme would be in raising men otherwise unobtainable, for they were to receive the same pay and rations as other soldiers.[5]

This experiment was disappointing. Secretary Seddon said that the bands did more harm to the people than the enemy and that they could seldom resist the temptation to "license and depredation. . . . " He recommended that they be merged into the troops of the line or be disbanded and drafted.[6] General Jeb Stuart said that the Rangers were detrimental to the best interests of the army, and that Mosby's Rangers was the only efficient band he knew of. Robert E. Lee recommended flatly that the law be repealed.[7] Since the United States had been strict in holding Confederate sympathizers responsible for Ranger activities, the continuation of activities would seem unreasonably harsh on these civilians. Congressmen from the West maintained that the conscription laws were so poorly applied there that their citizens had little alternative but to join the Rangers, and for several months persuaded Congress to withhold action. But by the end of 1863 so much evidence of their undesirability had accumulated that the bands obviously failed to merit continued existence. On February 17, 1864, Congress absorbed them into the regular army, with the exception that the Secretary of War could continue to use troops in Ranger capacity to serve within the enemy lines.[8]

During the winter of 1862-1863 Congress debated the advisability of drafting resident foreigners. In answer to inquiries about the matter, Attorney-General Thomas H. Watts advised the War

Department that a foreigner who planned to reside permanently in the Confederacy owed "the correlative *duty* of defending this country. . . ."[9] The majority in Congress, however, had no intention of drafting foreigners *en masse,* and Secretary Benjamin assured the worried British consul at Charleston that only foreigners who had "established themselves in these States without intention of returning to their native country" would be drafted.[10] This was borne out when the Senate, for fear of offending foreign nations, easily defeated Clay's bill to enroll all aliens. In the House Foote stated that "Jewish Shylocks" had flocked from all over the world by "mysterious process" to exploit the Confederacy's trials, but his proposal to draft them received the same treatment as Clay's.[11]

Congress had less respect for United States citizens. In January, 1863, George G. Vest of Missouri reported that there were 2,000 "blood-tub" Marylanders in Richmond who were always ready to break out into the strain of "Maryland, my Maryland" but who refused to strike a blow for their state.[12] He proposed to conscript all persons in the Confederacy who, if they were in the United States, would be subject to its conscription laws.[13] The House Judiciary Committee ruled the bill constitutional and on April 27 it easily passed. The Senate passed it two days before the end of the session, but Davis, seeing no reason to alienate the neighboring, and almost neutral, state for a few thousand troops, defeated it by pocket veto.

The first conscription law of April 16, 1862, had allowed a prospective soldier to furnish a substitute, who would be held to precisely the same terms as all other soldiers while relieving the principal of any further responsibility. Substitution was designed to benefit young businessmen who might be more valuable outside the army, but it soon was used by everyone who could afford it. The cost of substitutes rose from $100 to as much as $5,000, and brokers began to advertise them widely. Substitutes themselves were generally unsatisfactory soldiers. Most were over forty and from an undisciplined environment. Some hired themselves only to desert immediately and repeat the process, each time collecting their prices and exempting one more man by their "bounty jumping." Those who remained in service were seldom patriotic or industrious and soon earned the scorn of their associates. Men unable to afford substitutes condemned the law as class legislation, and the *Raleigh Standard* claimed that the practice "put the money of one man in one scale, and the blood of the moneyless man in the other. . . ."[14]

When the Conscription Act of September 27, 1862, extended the draft age to 45, few denied that substitutes between 35 and 45 were liable to military service in their own name. The difficulty arose when principals claimed that, since they had furnished substitutes according to the law, the government was under contract to continue their exemption indefinitely. Most state courts soon ruled that no contract was involved; therefore, the War Department claimed that principals were liable to service the moment their substitutes were subject to enrollment.[15] Generally it did not molest principals whose state courts sustained their exemptions, since it was administration policy to accept the findings of these courts whenever possible. For over a year, however, Congress refused to commit itself concerning principals from such states. Instead, contrary to advice from the Secretary of War, it chose to adjust rather than abolish the principle of substitution. Congress was reluctant to decide the issue, possibly because of coming congressional elections, but probably because most members felt that the home front needed such a law.

In August, 1862, the Senate Military Committee proposed and the Senate quickly passed a bill to allow substitutes only to men who the Secretary of War declared were skilled and actually employed in some "mechanical pursuit," or who were managing plantations with fifty or more slaves.[16] A supplementary bill forced the principal to guarantee his substitute by offering another or taking his place if the substitute deserted. Orr considered these measures both *ex post facto* and a breach of contract; the Military Committee agreed, but claimed that most principals had been aware of their substitutes' poor character and had thus entered the contract fraudulently.[17] The House refused to pass either of these bills. It usually defended the non-planting elements more than did the Senate and also hesitated to confer such powers of discretion upon the Secretary of War. The second bill was too poorly drawn to merit much consideration. It would force guarantees from those thereafter furnishing substitutes, but failed to demand the same from those already having them.[18]

During the last session of the First Congress, which met on December 7, 1863, opposition to substitution was impressive. The Secretary of War reported that substitutes were poor fighters but active deserters and had done little except excite discontent and impatience under service among the soldiers.[19] President Davis concurred and requested Congress to conscript both substitute and principal. He and the Secretary assured Congress that in accepting a substitute the government had not entered a contract but had conferred a temporary privilege, the time for which was now ended. The Mississippi legislature wished total repeal of the substitute law and John B. Jones wrote that Congress was particularly intimidated by petitions from several generals.[20]

In the first week of the session the Senate passed a bill withdrawing the right of substitution and drafting all principals outside the army. The House felt that the bill should be divided, for the second part involved an important issue of contractual obligation as well as one of policy. The Senate consented and the law of December 28 merely prohibited any further use of substitutes.[21]

Before drafting the principal the House sought to ease its conscience by inquiring about the substitute's good faith in entering the army. Seddon answered that substitutes frequently entered deceitfully and that over 10,000 men not in the army held fraudulent substitute papers.[22] The House Military Committee thereupon proposed to enroll any principal whose substitute had deserted or had been physically unfit at the time of induction, and to conscript those whose substitutes became liable to enrollment.[23] The majority considered this proposal too timid, for the principal would remain exempt if his substitute was otherwise acceptable and outside the conscription age. They amended the bill to draft the principal and to keep his substitute in the army even though the latter never became liable to service. This passed by a vote of 52 to 13 and, when only Senators Orr and Herschel V. Johnson opposed it, became law on January 5, 1864.[24] Orr then wondered if Congress expected the "special interposition of Providence" to feed the army as "God Almighty fed the Israelites. . . ."[25] The House tried to answer him by a proposal to allow substitution to men who, before January 1, 1864, were engaged in raising provisions, but the Senate refused even to bring this to a vote.

The state courts upheld both laws. They decided that the contract clause in the Constitution was a prohibition on the states and not on Congress. Permission to offer substitutes was an act of grace and a privilege, but this act did not grant exemption under future laws. Nor was it unconstitutional to refuse compensation to principals whose substitutes were drafted. Since there was no contract no compensation was legally due. The abolition of substitution was a healthy step; the army was not greatly increased, but an important cause of dissatisfaction was removed.

During 1862 and 1863 Congress also found several flaws in its exemption system, and here it had even more difficulty in striking a balance between the home front and the army. The most disagreeable problem was the "20 Nigger" section of the last exemption law, which exempted the owner or the overseer of plantations containing twenty or more slaves. A few newspapers conceded its validity, but most condemned the law as the grossest class legislation. Congressmen received scores of accusations that, though slaves caused the war, "those who own them . . . make the poor man do the fighting. . . ."[26] The legislatures of North Carolina, Louisiana, and Texas demanded either that the provision be changed or repealed. On January 12, 1863, President Davis finally advised Congress that the law was so detested that some means should be devised "for leaving at home a sufficient local police without making discriminations . . . between different classes of our citizens."[27]

Reuben Davis inaccurately recalled that after this message "Fifty members sprang to their feet" to demand the law's repeal,[28] but both houses quickly discovered that this particular exemption could not be divorced from others. For the past year President Davis and Secretary Seddon had criticized Congress's static exemption system. They felt that the use of able-bodied manpower was an administrative decision and wished Congress merely to establish the draft age and leave to the executive branch the choice of exempting or of detailing whomever it wished. This put Congress in a quandary, for it had little quarrel with the existing system. Even if it consented to study the exemption of overseers or any other class, it must decide whether to rely on its own judgment or that of the President. As a result, from January until May, 1863, both houses floundered in indecision and left the job only half done.

Congress disposed of the question of overseer exemption with relative ease, if with little finality, for both houses attacked only its worst faults. Barksdale considered the exemption "unnecessary, impolitic, unjust and prejudicial" and proposed its outright repeal.[29] This would have left plantation slaves relatively unsupervised, and the House adopted a substitute by Robert B. Hilton of Florida retaining a modicum of exemption. In the Senate the planters were ably represented by Hill, Orr, Yancey, and several others, who insisted that complete repeal would soon starve the army into submission. For several days the Senate wrangled unenthusiastically about "class legislation" and "the home front," with neither side making very telling points. In the end it decided to exempt only overseers employed before April 16, 1862.

Meanwhile the administration forces in both houses had undertaken the discouraging task of revising the entire exemption system. On January 20, Miles reported a bill from the House Military Committee delegating to the President and his Secretary of War the determination of all exemptions and details. The Senate Committee, less inclined to abdicate its authority, proposed to reduce the exemption lists by about one-third and to block the rush into exempt classes.[30] Neither bill had much committee support and congressmen in both houses who preferred liberal exemptions played havoc with both of them, repeatedly referring them back to their committee and proposing an almost endless number of amendments. Much of the time they entangled the matter with that of overseer exemption in an effort to make the latter's supporters accept their array of amendments. Representatives who disliked executive detail argued that Miles's bill destroyed the last trace of state rights, and would enable the President to establish a military despotism.[31] Foote added that congressmen were neither numbskulls nor impotent and could determine exemptions quite as well as the President could. The House proponents of liberal exemption revealed so much strength in exempting whomever they wished that it was useless to bring the bill to a vote. Senators from occupied states favored restricting exemptions, but were outnumbered and the Senate measure that finally passed on February 13 bore little resemblance to the original bill.

When the Senate bill, now with only slightly fewer exemptions than the law of October 11, reached the House it received so many new ones that a conference committee of both houses was ordered. This committee was largely composed of men favoring liberal class exemptions and reported a bill with such an exaggerated list that the Senate, contrary to custom, flatly rejected it.[32] At this point the administration despaired of overhauling the entire exemption system and Congress happily narrowed its attention once more to overseer exemption. The houses now established unofficial communication, and on April 27 the House Military Committee reported a bill which passed with dispatch and became law on May 31. The law allowed one exempted person

...... *Conscription under Attack* *81*

on each 20-slave plantation owned by persons physically or mentally unfit or in the army, provided the exemptee was so employed prior to April 16, 1862. Owners must prove their inability to hire a draft-exempt man and must pay $500 for each person so exempted. Even at this stage one concession had to be made to those desiring further exemption, and state officers whom their governors requested were added to the exemption list.[33] President Davis never officially expressed his keen disappointment at this rebuff and merely renewed his proposals at the next sessions.

This law would have injured agricultural production had not the War Department applied it cautiously. Many persons had already made their planting arrangements under the old law and requested that the Conscript Bureau be instructed to postpone its enforcement in view of the great demand for provisions. The administration consented and until the next autumn usually granted temporary exemptions to overseers engaged in raising provisions. This delay, plus the fact that the essential 20-Negro feature was retained, made the law poorly appreciated. The familiar theme of a "rich man's war and a poor man's fight" still plagued the government, for the poor considered the law discriminatory and the upcountry people protested it on sectional grounds.

Two other changes were made in the exemption system. In March, 1863, Postmaster Reagan reported that if his mail carriers were rushed into the army the efficiency of his department would be almost destroyed. The exemption of these 1,509 men could hardly wreck the army and he begged for their services.[34] Davis agreed that the appeal was urgent, and Congress immediately exempted most contractors and their drivers. On April 2 Congress authorized the discharge of any officer or soldier who was elected or appointed to Congress, to a state legislature, or to a number of other inferior state posts.[35]

By the end of 1863 the laws that Congress had written to enlist the Confederate manpower indicated by their very multiplicity that they were insufficient and inadequately enforced. By April the army had about one-half million men enrolled, but only half of them were present for duty, the others having been lost by shirking, disloyalty, and by poor machinery for enforcing the laws.

The system of class exemptions proved susceptible to wide abuse and there was a rush to qualify under some heading. Teaching became popular overnight and new schools were opened by young men who scratched around to get the required twenty pupils;

others opened "apothecary shops" that sold anything from strawberries to hair dye; still others became salt makers, tanners, or blacksmiths who did barely enough to warrant the name; many took small government positions for less than subsistence wages merely to occupy exempt jobs. Some physical infirmities now became blessings revealed, and gout, rheumatism, and "low back" pain were among the most cherished ailments. A number of doctors and enrolling officers were guilty in keeping friends out of the army and the ever-watchful war clerk John B. Jones reported that "for a price" they overlooked complete strangers.[36]

The army set up a Bureau of Conscription to carry out the laws of Congress. The Bureau was seldom vigorously managed, for reasons not always its own fault. Most of its officers were incompetents unfit for field service, and their subordinates were shirkers who preferred this easier duty and then performed it poorly. Several times Congress requested facts and figures from the Secretary of War, who at times was forced to reply that "the want of proper returns renders it impossible to supply the information sought."[37] The Bureau concentrated its work in the Atlantic coast states and congressmen from other states wrote that there was no need to make laws that would be ignored. For this reason General Braxton Bragg devised his own system of "enforced volunteering" in the area between the Mississippi River and the mountains. General Gideon J. Pillow was in charge of this operation and secured at least 25,000 men from districts which otherwise would have been almost untapped by the draft laws.[38]

In districts which the laws reached there was a wide range of enforcement. Senator Phelan informed the President that in Mississippi conscription was a farce, and the Acting Chief of the Bureau said that his enrolling officers were sometimes shot. Some of these officers were local citizens who showed partiality to acquaintances; others were young men whom the local citizenry overawed. Other enrolling officers showed too much zeal in their work. Malcolm D. Graham wrote that many Texans, "after being discharged on examination for *permanent* disability, to serve in the field, have been again & again, required to enroll themselves, and as often discharged."[39] A. T. Davidson reported that two of his friends from Asheville had been arrested and carried away to Georgia by an irresponsible man and forced to volunteer.[40] The *Florida Sentinel* wrote that its citizens were "hunted down, decoyed by blowing a horn, surprised and dragged off barefooted" into the army.[41]

Conscription under Attack 83

Recruits sometimes learned the discomforts of red tape before they became full fledged soldiers. A law of October 11, 1862, ordered a "place of rendezvous" in each county or city where men were to receive their physical examinations,[42] but the army found this frequency impractical and often forced men to travel more than a hundred miles for their examination. When they reported to camps of instruction they sometimes remained there for six months before being assigned to a regiment; meanwhile the army refused to consider this part of their enlistment term or to pay them anything for their stay. Such inconveniences, embarrassment, and discrimination antagonized the enlisted men.

One of the fundamental problems to be settled regarding conscription was its constitutionality. The Attorney General had declared the draft law of April 16 constitutional, but before it was completely safe it had to run the gamut of the state courts. Fortunately the idea of state sovereignty was more entrenched in government than in court circles; many state and Confederate judges had served in the United States and had retained a certain amount of nationalism. Some lower courts ruled against conscription, but by 1863 every state supreme court had accepted it as a part of Congress's war-making power. Except for Brown of Georgia the governors accepted these verdicts, though tending to add reservations as the war and conscription bore more heavily upon the states.[43]

Conscription fared poorer when it required writs of habeas corpus to enforce it. This "reign of habeas corpus" started when conscripts began to test their liability to military service by suing for writs from the lower state courts. Even though the slackers were eventually enrolled they would gain several months of respite during the trial, a delay at which the War Department fretted. President Davis sought to counteract this ruse through use of his authority to suspend the writ, but again the army was checkmated when a number of state judges would not surrender their ancient privilege. Chief Justice Pearson of North Carolina decided that his court could discharge any citizen who appeared to be unlawfully restrained by a Confederate officer and Governor Zebulon B. Vance boasted that no one in his state was ever denied recourse to the North Carolina courts. Other states sustained this opinion and the Richmond authorities were forced to concede defeat.

A leading objection to conscription was that it would weaken the states' local defenses. The West felt that its defense suffered by the concentration of armies in the East and by frequent drafts of its militia. Texas feared Indian trouble and felt aggrieved when the central government refused to suspend conscription or to accept Texas volunteers to be used only for frontier patrol. Some states protested whenever out-of-state enrolling officers operated within their state or when their citizens were commanded by men of other states. Others requested special favors from the War Department such as suspending the law in certain areas, exempting classes of men for peculiarly local reasons, and even the dismissal of soldiers needed at home.

After the first conscription act had taken men between 18 and 35 from state militia organizations, the states began to rebuild them with what manpower remained. The law of September 27, 1862, had stretched the conscription age to 45, but on October 11 Congress exempted all men "in active service under State authority" except those subject to the first draft law.[44] The result was that by 1863 the state militia organizations held back for local defense had reached their former size, with more than half of their men being between 35 and 45. Since these men were receiving poor training and less experience the War Department resolved to get control over them regardless of exemption. It contended that being only militia they were not in active service and therefore subject to the draft laws. Most of the governors, however, considered them "troops of war" and thereby deserving indefinite exemption. A number of state supreme courts decided that the state rather than the Secretary of War must decide what constituted active service, and the governors often refused to yield their able-bodied militiamen to the enrolling officers.

Since the Department could not force the release of militiamen between 35 and 45, it attempted to gain partial control of the whole body of state troops. Seddon asked the governors to organize all their available men into local defense and limited service companies under the acts of August 21, 1861, and October 13, 1862. He planned to requisition them for Confederate service, but the governors outmaneuvered him again. Practically none of them organized such troops, but took advantage of the requisition to acquire the residue of the able-bodied men for state forces, claiming exemption for them on the grounds that now they were in active service. Nor did they transfer these troops to the Confederacy for temporary service, but only lent them to district commanders during emergencies.

The states tried to safeguard their civil government as well as their local defense organizations. The exemption act of October

11 had been moderately generous regarding state officials and employees, but a number of governors continued to feel understaffed and undermined. Some of them even wrote their own exemption laws and their supreme courts were inclined to defend this practice as a right of a sovereign state. Congress therefore recognized the inevitable and on May 1, 1863, authorized state governors and legislatures to exempt any officer they wished.[45] Most of them exercised fair judgment in this privilege, but Georgia exceeded all bounds by exempting "all Civil and Military officers of this State."[46] Governor Brown even hampered the conscription of other men who he felt were more needed at home.

Section 3 of the first draft act required that state enrolling officers be used, and only on a governor's failure to cooperate could the President use Confederate officers in the recalcitrant state. The War Department found the state systems inept in this respect and soon made it clear that the states would be allowed little participation in conscription. The states conceded this point with good grace, though they might have contested its legality.

A final cause of discontent arose from the practice of executive detail. The second exemption law permitted the President to exempt anyone not included in the law, but this was not what he wanted. He considered class exemptions too rigid and preferred the more adaptable system of detail, whereby he could transfer a soldier from place to place, job to job, or even return him to the army, all the while retaining full control over him.[47] State rights defenders feared that using details would result in favoritism and prejudice, and before 1864 Congress allowed only the detail of officers for recruiting and of 2,000 soldiers as shoemakers. The absence of authority irked but failed to daunt the President, and he detailed soldiers about as he pleased. This left Congress with the unpleasant alternatives of censuring him or endorsing the practice against its own judgment.

MORE MEN!

BY THE WINTER OF 1863-1864 IT WAS STILL APPARENT THAT THE Confederate armies could not hold their own against the seemingly endless number of Northerners. General Lee had been begging for recruits for over a year and had advocated new laws, particularly the ending of all class exemptions, for the better use of the available manpower. William J. Hardee and twenty other generals proposed changes which would place all men, black and white, between 15 and 60 at the complete disposition of the military.[1] In his message of December 7, 1863, to the last session of the First Congress President Davis firmly stated that Congress must "add largely to our effective forces as promptly as possible." He advised it to substitute a system of executive detail for that of class exemption and to extend the draft age beyond 45, the older men to be used mainly to replace able-bodied men performing inactive duties.[2] The Secretary of War added two important requests. He explained that the first draft law had required all troops then in the army to serve for a total of three years. In 1864, 315 regiments and 58 battalions were eligible for discharge and he asked that they be continued in the army for the duration. He further suggested that Congress organize groups of non-conscripts and "the least available conscripts" to hunt down deserters and assist the enrolling officers when needed.[3]

Both houses contained men willing to go the limit and they vigorously sought the initiative. On December 11 Senator Wigfall proposed to draft everyone between 16 and 60 and leave their service almost entirely to the President.[4] Senator Albert Gallatin Brown of Mississippi, ordinarily opposed to extreme army measures, now demanded a levy en masse. He deplored the practice of frittering away the reserves by drafting a few men here and a few men there, and if his suggestion smacked of despotism he would save the country first and settle Constitution constructions afterwards.[5] On December 14 the Senate Military Committee introduced its famous Senate Bill No. 158, which encompassed the entire realm of military service. It drafted all between 16 and 60; those between 18 and 45 would constitute the field force, the remainder being combined with exempted and detailed men into reserve corps for local defense. It pared class exemptions to the bone, though it retained the controversial exemption of state officers.[6] The House Military Committee matched these heroics and in addition ended all exemptions except those in government offices and gave the President and his staff complete powers of detail.[7] Miles declared the existing system a failure and assured his listeners that Davis, though he liked power too much, could not misuse his authority, for the bill would allow him only to say where men would be of the greatest service.[8] Miles, usually imperturbable in the face of criticism, was nonplussed at the hostile reception to his bill, and the House quickly shifted most of its attention to the Senate bill.

Both houses amended the Senate measure a good bit, but did not alter its basic severity. The administration supporters accepted only a few additional class exemptions, mainly professional. They won an important victory in the Senate by striking out the provision that the reserve corps must be used only for local defense. Against the wishes of the Eastern senators they refused to liberalize the exemption of overseers, but let the President detail as many additional ones as were needed.[9] The only real setback they received in the Senate was the reduction of the draft age from 60 to 55. The House showed most concern about the handling of men over 45, who formed the backbone of the state militia. It changed the draft age limits to from 17 to 50, exempted men between 45 and 50 engaged in agriculture or mechanics, and required that less active duties be handled only by men disabled or over 50. It also placed several restrictions on the President's right of detail.[10]

When a conference committee met it had little trouble ironing out the disagreements, but reversed one decision of both houses. During debate the House and the Senate had agreed that men over 45 should be used only in inactive duty, which would have made them almost useless in military emergencies. Some members of the conference committee recognized the inadequacy of this restriction and considered allowing such men to perform their military duties in the state militia. Senator Sparrow of Louisiana, however, wrote Davis that the committee was still susceptible to advice and that a word from him would influence them to form a "Corps of Minute Men, for local & detail duty."[11] Davis hurriedly wrote Congress that allowing Confederate troops to serve in a state militia would give them poor training and might keep them away from valuable detail work. He wished them put into reserve corps for emergency military duty which would probably not require their absence from the fields and workshops more than two or three weeks at a time.[12] His suggestion was promptly worked into the committee report.

The law of February 17, 1864, conscripted for the duration all white men between 17 and 50. To prevent disrupting the army, those between 18 and 45 were retained under their same organization and officers. Men of 17-18 and 45-50 would constitute reserve corps for detail duty, and during emergencies could be used for military service within their home states. Provost and hospital guards and quartermaster and commissary employees must be physically unfit for active service or outside the draft age. All exemptions were repealed except the following: such officers as the President and the state governors certified were necessary; preachers; superintendents and physicians of benevolent institutions; doctors, teachers, and apothecaries who had practiced a certain length of time; one overseer on each plantation having fifteen slaves and otherwise unsupervised, provided the owner delivered to the government at impressment prices specified quantities of meat and sold his marketable surplus to the government at the same prices; finally, most railroad employees and all mail carriers specified by the act of April 14, 1863. The President might detail such overseers, artisans, mechanics, and scientists as he saw fit.[13]

The newspaper press generally complimented Congress for the new law and General Robert E. Lee urged that it be enforced to the letter. At least on paper it added thousands to the army lists. Most class exemptions retained were of the professional and public service type, while those abolished were agricultural and industrial to which the President could detail soldiers as he saw fit. While production and the Military were never completely coordinated, the law of February 17 probably enabled the Confederacy to approach such coordination as nearly as any country had in wartime.

The vigor of the law provoked strong criticism from those affected. The executive departments, contending that their few employees could be exempt without detriment to the army, were reluctant to give up their trained and able-bodied personnel. Members of obscure religious sects, dentists, students, accountants, and many other groups sought places on the exemption list. Planters feared that Davis would not detail enough help, particularly to places distant from the scene of battle. Congress and the President were bombarded with scores of requests for special favors. Virginia, for instance, led the demand for such favors in agriculture, but the Commissary-General of Subsistence reported that even there provisions were adequate. The firmness with which the administration handled these petitions increased the discontent.

The major repercussions came from the state governments, of which, until 1864, only North Carolina and Georgia had been overwhelmingly against conscription. The states had not forgotten that their courts refused to give their militia blanket exemption; under the law of February 17 they now saw their exempted militia endangered. Generally the courts again sided with the Confederacy by agreeing that youths in the state militia must, on reaching 17, be surrendered to the Confederate army.

Another issue that the new law revived was the drafting of state employees. The law of May 1, 1863, permitted governors to exempt whatever officials their state administration needed. The law of February 17 required governors to certify that each exemptee was absolutely necessary for the proper administration of his government. This, however, failed to embarrass most governors, who, according to the Superintendent of Conscription John S. Preston, certified "all persons in the service of the State, or in any mode employed by State authority. . . ."[14] The North Carolina legislature declared that the law tried to reduce states "to mere provincial administrations" and "to convert the Confederate government into a consolidated military despotism."[15] Other legislatures indicated that they would exempt whomever they wished. All governors drew up such exemption lists, with North Carolina and Georgia claiming over 25,000 exemptions between them.

The Second Congress, which began in May, 1864, contained a stronger state rights membership than its predecessor and the Davis administration hesitated to beard it immediately. Besides, the law of February 17 was too recent for proper evaluation and had disappointed Davis only in regard to soldier detail. At first, therefore, he and the Secretary of War asked little regarding manpower and on the whole were rather complimentary to the First

Congress. The new Congress, not yet bruising for a row, was content to stand pat. It debated organizing a separate Bureau of Conscription, but decided such was not really needed. When it resolved that the editor-exemption clause should include editors of all periodicals, Davis insisted that only newspapers were vital and Congress placidly respected his veto.[16]

During the summer of 1864 the increasing pace of the war proved the continuing inadequacy of all previous Confederate military laws. The draft ages had been pushed to its logical limits and attention now centered upon the more than 125,000 men on the exemption and the detail lists. Judge Andrew G. Magrath of South Carolina wrote Davis that improving the detail system would field 20,000 or 30,000 men from South Carolina and Georgia alone,[17] and General Lee asked Davis to make a thorough and vigorous inspection of the rolls of exempted and detailed men.[18] A governors' conference recommended that all able-bodied men who could possibly be replaced be sent to the front.[19] The Secretary of War wished to make the nation one great camp with Davis in complete charge, and Superintendent Preston stated that only the President was qualified to determine who should work and who should fight.[20] With this top brass support President Davis in his address on November 7, 1864, to the last session of Congress made a final effort to establish his dictatorship over the able-bodied men in the Confederacy. He asked Congress to replace the "unwise" class exemption system with one of executive detail and, now that he had despaired of the states' surrendering their remaining militia, to provide a law whereby he could requisition them bodily.[21]

The reaction of Congress to these suggestions was hardly enthusiastic, not because it doubted an emergency, but because it was still undecided on how much authority it should grant the President. Congress was by this time divided into three distinct groups of opinion on these matters, none of which could alone command a majority in either house. The radical state righters believed that they had "long since placed at the disposal of the Executive every able-bodied man in the Confederacy,"[22] and wished to restore class exemptions to the 1863 level. The middle-of-the-road group was the largest in both houses and was willing to make some small concessions. A few in each house wholeheartedly supported Davis's requests.

The handful who wished to repossess control of the army manpower made little impression on Congress. When Smith of North

..... *More Men!* 91

Carolina asked the House Military Committee to report any laws needed "to prevent the prostration of the industrial interests of the country,"[23] he was not rewarded with an answer. When Senator Orr questioned whether industry was getting enough detailed workers, the Military Committee assured him that the War Department was using proper discretion on every occasion.[24] For the most part the state righters recognized their own weakness and sought merely to sabotage the administration program.

The more moderate congressmen concentrated on tightening the laws around men whose absence from the field was questionable. Over a period of several months they proposed, among other things, the following: to end the exemption and detail of railroad workers, mail carriers, and overseers; to abolish all provost-marshalships except those with the armies in the field; to use only bonded agents outside the draft age for quartermaster and commissary duties; and to receive any volunteer group not ordinarily subject to military service. The deficiency of this program was that it involved only a small number of men, who performed such vital services that drafting them would create more confusion than it would military manpower. Most of the bills died in debate; the only one passing which would have appreciably increased the army — that replacing quartermasters and commissary officers with bonded agents — was vetoed on the danger of its "seriously impairing our ability to supply the armies in the field. . . ."[25]

While Congress dallied with its own solutions to the manpower problem, it also discussed the President's suggestions with as little profit. After being almost disrupted by the conscription law of February 17, 1864, the state militia had been re-formed with men outside the draft ages. Thus far, despite the War Department's constant supplications, the governors had lent these troops to district commanders only during emergencies and in their home state. This limited action made them so inexperienced as to be of little value in combat, and on November 7, 1864, Davis had asked for a law "organizing, arming, and disciplining" all state militia for use by the central government.[26] Concerning thousands more who were exempt because of holding state offices, though Davis discreetly avoided asking for them, his wishes were clear.

Congress hardly knew where to proceed upon such dangerous ground. On November 10 Waller R. Staples of Virginia proposed to investigate the value of an appeal upon the states to modify their exemption laws. James T. Leach of North Carolina considered it presumptuous to question a state's loyalty, but after a sharp debate the resolution passed. A week later a special committee advised joint action with the Senate both to see if the appeal was warranted and to ascertain the numbers exempt. Because the Senate, however, disliked the invidious implication of a joint resolution, both houses requested the same information independently. The figures that the Superintendent of Conscription compiled revealed that only North Carolina and Georgia allowed excessive[27] exemptions and both houses dropped the investigation.

Congress was even more reluctant to tamper with the state militia. On December 24 Clark of Missouri introduced a bill to commandeer the states' militia, but for two months the bill remained buried in the Military Committee. On March 13, 1865, Davis in bitter words again asked for complete control of the militia and this time did at least receive an answer. In the Senate Gustavus A. Henry of Tennessee introduced such a measure, but it failed by a tie vote. The House Military Committee resurrected Clark's bill and reported being unable to understand how it would help. The militia were "as efficient for State defense as if organized under Confederate authority," and Clark's bill was in reality the conscription of men over 50 and under 17, which the Committee was unwilling to recommend.[28] This report was defeated by a vote of 31 to 33, with the votes usually being determined by whether a congressman represented an occupied or an unoccupied district.[29] The bill passed the House on March 16 and was never acted upon by the Senate. The only concessions to the administration were two laws suspending for about four months the section in the law of February 17 preventing reserve forces from serving outside their state limits.[30]

The crucial recommendation of the President was the abolition of class exemptions. On November 7 when Mark H. Blandford of Georgia placed it before the House, discontent immediately rumbled. The *Montgomery Daily Mail* predicted that the measure would "convert the South into a howling desert,"[31] and Senator Graham of North Carolina wrote home of the "war fever" in Congress designed to "clothe the Executive, with still stronger powers."[32] But contrary to alarmist fears the House Military Committee would not be rushed. It was fairly well arrayed against the whole Davis military program by now and would allow neither the Superintendent of Conscription nor a long train of generals to intimidate it. On December 10 the Committee reported a bill which undoubtedly dismayed the anxious President. Its only significant changes in the existing laws were to transfer all overseers to the detail list and to reduce slightly the number of class exemptions. Even then the House shunted the bill aside for a month in favor of several financial measures. On January 11, 1865, the calendar was clear and for the next three months the Committee bill was intermittently discussed. It never provoked much enthusiasm, for another administration defeat seemed certain. Only the extreme state righters exerted any vigor and they tried to retrieve the ground they had lost the previous February by proposing numerous class exemption amendments. The President's friends accused them of trying to amend the measure to death, but, whatever their strategy,[33] it soon revealed that the President had lost strength on this issue.

After a week's debate, during which the administration was completely stalemated, attention shifted to a bill introduced on January 18 by Charles W. Russell of Virginia. He apparently feared that the administration was about to lose its gains of the last two years and wished to halt the trend. He proposed to repeal the exemption of overseers, leave the other classes untouched, and limit the President's right of detail to men over forty and to artisans and mechanics then working for the government. He hoped that the overseer exemption part would pass with the support of the non-planting element and that the administration would be relieved to see the exemption list remain the same; the limitation on executive detail was expected to attract moderate state-righters. Unheroic as was this strategy, it served its purpose. The radicals immediately lost much of their support and Russell's bill passed the House on January 23 with 19 of the 26 opposing votes coming from four Eastern states.[34]

Most of the Senate debate on Russell's bill was over Orr's test amendment to exempt all who might be more useful at home. He claimed that the present laws would be sufficient if applied correctly, but his motion narrowly failed when four senators from the South and East voted with the border states and the West against it. The Senate added two amendments to the bill: that the exemption of overseers past forty-five be continued and that all artisans and mechanics employed by the Confederacy or by a state government be exempt.

A conference committee advised acceptance of the amendments and the bill became law on March 16, 1865. The Senate amendments affected the bill very little. Had overseers beyond forty-five not been exempt, they would have remained at their jobs except for occasional reserve service. The amendment exempting artisans and mechanics did not contradict the House plan. During a worker's employment by the government he would be exempt; but his entire labor was the government's, for as a civilian worker he would be employed wherever the President desired. Were he to leave government employment he would be immediately drafted and then subject to executive detail. Whatever his army status, his labor was always available. The Senate amendment was intended to retain congressional determination of military service, not to deprive the government of its labor supply.[35]

Davis accepted this law reluctantly. He stated that it excused government workers from all military service, whereas if detailed they could be used for emergency local defense. He particularly criticized the provision "which revokes all details and exemptions heretofore granted by the President and Secretary of War, and prohibits the grant of such exemptions and details hereafter." Long experience had made some men in government service experts, and, as fewer than a hundred of them would be affected by the act, he requested Congress to amend it accordingly.[36] Congress immediately ordered that the President might detail not over one hundred indispensable department workers, and that the law of March 16 should not exempt artisans and mechanics from military service in the reserve force.[37]

Though these laws came so late that they amounted to no more than a defiant cry by Congress, this last bitter clash was a severe defeat for President Davis. Theoretically the laws put more men into the army, but not on the basis that he wished. The exemption system was hardly touched, whereas one of Davis's most cherished rights, that of detailing soldiers, was severely limited.

Congress's final experiment was an organizational change. In 1862 the War Department had set up a Bureau of Conscription to put the laws into effect. By 1864 the Bureau contained almost 3,000 employees who were not only exempt but who apparently were slipshod and inefficient. One of its greatest handicaps was that each man enrolled could legally apply for exemption; as his case sometimes required several months to be investigated, his military service was lost for that length of time. On March 7, 1865, Congress abolished the Bureau and installed a system operated by the army. The general officers commanding the reserves in each state were to direct and enforce all conscription, exemption, and detail laws. Conscripts might apply for exemption, but meanwhile were to be enrolled and trained without delay. A board of resident surgeons in each district was to visit around the counties every three months to ferret out available men.[38]

It is doubtful if this system was any over-all improvement. Though it would have eliminated the overcrowded state of the Richmond Bureau, undoubtedly the army's arbitrary tactics would have more than offset the system's accomplishments by thoroughly alienating public opinion. The obvious intent of the law was to intimidate would-be draft dodgers as long as the voters would tolerate this kind of military law.

While the Second Congress was embroiled in multifarious schemes to fill the army's thinning lines, it was also considering a total innovation, the arming of the slaves. The idea had been suggested as early as 1861, but the War Department stated that a "superabundance of our own color" was volunteering and that white soldiers preferred to do their own fighting.[39] By late 1863 this superabundance had vanished and some people began to consider the slaves more seriously as a source of manpower. In December General Patrick Cleburne designed a plan to draft Negroes, which he submitted to Joseph E. Johnston and an assembly of his generals. President Davis, however, not only scorned the idea but, for fear of bad publicity, requested that the plan be suppressed.[40] The few newspapers who deigned to consider the matter were in complete agreement that if the whites refused to support the war "with their persons and *property* let it go," for the Negroes must always be, in the Biblical formula, hewers of wood, and drawers of water.[41]

During the next year the press aired the question more thoroughly without much change in opinion. The great majority still believed that the white men were sufficient for the emergency and would be demoralized if compelled to fight beside Negroes.[42] The latter lacked courage, incentive, and intelligence, would soon become disobedient, and would desert at the first chance. The necessary reward of emancipation would embarrass the post-war South by creating thousands of free Negroes. They could be best used in menial jobs and thus release able-bodied white men for army duty.

The *Richmond Enquirer* and the *Montgomery Daily Mail*, the earliest converts to Negro conscription, maintained that freed Negro soldiers would be easily managed since the distinction between the races was not between freedom and enslavement but between Negro and white. Their emancipation was not abolition, but manumission, which had been practiced for decades. They considered themselves Confederates, loved their country, and wished to defend it. They would make good soldiers for they thoroughly understood obedience and discipline. Their conscription would indicate untapped manpower and added determination, and would not be a confession of weakness and exhaustion.[43]

The Davis administration was nonetheless unwilling at this time to defy public opinion. On September 6, 1864, Secretary Seddon wrote Governor Henry W. Allen of Louisiana that they should use every able-bodied Negro man as a soldier,[44] but a month later he stated officially that he could not yet perceive the necessity or approve the policy of employing slaves as soldiers.[45] Davis was just as evasive. On November 7 he refuted the need of Negro conscription, but confessed that "should the alternative ever be presented of subjugation or of the employment of the slave as a soldier, there seems no reason to doubt what should then be our decision."[46] This was one major issue that Davis was quite willing to leave with Congress and almost until the end he shunned it. He could hardly have done otherwise, for such an unorthodox proposal would fan the rumor that he was aiming toward dictatorship. He knew that several congressmen had corresponded with generals in the field over arming the slaves and hoped that Congress would be sufficiently impressed by their unanimously favorable response.

A few minutes before Davis's message of November 7 Swan of Tennessee attempted to place the House on record against Negro soldiers, but after hearing the President's cautious statements on the subject the House refused to commit itself either way. On December 29 the Senate tried to get Davis to take the initiative by requesting information on the condition of the Army, and the possibility of recruiting slaves.[47] When he failed even to respond, Congress in January, 1865, appointed a select committee to secure the information. The committee conferred with the President, but its report of March 16 carried no suggestion that he considered advisable the use of slaves as soldiers. Obviously when he wished the President could sidestep as well as Congress!

Meanwhile some congressmen favoring the use of Negro soldiers were becoming convinced that they could play politics no longer. In January they received word from General Lee, "whose opinions on all subjects are omnipotent," advocating the enlistment of Negroes and their subsequent emancipation.[48] Thomas L. Snead of Missouri said that Senate opposition to the employment of

Negro troops was growing weaker daily.[49] Some congressmen, by shifting the discussion of impressing slaves as laborers to their impressment as soldiers, tried to clear the air for a showdown. To head the movement off, the opposition introduced several resolutions similar to Swan's, which inspired heated and bitter debates. They usually hinged on the questions of expediency and necessity, though at times the state rights issue appeared.[50] Sometimes these debates degenerated into attacks on President Davis's ability as commander-in-chief. Senator Landon C. Haynes of Tennessee charged that his state had been lost by the mismanagement of the President.[51] Turner of North Carolina claimed that the country had been too long deluded and deceived by presidential "plans, projects and prophecies," and that the President had proposed abolition in a way that created suspicion as to his soundness.[52]

Finally Barksdale of Mississippi and Williamson S. Oldham of Texas agreed in private to bring the matter to a head and on February 10 introduced bills in their respective houses to arm the Negroes. They were alike with the exception that Oldham's Senate bill provided for 200,000 Negro troops while Barksdale's left the number to the President. Both left their organization to the War Department and both specified that freedom as a reward was entirely a state decision.[53] Opponents marshalled their forces and prepared to resist at almost any cost. Turner even postponed his return to comfort a complaining wife in order to "stay here and defeat the arming slaves. . . ."[54]

The House appointed a special select committee of one from each state to examine Barksdale's bill and on February 14 a majority of the committee reported it favorably.[55] The opposition relied on the strategy of a substitute motion asking the states for 300,000 men "irrespective of color," but at the height of debate Barksdale produced a letter from General Lee for which he had been frantically waiting. On hearing that the measure was finally before Congress Lee had hastily written that it was not only expedient but necessary, and that the enemy would certainly use Negroes if they could get them.[56] This warning influenced enough representatives to carry the bill and on February 20 the House passed it by a vote of 40 to 37, with North Carolina, Texas, Arkansas, and Missouri having a majority against it.[57] The fact that the vote showed no sectional or political alignment indicated that principle and conscience dictated the outcome and that Lee's influence confirmed the opinion of some and swayed that of enough others to secure passage.

Meanwhile the Senate Military Committee had quickly scanned Oldham's bill and on February 17 reported it favorably, with the amendment that all slaves so armed should, with the consent of their states, be manumitted at the end of their service. The influence of the administration and of General Lee was brought to bear in favor of the bill and Judah P. Benjamin wrote letters trying to persuade the army to declare for it,[58] but the Senate majority could not swallow the idea. It defeated its own bill by one vote and shunted aside the House measure for two more weeks. This time, however, the administration would not be denied. It begged help from the Virginia legislature then in session and the latter immediately instructed its senators to vote for the measure. The Senate then revived the House bill and, now with the approval of both Virginia Senators, passed it by a nine to eight vote.[59]

The passage of this bill by the Senate involved two significant questions, the first being the reason for the Senate's slowness in contrast to the House's speed. This difference may be explained in part by the fact that during these troubled times the Senate was generally more independent than the House and held back even after hearing from Lee. The Senate's choice of bills was another point of interest. Its own measure ordered the slave-soldiers freed, provided their state did not object, while the House bill evaded all constitutional difficulties by saying that "nothing ... shall be construed to authorize a change in the relation which the said slaves shall bear to their owners, except by consent of the owners and of the States in which they reside."[60] This was precisely in line with what both Davis and Lee were known to wish. Lee had advised Barksdale that the matter should be left, as far as possible, to the people of the States,[61] and had already asked the Virginia legislature to arm its slaves and provide a system of gradual emancipation. Considered in the light of the Barksdale letter, Congress had acted strictly in accordance with Lee's wishes; the error, if it may be called that, was that action came too late.

The act of March 13, 1865, authorized the President to ask for and accept from the states such numbers of slaves as he wished and to assign them to military service in whatever capacity he might direct. They were to be organized as the Secretary of War prescribed and should receive the same pay and rations as other troops. If this method proved inadequate the President might call on each state for its quota of 300,000 troops, to be raised from such classes of its population, "irrespective of color," as the state authorities might determine. Not more than twenty-five per cent of the male slaves between 18 and 45 in any state could be called, and nothing in the act should be construed to emancipate them.[62]

This law provoked a final outburst of bitterness between Congress and the President. Davis was overstrained and in a nervous condition and peevishly reproached Congress for its delay. He had been anxious to enlist the slaves and to use their emancipation as a diplomatic bribe and chided Congress for not passing the law the previous year.[63] The Senate defended itself vigorously, contending that "the President, in no official communication to Congress, has recommended the passage of a law putting slaves in the Army as soldiers, and the message under consideration is the first official information that such a law would meet his approval." The body recounted its efforts to elicit such opinion, and denied that its requests had ever received official recognition. "Under these circumstances, Congress, influenced no doubt by the opinion of General Lee, determined for itself the propriety, policy, and necessity of adopting the measure in question."[64] Congress made no effort to shoulder any blame for the delay and by implication expressed its habit of depending on the President for instructions. The fallacy in the whole argument was that no matter how much direct urging Davis might have given earlier, Congress itself was not ready to arm the slaves until the very last days of the Confederacy.

The Confederate naval forces require a brief and separate description. The early volunteer laws allowed the President to accept men from the state navies. When few volunteered under these laws Congress, in December, 1861, tried to secure 2,000 seamen for the duration, but even the munificent bonus of $50[65] failed to secure nearly that number. The first draft law allowed conscripts to choose their branch of service or to transfer to another branch of service after their enrollment. So few availed themselves of a naval career even under conscription that the courts later on recruited sailors by sentencing criminals to service in the navy.

The seamen and their officers received about the same pay and commutation as their landed brethren, and short-term volunteers were also continued in service until the end of the war by the draft acts. Secretary of the Navy Stephen R. Mallory had ambitions to build up a permanent navy and secured a school ship on which to train the 106 midshipmen allotted by law. In November, 1864, he asked for more midshipmen and six teachers, but Davis disliked the idea of a permanent naval officer personnel and vetoed the law of Congress to that effect. Mallory then had to be satisfied with the six instructors which Congress granted to teach his few midshipmen mathematics, English, ethics, and modern language, including one variously gifted person to teach drawing, drafting, and sword and bayonet exercises.[66]

The Confederacy, not being able to muster a navy capable of breaking the Northern blockade, soon turned its attention to the ancient profession of privateering. The United States had refused to sign the Declaration of Paris of 1856, which outlawed privateering; so the Confederacy had no compunction in using such an expedient. On May 6, 1861, Congress authorized the President to issue letters of marque and reprisal against vessels of the United States and set up rules and regulations which would prevent ships and crews from being classed as pirates. The law promised shipowners eighty-five per cent of the value of everything they seized, and encouraged privateers to attack enemy warships by offering a bounty of $20 for each person on board a captured or destroyed armed vessel. On May 21 Congress offered shipowners a bonus of twenty per cent of the value of each enemy warship sunk or destroyed.[67]

Privateering appealed to the adventurous, and on May 10 Davis granted the first commission. Soon a number of Confederates were roaming the seas and for a while threw consternation into the North. The tightening of the blackade, however, made them much less effective. Privateers found it almost impossible to get prizes back into Southern ports for disposition, and neutral countries refused to admit prizes into their waters. In the fall of 1862 Representative E. M. Bruce decided that Congress's "very stringent and unnecessary" regulations made it too difficult to secure a privateer's commission. He proposed simpler requirements that would let any "man of character" have a commission so that he could go to another country to buy and outfit his ship.[68] Congress passed such a law that October, but the administration at the time was formulating plans for a volunteer navy and Davis pocket vetoed the law.

During the spring and summer of 1861, B. J. Sage, a Louisiana planter, had popularized the idea of a volunteer navy that had certain advantages over regular privateers. The Navy Department finally became convinced of the value of Sage's idea and in January, 1862, Mallory informed Davis that a volunteer navy, invested "with a public character," would give the Confederacy the privateers which it needed. Members of the navy would receive almost the same returns and rewards as a privateer, but would have certain advantages. Whereas privateers operated only on the high seas, a volunteer navy vessel could seize ships and property on the coast, on rivers, or anywhere found.[69]

On February 12, 1862, C. J. McRae of Alabama proposed such a measure, but tried to make the volunteer navy too much like the regular navy[70] and the bill died in committee. In a few months Mallory and Sage collaborated on another bill more in accord with the latter's ideas, and it became law on April 18, 1863. The "Volunteer Navy" differed from privateering only slightly. The officers and crew were part of the Confederate forces; their vessels were to operate within "the ebb and flow of the tide," and the crew was to get half of the prize money or, if they captured a vessel of superior strength, all of it.[71] On February 11, 1864, Congress let the President issue commissions to officers to enable them to assemble ship and crew rather than force them to complete the latter task before being eligible for a commission.[72]

VIII

OF OFFICERS AND MEN

KEEPING THE RANKS OF THE ARMY FILLED WAS THE CONFEDERACY'S most difficult, though certainly not its only, military problem. New matters of organization constantly arose; officers had to be chosen, promoted, dismissed, and disciplined; enlisted men required a large amount of care, both of body and soul. The states had to be considered at every step, and when they proved intractable the administration had to decide whether to cater to or disregard them. The United States army organization and practices, while satisfactory for a beginning model, needed constant alteration. The South, with its military tradition and its experience in the Mexican War, always had enough officers, but too frequently the War Department had little jurisdiction over their appointment or promotion. Finally there was the problem of a president who would not hide his military light under an administrative bushel.

The Confederacy planned to organize defenses before the Lincoln government could take the initiative, and even before providing for executive departments Congress ordered its military and its naval committees to discuss jointly the resources of the country and how best to use them. The committees met on February 19, 1861, consulted with experienced military personnel, and worked out the main points of military organization.[1] On February 26, March 6, and March 16 Congress put the ideas of the committees into effect with laws establishing an army, a navy, and a general staff. The laws were almost identical with their United States counterparts and covered everything from pay to personnel. The haste with which they were written, combined with the outbreak of war, necessitated numerous amendments, but their basic structure remained the same. During this formative period the members of the military and naval committees were in constant touch with President Davis and his advisers and did little without consulting them.[2]

Davis had envisioned a military force composed of two complementary armies: the law of March 6, 1861, set up a Regular Army which was to constitute the nucleus of the defenses; the laws of February 28, March 6, May 8, May 11, August 8, 1861, and January 22, 1862, provided for an emergency "Provisional" or "Volunteer" Army composed of state militia and independent volunteers pledged to serve for stated enlistment terms. The Regular Army materialized only sketchily; the Provisional Army did the fighting and required most attention.

Early problems of organization usually stemmed from state-Confederate disputes, and the first of these concerned the officer personnel of the Provisional Army. The law of February 28 allowed the President, with the consent of Congress, to appoint only the general officers; state practice usually found the governors appointing regimental officers and the enlisted men electing their company commanders. Generally when the unit was being formed the governors commissioned all officers down from colonel and let them recruit their men. The War Department, unwilling to wait until a regiment was completed, wanted the governors to tender each company as it was formed and let the President organize them into larger units. But the governors jealously guarded their appointments and either waited until the regiment was filled or submitted "skeleton" regiments with a full contingent of officers and only a few privates. The Department disliked these skeletons, but often had to compromise and accept them with the understanding that the states would provide "bodies" as quickly as possible.[3]

A company or a regimental vacancy in the Provisional Army brought up the question of who had the right to fill it. The War Department assumed that after mustering the state militia into the Confederate service the Department had control over making promotions and filling vacancies, but in August Secretary Benjamin ruled that all troops tendered by the states remained subject to state laws. The governors took full advantage of this ruling and filled all vacancies during the first year of the war.

Adopting conscription gave Congress an opportunity to improve its officer selection practices but, somewhat appalled by its own daring, it decided against any drastic changes. The law of April 16, 1862, in continuing the twelve-month volunteers in service, allowed them to reorganize and elect new officers in the traditional fashion. The law also ordered that vacancies be filled by lower officers from the same military units, despite the fact that others might have a superfluity of good officers. The only improvement was to let the President fill all vacancies except in the lowest grade of company officers, who were still elected. Promotion, except for distinguished service, was still based on seniority.[4]

This system was not designed to give the Confederacy its best company and regimental officers. A principal evil of the arrangement was that company officers were usually chosen to begin with because of local political prominence. After a year's service most of them had become qualified leaders, but the twelve-month volunteers in reorganizing frequently discarded officers who had enforced discipline and replaced them with "good fellows" from the ranks. Since the law required that all the lowest commissioned officers be elected, the army was insured a steady supply of incompetents, and the principle of seniority required only that they remain alive to earn promotions. Lee and most other generals deplored both the election and the seniority principles, and Secretary Randolph reported that, in view of the Confederacy's short military history, seniority, which implied experience, was valueless.[5]

In September, 1862, Congress confronted the matter of promotions. Military experts in both houses maintained that the army's efficiency, not its happiness, should be sought. The President believed that the solution was a system whereby incompetent officers could be relieved by some means short of court martial.[6] Logic favored his suggestion, but the state rights persuasion was stronger. Senator Orr said that the administration was trying to cover up for General Bragg, who had degraded certain of his officers to the ranks. Yancey observed that Davis wanted a board of "young West Point officers," who might pose technical queries that would puzzle even General Lee.[7] The law that finally passed on October 13 was a compromise, allowing a commanding general to appoint an examining board to determine a particular officer's efficiency. If the board and the general found him incompetent, they could suspend him and refer their findings to Davis. If the officer was dropped, the next in rank whom the board found qualified would replace him. If none met the board's requirements, the President could fill the vacancy with someone from the same state to which the unit belonged. The deficiencies of the law were that it still recognized seniority as the basis for promotion and it left undisturbed the election of company officers.[8]

On January 3, 1863, Seddon reported that he was still dissatisfied. The seniority rule stifled ambition, for there were few promotions for extraordinary merit. He proposed that officer elections be confined to those recommended for candidacy by their commanders, and that the examining boards test the competency of everyone up for promotion.[9] But Congress, feeling that conscription alone caused enough ill-will, ignored the suggestion. During the debate in the winter of 1863-1864 some members even desired to reorganize the army completely to allow the men to rid themselves of all unpopular officers. Miles, however, convinced the House that reorganization would ruin the army, and Congress merely incorporated the old system in the draft law of February 17, 1864.

Until almost the end of the war Congress made only slight changes in officer tenure and promotion. On February 17, 1864, it allowed the President to discharge any officer whom his commanding general considered unfit for duty. A law of June 7 let generals dismount cavalry officers for the same reason and place them in the ranks.[10] Not until its death throes did Congress accept the fact that an "army is an army, and ought not to be an electoral college."[11] On March 9, 1865, the body ended all officer elections and gave the company captain, with the approval of his superiors, the right to nominate men to the lowest rank of commissioned officers. Officers above the lowest rank were to be chosen on the recommendation of their immediate superiors, the only requirement being that the nominating officer make his appointment from the same military unit.[12]

Officers guilty of more than incompetence were always liable to a court martial. Congress had adopted the United States regulations which required commanding generals when necessary to detail officers for court-martial duty, but generals near the enemy disliked excusing officers for this purpose. Even Lee was distressed about his army discipline and wrote Davis asking for a permanent system with authority to inflict the death penalty.[13] On September 11, 1862, Davis asked Congress for a permanent commission, dominated by civilian lawyers, for each army in the field to enforce discipline and to protect citizens from military trespassers. A month later Congress authorized such courts with jurisdiction over all soldiers and over any violation of the Rules and Articles of War or of Confederate and state laws. Penalties were to be in accord with the Rules of War; when the offense was not punishable by these Rules the courts could inflict any penalty, short of death, authorized by a Confederate or a state law.[14]

President Davis usually obtained well qualified men for these courts, and James Phelan, J. A. P. Campbell, Malcolm D. Graham, and Alexander R. Boteler were congressmen who later served on them. Secretary Seddon reported excellent results from the law, and in the next sixteen months Congress established similar courts in each military department, for each division of cavalry, and for each state within a military department. In February, 1864, it allowed the courts to summon any witness and force him to testify.[15]

Sometimes well adjusted and experienced officers became sources of embarrassment to the War Department. The first draft law did little to solve the problem of the "skeleton" regiments since it not only continued the twelve-month volunteers in their same organizations, but gave prospective conscripts thirty days' grace in which to organize and volunteer in their own outfits. The general practice was that, "having received a formal notice that by twelve o'clock on a certain day" they would be drafted, the men "never fail to volunteer, before the hour arrives, in some new company in process of formation. Thus they get the bounty of a volunteer, but frustrate the intention of the law. . . ."[16] Such behavior defeated the law's intent to fill up existing companies and regiments and brought in few unattached soldiers. As early as August, 1862, Secretary Randolph urged Davis to disband a number of regiments, put their officers "out of commission," and transfer their enlisted men to other regiments;[17] the next month Congress partially complied with Randolph's suggestion. The draft law of September 27, 1862, assigned all men raised by conscription to existing units from their home states; not until these were filled would new units be admitted. The law made no provision for consolidating any of the skeleton regiments.[18]

In the dreary winter of 1863-1864 the administration intensified its campaign to reorganize the army. Secretary Seddon, who hesitated to impair the camaraderie of old units, wished only to consolidate regiments from occupied areas, but advised President Davis to leave consolidation to the judgment of the commanding generals.[19] On December 7 Davis reported the growing impossibility of keeping all regiments at full strength and asked

Congress for a thorough-going law "disbanding a part of the officers and making regulations for securing the most judicious selection of those still retained while least wounding the feelings of those who are discharged." To round out the picture he requested an invalid corps to give retired officers an opportunity to serve in some capacity.[20] Miles, chairman of the House Military Committee, had Seddon write such a bill, and presented it exactly as drafted, but Congress at this time was in the process of extending conscription and was unwilling to attempt so much. The bill died in the Military Committee, along with several memorials from generals advising similar plans, and the only gains during the session were laws allowing Davis to discharge officers without command and providing for an invalid corps to perform such duties as the Secretary of War assigned them.[21]

At the beginning of the last session Davis renewed his proposals for army reorganization. Some brigades, he said, were smaller than normal regiments and generals were being forced to use unauthorized steps to handle their many corps. This time the House Military Committee gave Miles's bill its full support during debate. Opponents of reorganization attempted to add numerous conditions upon which consolidation would be permitted, but were largely unsuccessful and the measure passed on January 10, 1865. It had stopped short of complete reorganization lest it destroy soldier morale, and the Senate, considering such a bill inadequate, submitted a much stronger measure. The resulting conference committee was now inclined to believe that any change would be an improvement and adopted the Senate plan in toto. The law of February 23 allowed generals to consolidate companies having less than thirty-two enlisted men and with no hope of further recruitment. The general was to select the new officers from the disbanded companies, and those dispossessed could form a company of their own or, if unable to do so within thirty days, could wait and be drafted. Enlisted men from these companies could no longer insist on being in regiments from their own state.[22]

The management of general officers was a separate problem. Congress usually transferred United States officers to their equivalent rank in the Confederate army and the custom relieved Davis of considerable political pressure. The early military laws gave him the sole right, with the consent of the Senate, to appoint all general officers and Congress never directly interfered with this privilege. From time to time Congress gave Davis the right to appoint temporary or permanent generals and use them however he wished.

The first difficulty involving the appointment of general officers resulted from Davis's commendable practice of selecting them on the basis of merit. The law of March 6, 1861, stated that, "if necessary," he should apportion staff and general officers among the states according to the number of volunteers from each state; when Davis failed to find such apportionment necessary, Senator Yancey tried to force his hand. Yancey showed that Virginia had twenty-seven and Alabama only five brigadier-generals and stated that the discrepancy insulted his state. The Senate Judiciary Committee, however, replied that the President had the exclusive constitutional prerogative of nomination, while Congress could only approve or reject,[23] and the matter rested there.

Congress, even though it had made Davis commander-in-chief of the army and navy, did not intend for him to take active command, and in March, 1862, passed a bill providing for a commanding general who would reside at the capital or take command in the field as he wished. Davis approved the administrative features of the bill, but on March 15 he vetoed it on the ground that Congress could not impair his control of the army activities in the field.[24] An ex-congressman wrote that Congress was "raising a perfect storm" over the veto and would depose Davis if it had had any confidence in Stephens,[25] but this was wishful thinking, for the veto was sensible and only Joseph B. Heiskell of Tennessee wished to override it. The result was that for much of the war Davis used as advisors one or another of his "pet" generals appointed to command at the seat of government. On January 23, 1865, Congress finally instructed the President to appoint a "general-in-chief" who would be the ranking officer in the army and would command all the military forces of the Confederacy.[26] Everyone understood that Lee was to be appointed, but his unwillingness to desert Virginia for the broader command left the position a paper appointment.

During 1862 and 1863 newspapers and experienced field officers began to suggest an advisory military group similar to the Prussian General Staff. The Confederate staff law of February 26, 1861, which did little except authorize the officer personnel of the medical and the supply services, was inadequate for devising general military strategy, and in December, 1863, Davis asked for a better staff law. He avoided, however, the idea of an advisory body at the capital and asked only for improvements in the staff of each army. The weakness of his proposal was that, while it would render an army more efficient, it provided no better coordination for the several armies. The Senate Military Committee, working closely with General Beauregard, wrote a staff bill in the closing days of the session, but Davis again refused to sign it. At the next session he explained that the bill, in authorizing generals to make appointments to their staffs, deprived the President and the War Department of any voice in their selection. He also felt that the large staff proposed would be unwieldy and would take many good officers from the battlefield.[27] The next month Congress gave him precisely what he wanted, a small corps of experienced officers appointed by the President and assignable as he thought proper. Commanding generals in the field could ask for and receive an extra general officer to handle their administrative details.[28] The law disregarded the plan of an additional advisory body, and Congress was never able to saddle Davis with a vigorous body of military assistants.

Under the laws described in previous chapters most volunteers and conscripts who entered the military service found themselves with men from their home state. But many volunteers from Kentucky and Missouri had rushed into out-of-state units and soon began to repent at leisure. Willis B. Machen of Kentucky reported that his state had 20,000 men scattered throughout the army who wanted to transfer to home state regiments. Since refusal would contradict its policy toward other volunteers, on September 23, 1862, Congress allowed the Secretary of War to transfer enlisted men to regiments of their own state.[29] Neither the Secretary nor his generals approved of this principle and usually required the consent of the company commander before making the transfer. Some representatives from Missouri and Kentucky protested this restriction, but Congress refused to countermand it and on February 17, 1864, compromised only by granting the same right of transfer to whole companies.[30]

People at home took a normal interest in the welfare of the boys in the army and expected their congressmen to do likewise. President Davis did not approve coddling, but on this score generally went along with Congress unless the efficiency of the army was threatened. From time to time Congress reached the opinion that certain classes of men were due furloughs and bounties. On December 11, 1861, it offered a $50 bounty and a

60-day furlough to volunteers enlisting for three years, with free transporation to and from home. The next spring Congress incorporated this plan in the first conscription law, while the law of February 17, 1864, gave every enlisted man a $100 six-percent bond.[31] Congress balked at giving free transportation to ordinary soldiers on furlough. Soldiers wrote piteous letters about spending half their furloughs waiting in train stations, and wanted free transportation and passenger priority. The railroads, however, were already crowded and overworked, and not until its last day of existence did Congress grant free transportation to all officers and men honorably absent from duty.[32] The only time that Davis had to check Congress's generosity was on December 14, 1861, when he vetoed a bill granting furloughs or discharges to many soldiers who, "at the most trifling cost," could get a certificate of disability from a physician.[33] When Congress at a later session passed a similar bill he accompanied his veto with a hands-off declaration that it was "impracticable to administer an army in the field by statute."[34]

Early in 1862 Congress began to receive distressing news about hospital conditions and about the near impossibility of disabled men obtaining transfers or discharges. "Things is managed in an awful way hear in hospitals—there is hundreds here in them that . . . is kept here at a tremendous expence to the government when they could be furloughed. . . ."[35] Several congressmen surveyed the Richmond hospitals and indignantly reported that the doctors were insanely jealous of each other and put obstacles in one another's way and that the examining boards supervising the hospitals were negligent. William W. Clark of Georgia said that the doctors would not allow a patient a hearing before a board until he had been confined for three months, by which time he was usually well or dead. President Davis admitted to Congress as early as August 22, 1861, that the hasty organization of the Medical Department had injured its efficiency and that the examining boards which selected army physicians were known to have uneven standards for fitness. A special investigating committee reported that hospital conditions were generally good, but that the procedure for determining discharges and furloughs needed immediate revision.[36] Though the committee believed that legislation could not make the Medical Department more efficient, Congress thought differently and for the next year attempted several improvements.

Believing that the root of the evils was with the medical

personnel, Congress in October, 1862, attempted to reorganize the whole Department. Davis preferred to let the Department work out its own problems and detected so many flaws in the bill that he vetoed it.[37] Congress accepted the veto as a blanket discouragement of a general overhauling and aimed the remainder of its efforts at particular needs of the Department. On September 27, 1862, it voted $1 a day for hospital rations, allowed one suit of hospital clothing for each bed used for soldiers, and allowed more hospital personnel. On May 1, 1863, it ordered the boards of examiners to visit hospitals twice a week to examine applicants for discharge or furlough, with the final decision being left to the surgeon general or to the commanding general of the army to which the soldier belonged.[38]

Congress generally gave the War Department whatever labor it needed. The Secretary soon turned against detailed soldiers and civilians because the latter were expensive and the enlisted men were insulted when assigned to menial camp duties. The army almost inevitably turned to slaves and free Negroes, and from the first hired them as laborers and in emergencies impressed them. The owners generally acquiesced, though some feared that their slaves would be mistreated or would be taken when most needed at home. The War Department in turn was quick to compensate owners for slaves lost under impressment.[39]

Early in 1862 a number of government officials and newspapers began to urge a wider use of Negroes for camp drudgeries and heavy construction work. Congress willingly let each company hire four Negro cooks, but feared the planters' political strength and rejected a levy en masse. When the latter labor plan was proposed, Congress was evasive and merely sanctioned the existing army practice without suggesting any extension. It guaranteed owners against any losses of slaves hired by the army and, in 1863, allowed slave impressments according to the laws of their states. The owner received $30 a month for each slave used and full value in case of his death.[40]

In December, 1863, the labor shortage was more critical and Davis advised the extensive use of Negroes as "wagoners, nurses, cooks, and other employees as are doing service for which the negroes may be found competent."[41] The Secretary of War added that since slaves must be removed from the path of the enemy they should be worked until reclaimed by their owners.[42] General Joseph E. Johnston and so many other generals proposed that Negroes be impressed for long periods of service that Congress realized that now the planters must be defied. On January 5, 1864, the House Military Committee proposed to subject to a labor draft all free Negroes between 18 and 50 and to authorize the Secretary of War to hire or, if unable, to impress as many slaves as he needed. The proposal was amended to the effect that an owner should not lose more than twenty per cent of his slaves and that all free Negroes, since they produced little surplus, be taken first. The Senate limited to 20,000 the number of slaves that could be impressed, and the bill became law on February 17, 1864.[43]

The following November President Davis urged a "radical modification" of this law. The army had been able to hire and impress slaves for only a short period of time and usually had to return them just as they were becoming adept. Davis urged that the government obtain 40,000 slaves for public service and pay due compensation for them. To insure faithful service the government should promise them their freedom at the end of the war.[44] He had no premonition that Congress would question this policy, for only the Virginia delegation seemed convinced that the law of February 17 endangered the nation's economy; both he and the Secretary carefully guaranteed that these Negroes would never be armed.[45]

On December 6, 1864, the Senate Military Committee cautiously proposed merely to double the number of slaves to be hired or impressed. The House bill left the number entirely up to the War Department and became the basis of the new law of February 28, 1865. Most amendments proposed in the House intended to guarantee that no one owner or section should suffer discrimination. The Senate amendments tried to safeguard agricultural production against the demands of the army. Virginia senators offered many amendments, but were able to prohibit impressment only when state laws forbade it, in which case the state itself was to fill the quota. The law also stated that if a governor certified that slaves could not be spared in a particular locality the quota could be filled from the other sections of the state.[46]

When Congress first organized its army it established a pay scale for enlisted men ranging from $34 for a sergeant down to $11 a month for a private. Almost immediately people and the press began agitating for a pay increase, the *Wilmington Daily Journal* claiming that it "took a *gentleman* to fight for eleven dollars a month."[47] This agitation at first worried the

Provisional Congress, but General Samuel Cooper assured the members that the pay scale was in every way adequate.[48] For the next two years Congress was under attack on the matter of the army pay scale. The state legislatures joined the fray and passed more than a dozen resolutions asking for increases of from $4 to $9 a month. Both in 1862 and in 1863 the House voted enlisted men a $4 raise, but the Senate's purse strings remained tight. Those who opposed pay boosts denied that a few more dollars would help the soldiers, who would spend them idly and only the extortioners would profit. Besides, they added, inflation was getting so bad that a $4 increase would scarcely buy two weeks' rations of tobacco. The Senate Military Committee suggested that any increase made should be in "the indispensable articles of arms, food and raiment. Let us not promise more than we can perform, or fail to achieve our independence by destroying our credit."[49] It was not until the private's pay got down to the equivalent of 50¢ in specie that Congress, on June 9, 1864, raised the base pay to $18 for a private and $41 for a sergeant.[50]

The military laws enacted in the spring of 1861 prescribed rations and clothing quotas for officers and men, and for the rest of the war Congress tried to interfere as little as possible with the army's dispensing of them. Officers received no allowances except for forage, fuel, quarters, and traveling expenses when under orders. Enlisted men in the Regular Army received one ration a day of an unspecified nature and a similarly vague yearly allowance of clothing. Volunteers and later conscripts received the same except that, if the Secretary of War could not supply them with clothing, their allotment was commuted to $42 a year with which they must clothe themselves. In the summer of 1862 Quartermaster General Abraham C. Myers advised that this sum was so inadequate that the men only wasted it. Congress forthwith abolished clothing commutation and ordered the Secretary of War to provide the men with uniforms according to army regulations. Two years later the officers were allowed the same rations as enlisted men and could buy clothing at cost at the Quartermaster stores.[51]

This was about all Congress did directly to feed and clothe the men. In 1861 it directed the Secretary of War whenever possible to give the soldiers some "well baked bread"; three years later it ordered the Secretary to furnish every enlisted man one ration of tobacco and assigned a committee to see that it was of good quality.[52] Congress was of the opinion that it could do no more than pass adequate appropriation and impressment laws, and that any privation was the fault of the Quartermaster and the Commissary Departments. Congress could hardly have done more, and when General Lee wrote that congressmen did nothing but eat peanuts and chew tobacco, while his army was starving[53] he was, like lesser men, merely using Congress as a whipping boy.

Congress tried to make life easier for prisoners of war from both sides. At first it showed a great deal of interest in exchanging them, but in his message of December 8, 1863, Davis stated that the North generally refused to exchange prisoners and Congress left the matter to whatever cartel the Secretary of War could arrange. In May, 1861, Congress ordered the Secretary to furnish his prisoners of war with the same quantity and quality of rations that Confederate soldiers received. In March, 1862, it stated that he must supply Confederates in Northern prisons with whatever they needed and should credit the expense to the individual prisoner's account.[54] Twice during the war Congress investigated charges of prisoner mistreatment and both times exonerated the army. On May 1, 1863, a committee was appointed to investigate the management of prisoners at Castle Thunder in Richmond. The majority found the commandant Captain G. W. Alexander quite satisfactory on most scores, but Herbert of Texas and William D. Simpson of South Carolina considered his modes of punishment cruel and degrading.[55] On March 3, 1865, a joint select committee made a preliminary report to the effect that Yankee prisoners in the South were almost coddled, whereas Confederate prisoners were starved, smothered, shot, and robbed;[56] the war ended before the investigation was completed or before any recommendation could be made.

After a year or so of combat experience many soldiers lost their enthusiasm for fighting, and before the war's end more than 100,000 had deserted. Generals Lee and Jackson advised Congress to act ruthlessly, and in the spring of 1863 both houses discussed bills authorizing commanding generals to employ men to arrest deserters and return them to camp at $15 a head. Most members, however, considered such a plan too degrading and would have none of it. Instead Congress merely deprived officers and men overstaying their leave of a proportionate part of their pay and sentenced convicted deserters to death or imprisonment. After a year Congress saw that these laws were almost useless, but tried

...... Of Officers and Men 115

to reinforce them only by imposing a fine and imprisonment on anyone abetting deserters.[57] It never outlawed deserters or placed an open season on their capture.

Congress even made a few half-hearted efforts to improve the soldiers' morale. In the middle of the war it began to hear of army floggings and indignantly demanded an explanation. When the Secretary of War explained that Congress had sanctioned flogging and other severe punishments when it continued in force the main body of the United States laws, it immediately outlawed flogging.[58] The Senate even heard that some general officers had been shot without trial, but in September, 1862, Davis dismissed the reports as nonsense. In February, 1862, Congress learned that several officers had been found drunk on duty and, despite Wigfall's argument that one binge did not make a drunkard, ordered those guilty to be cashiered, suspended, or publicly reprimanded according to the seriousness of the offense.[59] It paid little attention to drunkenness among enlisted men and even contemplated authorizing the army to erect its own distilleries.[60] Toward the close of the war a law was passed which provided for free postage of newspapers to the soldiers, but Davis vetoed it on Reagan's advice that it violated the constitutional order that the Post Office Department be self-supporting. On this occasion Congress overrode a veto for the first and only time, but the passage of the bill on January 31, 1865, was too late to benefit anyone.[61] Finally Congress allowed the President to appoint whatever number of chaplains he wished and granted them officers' rations and pay.[62]

IX

ECONOMIC ORGANIZATION

One of the most basic and persistent problems in the whole war effort was the one of feeding the soldiers. The South, though predominantly agrarian, had poor transportation facilities for distributing farm produce, and as early as the autumn of 1861 the army was threatened with short rations. Prices were inching upward and farmers found it profitable to hold their produce in anticipation of gain. Even when produce was marketed, the government had difficulty buying it at reasonable prices. If the government paid market prices it would have to bid for goods against civilians, and the merchants would have overcharged both exorbitantly. In addition speculators soon became "worse than Hessians" in competing with Confederate purchasing agents. They would buy provisions at slightly more than market price, wait a few days until prices had risen a little, and then sell the goods to the government at market price and with a tidy profit. If government purchasing agents competed with them the army's budget would be disrupted and prices forced to ridiculous levels. Because of these conditions there was a real fear in Congress that part of the army would have to be disbanded for lack of food,[1] and a mounting determination to curb producers' and speculators' profiteering.

The result was that even in 1861 military commanders had begun to impress some of their supplies. They would take what they needed, give a note on the Treasury for what they considered a fair price, and thus write off much of the profit the producer would have made. The rules of war recognized the practice, but though the administration gave tacit approval, it was never happy with impressment and tried to keep it at a minimum. Commanders in the field, however, felt that they had no alternative and always relied heavily upon impressment.

...... *Economic Organization* *117*

A flood of complaints revealed that the system was widely abused. The businessmen of Petersburg, Virginia, said that they were afraid to buy and lay in stocks of provisions to meet current necessities,[2] and Senator Clay was informed that army officers made their own estimates of what had been consumed, and placed their own prices on it.[3] Impressing officers were supposed to pay fair prices for what they took, but often they underestimated its value or refused to allow the producer a reasonable profit. Producers and wholesale businessmen contended that a fair price was the prevailing local market price; they admitted that impressment was unavoidable, but denied that it justified license and robbery. To recognize their argument would have condoned speculation and officers seldom paid market prices.

Other criticisms pertained to methods of impressment. Farmers near battlefields suffered most and were the first to complain. Agents found it easier to strip almost bare a nearby vicinity than to glean lightly from a larger area, an expedient of military necessity but one subject to abuse. At times the press of battle made commanders reluctant to spare officers or responsible enlisted men for the task of impressment, and they assigned "the merest agents, the lowest subordinates" to the routine, though disagreeable, duty.[4] Since impressment was often a hurried process, unauthorized citizens could ravage farms under official guise. A slight show of command might suffice, but the marauders sometimes used displays of force and gunnery to overawe a planter or his family. Finally many people who endorsed impressment for army use opposed allocation of goods to civilian government employees or their sale for other army needs.

Though by the middle of 1862 Congress recognized the existence of these malpractices in impressment, it was not yet convinced that interference was required. Securing provisions had not quite become critically difficult, and the protests that besieged Congress hardly compared with those that came six months later. Virginia, however, heavily populated by soldiers of both armies, made early protests. In April and August, 1862, Virginians in the House introduced resolutions requesting inquiry into the need of regulating impressment, but both died in committee. In October the Senate asked the President by what authority officers along the several railroad lines were seizing produce and provisions. Davis apparently answered satisfactorily, for the matter was laid on the table uncontested.[5]

It was typical of Congress that even on this matter it left further initiative to the administration. On January 3, 1863, Seddon informed Davis that the army had to impress supplies, but that the practice was so liable to perversion and abuse that Congress should surround it with every safeguard.[6] Davis relayed the advice to Congress, which for the first time settled down to the issue. The problem was mainly one of balance. Had Congress catered to the demand of receiving just compensation at market prices, government expenses would have risen alarmingly and price restraints been seriously undermined. The question was how to regulate impressment without destroying its military and financial value.

In January, 1863, the Senate Judiciary Committee and Representative James B. Holcombe of Virginia presented measures to their respective houses embodying much the same procedures and restrictions. When all other recourses had failed, impressment agents could take property for military use. Disagreement over prices between the agent and the owner must be referred to a board of three disinterested persons from the vicinity. The Senate bill was slightly superior in detail. It allowed the impressment of homes for hospital use, it compelled all agents to be bonded, and it required the vicinage appraisers to declare that property was not essentially necessary for the producer's support before it could be taken. The House bill was superior only in that it also allowed the impressment of slaves.

A few Virginians grumbled about tolerating anything less than market prices, but on February 17 Holcombe's bill easily passed the House by a vote of 52 to 7. In the Senate Wigfall insisted that there was no antagonism between the army and the people,[7] but his colleagues thought otherwise. For several days they introduced amendments and substitutes, including a new approach by R. M. T. Hunter. He predicted that vicinage appraisement would be unsatisfactory, because the presumably disinterested appraisers would assess all property at unnaturally high prices for the purpose of putting the same valuation on their own goods. The fact that prices might vary in neighboring communities would provoke further trouble. He proposed a resident group of impressment commissioners for each state to determine prices of leading articles and to adjust these prices every two months according to the average market price for the preceding half year.[8]

The Senate was divided between those desiring limited impressments and local arbitration, and those preferring Hunter's plan. Apparently the latter seemed too authoritarian, for the tide slowly swung in favor of the more generous plan. The Virginia legislature instructed its senators to support vicinage appraisal, and the Attorney General warned Hunter that the Constitution might require the government to pay market prices.[9] Senator Clark said that the idea of state impressment commissioners was "the most pernicious proposition that had been made,"[10] and Simms of Kentucky warned that it would cause the people to revolt. On March 10 the Senate overwhelmingly endorsed the House plan with minor exceptions favoring the producing class. The Senate added amendments forbidding the impressment of slaves used in agriculture and of produce needed by the farmer; the House bill had allowed both.[11] A conference committee appointed to settle the points of disagreement presumptuously reinserted part of the state commission plan. Senator Orr protested the committee's right to introduce an original bill, but both houses followed the practice of accepting the judgment of a conference committee and the bill became law on March 26, 1863.

The law sanctioned impressment of two kinds of property, the first that which the owner had grown or had bought for his own use. If the needs of an army made it necessary, the supply officers or their agents could impress this produce for army use; if the Secretary of War considered it advisable, he could take it for public use. In either circumstance if the owner and the officer disagreed on a fair price, it must be fixed by two disinterested men from the vicinity, one appointed by the owner and one by the agent; if they disagreed they must appoint a third, whose decision was to be final. The second type of property considered in the law, that held for sale or resale, was handled more ruthlessly. The President and the governor of a state should each appoint a commissioner to fix a schedule of impressment prices; failing agreement, the commissioners could appoint an umpire whose function apparently was to arbitrate only the particular price in question. These schedules must be published in the newspapers at least every two months. All of the second type of property impressed was to be paid for according to this schedule, but differences between owner and officer should be settled by vicinage appraisement as outlined above. If the *officer* should be still dissatisfied he could appeal to the state board of commissioners, whose decision was final. Property necessary for the owner's support or his business was not subject to impressment. Slaves could be impressed for labor under the laws of their state, or, in the absence of such laws, according to rules set by the Secretary of War.[12] As the law worked out, those goods whose final valuation was determined by vicinage arbitration brought just about market prices. Most of the produce raised, however, was intended to be sold and was therefore subject to the low schedule prices.

Though there was some bitter complaint at the law, generally it was well received.[13] Most newspapers conceded that the government wished to treat producers fairly and begged their indulgence until the war was ended. The *Richmond Enquirer* admitted that the impressment measure was arbitrary, but denied that it was unjust; the *Houston Tri-Weekly Telegraph* predicted that it would prevent cotton from falling into enemy hands.[14]

During the same session Congress observed a defect in the law which needed quick attention. Impressing officers often encountered neighborhood combinations which greatly over-appraised goods. Rather than force the officers to await their appeals Congress allowed them to take what they needed at once, give a receipt for it, and let the commissioners determine later the necessary adjustments.[15] During debate North Carolina and Virginia, aided by a handful of lower South delegates, tried to force payment according to schedule prices for goods impressed and property destroyed before the law of March 26. This would have cost the government heavily, as schedule prices were quoted at inflation level, and Congress refused.

Congress had attempted the impossible in trying to regulate impressments. The need for such regulation, apparent from the beginning, was doubly increased by mid-1863; the action of Congress only made producers and wholesalers consider impressment as no more than legalized robbery. The experiments in price scheduling inhibited the sale of goods. As each schedule applied to an entire state it was bound to conflict with the law of supply and demand, and some districts always suffered discrimination. The schedules usually set different prices for the same goods in neighboring states, and Tennesseeans could hardly appreciate 30¢ a pound for bacon, which in Virginia was scheduled at $1.

In Virginia the board of commissioners had originally determined to resist inflation, and their first schedules offered less than half the market prices. By mid-1864 government prices were ridiculously out of line. The commission weakened in the face of criticism and in June and July raised the schedule level almost five-fold. Cries of "shame," "inflation," and "financial collapse" now poured in from other sources and the harried commissioners hastily back-tracked, defending their gymnastics on the grounds that the abundant harvest had relieved the immediate wants of the army.[16] With much the same happening in other states it is not surprising that the people used every trick to evade the law.

It soon became evident that the impressment laws had failed to stop illegal and arbitrary seizures. Bands of simulated government agents, often called "hog impressers," still scoured the country taking everything within reach, and the fact that they were generally indistinguishable from army agents, who legally could impress only surplus, reflected additionally on the latter. A number of state legislatures protested this thievery and Georgia asked Congress to use only Georgians as collectors[17] there. Regular agents sometimes took the farmer's subsistence and productive goods and often, lacking funds, gave receipts on the government rather than money. Senator Hill declared that in the very shadow of the commanding general's headquarters these illegal agents stripped persons of their last meals,[18] and Goode of Virginia stated that in his district agents had mailed instructions to farmers whom they could not reach to send their surplus goods to nearby army camps. Each congressman had his woeful tale to relate, but John A. Gilmer of North Carolina had a unique problem. Impressment agents took a large quantity of his own whiskey, and he agitated the matter so strongly that it was replaced, even though Commissary General Lucius B. Northrop insisted that it was "needed as a stimulant" for the Army of Northern Virginia.[19]

Other parts of the impressment system were criticized as severely. The government was accused of taking supplies, not to feed the army, but for sale and exchange;[20] often blanket seizures included items which were neither scarce nor even needed. A number of North Carolina and Virginia congressmen maintained that the government should not impress from areas near battlefields and should even give or sell provisions to these districts. Agents continued to bypass more remote farms and took property only near army camps along the main railroad lines. Sometimes they lurked around market places and frightened producers from bringing their goods to market lest they be seized in transit. Toward the end of the war, though the record is sketchy, the commissary officers seem to have become increasingly corrupt.

Finally it must be observed that the top echelon of the Commissary Department was not faultless. The Department's mounting disorganization and the inability of its heads to learn what their subordinates afield were doing made it frequently inexpedient or impossible for them to enforce impressment regulations. General Thomas O. Moore informed Secretary Benjamin of seizing pork against Benjamin's advice, to be rewarded with the reply that private rights should not be invaded, except in cases of necessity.[21] Congress cordially disliked Commissary General Northrop, who once rashly opined that nothing should be exempt from impressment,[22] and Davis would have done well to dismiss him and let Congress see that the emergency and not the man was to blame.

On December 15, 1863, Julian Hartridge of Georgia proposed to emasculate the law by abolishing the state commissions and accepting vicinage arbitration as final for all impressments. He admitted trying to establish market prices for all impressed goods, in consequence of the decision of the Georgia Supreme Court to this effect. Opponents contended that this "truckling to the *dicta* of every 'Supreme Court'" would place the government "at the mercy of extortioners and Shylocks,"[23] but the House Judiciary Committee favored the change and added a clause forbidding agents to seize property without immediate payment. The Committee had acted hastily and, in the opinion of the majority, imprudently, for the House referred the bill back for further study.

The second report on December 21 was more realistic, for it recognized the fact that local appraisers usually valued goods at higher than market prices. To forestall too-high local evaluation the boards of commissioners were retained, but only to hear appeals and to decide property value at the time and place of impressment. During debate the House further lightened the producer's burden by prohibiting, except at the order of a commanding general, the impressment of slaves employed exclusively in growing provisions. The amended report passed without a vote and was an admission that the House considered price control a failure and hoped only to keep prices from rising faster than the normal rate. The Senate readily accepted all concessions to the producing classes, but insisted on retaining the boards of commissioners at full strength.[24] The House capitulated in order to have something accomplished and the bill became law one day before the end of the First Congress.

This law, while it did not radically change the impressment procedure, relaxed it somewhat. The act of March 26, 1863, had allowed only the impressers the right of appeal to the commissioners; now the owner had this privilege. The ban on the impressment of slaves from grain-producing farms was extended to include those producing any kind of provisions. No impressment was allowed for the use or benefit of government contractors. Impressing officers must make cash payments only and at the time of seizure. The new law even made a concession to speculators, for it no longer required affidavits of property owners that their property was bought or raised for their own use.[25] Another law passed the next day clarified a disputed point in the impressment system. Many people contended that meat was not subject to impressment since it was not absolutely necessary for army subsistence. Congress had to decide whether the army or the civilians should be on short rations, and the law allowed the impressment, at the President's discretion, of as much as half of anyone's surplus meat.[26]

When the Second Congress met in the spring of 1864 it showed little inclination to tamper further with impressment. Complaints against the laws continued without abatement, for the collectors undoubtedly were becoming less respectful of citizens' rights; but the impending currency debacle so clearly revealed the value of impressment and taxation in kind that few in Congress had the audacity to protest either. To be sure, congressmen aired local grievances as never before, but for the most part the joint special committee established in May to handle the complaints resisted all efforts to weaken the system. Impressment was advisable economically and not overly dangerous politically, since discontent was concentrated mainly in a few Eastern states.

Actually most of the complaints were directed at the impressers rather than at faults in the laws, and the Second Congress concentrated on outlawing illegal and discriminatory practices. Several congressmen requested general investigations. Heiskell of Tennessee felt that the answer lay in correcting price inequalities; Chambers of Mississippi wished the President to appoint a supervisor in each district with full control over impressment activities; other representatives proposed all grades of punishments and penalties to control the agents. John D. C. Atkins of Tennessee was the only member from an occupied district to propose a basic change, and his suggestion reflected the viewpoint of the do-or-die element. He advocated a quarterly convention of all impressment commissioners to "fix the prime cost of all articles" and to permit the seizure of goods at not more than half of this figure.[27] Even department heads joined the fray with novel solutions of their own. Seddon believed that paying the cost of production with a fair profit would end all criticism;[28] Memminger believed that everyone would be delighted to receive for their impressed goods payment in certificates redeemable in gold two years after the war.[29]

While these ideas were well intended the majority in both houses was now convinced that the evils in question were irremediable. Oldham thought that jailing about 750 impressment officers would reform the system but would starve the army. Consequently the Joint Special Committee on Impressments suggested the unusual idea of legalizing all abuses. On May 28 the committee proposed in the Senate, and eventually pushed through, a bill to allow the seizure of any articles of property, except brood stock, in whatever amount the army needed. The only restrictions were that the post quartermaster must make immediate payment and must equalize his collections over his entire district.[30] This bill indulged the army without heeding citizens' complaints, neither easing the burden of legal impressments nor providing new safeguards against unauthorized seizures. The House spurned the measure and a small group even attempted to replace impressment with a purchasing department which would buy goods at their gold valuation. They failed decisively, but in turn were able to muster enough support to reject the ruthless Senate bill by one vote.[31] The lower South had allied with Virginia and North Carolina to defeat it.

To counteract its inability to curb the impressing agents Congress tried to relieve owners and producers from crushing losses. The law of June 14, 1864, established a claims system whereby in each congressional district an agent was to receive and audit petitions for property illegally impressed; valid claims were to be paid immediately.[32] This was tacit admission that the government could not effectively protect its citizens from damage, and a further indication that Congress would sanction any kind of property seizure. This law allowed the government to evade irate citizens by pleading non-responsibility and to appease them by immediate cash payments.

The agitation never ceased for market prices on goods impressed, but Congress exhibited commendable resistance. Not until February 2, 1865, did the Senate discuss a measure defining just compensation as the usual market price at the time and place of impressment.[33] During debate two novel, but thoroughly unsatisfactory, alternatives arose. Sparrow of Louisiana proposed to let the commissioners determine market as well as impressment prices, but the Senate could not assent to such thoroughgoing government control. On March 13 President Davis suggested the use of certificates of impressment guaranteeing future payment in coin, but his message on this and other matters defamed Congress so viciously that it was disregarded. Finally in the last days of the session Congress hurried through the Senate bill of February 2 and Davis signed it at the very last moment. The law of March 18, in addition to the above provision, abolished all price schedules and in case of appeal ordered the boards of commissioners to grant market prices on everything.[34]

While abandoning price control Congress steadfastly refused to starve the army by further restricting the impressing officers. A few die-hards still felt that new penalties and restrictions would "spike the guns of demagogues and disloyal men";[35] but the argument which prevailed was that in emergencies no law could prevent the military from taking what it needed, and that the government must accept the inevitable and rely on the claims commissions to adjudicate matters as fairly as possible. In further recognition of this policy Congress on March 18 allowed impressing officers to forego cash payments and force owners to take promissory notes for their goods.[36]

War Materiel and State Socialism

When the Confederate government began to take stock of its military assets, it found the country spirited but unequipped. There was no shipyard within the entire nation and the only important arms manufactory was the Tredegar iron works in Virginia. The nation was equally deficient in other war goods — clothing, shoes, distilleries, and the like — and communication and transportation facilities were far inferior to those in the North.

During the enthusiasm of the spring of 1861, the Confederacy could almost name the number of volunteers it wanted, but arming them was another matter and Congress and the War and the Navy Departments began scrambling around for what war materiel they could find. The seceding states, by commandeering the supplies in federal arsenals, acquired about 190,000 guns. Congress authorized the President to "receive" the guns from the states,[37] but several governors released only a part of them. In addition there were several hundred thousand guns in possession of the different state militias and of private citizens which the government also tried, with indifferent success, to secure. On March 6, 1861, Congress specified that volunteers must furnish themselves with arms, clothes, and horses.[38] Governor Brown of Georgia refused to let his militia take their arms out of the state, a distrust soon vindicated by the law of January 22, 1862. The terms of thousands of 12-month volunteers were about to expire, and Congress by this law ordered that they leave their guns behind for others.[39] The first draft law offered to pay each man arming himself either the value of his gun or one dollar a month for its use, though many of these weapons were undoubtedly not of battle caliber. At the beginning of the war pikes about seven or eight feet long were popular substitutes for bayonets, and in April, 1861, Congress allowed the President to organize large numbers of pikemen when firearms were not available. They were to serve as such until firearms became more plentiful.[40]

The act of March 6 had allowed volunteers to bring their own horses and to receive government forage for them. This ruse by the government to get cavalry mounts at little expense to itself caused all sorts of troubles. The law provided compensation for horses killed, but not disabled, a provision which the men considered unfair. Inflation soon made this compensation inadequate and cavalrymen began to take their steeds home and return to fight afoot. Those who had horses killed were promised furloughs to go home and buy a replacement, but toward the end of the war men began deliberately to kill their horses for this vacation. David personally felt that soldiers who owned horses considered themselves superior to those riding government property, and he wished that somehow the army could control all mounts. Congress, however, felt that pride of ownership created a strong *esprit de corps* among cavalrymen and hated to endanger it. Finally on February 23, 1865, Congress required the Quartermaster General to provide horses for dismounted soldiers and, on the recommendation of a commanding general, to buy the privately owned horses of any cavalry unit.[41]

But horses and heroes were not enough and for four years the government strove to build up and maintain its war materiel. While a good bit was captured from the enemy, the Ordnance Bureau, under the able guidance of Josiah Gorgas, secured far more from the Confederate manufactories. Considering the South's previous lack of skill and interest in such endeavors Gorgas's efforts were remarkable. Congress ordinarily took little initiative here, but was quick to carry out the President's suggestions.

The first concern was the manufacture of guns and powder. Guns could be either bought or made, though Southerners preferred the former. On the other hand gunpowder was made of nitre or saltpeter, charcoal, and sulphur, and the administration felt capable of finding enough of these ingredients. On February 20, 1861, Congress authorized the Secretary of War to contract for the purchase or manufacture of guns and munitions in any such method as the President wished.

When the Secretary continued to report difficulties Congress allowed him to make advances on these contracts up to one-third the value of the proposed output.[42] In March, 1862, the Secretary discouragingly reported that the manufacture of guns and powder was proceeding slowly. He had been unable to increase very much the production of saltpeter and doubted if the Confederacy could ever furnish more than one-tenth the small arms needed.[43] Congress forthwith lent what aid it could. In April it established a corps of officers to work government nitre caves and to contract for private deliveries whenever they could be secured. It also agreed to advance without interest 50% of the cost to any firm undertaking to manufacture saltpeter or small arms. Within the next year the provisions of these acts were extended to include the mining of any mineral.[44] By the end of 1863 the Secretary complimented these laws highly, stating that the production of powder and shot had increased so much that, except for a slight deficiency in nitre production, the Confederacy could arm itself for the rest of the war.[45] From time to time Congress checked with the President on the amount of arms and munitions on hand and on whether anything could be done to increase them. It always received encouraging responses and for the last two years had no occasion to act further.

Congress showed little interest in encouraging other kinds of manufacturing. It never interfered with the War Department's efforts to buy guns abroad and made duty free a number of goods and items to help their production. Through a system of detail and exemption Congress gave industry as much labor as could be spared, though skilled labor was always scarce. Occasionally bills were debated developing salt mines, encouraging clothing production, establishing government distilleries for medicinal liquor, and the like; but the army seemed to have had wartime production well disciplined without congressional aid and seldom asked for help. The army controlled labor, transportation, and much of the raw material production and could force private industry to conform to wartime production or go out of business. The administration was simply not interested in developing any industry of its own or any lasting control over civilian production. Since the plan was to exploit manufacturing only during the war, a comprehensive body of laws would seem to indicate a more permanent policy than was intended.[46]

When the war began the South was pitifully weak in naval facilities. The Navy Department had inherited only 10 vessels with 15 guns, and the only two naval yards, at Pensacola and at Norfolk, were soon lost to the enemy. Congress for the most part gave Secretary Mallory a free hand and he showed remarkable ability in assembling his fragmentary navy. He sought first to defend the coastal waters and navigable rivers, and this decision, plus his inability to construct larger vessels, necessitated the simplest type of warships. By the end of 1861 Congress had authorized the construction or purchase, almost entirely at the Secretary's discretion, of 113 gunboats and the conversion of an unspecified number of other vessels into "floating" river defenses. In May, 1863, Mallory was given the right to buy cruisers from Europe to harry the United States merchant marine.[47]

As early as May, 1861, Mallory had advised the Committee on Naval Affairs that an iron-clad ship could traverse the entire coast of the United States, prevent all blockades, and encounter, with a fair prospect of success, their entire Navy.[48] The puny little gunboats had proved almost worthless against the blockade, but the impressive feats of the venerable *Virginia* convinced Congress of the iron-clad's potentialities. On May 31, 1862, it authorized Davis to suspend construction on all gunboats and to have built at once as many iron-clad steam rams as possible. In April it allowed him to contract for the building in Europe of six such vessels.[49] From time to time Congress considered instructing Davis to increase the iron-clad program or to try new naval devices, but usually did nothing but pay for whatever the Navy Department billed it for.

Congress early in the war began to receive hundreds of requests for financial aid in developing new weapons or defenses for land and sea use. The correspondence of the chairmen of the military and naval committees includes petitions for aid in building anything from a new type percussion cap pressing machine to an "aerial caloric ship." Congress found only a handful of these ideas sufficiently promising to warrant immediate attention and for the most part referred such ideas to the War and the Navy Departments. Twice Congress considered establishing a bureau of polytechnics intended to examine inventions,

..... *Economic Organization* *129*

test them, and, if practical, requisition labor and material for their development. In February, 1864, such a bill passed the Senate, but the House believed that the War Department already had sufficient facilities and personnel for developing defense weapons and never approved the idea.

When the true proportions of the war were realized, Congress and the administration undertook to regulate certain vital phases of the Confederacy's economy. On May 11, 1861, Congress authorized the President, both to expedite defenses and to prevent information from leaking northward, to control telegraphic operations during the war, and if necessary to take them over. In April, 1861, representatives of the major railroads agreed upon postal rates low enough to satisfy the Postmaster General, and Congress established these rates by law.[50] Shortly afterward it considered the need of speeding up the transportation of men and supplies, but the Military Committee gave assurance that no further legislation was necessary.[51]

Later in 1861 the administration realized that certain gaps existed in the railroad system leading from Richmond to key positions southward. Private enterprise was hesitant to invest and on November 18 Davis asked Congress to complete an important link by connecting Danville, Virginia, to Greensboro, North Carolina. He explained that Congress should have no constitutional scruples against an appropriation for the railroad since it was for war and not for commercial construction. In February, 1862, Congress voted $1,000,000 with which Davis might aid a private company in the job.[52] Within the next year three similar appropriations were made but never without the stern opposition from the strict constructionists. They persistently denied that this was a constitutional function of the central government, and ten congressmen officially protested that such donations were without validity.[53] Not until March, 1865, did Congress ever make a sizable grant for railroad construction and repair, and by then it was too late even for the $21,000,000 appropriated to do any good.[54]

For four years extremists in Congress tried to establish complete government control over railroads. In August, 1861, both the Military Committee and a special investigating committee recommended commandeering the major roads, but the majority preferred to interfere only in specific emergencies.[55] On April 17, 1862, the House passed a bill establishing full military control over railroads, only to have the session end before the Senate could debate it. As yet the matter was not critical and neither Congress nor the President had convictions upon the subject. In fact about the only unqualified opinion expressed for the first two years was Quartermaster General Abraham C. Myers's remark that "railroad officers and workers would resign rather than be subject to the orders of officers wholly ignorant of railroads and their management."[56]

By 1863 the rails and rolling stock were rapidly deteriorating under the excessive war traffic, and Southern industries had shown little ability to maintain them properly. It was also becoming evident that the army intended to use the roads as it saw fit. During 1862 congressmen frequently heard that generals and quartermaster officers were forcing the roads to give government business first priority. Senator Hill considered this practice a nuisance to private business and even accused quartermasters of profiteering by passing speculators' goods off as war materiel.[57]

In January, 1863, the House Military Committee proposed to appoint a "Military Chief of Railroad Transportation" and a staff with authority to take over the roads completely.[58] The proposal got nowhere and attention turned to the more moderate Senate plan which allowed the Secretary of War in emergencies to commandeer any road he needed; if the owners were uncooperative he could seize the road outright. He could also shift any rolling stock or rails to more critical areas in order to reinforce those either insufficient or worn out. Orr was convinced that the owners could operate them more efficiently than could the government; Wigfall agreed, but added that the "rascally railroads" were generally so uncooperative that they must be coerced.[59] The bill passed in almost the same form and became law on May 1, 1863.

This law, though it did not stop the steady deterioration of railroad equipment, at least mobilized what remained of it. Congress admitted duty free all machinery and materials needed for railroad operation and asked the President to encourage the manufacture of equipment, but the facilities simply did not exist. The only remaining alternative was to ration what remained, and on February 28, 1865, Congress passed a law it had been avoiding for four years: complete government control over all transportation and communication. The Secretary of War was authorized to appoint men to supervise all railroads, steamboats, canals, and telegraph lines and to establish whatever rules governing them he wished. Their employees were to be considered soldiers in the field and their equipment was completely under government disposition.[60] This law, which would have been invaluable earlier, served no purpose because before it could be put into effect the war ended.

The readjustment of agriculture was another wartime problem of supply and demand. Within a year Southerners realized that large amounts of cotton and tobacco would soon glut the market and that food shortages were becoming critical. With Georgia taking the lead, one state after another imposed acreage limitations on cotton and tobacco production, so that by 1863 only Louisiana and Texas were without such laws and the cotton crop of that year was only one-ninth that of 1861.[61] Shortly before planting time in 1862 Congress considered supplementing the state restrictions with one of its own, but found itself divided both on the advisability and the scope of such a policy. On March 10 the House finally decided to recommend that planters emphasize provisions in their farm production. A number of senators preferred some compulsion and Brown proposed to limit staple crop production according to the number of farm hands employed by the head of a family. He held that such limitation was an accepted war power of Congress and disparaged the thought that it would encourage Europe to develop its colonial cotton production. Most of Brown's cotton belt associates maintained that the Constitution could not be interpreted so loosely, that the state regulations were sufficient, and that great accumulations of cotton would eventually win England's support.[62]

Probably because the state laws had not been properly tested, Congress decided against any action at this time, a decision justified by the sharp decline during 1862 in staple crop production. In 1863, however, many producers became convinced that the war would end that year, and Congress hurriedly corrected the impression that the need for provisions was almost over. On April 4, solemnly declaring that the people could only expect prolonged war, Congress asked the President to announce the "necessity of guarding against the great perils of a short crop of provisions. . . ."[63] Davis quickly complied, but it is doubtful that either appeal was needed. The 1863 cotton crop was only one-third that of 1862 and most of this was produced in the West where Confederate laws were inconsistently applied.

While staple crop production was thus partially curtailed, the Confederacy nevertheless found itself embarrassed by several million bales of cotton from previous crops. Yankee invaders pounced upon every bale they could find, and in March, 1862, the House Military Committee reported a bill authorizing military commanders to destroy cotton, tobacco, and any other property liable to capture. The surprising fact is that so many inherent objectors considered the bill inadequate. Foote believed that the provision "about to fall" into enemy hands would involve fatal delays and Jabez L. M. Curry of Alabama hoped that any man unwilling to sacrifice his property in this way would himself be burned by the invaders. W. W. Boyce wished Federals to find nothing before them but desolation; Roger A. Pryor of Virginia added that the "God of War is propitiated by no paltry sacrifice"; Conrad of Louisiana warned that war should not be waged against one's own people. But on the final vote only 13 representatives opposed the bill.[64]

The Senate meanwhile had worked out a similar measure which included a method of compensation; to avoid delay the House accepted it without study. The law of March 17 allowed the military authorities to destroy any property of value to the enemy and subject to capture, and vaguely promised compensation to owners out of the proceeds of confiscated and sequestered property.[65] The press and most of the people received the law well and there were accounts of cotton-burning as everyday events from Georgia to Arkansas.

Such an energetic law could hardly avoid injuring someone. For instance over-zealous officers sometimes destroyed property far removed from danger and were rewarded by an enemy retreat before the spot was reached. The *Richmond Enquirer* reported that *"The Yankees cannot do us any more harm than our own soldiers have done,"*[66] and Senator Phelan waged a vigorous crusade for repeal *in toto*. He had become convinced that in the battle between Southern cotton and Yankee bacon the Yankees had got the better of it and Southerners should even be allowed to swap their cotton to the North for provisions.[67] But the law was necessary and only in the closing days was it even amended. On March 4, 1865, Congress ordered generals at least to consider moving property to a safer place before destroying; it did not deny the army final right to destroy property at will.[68]

It seems strange that the President and Congress should have tolerated speculation so meekly. Oversupply of money and competition for goods drove prices upward all during the war and opened new ways for profiteering. Farmers and manufacturers

..... *Economic Organization* *133*

played the market ruthlessly, and speculators snapped up goods for further price increases. By 1862 four states had passed laws fining speculators and extortioners, but these were poorly enforced and from then on a national law was contemplated.

Nevertheless the government remained inactive, almost silent, on speculation. Though occasionally conscription put a scare into speculators, most of them were adept at bidding high on substitutes,[69] and the draft laws hardly touched them. Governor Milton asked the Florida delegation to outlaw the "villanous traffick" in the "prime necessities of life";[70] Representatives Lucius J. Gartrell of Georgia and James W. Moore of Kentucky urged price limits upon woolen goods and salt; Senators Sparrow of Louisiana and Augustus E. Maxwell of Florida and Representative Foote of Tennessee proposed to apply impressment prices to all goods; and Fayette McMullen of Virginia wished to ask the states to set maximum prices on major articles—and still Congress refused to comply. The committees to which these proposals were referred usually reported them unfavorably, and the only vote taken was on McMullen's bill, which received a bare 14 votes.[71] The majority in both houses undoubtedly felt that the authority of the government to control military prices did not extend to civilian goods. Such a law would also discourage producers from raising surpluses, and high prices were preferable to no goods at all.

The result was that the only vestiges of control over speculators were embodied piecemeal in other laws. It has already been shown that the impressment laws attacked speculation indirectly by exposing all surplus produce to the liability of immediate seizure at low prices. The military exemption law of October 11, 1862, exempted skilled workers and industrial management only so long as they sold their products at not more than a 75% profit.[72] Finally, it will be seen that the income and the profit tax provisions in the financial laws placed the greater tax burden upon the wealthier and thus indirectly penalized speculators. None of these laws, however, was severe enough to curtail speculative endeavors, and Congress's hesitancy to interfere in civilian affairs was yet another contributor to Confederate financial inflation.

Congress soon learned that few people expected to suffer direct financial loss from their war "sacrifices." The states wished to charge their initial war expenses to the central government, officeholders who transferred from United States jobs demanded their back salaries, and people who suffered property losses at the hands of the army lost no time in filing claims against the government. Congress, however, quickly indicated its hostility to such claims. On the question of compensating Southerners who helped prepare the census of 1860, the Committee on Claims reported in May, 1861, that, regardless of whether a moral right existed for such payment, the government should avoid overburdening itself financially during the war. It advised Congress to authenticate all claims while the evidence was fresh and to recognize the obligation for future payment.[73]

Congress accepted this way out and set about putting it into effect. Private citizens were to file claims against the government with the Attorney General, who was to report to each session what he had done about the claims. The Treasury Department was instructed to audit for future reference any state claim.[74] Neither act ordered a cent payment, and only the first implied compensation in the near future.

After establishing little more than a filing cabinet for claims, Congress refused to fulfill the constitutional order of a procedure for their investigation and settlement. From time to time during 1862 such proposals were made, but both houses believed that the settlement of claims should be postponed until peacetime. The influential *Richmond Enquirer* supported this viewpoint and bolstered Congress's courage with pleas that everyone must make some sacrifice. The Attorney General finally reprimanded Congress for its dereliction and on January 20, 1863, Senator Hill proposed a comprehensive claims system. It provided a stronger court of claims than existed in the United States, and even allowed it, with certain reservations, to make a direct draft upon the Treasury for payment.[75] The Senate passed the bill, but the House, convinced that it could only bring a "flock of sucking vampires to the government's pocketbook," postponed it indefinitely.[76]

No other claims bill got this far again. In September, 1863, the Second Auditor reported that he had on file 30,782 unsettled claims and that even this number was incomplete.[77] Congress was willing to pay for property illegally impressed, for the law had been broken, but it dared not open the gates to the multitude of legitimate claims involving no clear violation of a law. On February 9, 1864, the House Committee on Claims denied responsibility for property destroyed by the enemy and affirmed that the army's right to destroy private property for military reasons was inherent in the war-making power and compensable only by "grace" of the government. It conceded, however, that the government's liability extended to wanton destruction of property.[78] Neverthless to the committee's proposal to audit and pay claims for illegal property destruction, Congress gave no more respect than it had shown any other such proposal. The refusal to establish a general court of claims undeniably saved the Confederacy as much money as it earned ill-will. Some claims were settled by the executive departments and some by the Board of Sequestration Commissioners, but the vast majority of claims against the Confederacy were never heard.

Foreign Trade

When the Confederacy was organized Congress at first assumed that old trade habits would continue. During February and March the new country leisurely proceeded to re-knit foreign trade ties without much casting about for new practices. The outbreak of war, however, compelled Southern leaders to revise their plans regarding foreign trade and to concentrate their efforts into two narrow channels: to direct foreign commerce so as not to help the United States and to run the blockade.

On May 21 and August 2, 1861, Congress passed two laws designed to meet the first problem. Northern dependence on cotton was well known and large quantities could be slipped into the United States unnoticed by either government. The Confederate government attempted to block this commerce by prohibiting the export of cotton and most other staple crops except across the Mexican border or through Confederate seaports. When some of these ports were captured Congress forbade shipments to any Confederate territory in enemy hands.[79]

But army needs for certain goods became so critical that the War Department questioned the advisability of complete non-intercourse with the enemy. It began to exchange staple products for Northern munitions and to wink at much of the private trade that was taking place. This considerably embarrassed Congress, which neither wished to see its laws disregarded nor to impair the army's supply activities. Toward the last of 1863 Congress decided to discourage civilian trade with the enemy while leaving the government this privilege at its discretion, and the law of February 6, 1864, allowed staple crops to be exported only in accordance with regulations made by the President.[80] This law was sorely needed, for intercourse with the North had reached outlandish proportions and much of the goods received had no military value. Theoretically the new policy enabled the War Department to monopolize trade with the United States, but the extensive Confederate border made it almost a dead letter and private citizens continued this intercourse for the duration.

The law of May 21, 1861, permitting trade across the Mexican border placed Congress in another quandary. This trade was vastly important because Mexico was the only neutral from which the Confederacy could not be cut off and was also a route by which European goods could reach the South. Soon there was a vigorous border trade and Confederate purchasing agents found that they could get all manner of supplies in exchange for gold or cotton. The difficulty was that Texas speculators were constantly trying to buy all available cotton and thus to monopolize the trade across the Rio Grande. The cost of shipping government cotton from the East to Mexico would have been prohibitive, and agents were forced to compete with speculators for Texas cotton. By 1863 the army was impressing cotton and imposing unauthorized regulations upon private trade with Mexico. The Texas legislature protested this interference[81] and Senator Oldham charged that no Roman pro-consul was ever more absolute than the military commanders in the Trans-Mississippi department.[82] Nevertheless when General E. Kirby-Smith took command of the Department he arbitrarily established a Cotton Bureau, which would buy half the cotton of a planter and exempt the remainder from impressment.

It soon became evident that even the Cotton Bureau would have its troubles. Governor Pendleton Murrah began a practice whereby he would contract for all of a planter's cotton, ship it across the Rio Grande, and then give half of it back to the original owner. This put Texas cotton beyond the reach of the Bureau, since the impressment laws permitted the seizure of only privately owned cotton. Again Congress came to the rescue, and the second benefit of the law of February 6 allowing cotton exportation only according to the President's regulations was to hand Texas cotton to the Bureau on a silver platter. Soon, however, reports began to reach the East that unlicensed impressments still occurred and that false certificates of payment for cotton were being issued in enormous numbers. On August 5, 1864, the War Department abolished the Bureau and placed the entire Texas cotton exportation business in the hands of the

...... *Economic Organization* *137*

Treasury Department.⁸³ During all this time Congress had negligently refused to interfere despite many resolutions for an investigation. Not until March, 1865, did it belatedly initiate a series of investigations of the Western cotton question, and had the war not ended soon a major scandal might have been uncovered.

Trade across the Rio Grande and through the enemy lines only whetted the government's appetite, and once it recognized the failure of cotton diplomacy it sought to make the most of blockade running. This traffic had quickly reached large proportions despite its hazards and was enormously profitable to the lucky ones. On April 21, 1862, Congress permitted vessels to unload their cargoes anywhere on the coast in hopes that they could dash into out-of-the-way places; a year later it extended the same privilege to out-going ships. On April 4, 1863, it authorized the Secretary of the Navy to hire boats and pilots on such terms as he could make for running the blockade.⁸⁴

During 1863 the government became convinced that it was not getting its share of goods run through the blockade. Luxury items brought the greatest profit and shippers preferred to carry them rather than government supplies. Meanwhile several states had sent agents abroad and their competition with Confederate agents both increased the cost of goods and allowed the seaboard states to get the lion's share of foreign goods. Since the Confederate government possessed only a few small vessels, there was also competition for chartering blockade runners. In April, 1863, the government tried to compromise by renting one-third the shipping space on these ships; shipowners and states then devised a scheme whereby the state chartered or bought a share in private vessels which could still carry most of their cargo on private account while enjoying the protection of the state. When the government insisted on its cargo space the states protested so forcefully that a national law was needed to legalize the ruling.⁸⁵

On February 6, 1864, Congress passed two laws which had been partly devised by several Confederate representatives abroad and submitted to the President for his study. The first of these remarkably advanced examples of state socialism prohibited, except under the President's regulations, the exportation of cotton, tobacco, sugar, molasses, rice, and military and naval stores. The other law drew up a list of luxuries and some near-necessities and forbade their importation until after the ratification of peace.⁸⁶ At Memminger's instigation Congress also established a Bureau of Foreign Supplies to be in complete charge of government trade abroad,[87] but Davis pocket-vetoed this and a similar law the following May. He never explained the vetoes, though it may be that in February the Texas Cotton Bureau was handling satisfactorily the only sizable quantities of cotton being exported. The second bill was unnecessary, for by this time the President had already established an organization to buy cotton and sell it abroad.

With the law of February 6 now backing him the President ordered all ships to carry half their cargo on Confederate account. The states next tried to circumvent the regulation by permitting the transfer of private ships by charter to a state. The administration in turn countered by refusing clearance papers to ships not actually owned by the state unless the ships complied with the regulation. In April four governors protested that Davis had misinterpreted the law, which promised not to restrain state exportation, and they threatened to demand repeal if he continued to do so.[88]

When Davis was unimpressed, Hartridge of Georgia on May 3 asked the Ways and Means Committee to determine whether the law did "not expressly exempt from the operation of its provisions all vessels owned or chartered by the Confederate States or any of them."[89] Hartridge added that private vessels so much disliked dealing with the Confederate government that they were already half-rebellious. Within a month the confirmed anti-administration congressmen and other staunch state rights advocates passed a bill exempting from the President's regulations ships owned by a state or chartered by one of them for its exclusive use. Davis, who never claimed the right to regulate state-owned vessels, unhesitatingly vetoed the bill on the grounds that it would deprive the Confederacy of its main source of foreign supplies. He agreed to guarantee the states half the tonage of all ships, but felt that their needs were less important than the nation's. Despite the previous majorty, the veto was sustained, and in the House by the wide majority of 26 to 43.[90]

Thoroughly enraged, seven Eastern governors met at Augusta on October 17 to turn upon the President their full opprobrium. They formally asserted that the states had complete rights upon any vessels owned or chartered by them and asked him to remove all restrictions on their operations.[91] When Davis would not budge, Congress at the November session asked for an official explanation. The President then denied, in an excellent state paper, interfering with state commerce. The commercial policy of Congress had been to regulate commerce, so as to make it subservient to the success of the Confederacy; by taking half the space of private blockade runners the government neither impeded legal commerce nor questioned the right of the state to monopolize its own vessels.[92]

Davis's firmness was justified by the results of his regulations, for on December 20 he reported that blockade running was now immensely profitable to the war effort. Congress never undermined the program, but on March 8, 1865, made an important concession by permitting the states to export cotton freely in payment for army supplies.[93] The session ended before Davis acted on this meaure, though as it specified the importation of only army supplies he may have found it acceptable.

THE CONDUCT OF THE WAR

THE CONFEDERATE CONGRESS NEVER ESTABLISHED A COMMITTEE ON the conduct of the war as did the Congress of the United States. In fact, the former was consistently criticized for insufficient direction of military affairs. President Davis was far less bothered by politicians than was Lincoln, and the central Confederate administration ran more smoothly than did that of the United States. On January 11, 1865, William P. Chilton of Alabama proposed a committee of one from each state charged with duties touching the conduct of the war and the means necessary to its successful termination,[1] but the resolution was not adopted. Controversies abounded between Congress and the administration, but the former seldom asserted itself in military affairs, and even on those few occasions when it did act it did so cautiously and almost apologetically.

For about two years a group of congressmen chafed under the administration's defensive war policy. It is impossible to determine the number in this group, though its noise was undoubtedly out of proportion to its size. It first attracted notice when some congressmen expressed the opinion that the Yankees had not been properly chased during the Battle of First Manassas. Wiley P. Harris of Mississippi, speaking before a caucus of the Mississippi delegation, condemned strongly the army's inaction.[2] Reuben Davis of the Military Committee demanded bold, aggressive action, and resigned when the remainder of the Committee preferred caution and delay.[3] Louis T. Wigfall tried to gather evidence that President Davis had refused to attack in the autumn of 1861 when the enemy was supposedly reeling helplessly, but he never found enough evidence to support the charge.[4]

The climax of the issue came early in 1862 when Foote

introduced a resolution condemning a defensive policy and proposed to assail the enemy wherever they could be found.[5] When questioned he claimed to possess reliable information that Davis favored an aggressive war and that the generals alone were responsible for the non-action of Confederate forces.[6] The next day though several orators supported Foote's theme the resolution did not pass and Congress steered shy of telling the President how to fight the war. The House momentarily became enthusiastic when Lee invaded Pennsylvania in September, 1862, and Hilton of Florida proposed to compliment Lee for his advances. The Military Committee, however, was as careful as ever and re-worded the resolution simply into one of thanks for battles won.[7] After Lee's retreat, agitation for aggressive warfare practically ceased, and even Foote insisted only that no more Confederate territory be abandoned.

While Congress was unwilling to interfere in military strategy, it followed the war's progress closely, carefully scrutinizing all official battle reports and, when they seemed incomplete, asking for further information. The chairmen of the military committees kept in close touch with the War and Navy Departments and with certain leading generals, Miles in particular spending many evenings in conference with the heads of these departments. Congress adopted scores of joint resolutions thanking generals for particular victories and regiments for re-enlisting, resolutions which must have been valued, for General Joseph E. Johnston wrote Wigfall that his Army of Tennessee was irked that others which had done far less marching and fighting had been recognized by Congress while his had not.[8]

For the first half of the war Congress tried to investigate all major defeats. On February 8, 1862, a United States fleet suddenly attacked and overwhelmed Roanoke Island, a poorly defended spot off the coast of North Carolina. The *Richmond Enquirer* screamed for a vindication of the Virginian in charge, General Henry A. Wise, and two weeks later Congress ordered an investigation. The committee's report acknowledged Wise's efforts to persuade Secretary Benjamin to improve the island's fortifications and concluded that the latter's failure to do so placed the loss squarely on him.[9] General Benjamin Huger, a West Point graduate, had assured Benjamin that the defenses were adequate, whereas Wise, on taking charge, had reported the island to be almost defenseless. The Secretary had relied on the trained rather than on the political soldier, but was at fault for not checking

Wise out. Actually the blame could hardly have landed elsewhere. Congress by this time was gunning for Benjamin and much of the committee's evidence was based upon the reports and remarks of the humiliated Wise.

The committee assigned to investigate the losses of Forts Henry and Donelson and the evacuation of Nashville refused to place the responsibility anywhere.[10] Foote and Horatio W. Bruce of Kentucky asked leave to present a minority opinion, but this would have stirred a hornet's nest uselessly and the House refused. Congress had the same attitude toward the loss of New Orleans. Several Mississippi congressmen attacked General Mansfield Lowell, in charge of its defenses, for negligence; others accused the Navy of inefficiency and want of energy.[11] The investigating committee, however, exonerated both the General and the Navy and commended them and the War Department for heroic efforts.[12] In April, 1862, the House Naval Committee visited Fortress Monroe and complimented the authorities there on the excellent condition of the ram *Virginia*.[13] The committee must have been abashed when soon afterwards Commodore Josiah Tatnall found the vessel completely unseaworthy and scuttled it. In 1864 the House refused to investigate the cause of military reverses in the Valley of Virginia, announcing the pressure of other and more important work.[14]

Congressmen naturally spent much of their time championing local needs. The Trans-Mississippi states had a number of unique problems and kept a standing committee to work upon them. Texas and Arkansas in particular were burdened with Indian trouble. These states always felt that their frontiers were inadequately protected, and the fact that they suffered numerous and destructive Indian raids bore them out. Even the tribes presumably allied with the Confederacy were unprincipled enough to fight occasionally on either side, and when the Cherokees abrogated their treaty in February, 1863, several other tribes took advantage of Lincoln's amnesty proclamation and followed suit. Guerrillas from Kansas sometimes invaded Arkansas and Missouri; civilian thugs and soldiers plundered both sides indiscriminately all during the war. Davis was almost as unable as he was unwilling to give these states more support, and their congressmen maintained that they were largely ignored by the government.[15] Oldham told the Senate that the West was regarded as a fine source of beef and common soldiers and as nothing more.[16] This judgment was partly correct, for in their four-year siege of the administration for aid the Westerners obtained few tangible results.

Every state government was convinced that it had too few and too poorly equipped defenders; at times each made claims of being grossly neglected. When an army moved railroad equipment from a particular district its congressman usually insisted that his district was as important as any. Some pestered the War Department with demands that regiments from their state needed clothing, supplies, rest, a change in climate, or the like. Congressmen from the lower Mississippi River area demanded improved river defenses and often presented detailed defense plans as to location of cannon, breastworks, scuttled ships, and other obstructions. Floridians made similar requests but they received much less attention than most of the other suppliants.

Whenever a state was threatened with invasion its congressmen implored the War Department to send back its own regiments and whatever others could be spared. The Mississippi River, Charleston harbor, Mobile, Tampa, Atlanta, and any other threatened areas were variously declared to be key defense positions, an opinion defending generals were quick to substantiate. The hard-pressed Department juggled its men as best it could. Florida and the West were the most consistently denied and their congressmen felt that once their regiments left the state the Department would never return them. Oldham seems to have worked hardest to keep Westerners at home, while President Davis maintained that, once they had been sent East, they could do more good there serving cheerfully. When Vicksburg was under siege, the Mississippi delegation asked for 30,000 men to relieve it and received word that the redisposition of so many troops would cause the loss of half the area east of the river.[17]

After 1862 lower South states had many of their men transferred northward and made every effort to retrieve them. Miles and General Beauregard had done an excellent job in 1861 and 1862 in immobilizing infantry and cavalry around Charleston, and in 1863 when the War Department began to remove them Miles lost every trace of his ordinary aplomb. He wrote Seddon, "Don't strip us of troops—really of means of efficient defense. There are evidences of impending attack; don't invite it. I beg you to reconsider last order, and leave here what few troops left — much short of force here this time last year."[18] Enemy proximity caused civil disobedience and congressmen believed that the presence of a sizable Confederate command would keep order. The conscription, tax, and impressment laws at times needed military enforcement beyond the ability of local posts.

Many border state and Western congressmen had favorite schemes for winding up the war gloriously. They particularly disliked the administration's emphasis on protecting Richmond and magnified the importance of their own states. Russell of Virginia believed that West Virginia could be retaken with 10,000 troops. Delegates from Tennessee and Kentucky claimed that swift blows would win back their states. They became enraged when General Johnston retreated from Nashville to Murfreesboro and submitted to the President an elaborate plan for retaking Nashville.[19]

The War and the Navy Departments received a surprisingly small amount of outright condemnation from Congress, especially surprising since the Confederacy was waging a defensive and a losing war. The strident voices of Foote and Wigfall must not be considered as representative of the viewpoints of their respective houses.

While in the United States Senate President Davis had learned to respect the ability of Stephen R. Mallory, who was then chairman of its Committee on Naval Affairs, and without consulting the Florida delegation appointed him Confederate Secretary of the Navy. Present-day writers agree that Mallory did his job splendidly, but during 1861 and 1862 most people believed that the nation had great naval potentialities and fretted at his inaction in developing them. The loss of New Orleans set Congress off, and Charles M. Conrad, who was a personal enemy of Mallory and had just had most of his Louisiana property captured, instructed the House Committee on Naval Affairs to consider abolishing the Navy Department and adding its functions to the War Department. A week later Foote, who detested Mallory merely because of his membership in Davis's Cabinet, failed by six votes to put the House on record as lacking confidence in Mallory and was forced to be content with Conrad's proposal.[20] A joint investigating committee worked for the next year and a half, and on February 17, 1864, it completely exonerated Mallory and praised his accomplishments.[21] It appeared that most of the criticism of Mallory and his Department was much less a political attack upon the administration than an expression of Congress's frustration at a time when hopes were highest and important battles were being lost. By 1864 Congress was more familiar with and resigned to the Confederacy's naval deficiencies and the barbs against Mallory steadily diminished.

Congress's relations with the War Department were more personal. Davis nominated Leroy Pope Walker as his first Secretary of War solely on the recommendation of Clay, Wigfall, and other friends; his younger brother, Richard Walker, then heading the Alabama delegation, persuaded Congress to accept Leroy, an Alabama fire-eater, for the post.[22] Davis had no confidence in Walker and entrusted him with little responsibility. Congressmen found relations with him trying. They bristled under his high-minded refusal to grant official favors, and Walker's letter books reveal a curt and none too cordial relationship with them. Continuous congressional inquiries so interfered with his attention to routine duties that in August he began receiving them only between 9 and 10 A.M. Members of Congress generally lacked confidence in Walker. Thomas R. R. Cobb considered him utterly unfit as a department head and deplored the inefficiency of the War Department.[23] Those who felt that Walker was not developing the war machine rapidly enough condemned his management of the Department so heartily that at length a committee was appointed to investigate the medical, commissary, and quartermaster branches. Before a report could be made, however, Davis willingly eased the controversial Secretary out of office in early September.

Judah P. Benjamin, Walker's successor, never had a fair chance in the position. Administration opponents scorned his subservience to the President, and congressmen favoring an aggressive war policy found him too intent on defense. He, like Walker, angered members by the tone of his correspondence, but the most damning factor against him was the series of military reverses during his term. For the most part Congress blamed Benjamin only indirectly for the defeats, though it placed the responsibility for the Roanoke Island loss directly on him. Davis, however, liked Benjamin's self-effacing qualities and, on seeing that the Senate under the Permanent Constitution would not continue him in his post, promoted him to head the State Department.

The succeeding Secretaries of War found Congress quite friendly. By now the body had accepted a defensive war policy and had realized that it could not win the war by meddling with the Department. George W. Randolph occupied the post until November, 1862, and left almost no impression on it. James A. Seddon, Secretary from November, 1862, to February, 1865, was an intimate friend of the President and influenced military strategy more than any other Cabinet member. Except for Foote, who considered Seddon a "foul and incompetent Secretary,"[24] congressmen seldom attacked him openly. When at last Seddon resigned it was mainly for political reasons. John C. Breckinridge, who then served until the end of the war, was one of the most popular men in the Confederacy and was appointed primarily to appease Congress. He enjoyed his popularity, although he contributed little time or thought to his job.

The Quartermaster and the Commissary Departments, two branches of the War Department charged with providing the soldiers with food and subsistence, fared poorer at the hands of Congress. The policy of impressment and the rumors of inefficiency and corruption in the departments gave them a bad name by mid-1861; since their services were administrative rather than policy-making, Congress stood in no awe of them and in August decided to investigate thoroughly their organization and administration. The War Department graciously gave the five committeemen free railroad passes and carte blanche to pry where they wished; so between sessions they roamed the army camps. Their report of January, 1862, disclosed only a lack of supplies and transportation facilities and found the Departments guiltless of fraud or inefficiency.[25]

Nevertheless, rumors continued and by 1863 were so widespread that Foote and Hill proposed a new investigation. Sparrow, however, informed the Senate that the War Department was then making just such a study, the results of which Congress should await. The House Committee on the Quartermaster and the Commissary Departments was also looking into the army flour contracts with Hexall, Crenshaw and Company of Richmond, with specific interest as to whether Commissary Major Frank Ruffin was profiteering from them. By the end of April everyone had been absolved, and the only tangible results of these disturbances was the law of May 1, 1863, to prevent fraud in the two Departments.[26] The law served no real purpose, for it only outlawed a few practices already illegal under general army regulations.

For the remainder of the Confederacy, Congress discussed numerous resolutions and bills to reform these Departments. The resolutions usually denounced various abuses and speculations practiced by government employees; the Bills established minute regulations for the conduct of each Department. None had any

...... *The Conduct of the War* *147*

success, for the majority in both houses not only realized the impossibility of ending these practices in question by law but also acknowledged the efforts of the War Department to combat them. The Department, to its credit, emerged almost unscathed from these attacks. In March, 1865, Congress indiscreetly drafted all quartermaster and commissary workers under 45 at posts and depots, but Davis vetoed the bill on the grounds that the few additional soldiers would not compensate for the injury done to the supply system.[27] Congress's over-all evaluation of these Departments was that abuses in them were not flagrant, their inefficiency was not excessive, and, while the army was often underfed, the Departments were doing their best.

Telling the President how to use his generals and how to conduct the war were different matters according to some congressmen. Each general had at least one determined supporter, sometimes more, in Congress, usually a personal friend who did not hesitate to promote his favorite's cause. High officers naturally carried a great deal of weight during wartime, and congressmen in turn often expressed their viewpoint of war policies by means of criticizing or championing certain ones.

Early in January, 1862, there was a long and sharp secret debate over General Beauregard's report on the Battle of First Manassas. Part of this report censured the President for refusing to permit an immediate advance upon Washington and another section criticized the Quartermaster and Commissary Departments for supply shortages at critical moments. The report had created some little stir during the previous autumn and Davis accentuated it when he added to the document his own comments about Beauregard's ability and veracity.[28] Beauregard had anticipated the consequences of his report, but, on being asked whether he wished it printed in entirety, had replied "Let Congress do for the best."[29] Congress judiciously published the report without the belittling remarks of either accuser and thereby spared Davis the indignity of being officially declared incompetent.

After Shiloh, Davis distrusted Beauregard's ability and replaced him as commander of the Army of the West with General Bragg. The Trans-Mississippi delegates, who had originally secured Beauregard for this command, in September petitioned that he be restored. Semmes and Sparrow took the petition to Davis, who disconcerted them by reading it aloud in their presence, interspersing his reading with caustic remarks. He then declared that Beauregard was needed at Charleston and that his return West was out of the question.[30] Meanwhile Davis's apologists in Congress stated that Beauregard had acted too independently of the War Department and deserved his come-uppance. South Carolinians were delighted with this exchange, while the West felt keenly rebuffed.

Bragg had his supporters in Congress, but the majority regarded him as a bloodthirsty martinet and were inclined to believe any unfavorable tale about him. They also felt that, as a "pet" of the President, he received honors that others deserved more. He tended to blame defeats on his subordinates, and since most of these also had their sponsors in Congress he soon built up a strong anti-Bragg clique. Wigfall and Henry C. Burnett of Kentucky claimed that he browbeat his generals and refused to report cases in which enlisted men had been summarily executed. In March, 1863, the Tennessee delegation asked Davis to remove Bragg from that state as his presence depressed the entire population.[31] Accounts of Davis's reply vary, but after a few months Bragg was demoted to the relatively unimportant post of commanding general at Richmond. Even here he was not free from congressional heckling. Several members considered his new appointment a reward and continued to watch him closely and even tried to reduce his pay. The administration was fortunate in that Bragg's severest critics were from Western and border states which otherwise were most cooperative.

General Joseph E. Johnston was another storm center of the army. His over-cautiousness was the despair of those wishing to drive the enemy from Tennessee and Kentucky and his querulous nature caused him to complain incessantly of executive discrimination. The above states' delegations were divided concerning his ability, but the entire Georgia delegation demanded his removal when he began his Fabian tactics before Sherman's army. Finally, on July 17, 1864, the War Department rendered Sherman an invaluable service by replacing Johnston with the "fighting general," John B. Hood.

There were several other generals whose personalities and policies resounded through Congress. Most of them, particularly in the Trans-Mississippi Department, faced such insurmountable obstacles that they could not afford to curry popularity and usually took for granted their embroilments with congressmen. During 1862 the Tennessee delegation believed that Albert Sidney Johnston was usually at the wrong place at the wrong time. When they asked Davis to remove him, they hardly appreciated the President's loyal reply that "If Sidney Johnston is not a general, the Confederacy has none to give you."[32] Kentuckians showered most of their compliments on John C. Breckinridge and few elsewhere. South Carolina congressmen disliked John C. Pemberton's defenses for Charleston; when he was transferred westward only to lose Vicksburg congressmen there advised the War Department that he was ruinous to the cause.[33] Senator Brown had become enraged at the way David R. Jones had handled his regiment in July, 1861, and almost persuaded the Senate Military Committee to refuse him a brigadier-generalship. Several senators thought that Jubal A. Early had been drunk while losing battles in the Shenandoah Valley. Early demanded an investigation, but the Senate decided that it would solve nothing.[34] Boteler of Virginia wrote that the enemy was treating his district dreadfully and begged Seddon to send General Fitzhugh Lee "or some such dashing officer, to the Valley in the place of General Jones."[35]

The Trans-Mississippi Department, half separate from the interest as well as the jurisdiction of the Richmond authorities, had its own brands of general officer troubles. Their civil usurpations continued through the war. Some Western congressmen felt that the Department was a dumping ground for unfit officers, and Snead of Missouri was terrified at the rumor that Bragg was to take command there. Davis intended to appoint Henry Heath of Virginia to command in Missouri on the grounds that Westerners could be brought into co-operation only by a man not a resident of a Western state.[36] When the Missouri delegation stated that their citizens would enlist poorly under any general except Sterling Price, Davis was firm and even impatient in his opposition to their views.[37] They then sought assurances within Congress that Heath would not be confirmed and finally the latter persuaded Davis to withdraw his nomination.[38] General Thomas C. Hindman had made himself unpopular by enforcing conscription and by numerous *habeas corpus* suspensions, and in January, 1863, Davis transferred him to Vicksburg. Arkansas tried to dispose of Theophilus Holmes for the same reasons, but Davis liked Holmes and held on to him tenaciously. The favorite generals were E. Kirby Smith and Sterling Price and Western congressmen seldom criticized either.

THE WRIT OF HABEAS CORPUS

IN COUNTRIES WHERE ANGLO-SAXON CONSTITUTIONAL PRINCIPLES rule, wartime usually provokes the controversy of whether in emergencies the government should, or even could, tamper with its citizens' fundamental rights. The Confederacy, though a nation of emergencies, was remarkably free of this problem, for its state rights heritage had almost settled the question before it arose. The only liberty actively threatened was the right of habeas corpus. By early 1862 the nation seemed falling apart. The likelihood that the twelve-month volunteers would refuse to re-enlist endangered the nation's defenses, conscription did not yet exist, and a number of cities contained lawless elements. As early as 1861 reports began to reach Congress that some commanders already were suspending civil rights as the occasion demanded.

To cover such emergencies Congress on February 27, 1862, and apparently at Davis's unofficial request, hurriedly allowed the President to suspend the writ of habeas corpus in cities, towns, and military districts when in his judgment they were in such danger of attack that proper defense required martial law.[1] Wigfall had assured his fellow senators that the law would seldom be applied and that it was primarily intended to cover Norfolk, Portsmouth, and the surrounding country; Davis immediately placed these areas under martial law with the suspension of all civil jurisdiction. Richmondites were so excited that the next day the Senate did not convene and the House adjourned after the opening prayer. Davis, however, was not fazed and on March 1 extended the suspension to Richmond and the area ten miles around it.

Congress soon was able to witness martial law in action. General John H. Winder, in charge of military affairs in Richmond, used his provost marshal "Plug Uglies" rather arbitrarily and members

......*The Writ of Habeas Corpus* 151

could glimpse from their windows the "glitter of bayonets in the streets. . . ."[2] By mid-April Congress had re-examined martial law from the viewpoint of its inherent excesses and on April 19 added two important reservations to the law of February 27. Suspension of the writ of habeas corpus was limited to arrests made by authorities of the Confederacy and for offenses against it; the act itself would expire thirty days after the next meeting of Congress.[3] These provisions were designed to prevent any interference with the normal operation of state courts and to make sure that military government would only supplement and not supersede ordinary civil government. It was made plain that the writ could be withheld only in offenses against the Confederate laws.

Unlike Lincoln, Davis applied the law sparingly, singling out the danger spots and leaving the rest of the country unmolested. Even then he attempted to avoid shocking people, and often the civil courts continued limited operation. Nevertheless suspension aroused much hostility. Congressmen disliked carrying passes wherever they went, and complained that provost marshals enjoyed poking their bayonets at people. They maintained that these officers pre-empted undue authority over civilians, were too expensive to warrant their picayune duties, and retarded traffic by continually requiring passes. John B. Jones observed that others considered suspension a failure because top government secrets continued to reach the enemy from Richmond. Generals in restricted areas sometimes exceeded their authority by confiscating property and by prohibiting the employment of soldier substitutes. Finally suspension was unpopular because it enabled Confederate enrolling officers to reach men being protected by the authority of a state court.

Western generals were the worst offenders under the law. Indians, speculators, and smugglers were so troublesome that generals felt compelled to take the law into their own hands, the distance from Richmond giving them courage to do so. They presumed to exercise the same privileges of suspension that Congress had granted the President, and Generals Peter O. Herbert, Earl Van Dorn, and T. C. Hindman soon blanketed most of the West with martial law. Western congressmen protested vehemently and Davis, though too far removed for much success, did his best with these outpost difficulties. He rebuked the three generals for acting without authority, issued General Order 66 annulling their proclamations, and later replaced them with more popular officers. This shift of command, however, was ineffective, for the need for summary action continued and was satisfied in the same way.

Radical state righters everywhere warned that suspension of the writ was but another step toward despotism; those too timid to hurl this charge at Davis loosed it against his generals. The *Texas State Gazette* said that the administration consisted of "but men," and extraordinary powers "might make them our master, and us their slaves"; military necessity could "claim no such sacrifice at our hands."[4] The *Mercury* warned that Davis would abuse this "bulwark of our liberty if given the chance."[5] In Congress Reuben Davis predicted that the President might even dissolve Congress.[6] After the war Henry Foote recited a "shocking catalog" of persons arbitrarily imprisoned, and almost triumphantly claimed that most of them died from their confinement.[7]

Nevertheless Davis found the suspension laws invaluable and in August, 1862, Ethelbert Barksdale, his spokesman in the House, proposed to repeal the time limit and make suspension part of the permanent war effort.[8] He was bluntly rebuffed when both houses postponed the suggestion and undertook to re-examine the wording of the laws. The first law had carelessly used interchangeably the terms "suspension of the writ" and "martial law," but many congressmen insisted that they were dissimilar. The discussion was more than academic, for in practice most officers made no distinction between them and had frequently established martial law as a concomitant of the right to suspend the writ.

These interpretations were controversial enough to warrant study by Congress. Suspension of the writ of habeas corpus meant only that the civil courts would be powerless to free a man held by Confederate military authorities. The fact that its authorization was in the section of the Constitution dealing with the legislature apparently made suspension a congressional decision; but Davis might have used Lincoln's argument that his oath to "preserve, protect, and defend the Constitution" allowed him to use his powers as commander-in-chief of the military forces in any manner he thought necessary. He never encouraged this interpretation, however, and the distinction between martial law and suspension of habeas corpus was the only question involved. Martial law meant the placing of a whole community under a military regime with the ordinary processes of justice suspended. Its advocates have maintained that declaring a state of martial law is a part of the president's war powers and that he can proclaim it without authorization from Congress. Resort to this extreme procedure

......*The Writ of Habeas Corpus* *153*

has been rare both in England and America, and during the War of 1812 General Andrew Jackson was fined $1,000 for imposing martial law over civilians in Louisiana. At this stage, the question was not whether the right of habeas corpus could be suspended, but whether the entire civil government could be replaced by martial law.

In August, 1862, some congressmen determined to end this uncertainty. At the instigation of Vice-President Stephens, Senator Semmes asked the Judiciary Committee to report what laws were needed to prevent military commanders from usurping power under guise of the suspension laws. Semmes was primarily interested in Western affairs, though Landon Haynes stated that martial law existed everywhere and tried to instruct the Committee to rule that it was not authorized by the Constitution. This bellicose resolution, which would have predetermined the nature of the Committee report, was tabled.[9] In the House Muscoe R. H. Garnett of Virginia, recounting how generals muzzled the press and fixed agricultural prices, merely asked the Judiciary Committee to look into the whole matter of martial law. He was supported by Thomas M. Jones of Tennessee, who cuttingly defined martial law as the will of the officer declaring it,[10] and by Foote, who promised to order his constituents to "put down the domestic tyrant who thus sought to invade their rights."[11]

Not everyone disparaged martial law. Clark of Missouri refused to criticize "every little stretch" of the Constitution or officers taking "enlarged views" of their duties.[12] Phelan, using the traditional argument that attempts to define fundamental rights, would imply unintended limits to them, noted that the Constitution already protected freedom of speech and of the press and needed no further implementation. In the House Dargan of Alabama explained that martial law was a power incidental to the office of commander-in-chief and must be tolerated for the sake of survival. Congress had constitutional jurisdiction only over the right of habeas corpus, while martial law was an implied war power of the President. He concluded with the apology that martial law did not suspend civil law between citizen and citizen, but only between citizen and the army, and that Davis and his generals, by including both relationships, had violated an important principle of martial law.[13]

The Senate Judiciary Committee bypassed the issue and merely added to its bill of September 20 the reservation that it should not be construed to countenance martial law. The House Committee, however, made a thorough study of the distinction between the two concepts. It admitted that the first suspension act had been too general, and that the President, while using moderation, had gone far beyond a mere suspension of the writ of habeas corpus. The Committee then investigated martial law in English history and arrived at the definition, "absolute power administered by military courts in summary proceedings. . . ." In the Confederacy this definition held true for military law, the legality of which was unquestioned, but the point at issue was whether the law pertained as well to civilians. The Committee contended that neither in peace nor war could citizens be subject to any power inconsistent with the Constitution or laws. Congress might suspend the habeas corpus or even authorize military commanders to destroy private homes, but neither Congress nor the commander was herein acting arbitrarily. The Constitution delegated to Congress a number of war-making powers that on occasion might be violations of basic rights, but even these violations were justified by a constitutional principle, and not by a suspension of the Constitution. Any unauthorized violations by the President or his generals were "simply impossible." The only kind of martial law permissible would be for Congress to grant certain powers to the President and call them "martial law." The President indeed was commander-in-chief of the army, but his authority was still subject to the regulations enacted by Congress in pursuance of the Constitution. The Committee concluded with the statement that "the laws can be suspended only by the law-making power," that if martial law was needed "it should be regulated and defined in a sense consistent with the Constitution by distinct enactments."[14]

The pronouncement was largely wasted, for neither house was inclined to make rules which in emergencies would be ignored. No doubt Congress was also impressed with Davis's sincere intentions in applying the first suspension law. Senator Semmes introduced a bill to prohibit martial law, which was narrowly defeated. Foote tried to order the President to respect the Constitution and Francis S. Lyon of Alabama would let him proclaim martial law only in times of invasion, but both resolutions failed. The year 1862 ended with the only ruling on martial law being a Senate joint resolution, ignored by the House, that the War Department had no authority over civilians or the civil courts.[15]

Once that question had been dodged, Congress re-enacted without mishap a second habeas corpus suspension. Conditions in threatened areas were still troublesome, and in Richmond Con-

...... *The Writ of Habeas Corpus* *155*

gress was startled into action within one day by "a murder on 10th street, a riot on 17th, a fight and a banging away with pistols on Franklin street, and sundry robberies and rascalities. . . ."[16] The Senate bill of September 20 defined too precisely the conditions of suspension and required an awkward system of tests and measurements to determine if the conditions existed. The House bill re-enacted the first law, time limit and all, with the exceptions that it omitted any reference to martial law and stated that arrested persons should be investigated immediately. These safeguards satisfied both houses and the law passed on October 13, 1862.[17]

Opposition to this second law reached such a high pitch that the administration was unable to follow it immediately with a third. Governor Vance anticipated "a vast tide of inflowing evil from these inordinate stretches of military power,"[18] while Vice-President Stephens and Governor Joseph E. Brown collaborated to denounce the law. The *Charleston Mercury* declared that state treason laws were adequate and that the President should have no power in a state beyond the lines of the army.[19] By this time large numbers of unwilling conscripts were seeking deliverance from the draft laws through their state courts. These men, most of them recently elected petty officials, or principals whose substitutes had been drafted, had considerable success in getting court writs to protect them from enrolling officers. It was primarily to deny these men the protection of their courts that President Davis desired to end the "reign of habeas corpus."[20]

During the first half of 1863, however, Congress hardly bothered to discuss the matter. Because of the widespread confidence of victory, the majority disliked antagonizing the people so near election time. The Senate completely ignored habeas corpus, and the House Judiciary Committee persuaded the members to reject bills by Gartrell and Barksdale re-enacting the law of October 13. The Committee approved A. H. Garland's resolutions condemning martial law, but the majority considered them "abstractions, the passage of which could do no possible good."[21]

By the end of the year the tide of war was more disheartening. The *Richmond Enquirer* now begged for a new habeas corpus suspension lest civil order in Richmond completely vanish. In Congress also the wind had begun to shift. On December 10 the House ordered a select committee to determine whether the army was violating the constitutional rights of citizens. Four of the five members had consistently opposed suspension, but the failure of the Committee to report indicated either inability or unwillingness to indict the President and his generals.[22]

Encouraged, Phelan and Gartrell tentatively broached the matter of suspension, but both houses preferred to await Davis's signal. On February 3, 1864, Congress heard his request for a new law. After describing several cases of treason he reported that guilty persons were often released under writs for want of competent legal testimony. In the absence of summary action valuable information was leaving Richmond, and a United States plot to incite slave rebellions had just been discovered. In some states civil process had been brought to bear upon the army with disastrous efficiency, for judges were releasing hundreds of men liable to conscription. Davis ended on the conciliatory note that only Congress could suspend the writ.[23]

Though John Baldwin of Virginia warned that it "would be the last organized act of the Confederacy,"[24] both houses were ready to comply. Their judiciary committees had already prepared bills which they introduced almost immediately. On February 5 the House passed its bill by a vote of 58 to 20; the Senate then dropped its measures, amended the House bill slightly, and on February 11 passed it by a 14 to 10 vote.[25]

During its passage two significant facts emerged: a general recognition of the need for suspension and a conviction that executive and military discretion must be strictly contained. Both bills and all substitutes reveal the determination of Congress to write a law that could not be loosely interpreted. They abandoned the former technique of blanket suspension and instead drew up lists of treasonable practices which would warrant suspension. Baldwin and Oldham led small groups in their respective houses opposed to any suspension and sought to defeat all such bills by overcomplicating the procedure of suspension. They had no success and most of the effective defensive work was done by those who only tried to pinpoint the conditions allowing suspension. Opposition to suspension bills, based more on doctrinal hostility than on local oppression, was, unlike opposition to most administration measures, well scattered geographically. This fact explains why the history of most suspension bills was decided without loose ends or hesitation. When the administration majority felt compelled to act ruthlessly it could usually pass a suspension bill with great speed.

The law of February 15, 1864, differed from the sweeping measures of 1862. It was realistic enough in that it gave the President, the Secretary of War, and the commanding general of the Trans-Mississippi Department power to arrest suspected traitors; it also released military officers from all obligation to surrender their prisoners to civil authorities. The innovation was that, in an effort to prevent discretionary action, the law listed specific causes for which the writ could be suspended and required the President to investigate all cases of persons so arrested.[26] It is difficult to see how this new approach was any improvement. Davis had his generals under fair control and most of the suspensions which he himself had ordered were against the treasonable practices defined under this law. Perhaps its virtue was that it might restrain excessive violations of civilian rights under the name of suspension.

Congress received a few accolades for the law, but scarcely enough to feel complimented. The *Savannah Republican* believed that "only bad men should disapprove of it,"[27] and the *Richmond Enquirer* thought that Confederates should not wage "mockheroics" over civil rights until after the war.[28] But most public statements were derogatory. The Mississippi legislature urged repeal on the grounds that the law was dangerous and unconstitutional, and tended to make the civil power subordinate to the military.[29] At Stephens's advice the Georgia legislature took similar action, at the same time professing undiminished confidence in the integrity and patriotism of the President.[30] On October 17 the Eastern governors jointly condemned all suspension and urged Congress to repeal the law.[31] North Carolina felt, with much justification,[32] that it was aimed especially at her and Governor Vance warned Davis to use suspension lightly. Chief Justice Pearson decided to continue issuing writs to all principals of substitutes seeking them, and the state legislature finally ordered the other judges to follow suit.

When the Second Congress met on May 2, 1864, several representatives believed that they had a mandate to undo the law of February 15, which would expire in less than 90 days. Marcus H. Cruikshank of Alabama was one of these representatives and on the opening day proposed outright repeal. Five of the nine members of the Judiciary Committee had previously favored suspension laws, but the Committee now recommended unanimously that Cruikshank's bill be tabled. A. H. Garland explained that the pressure of federal armies around Richmond was so disturbing that it should be deferred.[33] Only North Carolina favored an immediate showdown, and the House majority preferred to ask whether the law was still needed. The alarmed President hastily replied that suspension had been "most salutary," and that its discontinuance during the existing military crisis would be dangerous, if not outright calamitous.[34]

A majority of the Judiciary Committee supported Davis's opinions, but Gaither and Garland submitted a minority report explaining their support of repeal. They contended that by allowing the President and his subordinates any discretion in determining who should be arrested the law had obliterated the lines between the two branches of government; that it required much elasticity of construction to hold that Congress could vest such great power in the Executive. Moreover, the law violated judicial independence by letting the President appoint investigating commissions to study matters ordinarily handled by the courts. Finally, the law was unnecessary. Confederate soldiers were loyal and confident, but violations of individual liberties had dampened popular enthusiasm. Suspension only dismayed the people, who felt that they were living under a despotism doing everything possible to save itself.[35]

The Senate handled the matter more discreetly. Wigfall attempted to define both Confederate and state jurisdictions over civil liberties; though he supported his resolution with the best speech of his career, the majority avoided argument by tabling it. Sparrow then tried to instruct the Judiciary Committee to inquire into the need for another suspension law, but again the majority preferred to ignore the whole issue.

The fact that the struggle over suspension during this session had been inconclusive was a negative victory for the administration. While Congress never seriously considered extending the law of February 15, 1864, past its expiration date of July 31, Davis had only insisted that it be continued for its assigned duration. The administration forces might even have managed another suspension, for they showed their strength more positively at this point by burying a resolution denying the right of Congress to let the President arrest persons without due process of law.[36] But the recent conscription and funding laws had so dismayed the seaboard states that the administration preferred not to test their breaking point.

At the beginning of the last session, when Sherman was coasting through Georgia and Grant was steadily increasing the pressure on Richmond, Davis once more asked for another suspension law. He described a dangerous conspiracy in parts of Virginia, North Carolina, and Tennessee which could not be otherwise suppressed;

unofficially he fortified his request by revealing a letter from Lee asking for just such a law.[37] The administration now felt compelled to exert its full strength and on November 11 the House Judiciary Committee introduced a bill almost identical to the law of February 15.[38]

Despite Foote's threat to resign if the bill passed, the administration had the House well in hand at least on the matter of suspension. The House acted cautiously, however, and for three weeks willingly entertained any amendment that did not diminish the effectiveness of the act. Amendments were accepted requiring that all arrests be accompanied by written evidence, that writs be given to men wishing to test their legal liability to conscription or claiming exemption as state officers, and that the law could not be retroactive. On the other hand, the majority consistently defeated all efforts to weaken the bill by emasculation or by overcomplication: it refused to let state judges investigate suspension cases, to guarantee that the law would not change the law of arrest and commitment, to let the right of suspension be delegated to generals, or to prescribe punishments for violations of the law. The bill passed the House by a vote of 50 to 44; half the opposing votes were from North Carolina, South Carolina, and Georgia, while the strong support of the occupied states and Virginia carried the day.[39]

The Senate had before it a similar measure, but to save time took up the House bill. Matters were different here, for the Senate was particularly suspicious of administration measures having strong state rights implications, and by one amendment destroyed the value of the House bill. The latter was lenient enough toward men with good claims for military exemption, but refused to interfere with the enrollment of out-and-out draft dodgers. The Senate's amendment, which insisted that Confederate officials must honor all state court writs pertaining to any matter of military service,[40] conceded the superiority of the state courts over both military and federal officials, and would have rendered the law worthless.

The House declined to contest this obvious impasse and for the next month only toyed with its rejected bill. On March 17 Davis cracked his whip once more and advised Congress that suspension was not merely advisable and expedient, but almost indispensable to the successful conduct of the war.[41] The House compliantly rushed through a measure granting complete powers of suspension to the President, the Secretary of War, the commander of the Trans-Mississippi Department, and to any general officer commanding an army or a military district. The Senate rejected the measure without debate,[42] and Congress ended the next day, having suspended the writ of habeas corpus for only sixteen months during the war.

FOREIGN AFFAIRS

IN THE FIRST STAGES OF ITS EXISTENCE CONGRESS BELIEVED THAT ONE of its most urgent tasks was to establish the Confederacy and make the new country known in the family of nations. Most Southerners felt confident that, because of their cotton, the new nation would be universally welcomed. During the first two months Congress thereupon organized a State Department and authorized the President to appoint consuls and commissioners to other countries and to instruct them as he thought advisable. Rhett wanted the post of Secretary of State, but his cooperationist delegation would not support him and Davis offered it to Robert W. Barnwell of South Carolina. Barnwell, however, wished to concentrate his influence on making Memminger Secretary of the Treasury and declined. Though Davis preferred Toombs for this position, he yielded to South Carolina and made Toombs Secretary of State.

On February 12, 1861, Congress took charge of the questions and difficulties between the Southern states and the United States relating to occupation of forts, arsenals, navy yards, and the like; it then authorized the President to appoint three commissioners to settle the problems amicably and to seek recognition from the United States.[1] Lincoln thoroughly snubbed these commissioners, and when the Fort Sumter fracas precipitated a shooting war Davis called a special session of Congress for April 29 and described the complete breakdown of relations between the neighboring countries. On May 6 Congress recognized the existence of war and instructed Davis to use the whole land and naval force.[2] Finally, Congress ordered that all citizens of hostile nations be declared alien enemies and be either removed or jailed unless they showed intent to become Confederates.[3] From then on intercourse between the two nations was largely on matters over which Congress legally had no control.

161

Some delegates reached Montgomery determined to rewrite the United States naturalization laws so as to keep the Confederate breed uncontaminated. They accordingly sought to enact strict naturalization rules, but the majority in Congress were unwilling to be so exclusive and ultimately changed the old laws only to confer temporary citizenship or quick naturalization on foreigners in the Confederate army. Thereafter Congress preferred to wait until after the war to see specifically what laws were needed. At the close of the Provisional Congress T. R. R. Cobb pushed through a bill designed to keep Northerners out of the South *after* the war; the bill threw the problem of naturalization to the states by repealing the United States laws on the subject without providing any replacements. Davis forthwith vetoed it on the grounds that only Congress could determine citizenship and that the law would mistreat aliens who had already begun naturalization proceedings.[4]

In the meantime Congress was making desultory efforts to lure some of the Northern states out of the war. The Mid-West had depended on the Mississippi River for much of its contact with the outside world, and the Confederate government hoped to use the river to persuade the Mid-West to be neutral or even to form a Western confederacy. This delicate strategy required only the slightest pressure, and in February, 1861, Congress made its first move by exempting from duty almost everything the Northwest produced and by granting free navigation of the Mississippi to the citizens of all states bordering the river or its navigable tributaries.[5] The joker was that while these states were a part of a foreign country they could use the river only for access to the ocean. The fact that local river traffic was not theirs except in full payment of the regular tariff duties was an important reservation, for most of the Northwest's trade was with the Southern states rather than abroad.[6]

When war began some congressmen wished to deny the Northwest the use of the Mississippi, but the Committee on Commerce argued successfully that the Confederacy needed access to the United States granaries. By the fall of 1862 this river diplomacy was a failure and the House Foreign Affairs Committee investigated to see why. On deciding that the Northwest believed that the outbreak of war had revoked the right of transit, the Committee asked the President to reiterate the guarantee of free navigation and to offer a commercial treaty to any state that desired one.[7] Davis undoubtedly agreed with the Committee minority

...... *Foreign Affairs* *163*

report that the likelihood of secession in the Northwest had vanished, for he refused to offer such a treaty.

Until the end of 1864 Congress intermittently debated propositions that offered commercial advantages to any state declaring its peace with the Confederacy, and rejected all of them.[8] After 1862 almost everyone had abandoned hope of other states seceding and the "more sensible members laughed and walked out" when Foote announced in January, 1863, that Kentucky had rebelled and that Indiana and Illinois would quickly follow suit.[9] By 1863 about half of the representatives from states bordering the Mississippi wished to continue efforts to spread secession, while the rest of Congress considered such efforts futile.[10]

The Confederacy had strong expectation that Maryland at least would secede with the other slave states, and at first Wigfall went "on a warpath . . . to strike for Maryland."[11] The Provisional Congress exempted Maryland from several of its tariff and alien laws, and as late as December, 1861, expressed sympathy for the sufferings of Maryland and promised to conclude no peace without insuring her a chance to join the Confederacy.[12] Russell of Virginia even proposed to allow her a non-voting congressman, but Confederate sympathizers there had not even erected a provisional government and the resolution was tabled. After three years of anticipation some disgusted congressmen wished to retract all favors shown Maryland. In January, 1864, Congress even debated drafting Marylanders residing in the Confederacy, who were otherwise exempt by their status as foreigners. The obstacle was that such a policy would have precipitated the embarrassing question of whether to draft Europeans as well. This would undoubtedly have created a serious diplomatic crisis, and the movement to draft Marylanders was probably dropped to avoid the related question of other aliens.

Some of the most bloodthirsty moments in Congress concerned retaliation to enemy outrages. In the summer of 1861 Lincoln threatened to treat the crew of the captured Confederate privateer *Savannah* as pirates rather than as regular prisoners of war. Davis indignantly reported Lincoln's threat and other standard instances of torture, outrages, and depredations, and Congress granted him permission to inflict upon United States prisoners the same punishment applied to the *Savannah* crew.[13] The Northern jury, however, did not convict the crewmen of piracy and this particular incident settled itself.

By the next summer discussion of retaliation was began again and continued intermittently for the rest of the war. The time for "rose water philanthropy and womanly tenderness" was over and the South must extract "blood for blood."[14] Among other things the Yankees were accused of destroying or confiscating civilian property, imprisoning Confederate sympathizers, executing prisoners, and using Negroes as soldiers. Confederates usually advocated the general rule of an eye for an eye for these crimes, but Lincoln's Emancipation Proclamation aroused their most furious indignation. Beauregard wrote that it was "high time to proclaim the black flag," and many congressmen agreed.[15] Senator Clark said that the Confederacy should neither ask quarter for its soldiers nor extend it to the enemy,[16] and both houses entertained resolutions to enslave Negro soldiers captured and to execute their white officers.

In October, 1862, Congress debated these resolutions, but on thinking better finally passed a much less resounding one offered by Barksdale. It described the atrocities committed by Northern soldiers, explained how Lincoln had intended his Proclamation to foment slave revolts, and promised to sustain the President in resorting to such measures of retaliation as in his judgment should be demanded by the lawless and barbarous conduct of the enemy.[17]

Congress and the President could never agree on how to follow up this resolution. The next January Davis reported that unless Congress objected he would consider the enlisted soldiers as unwilling instruments in the commission of all the crimes and would hand their officers over to the states to try as ordinary criminals.[18] The Senate Judiciary Committee would not agree that state laws were in force against the enemy and stated that retaliation was a function which could only be exercised by a belligerent nation. The Committee presented its own plan, which finally passed after many stump speeches. Officers of Negro soldiers were to be considered as inciting servile insurrection, and the military courts before which they were to be tried could exact the death penalty. Captured Negro soldiers should be handed over to the state government in which they had been seized.[19]

Nothing came of this joint resolution, for neither Davis nor a state ever executed anyone under it. On February 8, 1865, Congress opened the way for its own use of Negroes by striking out of the resolution the pronouncement against Northerners using "negroes" as soldiers and only forbade them to use "our negro slaves."[20]

...... *Foreign Affairs* *165*

Robert Barnwell Rhett had hoped to become either Secretary of State or ambassador to England; when he obtained neither he happily accepted the chairmanship of the Committee on Foreign Affairs. Rhett, who believed that Davis and many others had seceded only in order to get favorable reconstruction terms, hoped to commit the Confederacy to an aggressive and irrevocable foreign policy before Davis took office. On February 13 his committee recommended that three commissioners be immediately appointed and sent to Europe. After the inauguration they would be under the President's direction, but their first instructions would be formulated by Congress under Rhett's guidance. Through his early control of foreign affairs he hoped to establish the following as bases of the new foreign policy: a 20-year commercial alliance with England and France conditional on their recognition of the Confederacy, a promise of a 20% maximum import duty, and an offensive and defensive league with European countries to defend their possessions in North America. To his dismay a majority in Congress liked neither these tactics nor their free trade implications. They rejected the initiative by amending the report so as to leave the appointments and the instructions to the President.[21] It is hardly surprising that Davis withheld any diplomatic post from Rhett.

Davis quickly appointed William L. Yancey, Pierre A. Rost, and A. Dudley Mann as commissioners to Europe and Rhett anxiously questioned Yancey about his instructions. He was enraged to learn that the group had orders only to secure recognition by threats of a cotton embargo, with no authorization whatever to make commercial treaties. Rhett advised Yancey that unless he went prepared to conciliate Europe by irresistible proffers of trade he could expect no success,[22] and determined at the next session to contest the President's reliance on cotton diplomacy.

In May Rhett prepared a resolution empowering the commissioners to promise a 20% maximum tariff to any nation making a satisfactory treaty with the Confederacy. Secretary of State Toombs approved the resolution and urged it on the Foreign Affairs Committee. The Committee endorsed the resolution, unanimously according to Rhett, and on May 13 he introduced it before Congress. The protectionists then asserted themselves and, on the ground that continued free trade would handicap Southern manufacturing, limited the proposed treaty to five years. Rhett, who had always contended that only a 20-year guarantee would tempt England and France to risk antagonizing the United States, sulkily had the resolution tabled.[23]

The implication of Rhett's defeat was that the administration had decided to stake its European diplomacy upon cotton. "Cotton is King" was a byword with Southerners, who believed that England and France would defy the United States to secure Confederate cotton. Nineteenth-century international law required that a blockade, to be legal, be effective enough to prevent its being violated. In the spring of 1861 the Northern blockade was mainly on paper and Confederate strategy was to hold cotton until Europe came and got it. Secretary Memminger and a few others preferred to build up foreign credit before the blockade became effective, but they were hopelessly outnumbered. Most of the press, merchants, planters, cotton factors, governors, and legislatures believed that the cotton embargo would earn recognition from abroad, and state and local authorities sought to prevent exportation. Several congressmen in informal conversation with foreign representatives had received satisfactory encouragement. Benjamin H. Hill expressed their opinion when he stated in Congress his complete faith in "that little attenuated cotton thread, which a child can break, but which, nevertheless can hang the world."[24]

Congress did not convert this sentiment into a direct embargo. It frequently debated doing so and passed several laws pointing toward an embargo, but then stopped short. The reasons for avoiding this final step lay in the President's interpretation of Europe's mood. He believed that a Confederate embargo would only alienate Europe. He preferred to depend on other factors to keep cotton from Europe, while his administration appeared as the last restraint upon a Congress always threatening an absolute embargo. Therefore he encouraged Congress to talk freely and never act. Meanwhile the nationwide enthusiasm for cotton diplomacy was making the embargo an accomplished fact. State legislatures and citizens' extra-legal devices very effectively prevented most cotton from leaving the country in 1861, and Consul Bunch at Charleston thought that an act of Congress would be superfluous.[25]

This explanation clarifies congressional action during 1861 regarding the exportation of cotton. On May 10 Congress stopped all trade with the United States.[26] Since Europe got most of her cotton through the North, Consul Bunch wrote that Congress had already begun to apply pressure to England. On the same date Congress debated a complete embargo, but the law of May 21 only prohibited, except through the Confederacy's own seaports and through Mexico, the shipping of cotton during the blockade.[27] The law would prevent cotton from being sent abroad through the United States, would allow the Confederacy to get necessary supplies through Mexico, and would force Europeans to come directly to Southern ports for any sizable quantity of cotton. In July Congress instructed the Committee on Foreign Affairs to study the advisability of an embargo on cotton, tobacco, and naval stores, but it never reported. Underneath all this indecision can be detected the operation of Davis's strategy. He directed foreign policy completely and an embargo law was not remotely possible.

Congress passed two other laws to support its cotton diplomacy. In August it declared its adherence to the Declaration of Paris of 1856 that neutral countries might carry non-contraband enemy commerce and that blockades, to be binding, must be effective.[28] By this time it was apparent that the Yancey-Mann-Rost mission was getting nowhere, and Davis decided to concentrate on England and France. Several lower South members felt that they should stop begging for recognition and let cotton do the job, but the majority consented to the appointment of James M. Mason and John Slidell to whatever extra foreign duties the President might assign them.[29]

By the end of 1861 cotton diplomacy had proved less than successful; it had created a cotton famine abroad, but unforeseen factors had weakened it. The enormous crop of 1860 had enabled England to accumulate a surplus of raw cotton that would last her through 1862. Also she had so successfully encouraged cotton growing in Egypt and India that by 1865 both countries were sending her large shipments. Meanwhile the United States had vowed to defend its blockade with force if necessary, and England had no wish for war at this time. France would do nothing without English leadership and the Confederacy gradually realized that the embargo had failed.

The last spark of hope came in the spring of 1862 when Robert Mercier, the French minister to the United States, visited Richmond. In his talks with Conrad, Wigfall, Clay, James L. Orr, and others he became convinced that the Confederacy was unconquerable. Judah P. Benjamin hoped that Mercier's admiration had influenced the French government and on April 12 made an offer to Napoleon III of 100,000 bales of cotton and free trade in exchange for recognition and help in breaking the blockade. Benjamin's enthusiasm was contagious and on April 18 the Senate optimistically requested Davis to make commercial treaties with France, England, and Spain.[30] This request assumed that Europe had succumbed to cotton diplomacy and was ready for trade at all costs; Davis, who knew that this was not the case, ignored the request. By this time some supply shortages were becoming critical, and the government reluctantly abandoned the entire program; by mid-1862 the Confederacy was trying to get cotton abroad in any possible way.

Confederates were as angry as they were disappointed at this European cold shoulder. By 1862 the newspapers were criticizing the Southern insistence on the supremacy of cotton,[31] and began to suggest that the government abandon blind reliance upon foreign nations.[32] When the failure of diplomacy became complete, there then grew up a violent sentiment against "waiting in the servants' halls and on the back stairs" for foreign recognition[33] and a feeling that the Confederacy should "discard the maudlin balderdash about our 'Anglo-Saxon kindred'" and withdraw its commissioners from Europe.[34]

A number of congressmen held this viewpoint and occasionally proposed to recall all diplomatic agents. The majority, however, respected the President's control of diplomacy and, knowing that he disliked breaking all ties abroad, never took action against Confederate agents already commissioned to Europe. Increasing their number was another matter. In November, 1862, during a recess of Congress, Davis had appointed Lucius Q. C. Lamar as minister to Russia. Instead of confirming him at the next session in February the Senate asked why it was necessary to send anyone to Russia. The Secretary of State replied that an effort was being made by the Emperor of the French to obtain the concurrence of St. Petersburg to put an end to the war, and a Confederate agent was needed there.[35] This answer failed to convince the Senate, which resolved that no confirmation of envoys should be made to any foreign court, until the Confederate States had been recognized by the respective powers.[36]

A related problem concerned the status of consuls stationed in Southern ports who represented nations which had not recognized the Confederacy. Sentiment against them grew rapidly, and the origin of their exequaturs was considered as justification for expelling them. These consuls had received their exequaturs from the United States, and the Confederacy had simply recognized and continued their official status. When their governments continued to withhold recognition the question arose over the exercise of consular functions under an enemy exequatur. Secretary Benjamin maintained that secession did not automatically invalidate the prior obligation of the states in receiving these consuls, who should be tolerated as long as they exercised their duties properly.[37] But no foreign agent possessed an inherent right of residence, and the consuls were always liable to expulsion.

In April, 1862, Congress debated expulsion of these consuls, but, still hoping for recognition from foreign governments, at the time took no action. By the end of the summer the picture was clearer, and both houses asked their foreign affairs committees to consider severing all relations with Europe. The Senate Committee never acted, and that of the House knew so little about executive policies that it asked for more time to query the State Department. When Benjamin would not release state secrets the committee reported that it could not make a judicious recommendation. It added that since hope of recognition remained the Committee members would not advise the immediate recall of commissioners nor recommend the dismissal of the consuls of foreign nations.[38] The administration preferred to keep the existing arrangement as long as it was advantageous. Foreign consuls communicated with their governments through their ministers in Washington, and the Confederate State Department reached other countries through these channels.

The only action against foreign agents arose in October, 1863, when some British consuls assumed quasi-diplomatic status and advised British citizens that they were not liable to Confederate military service. Davis was visiting the army in the West, and Benjamin called a Cabinet meeting which was unanimously in favor of expelling all British consuls. Benjamin informed the latter that their efforts "to arrogate the right to interfere directly with the execution of the Confederate laws" rendered them *persona non grata*.[39] Benjamin immediately wrote Davis that the presumptuous action of the consuls was a stroke of fortune in that "it enabled us . . . to satisfy public sentiment which would have been quite restive under their continued residence here. . . ."[40]

These scattered incidents reveal Congress's insignificant role in diplomacy. Members were generally uninformed as to diplomatic intricacies and Davis made little effort to enlighten them. Congress occasionally asked for information about correspondences of the State Department, the number of agents abroad, their names, expenses, location, et cetera. Usually the information was given, but was twice withheld on the grounds that what was requested was too confidential.[41] The fact that administration opponents presented most of these requests indicates that they were primarily expressions of political emotions, not efforts by Congress as a whole to take a stronger role in foreign affairs.

XIII

THE PEACE MOVEMENT

Congress was most active in foreign policy in regard to the opening of peace negotiations with the United States. The unofficial peace movement in the South was as old as the Confederacy. Portions of the Appalachian and the Trans-Mississippi regions had opposed secession, but were forced into the Confederacy as minority sections of seceding states. They remained passively Confederate during the first two years of the war but camouflaged their activities by resorting to secret societies. There were three well-developed peace organizations extending from Arkansas to Florida and many smaller local organizations. Some were formed for treasonable purposes and maintained close contact with the United States; others were organized to offer only constitutional opposition to the Confederacy and to induce it to open negotiations based on independence. The extremes grew farther apart as the war progressed, until the constitutional wing either withdrew or ceased to exist and the other became, from the government's point of view, wholly treasonable.

Peace talk occasionally arose even in official circles as early as 1861. Many believed that the North would recognize the independence of the Confederacy if it could avoid the stigma of opening negotiations. Some thought that First Bull Run afforded the South an opportunity to take the initiative without losing face, and a few congressmen discussed this possibility in private conversation. There was a rumor in Montgomery that President Davis himself sympathized with this view, though he firmly denied it.[1]

The first official peace proposals in Congress were made on September 16, 1862, when Foote of Tennessee and Hines Holt of Georgia suggested that commissioners be sent to Washington to seek a just and honorable peace. These resolutions were tabled by a vote of 59 to 26,[2] and the lack of uniformity on the vote indicated a complete absence of organization among peace agitators. When compared with other issues, peace negotiation was not anti-administration nor was it a project of former Whigs or Unionists, for each of these three cliques opposed the resolutions by about a two-to-one majority. The consensus among the newspapers was that peace could be won only on the battlefield and that Congress had more important matters to consider. Foote's plan was proposed in the House on several other occasions during the spring of 1863 but met defeat at every turn.

By the end of 1863 the peace movement had gained considerable strength. Its strength might be attributed to an increasing dislike of certain Confederate policies, a fear of the growing strength of the central government, a belief that the North would negotiate on the basis of Confederate independence, and a defeatism among the people due to the unfavorable tide of battle.

Various policies of the government offered a fertile ground for peace agitation. Impressments, conscription, suspension of the writ of *habeas corpus,* the cotton embargo, and other measures were sources of popular dissatisfaction; and the daily privations of life gradually exhausted the patience and perseverence of both soldiers and civilians. Border states complained incessantly of danger from Indians and marauders, and began to desire peace on any terms. All states at some time protested against outsiders in local offices, for, in spite of every precaution by the War Department, district military commanders were frequently citizens of another state. The Gulf states protested the disproportionate number of general officers from the Atlantic seaboard and demanded that the Department establish a ratio between the generals and the number of soldiers from each state. Planters frequently felt that the employment of slaves as laborers and soldiers might lead to emancipation; rather than await this eventuality they preferred to risk opening negotiations based on independence. No one grievance was a major cause of the peace movement, but general irritations caused by the war combined often to induce a receptive mood for peace discussions.

The drift of the Confederate government toward extreme measures caused many to visualize a military despotism dominating the state governments. In a sensational open letter to President Davis in September, 1864, W. W. Boyce brought a severe indictment against the government for all manner of abuse and incompetence. Among other things, he asked what greater powers could Davis exercise if he and Congress had been granted unlimited power; he then went on to answer himself at length by demonstrating how the government had implanted a centralized military despotism over constitution, state, and individual.[3] Though most newspapers and public figures regarded this attack as something between poor taste and treason, it received enough commendation to seem impressive.

The vigor of the government's war action, combined with a seemingly endless war, induced no little defeatism over the Confederacy. Desertions from the army increased, and investigating congressmen reported conditions "gloomy" and soldier enthusiasm cold.[4] Lee's failure in Pennsylvania and the failure of cotton diplomacy caused most people to despair of foreign intervention. Boyce felt that even if the South should be victorious the North would recoup its forces and soon hatch another war. A leading cause of defeatism was that most enlisted men felt they were waging a "rich man's war and a poor man's fight." The non-slaveholder felt that he had nothing to lose by emancipation. From the planters' point of view, when slaves were impressed their owners lost the immediate use of their labor, and when the government contemplated emancipation to curry European favor the owners felt that all abolitionists were not in the North. Several state governments had collapsed by 1863 and many members of Congress believed that the Confederacy could not stand another campaign.[5] Some congressmen despaired of their own ability and talked of establishing a military dictatorship under Lee. None, however, admitted less than complete loyalty to the cause. North Carolina, for instance, felt snubbed and insulted by the central government; Senator Reade admitted that dissatisfaction was rampant, but claimed that it was justified and that it did not imply disloyalty.[6]

A large number of optimists believed that the United States would welcome peace overtures based on Confederate independence. They supposed that both belligerents were equally war-weary and that once the South had expressed desire for peace the Northerners would force their government to negotiate. The Democratic platform in the United States election of 1864 favored a restoration of peace, but Confederates failed to realize that it presupposed reunion and was not a declaration for peace at any price. The re-election of Lincoln at first discouraged Southerners, though they quickly rationalized it as a triumph of political chicanery rather than any positive expression of public opinion.

But while everyone longed for peace, the road was clouded and treacherous. As the war progressed the treasonable peace movement became bolder, and as guilt-by-association is by no means a twentieth-century monopoly, men favoring the opening of negotiations might find themselves classed as reconstructionists, cowards, or even traitors. All peace advocates insisted that the United States would accept Southern independence and promised that if overtures were rejected they would agree to continue the war indefinitely. Nevertheless outside their own circles peace agitators were looked upon with suspicion and were publicly condemned for demoralizing the war effort.

A peace movement began in North Carolina on March 15, 1862, when a meeting near Ashboro prayed for peace; within eight weeks after Gettysburg over a hundred peace meetings had been held throughout the state. Editor Holden of the *Raleigh Standard* proposed that the congressional elections for the Second Congress turn on the proposition that Congress make an honorable adjustment,[7] and several candidates ran on this platform. In Georgia the quarrels of Governor Brown with the Confederate government set a pattern of protest all over the state, and several candidates campaigned on the vague platform of "a just and honorable peace." In Alabama the former cooperationists tended to re-form as the peace group and some of the candidates were rumored to be reconstructionists. In the Trans-Mississippi Department there was even talk of a Western Confederacy which would be neutral in the North-South war.

A major obstacle to peace hopes was finding an approach to negotiations which, if it failed, would not endanger the Confederacy's morale. Some felt that Congress should order President Davis to take the initiative, while others wished the body to appoint commissioners of its own. Senator Hill belonged to a group favoring a Southern convention to negotiate with the Lincoln government, with any decision subject to separate state ratification. The more radical elements despaired of collective initiative and favored separate state action of one kind or another. Usually the radicals rejected the idea that states should make peace separately, claiming that individually a state could only lead the way to a Southern convention or lay the groundwork for a *rapprochement*. Though this group consistently denied the charge, their political opponents claimed that they were surreptitiously seeking reconstruction on the best terms available.

The leadership of the official peace movement came from North

The Peace Movement

Carolina where on December 30, 1863, W. W. Holden proposed in an editorial that the state begin negotiations of its own by means of a state convention.[8] Vance, who differed consistently with the Confederate government over other matters, now promised he would see Holden "in hell" before consenting to a course that would bring dishonor and ruin upon both state and Confederacy,[9] and was finally able to block the convention movement. Holden, like others favoring separate state action, never explained what he wanted his convention to do, but he was suspected of being a reconstructionist and on one occasion was the victim of a mob which broke into his printing establishment and destroyed much of his equipment. Friction on the home front was influential, for many of the thousands of North Carolina deserters confessed that they were influenced by home activities. News of this disaffection reached the United States, where people thought that North Carolina was about to secede from the Confederacy.

Despite the hope that the government would in some fashion negotiate an honorable peace, President Davis was convinced that any overture would be fruitless and feared that it would irreparably injure public morale. Individual congressmen and sometimes whole delegations sought to convince him to try negotiation, but he remained adamant. He explained to Senator Dortch that he would think about the matter but was not convinced of its propriety.[10] The North Carolina delegation advised that he could remove the sources of discontent in the state and quash all convention talk by showing a willingness to negotiate.[11] Davis pleasantly invited suggestions as to the methods of opening negotiations and the terms to be offered, but added that the delegation was probably not aware of the obstacles involved.[12]

The First Congress respected Davis's leadership in foreign affairs even more than along domestic lines and its only action resembling a peace proposal was an *Address* to the people of the Confederacy in relation to the war. After justifying secession and recounting the many crimes of the Republican party and the United States, the *Address* stated that unless the United States gave some evidence that efforts to negotiate would not be spurned, Congress could only repeat its readiness to accept terms consistent with the honor and dignity and independence of the States.[13] This manifesto was published throughout the South and was sent to France and Belgium.

Hiram P. Bell of Georgia wrote that the election of 1863 had sent to the Second Congress a number of men who hoped to save what they could of the Confederacy.[14] On May 23, 1864, James T. Leach of North Carolina, a fiery and sarcastic newcomer, proposed that delegations from each state should request the President to offer the United States a 90-day armistice preliminary to negotiations for peace upon state sovereignty and independence. If the North offered peace Congress should submit the terms to each state for ratification or rejection.[15] This procedure reserved to the states important controls over a peace movement, but not even Leach dared suggest that Congress pre-empt the President's constitutional functions, and so the matter of negotiations was left entirely to him. Leach stated that his resolution contemplated neither state action nor reconstruction and would probably be fruitless, but that he felt that a peace effort should be made.[16] After a few minutes of words and name-calling, in which the vitriolic Leach more than held his own, the resolution was tabled by a vote of 62 to 21, with fourteen of the nays coming from North Carolina and Georgia.[17]

A month later, Lee's victories at Spotsylvania and in the Wilderness convinced the peace advocates in Congress that their most opportune moment for successful negotiations had arrived. This time they planned more carefully; Graham of North Carolina, Johnson of Georgia, Orr and Boyce of South Carolina, and several others gathered in the suite of Senator Watson of Mississippi and, after rejecting reconstruction, agreed to work simultaneously in both houses for negotiations based on Southern independence.[18] The next day, June 2, Foote and Orr proposed resolutions that the Confederate government dispatch peace commissioners to Washington. Concerted effort, however, had no effect on the majority, for neither house was yet inclined to instruct the President as to his duties and both resolutions were tabled by comfortable margins. Congress could only agree upon a harmless manifesto, similar to previous ones, presenting the principles, the sentiments, and the purposes of the Confederacy and leaving the initiative to the United States.[19]

Thus the first session of the Second Congress continued to pussyfoot. McClellan was then campaigning against Lincoln on what to the South appeared to be a defeatist platform, and most Confederate leaders preferred to await the outcome. The next session of Congress would commence at approximately the same date as the United States elections and would be the most propitious moment for an all-out peace offensive.

...... *The Peace Movement* *177*

Those opposing delay found solace in the aforementioned letter by Boyce, who pleaded for a political policy to supplement the military effort. There was no hope of Lincoln as a peace maker for he was committed to the most violent course and was no more than an instrument of the mob. Nevertheless the Democrats, who were rational on the subject of slavery, had proposed an armistice to discuss peace. The Confederacy should abet them by expressing willingness to an armistice, and a convocation of all the States in their sovereign capacity to consider peace. Such action would thoroughly invalidate Lincoln's claim that the sword was the only arbiter.[20] Boyce hoped that his letter would either force Davis to act or persuade Congress to take negotiations under its own jurisdiction.

As a matter of fact, Boyce's violent attack served only to rally support to the President. The *Augusta Tri-Weekly Constitutionalist* condemned the convention idea because the South would still be out-voted as before the war. The *Montgomery Daily Advertiser* maintained that peace was possible only by convincing the enemy that his attempt at subjugation was hopeless.[21] The *Richmond Enquirer* claimed that the matter was entirely an executive decision. Others said that the proposition was subversive and that the North would never consider terms while victory was remotely possible. Senator Semmes warned that a convention would divide the Confederacy irreparably; Johnson of Georgia, an earnest peace advocate, advised his constituents that Boyce's letter could only demoralize the South and encourage the North. The *Raleigh Standard* and the *Montgomery Mail* were alone in defending Boyce. They contended that the mutual desire for peace would simplify the convention's problem, and the *Mail* added that in view of the President's non-action the next move was up to Congress.[22] Alexander H. Stephens personally liked the idea of a convention of all the states, but chose to unburden himself only within his bitter little circle of friends.

Encouraged by expressions of confidence, President Davis took pains in his speeches during the next month to criticize Boyce's position. In his opening message of November 7, 1864, to what was to be the last session of Congress he restated his policy of the last three years. The Confederacy's disposition for peace was well known, but the enemy authorities had clearly expressed their resolution to make no peace, except on terms of unconditional surrender. He added that when the enemy expressed a desire for peace, there would be no difficulty in finding means for accomplishing so desirable an end.[23]

Meanwhile, with Sherman marching through Georgia and Grant delivering trip-hammer blows around Richmond, many considered that the last opportunity was at hand to secure peace without reconstruction. The legislatures of Alabama and North Carolina discussed the advisability of separate state action, and the failure of resolutions for such action did not entirely dispel the impulse which prompted them. There was also a rumor that Sherman had invited Herschel V. Johnson and Joseph E. Brown to a meeting with him to confer on terms by which Georgia could re-enter the United States.[24]

By this time Mrs. Chesnut wrote that a Boyce party was forming in both houses.[25] Though only informally organized, it had a recognized group of leaders who met occasionally to exchange ideas on peace negotiations. The group never formulated a definite plan of action within Congress, as is witnessed by the variety of their propositions, but their essential unity is evident in the consistency with which they supported each other's resolutions. They conceded that Lincoln's re-election ended their hopes that the North would begin negotiations, though they firmly believed that war-weary Northerners would force Lincoln to meet halfway any Southern proposition. Upon hearing Davis's disappointing remarks on November 7, the peace group in Congress staged its final bid for negotiations leading to an honorable settlement between the two nations.

The loudest peace agitators were in the House, and the Senate was content to let them have the initiative. Senator Maxwell asked whether any Northern state had made separate peace overtures, and was satisfied with Benjamin's assurances to the contrary. Graham of North Carolina and William C. Rives of Virginia outlined in private a resolution calling for reconstruction on the basis of equality with the other states, but such a resolution would have stigmatized the peace party while accomplishing nothing and was never offered. Meanwhile the peace members in the House had introduced several positive resolutions proposing negotiations based on Southern independence.[26] Some of the resolutions dared to instruct the President how to act or even authorized Congress to negotiate in the case of his non-action. These innovations were particularly bold, for this was the first time that anyone had tried to divide the responsibility for making peace between Congress and the President.

Barksdale, speaking for President Davis, retorted by resolving that the Constitution afforded ample means for making peace without congressional interference, and that the initiative must come from the North.[27] All the resolutions were referred to the Committee on Foreign Affairs for a final clarification of the Confederacy's peace program.

The Committee mulled over the resolutions for almost a month and its procrastination was undoubtedly due in part to the presence in Richmond at that time of Francis P. Blair.[28] Early in December he had asked for permission to attempt peace talks with Confederate leaders. Lincoln postponed his reply until after the fall of Savannah, and not until December 28 did he issue Blair a pass through the Northern lines. Blair was convinced that the Confederate government would never abandon its face-saving maneuverings regarding peace, but believed that Confederate leaders were willing to consider reconstruction under satisfactory terms. Lincoln was willing for Blair to attempt peace overtures, but never authorized him to offer any terms except unconditional surrender.

Before the war Blair had been on familiar terms with several Confederate congressmen and on reaching Richmond he quickly got in touch with key members of the "Cabal" opposing the administration. This diplomat without portfolio argued that the disparity of resources made Southern victory impossible and that further warfare would make amicable reconstruction more difficult. In addition he gave personal assurances, completely unauthorized though convincing enough to those clutching at straws, that Confederate congressmen would be transferred in full force to seats in the United States Congress, that the United States would adopt a 30-year gradual emancipation program, and that Lincoln would yield everything desired except independence.[29] By this time a number of members were reconciled to reconstruction and considered the terms set forth ideal. Experience, however, had proved that it would be foolhardy to air them in Congress. Instead, at a meeting in the Ballard House, the group agreed to throw full support behind the peace resolutions pending, knowing full well that the resolutions could lead at best only to an honorable reconstruction.[30] It is impossible clearly to separate this group from those men who still expected to secure Southern independence, and, for practical purposes, it is unnecessary, because in Congress they all worked as one.

On January 12, 1865, the House Committee on Foreign Affairs

reported favorably for opening negotiations. It requested Davis to appoint three men from each house to seek an informal interview with the Lincoln government to discuss peace terms and to plan joint action against the French in Mexico.[31] Such an interview, possibly held outside of Washington, might permit Lincoln to avoid political recriminations. The Maximilian regime in Mexico was a known embarrassment to Lincoln, for he could not enforce the Monroe Doctrine while quelling a rebellion; Davis himself believed that this point might constitute a basis for peace. Despite these apparently favorable conditions and the fact that the Committee report was couched in terms designed to please him, Davis was still unalterably hostile to congressional interference and used his executive influence[32] to have the Committee's report postponed by a vote of 42 to 38, with only North Carolina, Georgia, Tennessee, and Kentucky willing to force his hand.[33]

This close vote and the debate upon it apparently convinced Davis that his control of the peace movement was in danger. To ignore the matter any longer might discredit his administration, and Stephens wrote that the whole arrangement with Blair was planned with a view to stop the action of Congress.[34] The Vice-President was referring to the fact that on the date of the defeat of the House Committee's resolution Davis had invited Blair to the first of several interviews. There is no evidence, however, that the invitation hoodwinked or even displeased Congress. Josiah Turner of North Carolina reported signs of peace because Davis was bending;[35] William A. Graham was intensely pleased that Davis had not continued to reject all intercourse with Lincoln as formerly.[36] The majority in Congress were so delighted to be relieved of the responsibility that they "adjourned such questions to give him time to act. . . ."[37]

Davis knew that Lincoln had advised Blair of his willingness for peace only to the people of one common country, and in the interviews he expected and received nothing but an offer of honorable reconstruction. Blair praised the old Union and warned that if the war continued its institutions might be overthrown by monarchism in the form of Napoleon and Mexico. As the South was planning to arm and then free its slaves, slavery as a cause of separation had disappeared, and with slavery gone all reasons for Southern independence had ceased to exist. Blair proposed that the South abandon slavery by gradual emancipation, that the two sections unite against

...... *The Peace Movement* 181

Mexico, and in return he promised blanket amnesty for all Southerners.

Finding these terms thoroughly unacceptable, Davis proceeded with his original design to show the futility of negotiations; toward the end of January he appointed Stephens, Hunter, and Judge John A. Campbell to meet Lincoln and William H. Seward at Hampton Roads, Virginia.[38] Since all three commissioners were peace men, and Stephens a suspected reconstructionist, Davis felt compelled to instruct them to treat only on the basis of Southern independence. Such instructions of course effectively destroyed any bargaining power the commissioners might have had. At the meeting Lincoln insisted on re-union and emancipation and refused to discuss any details of his terms; the Southerners declined to violate their instructions and the failure of the conference was complete. On February 6 Davis could only report to Congress that the United States had refused to enter negotiations on any other basis than unconditional submission.[39]

The reaction throughout the Confederacy to this conclusive failure of negotiations was everything that President Davis had anticipated, for a final wave of desperate determination swept through everyone. When Davis's report reached the streets, congressmen, Cabinet members, and private citizens addressed mass meetings and exhorted the people to greater sacrifices. The few remaining newspapers advised their readers to resign themselves to more years of war. Senator Hill rejoiced publicly that the Hampton Roads conference had failed and hurried home to rally his fellow Georgians. Even W. W. Boyce admitted no alternative but to continue fighting and wished Lee to fall back into Tennessee for last-ditch mountain defenses. The Virginia delegation in Congress assured Lee and Davis that Virginians would be ready and willing to meet any requisition made upon them.[40]

Even those who were dissatisfied with the conduct of the conference with Lincoln saw the futility of more discussion and resigned themselves to the inevitable. Congress heard little more from its peace party. Some members believed that Lincoln had made generous concessions which Davis had withheld from his report lest Congress demand their acceptance. The Senate timidly requested a full report of the conference proceedings, but when Davis ignored the resolution, never broached the subject again.[41] Secretary Mallory later stated that had the Senate advised accepting Lincoln's terms, it would have divided the responsibility with the President, and peace short of unconditional surrender would have resulted. He added that the Senate shrank from this responsibility and probably would have accused Davis of treason had he surrendered to Lincoln's terms.[42] In the House a small group, mainly from North Carolina, proposed an American diet with each nation having one vote and with the two members constituting a single economic unit.[43] When this proposal failed, the House adopted a Senate resolution on peace with only the objecting vote of James T. Leach. In this manifesto of March 14 Congress declared that rather than accept terms of peace at once ruinous and dishonorable it was determined to prosecute the war until the independence of the Confederate States was established.[44]

Since Congress would not contemplate reconstruction even in its death throes, some members hoped that individually they could salvage part of the wreckage of the Confederacy. Even before the result of the Hampton Roads conference was known, Foote, claiming the approval of the Tennessee delegation, slipped northward to inform Lincoln that the South would abolish slavery if assured honorable reconstruction. He was arrested while trying to cross the Potomac and hauled into a Confederate district court. A special committee of the House advised that Foote be released, but that for the good of the country he not be compelled to attend Congress. When Barksdale proposed to expel him Foote appeared before the House and was allowed to defend himself; but when he proceeded to present his case the Speaker declared him out of order and sent him to his seat. Though a motion to expel Foote failed, members voted unanimously that he had been properly arrested and deserved the House's censure.[45] His next attempt to escape northward was successful; however, Lincoln refused to see him and, on being given the choice by Secretary of War Stanton, Foote went to Europe instead of returning to Richmond.

Judge Campbell had returned from the Hampton Roads conference with the belief that another meeting would find Lincoln in a more receptive mood. A small group of senators decided to test Campbell's opinion, and asked other congressmen to stick to their posts until they had "broken the ice in a new direction."[46] In mid-February Graham, Hunter, and Orr visited the President, supported Campbell's viewpoint, and advised Davis to work for favorable reconstruction terms. This was the first time the peace leaders had proposed anything short of independence and Davis disdainfully asked them to make their proposal through formal Senate channels.[47] Both he and they knew that honor forbade such action, and Congress ended with at least the satisfaction of never having begged for mercy.

XIV

FINANCING THE WAR

THE CONFEDERACY HAD HARDLY BEEN FORMED WHEN SECRETARY OF the Treasury Christopher G. Memminger aptly pronounced economy to be desirable in every government but in the Confederacy to be a necessity.[1] The ante-bellum South had never possessed much financial surplus and a combination of circumstances during 1860 and 1861 had made it even more limited. The rapid growth of the states for the past few years had exhausted their credit and they were burdened with fiat money and large bond issues. At Lincoln's election the Northern banks had cautiously reduced their loans to the South; soon after the war began, the absence of specie caused most Confederate banks to suspend specie payments and curtail their credit. The states had lost much of their remaining cash in meeting the heavy expenses of secession. As a result, the Confederacy was forced to wage a four-year war on approximately $25,000,000 of gold. A further embarrassment was due to the fact that Southern merchants had restricted their orders during secession and when war commenced their stocks of goods were low.

To tide the government over until a revenue system could be established, the Alabama legislature lent the Treasury $500,-000. With this small fund Congress set about putting the nation on a paying basis. The United States tariff rates of 1857 had been carried over by the blanket transference of laws; on February 14 Congress continued in office the same customs personnel with the request that Memminger formulate a plan to halve the expenses of collection.[2] Congress then established a Treasury Department, provided for clerical help, designated ports of entry, set up minting, assay and coinage facilities, and provided for disbursing functions. After the spring of 1861 the only significant changes in the Treasury organization were the addition of certain offices to handle loan and tax programs and the establishment of semi-independent bureaus in the Trans-Mississippi Department.

Most members of Congress assumed that the tariff would be the main source of revenue. Since for a few months, however, its proceeds would be small, the administration felt compelled to devise quicker ways of raising funds. The alternatives were taxes, loans, fiat money, or a combination of the three; opinion predominantly favored fiat money and loans. Southerners were hostile to direct taxes and "would sooner give ten dollars which they have never seen, than one they have had in their pockets."[3] Even a makeshift tax system would require several months to be put into operation. Memminger personally desired taxation, but declined to advocate it either as Cabinet member or congressman and for a year taxation received no real support. The result was that the government placidly resorted to time-honored credit policies. Few expected a long, costly war and credit advocates thought the early loans would be the last ones.

On February 25, 1861, the Committee on Finance proposed the first Confederate loan. It was designed to give the Treasury an immediate supply of money and authorized a $15,000,000 loan in the form of certificates of stocks or bonds bearing 8% interest payable in specie. The certificates were issued for ten years and were redeemable by the government after five. The loan was guaranteed by a duty of ⅛¢ a pound on all raw cotton exported, the total proceeds of which were pledged to amortize the loan; when the total debt was extinguished the export duty should cease.[4] At this early date when harmony vied with secrecy in legislative proceedings, Congress handled the bill with dispatch. The only significant attempted alteration, an unsuccessful effort by Florida and Alabama, would have raised the rate to a 1% ad valorem export duty on most field and forest products.

Because of the severity of the blockade, the export tax was not successful,[5] but the loan provisions were the soundest of the war. Subscribers at first had difficulty meeting the required down payment of 6% in specie, for most banks refused to exchange their gold for paper currency. At Memminger's urging the banks agreed to redeem in specie all notes used in buying these first bonds and by November the full amount was subscribed. Until the middle of 1862 the bonds were quoted in currency at par and by 1865 had fallen only six or seven per, cent. Other bonds raised little specie, for it soon went abroad in exchange for military supplies. The small revenue from the cotton export duty was never diverted to other purposes, and these bonds assured at least a trickle of gold for their redemption and interest.

The other initial financial step was the act of March 9 authorizing the issuance of $1,000,000 in Treasury notes bearing 3.65% interest. They were to be issued in denominations of not less than $50 and were redeemable one year from the date of issue.[6] Their large size and their transferability only by endorsement showed that they were intended for investment, not for general circulation.

The new financial needs after the outbreak of war proved this shoe-string financial system hopelessly inadequate; on May 10, 1861, Memminger proposed a general overhauling. He predicted a deficit of $38,000,000 for the next year and estimated that a tariff averaging $12\frac{1}{2}\%$ would net somewhat less than $13,000,000. To make up the remaining deficit he suggested three other sources: $20,000,000 more in Treasury notes; a war tax designed to raise $15,000,000; and a $50,000,000 bond issue paying 8% interest. This program was so commonplace that he only bothered to defend the issuing of more Treasury notes. He explained that although they would never constitute a major source of income, money was becoming tight and Treasury notes could be used immediately in anticipation of proceeds from slower sources. The first notes were circulating at par with gold and there was no danger that $20,000,000 more would cause inflation. He expected the people eventually to accept them as a permanent loan to the government.[7] Congress immediately set to work to put Memminger's ideas into effect.

Deciding precisely how to establish a truly "Southern" tariff system was difficult. On February 18 Davis had delighted the free traders by advocating the freest trade which necessities permitted,[8] and there were good arguments in favor of free trade. The commercial interests preferred it, and it might pacify the North. It would solve questions concerning Mississippi River traffic and would undoubtedly please France and England. But even Davis's statement had a tariff reservation and from the beginning most informed sources advised that free trade was not yet practicable but must come gradually.[9] Border states feared that their business interests would suffer under the free-trade principle of the lower South. The Louisiana sugar and the Virginia iron interests openly advocated protection. Others hoped that a tariff would make the South economically independent of the North. Most important was the question of revenue. Congressmen realized that Southerners disliked the tariff, but preferred it to taxes. They believed that a tariff of from 5% to 15% would support the government, avoid the need for taxes, and still would not hinder European commerce. This was precisely what the South Carolina free traders had feared when the Permanent Constitution placed no limit on duties that Congress might impose. The result was that few supported the strategy of opening the Southern market to foreign manufactured goods, and cotton diplomacy remained the only force behind Confederate foreign policy.

In mid-February the Committee on Finance reported that tariff rates could be safely reduced, and Congress immediately began lowering them. On February 18 it placed upon the free list most foodstuffs and military equipment; a month later it reduced to 15% the duty on coal and most crude wood and iron goods. Both to gain access to their farm produce and to create stronger ties with them, Congress made duty free all imports from Virginia, North Carolina, Arkansas, and Tennessee.[10] When the Committee on Finance reported on March 9 a plan for a general tariff revision, the session was too near ended and Congress postponed consideration until the next session. By that time the need for action was pressing, and the Committee report passed with only the opposition of Georgia and Mississippi; it became law on May 21, 1861.[11]

This law defined the Confederate tariff policy for the war. It had few protective features, and rates were designed to derive the most possible revenue. The leading rate of the 1857 tariff was 24%, while that of the May 21 law was 15% and lower. A large number of ornaments, fine pieces of furniture, table delicacies, and foreign specialties were taxed at 20% or 25%. Many commonplace items, including textile and metal goods, were placed at 15%. Drugs, fruit, plank, coal, metal ingots, ores, rawhide, plants, wood, and a variety of other unfinished products and raw materials paid 5% or 10%. Books, cultural aids, scientific instruments, gold and silver bullion, meat, grain, war materiel, and tools were on the free list.[12] In general this tariff was designed to achieve the opposite of what the North had recently sought in the Morrill tariff.

Free trade agitation remained strong for another year. The *Examiner* claimed that the tariff was playing directly into the hands of the manufacturers around Richmond,[13] and some other papers desired at least the remission of duties on cargoes eluding the blockade. The important Commercial and Planters Convention at Macon, Georgia, suggested that all foreign vessels bringing goods into the Confederacy be guaranteed return cargoes.[14] The legislatures of Georgia and Texas requested free trade for the remainder of the war.[15] However, when on April 14, 1862, the House Committee on Commerce tested sentiment by proposing free trade with all but the United States, its bill found favor with only four states.[16]

The last concerted effort for free trade came after the conclusive failure of cotton diplomacy. Perkins of Louisiana declared that free trade would induce Europe to break the blockade, though the opposition insisted that it would not cause France and England to risk war.[17] The House, with only scattered border state opposition, then impulsively removed all import duties, but the Senate refused to condone this complete reversal of policy.[18] By this time free trade was bereft of its chief recommendation, for the blockade had become effective. Europe was thoroughly intimidated and free trade would deprive the Treasury of the specie obtained from duties paid by blockade runners.

Congress thereafter refused to change its tariff except to place on the free list machinery needed to maintain railroads, textile mills, or "any of the mechanical arts" in the Confederacy.[19] On February 27, 1865, the House approximately quadrupled the tariff rates; but the Senate refused even to consider the change, and the law of May 21 remained practically intact throughout the war.

Both constitutions allowed export duties for revenue purposes, but the government's foreign policies prevented these provisions from being used profitably. The small export duty on cotton raised only a few hundred dollars a month, and Memminger often urged that the duty be increased as well as extended to other items. Several times a year the House received such proposals, but for three years none ever got past the committee stage. When, on December 13, 1864, the Ways and Means Committee finally proposed a duty of 5¢ a pound on all cotton and tobacco exported, the House was pressed for time and refused to consider the change.

On May 16, 1861, Congress adopted Memminger's credit recommendations by means of its first "Produce Loan." Edward A.

Pollard attributed to President Davis the idea of using staple crops as a basis for credit;[20] Davis passed the compliment on to Congress, probably referring to its decision to consider soliciting of subscriptions of cotton, tobacco, and sugar in exchange for bonds and Treasury notes.[21] Actually this plan had been publicly discussed for several weeks, and on April 8 the South Carolina convention had promised to subscribe their state's share of any produce loan floated.[22] Besides forming the basis for additional credit, such a loan could secure provisions for the army, keep cotton away from seaports where it was most likely to be captured, regiment the cotton crop for diplomatic purposes, and relieve the planters financially.

On May 14 the Committee on Finance reported a bill in accord with Memminger's requests, and Congress changed it only to increase the bond interest to 8%. The law authorized the Secretary to issue $50,000,000 of 8% bonds payable in 20 years. They were to be sold for specie, military stores, foreign credit, or proceeds of the sale of manufactured articles and raw materials; however, they could *not* be exchanged for Treasury notes or for commercial paper. Of the issue, $20,000,000 could be in non-interest-bearing notes of not less than $5 denomination which would be receivable for all Confederate debts and taxes except the export duty on cotton. The notes were payable after two years in specie or were convertible at the option of the holder in 8% bonds. No specific guarantee was pledged to the bonds or the notes except faith in the government.[23] This law differed significantly from the Secretary's recommendations only in that he desired part of the notes to be interest-bearing so that they would be held as an investment.

The plan was immediately put into operation under the direction of the eminent economist James D. B. DeBow. It was based upon the assumptions that the planters had considerable produce but little cash, and that, while awaiting the latter, the Treasury could use the produce for establishing foreign and domestic credit. Treasury agents and congressmen canvassed districts for subscriptions. At each locality they advertised their presence and shortly afterward addressed the planters. They argued that "You must wait for your crops, before you can employ your contribution to the support of the credit of the Government. But the Government must have money at once." The subscribing planter was to indicate that portion of his crop he was willing to subscribe, the time and place of delivery, and the factor who would handle its sale; finally the factor was to be instructed to buy 8% bonds with the proceeds of the crop subscribed.

Memminger's tax suggestions received much colder treatment. Most congressmen inherently disliked taxation and felt that other revenue would suffice for the expected short war. Nevertheless the Secretary had boldly asked for a war tax designed to raise $15,000,000; to speed its collection he advised Congress to assess the amount through the states' existing machinery and to give a discount to each state that assumed its citizens' quota and paid it immediately.[24] The next day in his capacity as legislator he attempted to add these proposals to the pending loan measure. His colleagues declined to be rushed and instructed him to collect information regarding the state revenue systems looking toward raising $10,000,000 within the next fiscal year.[25]

At the next session Memminger reported that the state tax systems were too diversified to be used and that Congress could more easily levy an ad valorem tax on certain items of property common to all states. He estimated the value of all real estate, slaves, merchandise, corporate stock, and money at interest to be $4,600,000,000 and informed Congress that a uniform rate of 54¢ on each $100 of this property would raise about $25,000,000.[26] The Committee on Finance believed that this rate would net only about $13,000,000, but, not favoring an increase, introduced a bill strictly in accord with Memminger's suggestions. During debate North Carolina and Virginia favored lower rates. The other states, however, blocked their efforts, and the unanimous final vote on the original plan evidenced general satisfaction with its moderation.[27]

The law of August 19, 1861, levied a tax of 50¢ on each $100 worth of goods named by Memminger and a few luxury items tacked on during debate. It exempted from taxation Confederate bonds, $500 worth of property for each family, and all property of educational, charitable, and religious associations. Each state constituted a tax division and was granted a 10% rebate if it paid its citizens' taxes before April 1, 1862. Otherwise the Treasury Department must compile its assessment lists by October 1, 1861, and collect the taxes by May 1, 1862.[28] Most of the press approved the modest proportions of the law, the few newspapers that criticized it doing so on the ground that taxation was entirely a state prerogative.

The remaining significant financial policy begun during this formative period was expressed in the sequestration law of August 30, 1861. The law of May 21 required Southerners indebted to Northerners to write off their debts by paying the amount into the Confederate Treasury.[29] Most people, however, preferred to let their debts stand until the end of the war, for should victory be incomplete they might have to pay them again. In July and August the United States passed laws confiscating Southerners' property in the North. The Confederate Congress followed suit, with full regard to the propaganda effect, declaring that it must indemnify Confederate citizens for their losses, and restrain the wanton excesses of the enemy. All enemy property was ordered sequestered and used to repay Confederates affected by the Northern confiscation laws.[30]

For the next year and a half the finances of the Confederacy followed these familiar themes with few variations. It was not that Congress and the administration were proud of their handiwork, but that it seemed to be operating with fair success and supposedly would see the nation through the war without bankruptcy. Few people genuinely believed that the system contained inherent dangers. Whenever references to inflation arose, for instance, Memminger, Congress, and the financial wizards writing the newspaper editorials agreed that everything was not perfect and pretty much left the matter there.

The Treasury Department had difficulty even collecting the slight tax levied by the Provisional Congress. In September, 1861, the Department set up a War Tax Bureau, which administered the law so slowly that on December 19 Congress extended the time of assessment to January 1, 1862, and authorized further postponement at the discretion of the Secretary. When the collection proceeded as slowly, Congress had to extend the office of the War Tax Collector until October, 1863. Because the presence of the enemy made collection impossible, Congress suspended the tax in areas occupied or laid waste by the invader. The use of state tax systems caused confusion as to what was taxable and how much it was worth, and congressmen received many complaints that property had been over valued. By the end of 1862 somewhat over $16,600,000 had been collected and the final figure was $17,446,000.[31] Only three states collected the tax through regular channels; the others simply added to the redundancy by floating loans to pay off their tax in state bank notes.

Ineffective as this tax was, the administration and Congress saw no immediate occasion to improve or expand it. Secretary

Memminger, who should have taken the initiative, was reluctant to push an unpopular measure, and felt that the nation could depend on credit without undue embarrassment. It was not until March 14, 1862, that he again broached the subject. In his "Review of the Financial Measures of the Provisional Government" he admitted that only taxes could provide a solid basis for loans, but he merely suggested that the existing rates be increased.[32] Without more guidance Congress was complacently inactive. On March 11, 1862, the House instructed the Ways and Means Committee to study the situation; the Committee did not report until September, when it offered a bill levying a 20% tax on agricultural products, naval stores, livestock, and all incomes. Each taxpayer would receive 6% "Income Tax Bonds" to the value of his payment, which, in effect, constituted a forced loan.[33] The consensus was that, however objectionable, taxation was constitutional and a forced loan was not, but the debate was purely academic, for the House would have neither.[34]

This history of taxation for the first half of the Confederacy proved that, regardless of his private opinions, Memminger would not insist upon heavy taxes; and that, even had he done so, Congress would undoubtedly have ignored him. Hence, the Secretary expediently, if not wisely, based his financial recommendations primarily on the credit system described above. Between bonds and Treasury notes, bonds were safer, and Memminger originally hoped that high interest payments would make them attractive investments. He thought that in an agrarian nation the Produce Loan would be most remunerative, and he freely advised Congress on ways of improving it. Unfortunately people soon realized that even 8% interest was a meager dividend in an inflating currency and preferred to invest in businesses promising speedier returns. On August 18, 1862, Memminger regretfully announced that public reluctance to buy bonds had resulted in only a small portion of the government's revenue coming from their sale.[35]

The other alternative to taxation was to see the war through on Treasury notes. The Southern currency circulation was small at first and the nation easily absorbed the first experiments with notes. Accordingly in most of his reports for 1861 and 1862 Memminger asked for additional issues. During 1861 he repeatedly assured Congress that talk of inflation was unfounded and his only recommended safeguard was that part of the issues be made in interest-bearing notes of large denomination, suitable for investment. During these two years he occasionally proposed new ways of getting people to fund their notes into bonds, but none of his suggestions had much success. In 1862 he was hardly less optimistic. At times he mildly warned against inflation, and on August 18 he advised that the currency needed reducing; in the next breath he announced that there was no lack of confidence in the currency. Meanwhile he continued to accompany his currency requests with requests for further bond issues to absorb new issues of Treasury notes, all in the face of his admission that bonds sold poorly. During these two years Congress continued complacent and did little but enact Memminger's conservative recommendations.

J. D. B. DeBow, who served as Chief Commissioner of the Produce Loans until January, 1862, had set up his organization soon after the passage of the first loan. His agents appealed to the patriotism of the producers with only fair results. They canvassed Georgia, Alabama, and Mississippi thoroughly, and DeBow wrote that their planters subscribed from one-third to one-half of their crops. Subscriptions in other states were far less. By the first of 1862 Memminger reported that almost 500,000 bales of cotton and lesser quantities of tobacco, wheat, rice, and sugar had been subscribed, with hopes of more to come.[36]

The main criticism of the Produce Loan came from the planters, who found it impossible to get decent prices for their crops in a deflated market. They felt that the government should devise a more generous credit system than the limited arrangements of the first Produce Loan. They wished the government to purchase outright at a fair price the entire cotton and other usable crops and to continue doing so until the foreign markets were regained. The planters were ably sustained by several lower South newspapers, which concealed their planter sympathies behind the argument of establishing a strong credit basis. Vice President Stephens was told that the planters of Georgia were mad upon the subject of the government's buying the cotton crop,[37] and Stephens himself felt that the government should buy cotton at 8¢ a pound payable in 8% bonds.[38] The administration never liked this plan. At the first Cabinet meeting Benjamin proposed that the government buy at least 100,000 bales of cotton for shipment abroad, but others ridiculed the idea. Memminger had at first favored some plan of basing Confederate credit on the value of cotton, though by October had reversed his judgment and considered any such plan extravagant, impolitic, and unconstitutional.[39]

In July, 1861, Memminger stated that the nation could handle a currency of $150,000,000 and asked for more bonds and notes. Congress momentarily hesitated between extending the Produce Loan system and ordering the government to buy the entire sugar, cotton, and tobacco crops. It finally decided that accumulating crop stockpiles would not cure the financial troubles and followed closely Memminger's recommendations. The law of August 19 authorized $100,000,000 in Treasury notes receivable for all public dues except the export duty on cotton. It extended the bond issue to the same figure and now permitted crop subscriptions pledged to be paid in notes. The first loan had allowed monetary payment only in specie or foreign bills of exchange, but the public was running short of both. Permitting payment in notes would both increase the Treasury's income and reduce the currency. Congress took significant exception to Memminger's requests, however, in continuing to make all notes non-interest-bearing.[40]

This new form of Produce Loan by no means settled government purchase of staple crops, and in the first session of the Permanent Congress Representatives Holt of Georgia and Foote of Tennessee renewed the question. Holt was a friend of the President and Foote a political and personal enemy, but neither saw his proposal past a first reading. During the same session the Senate Committee on Finance reported unfavorably on three such motions.[41] On January 28, 1863, James Phelan made the final attempt when he proposed that the government seize all cotton and give bonds in return at the rate of 15¢ a pound.[42] By now conditions had changed. The small crops of the previous years and the abandonment of cotton diplomacy had raised cotton prices and Phelan's measure seemed inadequate. The cotton press therefore denounced it as arbitrary and tyrannical and an attempt to convert the Confederacy into a firm of cotton brokers. So the government's taking over the cotton crop was laid to rest.

On December 24, 1861, Congress took its first positive step to prevent inflation. Under the law of that date the Secretary of the Treasury could issue $30,000,000 in 20-year bonds bearing 6% interest. These "Call Certificates" were convertible interchangeably into Treasury notes, and Congress hoped thereby to make the issue either a circulating medium or an investment at the discretion of the bearer.[43]

On March 14, 1862, Memminger for the first time expressed

genuine concern over his finances. The amount of $214,000,000 would be needed for 1862 and most of it would have to be raised through credit. Ordinarily bonds would provide only about $38,000,000. Memminger, however, insisted that there was no limit to their sale so long as their interest was guaranteed by a war tax and claimed that now the people simply did not have their purchase price. He then asked that the government be allowed to sell the new bonds for articles in kind as well as for currency. Finally he denied that the saturation point of notes had been reached despite some "evidence of redundancy" and asked for $50,000,000 of them.[44]

Within a week the House Ways and Means Committee began reporting bills in accordance with the Secretary's suggestions and the bills slipped through practically intact. The law of April 18, 1862, authorized the Secretary to issue $50,000,000 more of notes and $165,000,000 of 8% bonds payable in 30 years; it also extended the Call Certificate program by allowing $50,000,000 in notes to be converted into 10-year 6% Certificates, the latter always to be reconvertible into notes. On April 17 Congress allowed the Secretary to use as much as he wished of the $165,000,000 bond issue in the form of $100 Treasury notes bearing 7.3% interest. On April 21 Congress allowed him to exchange bonds for any article in kind needed and to use the produce as he saw fit.[45]

These three laws had mixed success. The plan of making notes and Call Certificates interchangeable made the latter good short-term investments; by the end of 1862 almost $60,000,000 of the certificates had been issued. Their flaw was that they soon began circulating as currency and eventually had to be funded as did Treasury notes. Much the same happened to the $100 interest-bearing notes. Memminger reported that by January 1, 1863, almost $114,000,000 had been issued; but their high interest rate did not keep them from circulating almost as freely as did other types of notes.

The main result of the Produce Loan of April 21 was to increase the government's supply of cotton. Agents traveled around exchanging the bonds for cotton at its market value, with the cotton farthest from the enemy bringing the best prices. By 1863 the loans had raised about 450,000 bales. The Treasury Department in turn issued cotton certificates of $1,000 each and whenever possible exchanged them for military supplies. Even though the blockade limited cotton exports, some Europeans were willing to speculate on future profits. On October 28, 1862, John Slidell contracted with Erlanger and Company of Paris whereby the latter would float a $15,000,000 bond issue secured by cotton certificates valued at only six pence a pound. The market price of cotton in Europe was four times that amount, but investors knew that if the Confederacy collapsed their bonds would be worthless. When asked for their approval, some congressmen felt that the President did not need Congress's permission, while others wished to make the loan $50,000,000. When Memminger insisted on his original figure, Congress meekly ratified the loan as requested.[46]

The first objection to the sequestration laws came from the merchant class. The war found merchants in possession of considerable enemy money, and by law they were required to turn it over to the sequestration officers. The merchants were convinced that this loss, plus their curtailed business, would bankrupt them, and wanted the government to take evidence of the amount involved, and collect it after the war. On February 15, 1862, Congress granted merchants the use of what enemy money they possessed until a year after peace.[47] This moratorium greatly decreased the income from sequestration and the Confederacy never collected these debts.

Sequestered property that was put up for sale generally brought a poor price. To avoid any loss the government decided to wait until after the war to sell most of it. In April, 1863, Congress allowed short-term leases of any sequestered property containing mines or mineral deposits.[48] Border state representatives, who had suffered the greatest property losses, generally advocated a more ruthless confiscation policy. In September, 1862, Senator Henry of Tennessee proposed to sequester the property of every Southerner who proved less than 100% loyal, but Congress decided that Confederates within enemy lines should be proved enemies before being despoiled. President Davis applied the law against these people compassionately and in February, 1863, stated that he had confiscated no Confederate property. Toward the end of the war Southerners began to skip Northward to avoid the draft laws, and on February 3, 1865, Congress sequestered the property of anyone leaving the Confederacy without permission.[49]

The exception to these conservative financial measures was the final recognition of how vulnerable the currency was. By the end of 1862 there were outstanding over $289,000,000 of

...... *Financing the War* *197*

non-interest-bearing and $121,000,000 of interest-bearing notes. Every major note issue had been accompanied by bonds for the absorption of these notes and for the past year and a half Memminger had proposed and Congress, somewhat belatedly at times, had offered inducements for voluntary funding. Despite some success, the outlay of notes so far exceeded their funding that on October 1 Memminger reported that the desirable maximum of $150,000,000 would soon be doubled.[50] Voluntary funding had failed largely because the public preferred other investments for their depreciating currency than long-term bonds which steadily declined in value.

On October 6, 1862, Memminger courageously proposed a forced loan of 20% on all income and a reduction of the interest on bonds into which notes could be funded.[51] Three days later the House Ways and Means Committee reported a bill simply reducing the rate of interest on the funded debt. The bill provided that all Treasury notes issued after December 1, 1862, should be fundable only in 6% bonds. The Senate raised this interest to 7% and on October 13 the first mildly forced funding law went into effect.[52]

THE FINANCES OF INFLATION, 1863-1865

The convening of Congress on January 12, 1863, opened the next financial period of the Confederacy. The war's end nowhere in sight, few remained blindly confident that the nation could muddle through with its original financial program. Opinion differed now not concerning whether emergency financial measures were necessary, but how drastic they were to be. One newspaper after another faced the inevitable and began to urge the government to consider stronger tax and funding programs. A few wished Congress to limit, or even to abolish, state currency and credit. Some states in turn realized that their individual credit was sounder than that of the Confederacy and, provided all others cooperated, promised to guarantee their share of the national debt. By 1863 the government was even having difficulty securing enough cotton for its foreign business. States and private citizens competed with the Confederacy in buying cotton and were so successful that the government sometimes had to impress cotton to meet its needs. It is significant that to face these issues Congress and Secretary Memminger became equally courageous at the same time.

On January 10, 1863, the Secretary offered his boldest currency program to date. Existing funding acts were patently inadequate and were absorbing only about $3,500,000 a month. Meanwhile expenses were increasing and additional Treasury notes would push the total circulation far past the danger mark. To prevent this the amount of currency must be reduced by two-thirds. Memminger proposed that after a certain date notes issued before December 1, 1862, should cease to be fundable, with notes not funded being unacceptable as currency. This plan would force all old notes into bonds and clear the way for a new issue of $200,000,000. He wished this compulsory funding program to be supplemented by a comprehensive tax plan, which would serve the dual purpose of taking even more money from circulation and of affording a guarantee for new bond issues. He preferred income and property taxes to stamp duties and excise or license taxes, the collection of which would necessitate a vexatious and expensive machinery. His proposal was a 1% property tax and a 10% income tax, which would raise almost $65,000,000. This program violated no contract, since a "limitation of time for the performance of contracts has never been considered an infringement where sufficient opportunity is given to claim performance." Neither was the program repudiation, for non-fundable notes would retain all other guarantees including ultimate payment, and the remaining currency would have the same value as the old volume in circulation. Memminger's final suggestion was that the states guarantee their quota of the Confederate bonds outstanding.[53] When President Davis promised that the people of the Confederacy would agree to taxation adequate for the maintenance of the public credit and the support of the government[54] Congress then had the active leadership that it usually needed on such occasions.

On February 25 the House Ways and Means Committee proposed a tax of 1% on all real and personal property, a system of business and sales taxes, and a 14% tax on incomes up to $10,000 and 24% on those over that sum.[55] The fact that at this time two-thirds of the taxable property was in land and slaves made the House uneasily cognizant of a constitutional obstruction. The writers of the Permanent Constitution had thoughtlessly included the United States requirement of a census within three years after the first meeting of Congress, that is, by February 18, 1865. Since the same paragraph required direct taxes to be apportioned among the states according to their population, it was questionable whether Congress could tax land

and slaves until the number of people in the Confederacy was known. The small group of absolute anti-tax men failed miserably, however, when they demanded an entirely new census before levying any direct tax. Most of the debate was on whether to accept the United States census of 1860 as a proper basis for direct taxation or whether to ignore the issue on the assumption that taxes on land and slaves needed no apportionment. Davidson of North Carolina reported frantic efforts of the cotton members to have a direct tax levied according to representation.[56] Lower South representatives generally preferred the former interpretation, since an apportioned direct tax would place the greatest burden on the populous border states. The border states, on the other hand, desired a straight ad valorem tax on land and slaves, and their viewpoint prevailed. When the cotton representatives proved unwilling to wreck the tax program on constitutional grounds, the bill passed the House by a safe 50 to 30 margin.[57] Though Davidson considered it a "rip snorter," it was about what most people expected and some considered it inadequate.

The Senate Finance Committee, which had more constitutional scruples than did the House, was convinced that a tax on land and slaves would be a direct tax, and so offered a substitute bill on April 2 omitting completely the 1% property tax. It also lowered the income tax rates. The maximum tax on salaries was placed at 2%; incomes from business were taxed from 5% on $1,500 up to 15% on all over $15,000. Finally the Committee added a new "tax-in-kind" which levied a 10% tithe on all agricultural products in the hands of the producer. Chairman Hunter estimated that such a tax-in-kind would yield $130,-000,000, almost one-third of the war expenses, and would feed the army, reduce government expenses, provide a basis for foreign credit, and help the government retire its Treasury notes.[58] The idea so delighted Memminger that he quickly recommended it to both houses as a financial panacea.

When the Senate adopted Hunter's bill the House disapproved of easing the burden of the propertied classes and insisted on a conference committee. Contrary to the expectations of Senator Johnson of Arkansas who looked for an "earnest & bitter & perhaps relentless conflict between the two Houses,"[59] high tax men dominated the committee and worked out a satisfactory compromise without injury to the Treasury. While the Committee dropped the House property tax and kept the tithe, it placed the fees and other taxes higher than the Senate desired.

Even now the House was rumored to be unreconciled to the tithe and Wigfall stormed across the hall electioneering among the members of the house for the committee report.[60] His invasion, however, was needless. About two-thirds of the lower South preferred lower or direct taxation, and thoroughly detested the tithing principle; but they received little support except from North Carolina and eastern Virginia, and the bill became law on April 24, 1863.

The new tax law dodged the question of direct taxation and tried to touch everything else. It levied an 8% property tax on the value of naval stores, salt, wine, liquor, and all agricultural products held on July 1, 1863, with deductions for articles needed for home consumption. It placed a 1% tax on money and credit held on July 1, 1863. Speculation was penalized by means of a 10% tax on profits by wholesalers from food products, iron, shoes, blankets, and cotton cloth. Licenses, costing from $40 to $500, were required in most businesses and occupations; when selling was involved taxes had to be paid on gross receipts varying from 2½% to 20% according to supposed lucrativeness. On all income except salaries the act levied a graduated income tax scaled from 5% to 15%, with a $500 exemption and with certain specified deductions. Salaries were taxed 1% on the first $1,500 and 2% on the excess, with a $1,000 deduction. Finally the law imposed a 10% tax-in-kind on all agricultural products and slaughtered hogs for 1863, deliverable by the farmer to the post quartermaster-general.[61]

Generally the press received this law favorably, crediting Congress with a job well done in fixing tax rates best calculated to help the Treasury. Most newspapers felt that the tithe, which bore heaviest on hoarded produce, would end agricultural speculation; they denied that the tithe was unjust, for it was the only major tax on agriculture. They observed that removing the money element from agricultural taxes would keep the farmers from delaying payments in expectation of better prices.

A few newspapers were less complimentary. The *Richmond Enquirer* said that the license and gross sales taxes were trade regulations rather than taxes and were therefore unconstitutional.[62] Some farm papers protested that the law was double taxation in that it taxed both the farmers' capital and the value of that capital's produce. Most criticism was against the tithing principle. Farmers disliked not having a chance to market their crops profitably. They had few resources except their crops, whereas license and income taxes applied to classes that could borrow. The *Raleigh Standard* complained that the absence of a tax on slave property hurt the small farmer, who now would have to compete on equal terms with the planter.[63] The agricultural press generally believed that farmers paid proportionately more than anyone else, and that a tax on their profits would have been fairer.

Faults soon appeared in the tax-in-kind. Potatoes were so perishable that by the time they were collected, stored, and distributed they were often spoiled. On December 28, 1863, Congress allowed farmers to commute this tithe into money at impressment rates. Another act remitted the tax on property which had been destroyed by the enemy or by order of the government. On January 30, 1864, Congress transferred the collection of the tobacco tithe from the War to the Treasury Department.[64] As long as the post quartermaster collected the tobacco it was distributed among the troops; by entrusting collection to the Treasury officials the government acknowledged the desire to acquire tobacco for foreign trade.

The income from this tax law proved disappointing. The law itself, with its multiplicity of taxable items and its numerous differences of time for their collection, was confusing enough; but on May 1, 1863, Congress set up a system of assessment and collection that was at least as complicated. Both laws proved so ambiguous that the rulings of the tax commissioner were often as important as the laws themselves. The enemy interfered with execution of the laws, speculators and businessmen found them easy to evade, and the money came in slowly. During its first year the law of April 24 brought in only about $82,000,000.[65]

A week after Memminger's report of January 10, 1863, the House began considering various forced funding measures. Such measures usually allowed a short time for funding notes, then forbade their use as currency except in payment of taxes and debts to the government. None gained very much support and the House did little but muddle around with them for the next two weeks. Meanwhile Senator Hunter, one of the nation's best financial minds, had prepared a clear-cut measure. The Senate rejected Phelan's weak suggestion merely to reduce the interest on bonds and passed Hunter's bill almost intact. The House, glad to escape its dilemma, quickly took up the Senate bill. Its Ways and Means Committee suggested limiting the new issue of Treasury notes to $12,500,000 a month, but the majority rejected the limitation, as it did the proposals to continue indefinitely the right of funding notes into low-interest bonds. The only significant House amendment was a three-months extension of the funding privilege.

Under the act of March 23, 1863, non-interest-bearing notes were divided into two classes. Those dated before December 1, 1862, were fundable in 8% bonds until April 22, 1863, and in 7% bonds until August; thereafter they could not be funded, but were still receivable for government dues and payable six months after peace. Those dated between December 1, 1862, and April 6, 1863, were fundable in 7% bonds until August 1, 1863, and thereafter in 4% bonds; they continued to be receivable and payable as the first class. Eight per cent Call Certificates were fundable in 8% bonds if offered before July 1, 1863; thereafter they were fundable only in 6% bonds. The Secretary was permitted to buy Treasury notes whenever able with a view to reducing currency circulation to $175,000,000. The main difference between this program and Memminger's was that the Secretary, while he intended to redeem in specie all notes after the war, wanted those not funded to be unacceptable as currency during the war; the law of March 23 continued them as currency by making them acceptable for government dues.

The remainder of the law dealt with the inevitable problem of the continued support of the government. It allowed the Secretary to sell $200,000,000 of 6% bonds to the states or to anyone else if the states guaranteed the entire issue. It also authorized a $100,000,000 issue of 6% bonds with interest payable either in currency or in cotton certificates, with cotton deliverable six months after peace and valued at eight pence sterling a pound. Finally the Secretary was authorized to issue monthly up to $50,000,000 of non-interest-bearing notes and make them fundable in low-interest bonds.[66]

This act at first caused a sharp fall in prices, but increased confidence soon gave way to distrust of the government's promises. Instead of correcting the inflation the act discredited previous notes and dragged down subsequent ones to their level. While voluntary funding of old notes presumably ended in July, they continued to circulate at a reduced rate because they were eventually redeemable in specie. Bonds still were considered a poor investment and a noteholder could make a larger profit on anything he might purchase than by investing in Confederate bonds.[67] Only $21,000,000 of notes were funded under the law, and by September 30 there were $616,000,000 of non-interest-bearing notes in circulation. Governor Brown maintained that Georgia could not guarantee its portion of the $200,000,000 bond issue without dangerously stretching its credit and refused to let Georgia assume her portion. The other states would not place themselves at a disadvantage in relation to Georgia, and Memminger placed the blame for failure of the plan squarely on Brown.[68]

A month later Congress made a final effort to improve the use of cotton as a source of credit. Planters could now usually get better prices than Produce Loan agents offered, and, both to obtain cotton and to help the currency, Congress on April 30, 1863, passed its last Produce Loan. It authorized the issue of $250,000,000 of 6% bonds payable in 20 years. Attached to the bonds were interest coupons payable either in coin or in cotton valued at 12¢ a pound delivered at one of seven ports specified by the law. The bonds were to be sold for Treasury notes, with the stipulation that the Secretary use part of their proceeds to buy agricultural products under the act of April 21, 1862.[69]

Regardless of the success of the financial measures of the spring of 1863, they served at least to acquaint the Southern people with stronger measures. During the continued and increasing financial trouble of succeeding months it was the press, strangely, which insisted on even greater sacrifices. The influential *Richmond Enquirer* urged Congress to "Stop the Press!" and most important papers advocated stronger compulsory funding and heavier taxation. Among the leading papers, only the *Charleston Mercury* and the *Raleigh Standard* held back, claiming that such laws, besides being unconstitutional, would injure legitimate business as well as speculators, would make subsequent Treasury notes worthless, would destroy faith in the government, and would provoke revolution.

In his report of December 7, 1863, Memminger presented the distressing financial situation in far his most positive terms to date. He confessed that existing funding and tax laws would fall far short of reducing the currency from $700,000,000 to the desired $200,000,000. To absorb the excess and to meet current expenses he proposed an issue of $1,000,000,000 in 6% 20-year bonds; to encourage funding he included several new principles. He proposed that the new bonds be tax exempt at a steadily diminishing allowance until April 1, 1864 (July 1 west of the Mississippi). After this date tax exemption should cease, the privilege of funding old notes should no longer exist, and those remaining should be considered totally repudiated. For the new currency Memminger asked for $200,000,000 of new Treasury notes, which amount must never be increased.

To supplement this loan the Secretary proposed to raise $120,000,000 by means of a 5% tax on all property and credits. Half this amount should be used for buying supplies and the remainder for paying the interest on the new loan. Taxpayers should be required to make half their payments in Treasury notes and half in interest coupons of the $1,000,000,000 or in coin.

Memminger admitted that the letter of the Constitution required a census before a direct tax could be levied upon land and slaves. It would be illogical to presume, however, that "all the States which had ratified the Constitution . . . excepted from the contribution to maintain [the] war the very property for which they were contending." A better interpretation was that the 1860 census could be used until a new one could be taken. The Secretary recognized that repudiating any currency impaired the contract between the government and the noteholder, but minimized the infringement. The government had "provided a fund as nearly equal to specie as is within its power"; it would, like any honest debtor, recognize its debt, offer the best security it could, and ask for time.[70]

In December the House entertained several bills incorporating this plan and also some others. The majority preferred not to experiment and on December 31 the House Special Committee on the Currency reported a bill which became the basis of the new tax law. Since Memminger had offered only the sketchiest guidance, the bill was the usual combination of boldness and timidity. It contained the 5% property tax, but included seriously weakening exceptions: it made the tax on agricultural products deductible from the tax-in-kind, it undervalued the taxable property five-fold by using 1860 valuations, and it exempted from the income tax all property subject to the ad valorem tax. In a stronger vein, the bill increased the number of products subject to the ad valorem tax, at least doubled most other taxes, and added a 5% tax-in-kind on foreign credit and raw gold and silver.[71]

During debate several representatives, generally from unoccupied districts, strove to reduce or abolish certain taxes, but more than a third of the members from such districts favored heavier taxation and swung the balance in that direction. On the final vote only the Virginia delegation contained a majority against

...... Financing the War 205

the bill.[72] The Senate, however, was at loggerheads with the administration on taxation, and after considering the House bill from January 25 to February 12 its Committee on Finance reported a version which practically halved the House rates. This bill passed the Senate near the end of the session and a conference committee was hurriedly appointed to reach some compromise. At this stage the Senate tax philosophy was clearly untenable, and the committee report was almost a total House victory.

The tax on February 17, 1864, in addition to existing taxes, levied a 5% tax on all real and personal property according to its 1860 valuation. The tax-in-kind was deductible so as not to impose double taxation, and the income tax of the previous law was credited against the ad valorem tax on property. To penalize speculators all land, slaves, cotton, and tobacco bought since January 1, 1862, were assessed at the price paid for them. New taxes included the following: 5% on gold and silver coin, dust, or bullion, on all corporation stock and solvent credits, and on all bonds and paper currency except non-interest-bearing Treasury notes; 10% on gold and silverware, on jewelry, and on profits made in trading in agricultural and manufactured goods; and a 25% tax on all corporation profits over 25%. Taxes were to be assessed at once and collected on July 1, 1864, or as soon thereafter as practicable. The previous tax law had no general system of exemption; now each head of a family received a $500 exemption, with $100 extra for each minor child, and $500 for each son in the army. Widows and soldiers received $1,000 exemption.[73]

A similar spirit of enthusiasm prevailed in this last session of the First Congress in regard to remedying the nation's credit troubles. Even before the session began observers in Richmond noticed that the gathering congressmen seemed profoundly impressed with the necessity of curbing inflation by kill-or-cure legislation. Francis B. Sexton, for instance, personally preferred heavier taxation to any other solution, but admitted that such extraordinary times might force him to yield more to the tyrannical argument of "necessity" than ever before.[74] During the first days of the session the House appointed a Special Committee on the Currency, which soon received bills incorporating almost a dozen financial schemes. These bills contained one of two devices to compel funding: some set a date after which old notes would be repudiated; others imposed a tax on all notes which, unless they were funded, would eventually tax them out of existence.

In addition each bill contained one or more supplementary inducements, such as specie payment of bond interest, making all new Treasury notes legal tender, or a high profit tax.

A political enemy of the Davis administration wrote that the Secretary's scheme was not approved in toto by a single member of the Special Committee,[75] but five of its seven members had favored compulsory funding the previous spring and half-way measures now would surely not satisfy them. On December 31 the Committee reported a comprehensive bill to tax, fund, and limit the currency. It allowed all non-interest-bearing notes to be funded in 6% bonds until March 1 and in 4% bonds until May 1; for the next three months they were fundable at a reduced rate of 25¢ on the dollar each month, and after August 1 those unfunded would be repudiated. To replace all these notes the Secretary could issue $200,000,000 in new notes with a guarantee of a maximum future circulation of $250,000,000. He could also issue $500,000,000 of 6% bonds, the principal and interest to be forever tax exempt, and the entire net receipts of all import duties were to be pledged to their payment. In a minority report Boyce explained that since notes were worth about 5¢ on the dollar the government should accept that as their real value. The need of compulsory funding would thus be removed, for the currency would no longer be inflated.[76]

For the next two weeks the House discussed various funding bills, none of which was promising enough to replace the vigorous Committee bill. The Atlantic coast states, plus Alabama, those with the greatest concentration of currency, tried unsuccessfully to moderate the measure by extending the funding deadline or by opposing repudiation. Ayer of South Carolina wrote that many members from other states had been ruined and impoverished by the enemy and rendered so desperate and reckless that they would support the most crushing financial policy.[77] His prediction was correct and their four-to-one support of the Committee bill overwhelmed the two-to-one opposition from the Eastern states; on January 16, 1864, the bill passed the House by a vote of 38 to 32.[78]

Meanwhile the Senate was discussing several currency propositions of its own. On January 25 the Committee on Finance criticized the House bill on two scores. It believed that as long as old notes were payable for taxes they would circulate along with the new issue at a depreciated rate. A more serious criticism was that, in addition to seeing the government break its contract, the people would be exhausted by the payment of an onerous

...... Financing the War 207

tax for no other purpose than to satisfy public creditors who had given bonds in exchange for securities. The Committee preferred simply on April 1 to tax away two-thirds of the currency; the remaining one-third would be equal to the original amount in purchasing power and would violate no contract. Until then old notes should be fundable at the rate of three to one and afterwards only at their nominal value. New notes should be issued to the extent of one to three of the old notes funded.[79]

After the Senate had haggled a week to no avail, the Committee tried another approach. After May 1 Treasury notes should no longer be receivable for public dues or funding. Until then they could be converted at 90% value into bonds or at 10% value into "Exchequer notes," the latter not fundable but receivable for all public dues except the export duty on cotton.[80] Exchequer notes would supposedly circulate at par, while the Treasury notes, still payable after the war, would remain circulating at a reduced value. The Senate passed this bill mainly to have something upon which it agreed; when the House insisted on a conference committee the participating senators admitted that their plan would only further complicate the currency and accepted the House plan. The final bill was quite severe, despite substantial concessions to the Senate's moderation; of the 34 votes against the final version 25 were from the Atlantic states and Alabama.[81]

The currency act of February 17, 1864, divided non-interest-bearing notes into four classes. Those of less than $5 were not bothered. Until July 1 $5 notes were receivable and fundable at par into 4% registered bonds; until January 1, 1865, they were fundable at two-thirds their face value, and thereafter were abolished by a 100% tax. Notes between $5 and $100, comprising a majority of the circulation, were treated as the $5 notes except being fundable at par only until April 1. The most severe treatment was in regard to the $200,000,000 of $100 notes. Those not funded by April 1 were no longer receivable by the government and, in addition to an immediate 33 1/3% tax, were to be taxed 10% more a month until funded.

To avoid sudden contraction the Secretary of the Treasury could issue new notes which, until January 1, 1865, were exchangeable for old notes at the rate of three old for two new ($100 notes not included). After that date this privilege ceased and all old notes were to be considered worthless. To prevent further inflation new and old notes were exchangeable for 4% Call Certificates during this period. The law provided for additional government expenses by authorizing the Secretary, in emergencies, to buy supplies with 6% non-taxable certificates of indebtedness from anyone who would receive them. Finally it authorized a new issue of $500,000,000 of 6% 30-year tax-free bonds which could be used for funding or in exchange for goods.[82]

It is interesting to compare the tax and currency laws of February 17 with Memminger's official recommendations; there seem to be eight significant points at which they differed. (1) Memminger asked for $1,000,000,000 of bonds; Congress granted half that sum. (2) Memminger wished a 5% tax on property and credit; Congress ratified this, but used the 1860 property valuation.[83] (3) Congress made a number of tax exemptions that Memminger did not recommend. (4) Congress increased several ad valorem and property taxes that had not been requested. (5) To reduce the circulation Memminger wanted money taxes payable only in Treasury notes; Congress allowed tax payments in notes, 4% bonds, or certificates. (6) Memminger wanted the old notes repudiated after April 1; Congress postponed repudiation for most notes until January 1, 1865. (7) Congress's plan to reduce the value of notes until funded or repudiated was more gradual than Memminger had proposed. (8) Memminger did not recommend the idea of swapping three old for two new notes.

The Secretary felt that these differences constituted a legislative repudiation of his suggestions, and on May 2 reported that he had offered one scheme to cure the currency, but that Congress had tried its own, which did no more than seek the same object by different means.[84] Memminger's straightforward funding plan was unquestionably the better of the two. Senator Johnson of Missouri said that Congress's bill was the result of a compromise among conflicting views,[85] and so was over-complicated and somewhat slower acting than the Secretary wished. Nevertheless the two plans differed in detail rather than in principle, and Memminger exaggerated when he claimed that his program had been rejected.[86]

Except for minor adjustments the laws of February 17, 1864, represented the extreme in financial daring by Congress. Most newspapers defended the currency act. They admitted that it was severe, but necessary. They urged people to fund their notes immediately and not indulge in an orgy of speculation from then until April. They agreed that the public had not been defrauded by the repudiation of two-thirds of the currency, for the remaining notes would quickly rise in value. Public reaction, however, was almost one of panic. Many people refused to receive any bill over $5; some banks would give out no small bills when people rushed to secure them; for a time brokers would not sell gold on any terms, and all securities rose rapidly. Merchants raised prices to make their profits before the old notes were withdrawn, and many accepted only the small ones. Governor Thomas Reynolds wrote that most of his fugitive government's funds were in notes and bonds, and begged that Missouri's $350,000,000 of old notes be placed on an equal footing with the new currency.[87]

Partial repudiation did not greatly reduce the currency nor increase the value of that remaining. By April 1 nearly one-third of the non-interest-bearing notes had been funded and the situation temporarily improved. But then when the Treasury began exchanging new for old notes, the value of the currency again began to fall and new and old notes circulated almost equally, with the value of both steadily declining after July. The $500,000,000 bond issue went poorly and by January 28, 1865, only about a third of it had been sold. Government contractors were unwilling to accept the 6% certificates and by November less than $2,000,000 had been issued.

On May 2, 1864, Memminger pulled out his rusty guns and fired away at the financial ogres as ineffectively as ever. He admitted that the currency law should already have caused a decline in prices and placed the blame for its failure to do so mainly on the law's not touching the $5 notes. He also criticized the exemption of agriculture from money taxation and insisted that if Congress remedied these faults prices must fall. He added that the exchange of old for new notes at three for two would place the currency at $414,000,000 and proposed to halve this amount by a new issue of tax-free 4% bonds. He was convinced that the recent $500,000,000 loan would soon be taken. Finally he asked Congress to abolish any remaining redundancy by a tax payable only in Treasury notes.[88]

On May 13 faithful Senator Barnwell introduced a catch-all bill incorporating these ideas and saw it ignored. A week later Memminger desperately proposed another scheme whereby all articles impressed would be paid for in certificates of indebtedness payable two years after peace. The Senate liked this scheme better and on May 26 authorized such certificates for any property bought or impressed, with interest to be paid in specie beginning immediately. The House rejected the plan on the grounds that it was organized robbery and would only create a new form of redundant currency.[89]

The fate of these bills indicated, among other things, that Congress accepted the inevitability of inflation and believed that it was useless to follow Memminger's variations upon the same old themes. Congress now sought to make the funding system as equitable as possible. On May 17 Barksdale proposed to extend the time for funding notes held by Confederates within enemy lines. Despite the warning of the Senate Finance Committee that extension would cause innumerable frauds and would be "manna to the speculators," the proposal passed both houses. President Davis disliked this catering to individual and state complaints and gave an emphatic veto.[90]

Senator Johnson of Missouri tried to keep his state from being penalized by the rapid devaluation of currency enforced by the funding act. Fugitive state governments had most of their money in currency and Johnson proposed that they be allowed to fund or exchange it at par until 1865. The Senate decided to let them exchange half their old notes for new ones at any time and the House accepted this compromise. Also, any state that had funded so much of its old notes that it had difficulty meeting expenses was allowed to reconvert its bonds into notes of the new issue.[91]

After Congress so thoroughly disregarded his suggestions Memminger resigned in June, 1864. He was replaced by George A. Trenholm, a wealthy Charleston merchant, whom congressmen liked personally but whose advice they generally disregarded. On November 7 Trenholm reported that gold was selling at a premium of 25 to 1 and that Congress must stabilize the value of Treasury notes or abandon them as currency. To encourage stability he offered a four-point program: that all notes be tax exempt, that Congress promise to issue no more notes, that part of the tax receipts be allocated to reducing the currency to $150,000,000, and that the tax-in-kind be continued several years after the war so as to redeem the entire circulation.[92]

On November 25 the House Ways and Means Committee reported a bill which for the next month was discussed almost daily in committee of the whole. It differed from the Secretary's program in several instances. Instead of making all notes tax exempt the Committee's bill included only those issued after February 17. Twenty per cent of all notes received thereafter by the government were to be cancelled until the circulation reached $150,000,000. Four-ninths of the corn tithe and one-ninth of the wheat tithe were pledged to redeem the notes after peace until all were absorbed.[93]

..... *Financing the War* *211*

House opinion on this bill was almost equally divided. Its proponents felt positive that the tithe continuation would raise Treasury notes back to par value. Arthur S. Colyar of Tennessee and James Lyons of Virginia maintained that since currency would be based on the tithe, no more notes would have to be issued to purchase government supplies. Fayette McMullen and Josiah Turner, administration opponents, contended that the bill was the worst sort of discrimination, for it forced agriculture to support the government's credit. Perkins of Louisiana wished to broaden the scope of the tithe pledge. James Echols, a Georgia cotton planter, preferred an annual sale of government cotton to provide funds for withdrawing notes from circulation. The majority, however, could not be persuaded to change the Committee plan and passed it almost as introduced. The Senate considered it too strong and toned it down considerably. As it passed the Senate near the end of January, 1865, the bill made Treasury notes only partially tax exempt, placed the desired currency circulation at $200,000,000, and opposed the reissue of notes received through taxation.[94]

After discussing these bills for a month, the conference committee reported its inability to agree and was discharged. The report was less the result of disagreement than a decision to drop the whole subject. Congress felt that the paper money policy was already past any remedy and that no tinkering could help. The government could only continue to pay its way with notes and to hope that peace would come in time to prevent complete financial collapse.

Most currency bills passed during the last session of Congress reflect quiet desperation. On December 29 the term for exchanging old notes for 4% bonds was extended to July 1, 1865, and the 100% tax on them was likewise postponed; all old notes were again made tax receivable for six more months. Another burden was added to the currency when all certificates of indebtedness were made receivable for all public dues except the export and import duties.[95] Finally, Congress authorized a new issue of notes to pay the arrears due the army, but Davis vetoed this on the grounds that it violated the pledge of the law of February 17, 1864, not to increase the currency circulation further.[96]

A final and separate effort to restore some degree of solvency was made in 1865 by using all available means to obtain specie. Trenholm announced that he could negotiate a foreign loan of 15,000,000 pounds sterling, and on January 4, 1865, Congress authorized him to do so on such terms as were agreeable.[97] On March 13 it allowed the Secretary to receive contributions of specie and jewels and to publish in daily newspapers all such contributions and the names of donors. The same day Congress authorized him to borrow from any individual or corporation as much as $30,000,000 of specie to be used in buying outstanding Treasury notes. Four days later this order was superseded by a smaller specie loan, which allowed the Secretary to borrow $3,000,000 in coin in exchange for 6% bonds. The loan was secured by a pledge of 50,000 bales of government cotton deliverable at suitable shipping points and valued at 15¢ a pound. Bondholders receiving cotton through this loan could export it wherever they wished. If this loan should be unsuccessful the Secretary could levy a 25% tax-in-kind on all gold and silver coin, dust, and bullion in the Confederacy and on all foreign exchange.[98] The government obtained somewhat less than $2,000,000 in donations and approximately $300,000 from the specie loans.

The story of taxation during the last year of the war was much the same as that of the currency. After adopting the comprehensive tax law of February 17, 1864, Congress relaxed somewhat. People were being asked to pay the heaviest national taxes in American history and Congress felt that their limit of tolerance had been reached. Its main concern from here on was to remedy flaws in the existing laws. Memminger had much the same thoughts, but with different ends in mind. Whereas the main interest of Congress was in relieving anyone mistreated by the laws, the Secretary wished to tighten the laws and make them more profitable for the Confederacy. This conflict was yet another factor in Memminger's decision to resign.

The tax-in-kind had turned out to be a valuable source of revenue. In May, 1863, the Quartermaster General's Department set up the organization for collection, and by March, 1864, had received about $40,000,000 of goods. The tax was quite bothersome. The major criticism was that it bore too heavily on agriculture. Producers claimed that inflation had made the money taxes easily payable, but that the value of the tithe was stationary and therefore amounting to relatively more each month. This argument was particularly applicable in regard to taxes estimated on an 1860 valuation. Two-thirds of the tithes collected came from North Carolina, Georgia, and Alabama, and these states besieged Congress with requests for relief. Some of their congressmen said that many Treasury agents refused to arbitrate disagreements with the producers and often seized whatever they wanted under the guise of "collecting the tithe."

Objections had arisen to other parts of the tax system. Assessments varied from state to state, with the variations depending on the opinion of the assessor, whether he was energetic enough to visit isolated areas, and on the market value of an item at a particular place or time. Congress received many complaints that taxes were so high that only the wealthy and the speculators could afford to pay them. Banks and corporations criticized the tax on two scores. They claimed that taxes on capital stock and bonds and also on their solvent credit was double taxation. They also said that property was taxed at 5% of its 1860 valuation, which really amounted to less than 1% of the 1864 market value. Stocks and credits, however, being taxed according to their market value, were overloaded unfairly.

On May 2, 1864, Memminger proposed three significant changes in the tax laws. He believed that agriculture was escaping too lightly and asked Congress to increase its load. Specifically he recommended the repeal of the section in the law of February 17 which let farmers deduct the value of their tax-in-kind from the amount of the 5% property tax. He also advocated the repeal of the section allowing the 5% property tax to be deducted from the income tax. He agreed that taxing capital stock and solvent credit of a firm was double taxation and that it should be adjusted.[99]

Three weeks later the House Ways and Means Committee ignored Memminger's suggestions and reported a bill remedying what it considered the flaws in the tax system. The bill specified that the property tax should not be determined until after the tithe had been assessed and delivered; it ordered that all property be assessed according to the 1860 valuation only if owned before 1862; it acknowledged one of Memminger's points when it outlawed double taxation by ending the tax on bank deposits and on stock held by Confederate citizens.[100] The fact is striking that two of these provisions would have materially reduced the income from the tax laws, and that the other was designed to penalize speculators rather than to raise more taxes. The bill was considerably amended in its passage through Congress, but the only seriously contested provisions were those concerning corporation taxes. The West was innately hostile to corporations, and the border area, now almost completely lost, opposed any tax relief. Colyar of Tennesseee offered a minority report protesting any leniency to corporations. He contended that if business assets were reckoned at their 1860 valuation the 5% tax would actually amount to only one-sixteenth of one per cent.[101] The border and Western representatives almost defeated the plan to relieve business from double taxation, but the East and lower South combined to see it through. Edward Sparrow was the only lower South senator opposing the bill on its final passage.[102]

The law of June 14 changed the tax laws in four significant respects. It ended double taxation of agriculture by ordering that the tithe be completely assessed and collected before the levy of the 5% property tax. Banks were relieved of the tax on deposits, and corporation stock was made tax exempt. Two provisions were curbs on speculation. Any property owned before 1862 was to be taxed according to its 1860 valuation; that acquired afterwards, according to the price paid. Finally, an additional 30% profit tax was placed on all trading and selling between February 17 and July 1, 1864.[103]

Otherwise Congress preferred not to experiment until there was further information on the effectiveness of existing laws. There was not even a concrete effort during the first session to abandon the tithe, since its value was obvious. The only other tax changes made during 1864 were to remit the tax on property and slaves lost or destroyed, to allow the commutation of corn into its money equivalent when the producer's amount was insufficient for his own needs, and to exempt garden products and fruit.[104]

In his first comprehensive report on November 7, Trenholm presented a set of ideas reminiscent of Memminger's. The 5% property tax was based on 1860 valuations, which were the equivalent of gold, and amounted to about .5% in currency. He wished all taxes to be assessed at their existing value. He advised the repeal of all tax abatements and estimated that this alone would increase the revenue by about 7%. He maintained that private citizens owned the bank deposits, while bank stock was held by stockholders; since these were different groups, the tax on deposits, which the law of June 14 had removed, could be reimposed without causing double taxation. On January 9, 1865, he recommended doubling all existing taxes, with the augmented tax-in-kind payable in Treasury notes, and selling government cotton in the domestic market.[105]

Though several such bills were introduced, Congress rejected Trenholm's advice to double the tithe. Both houses wrangled intermittently about whether agriculture paid too much or too little in taxes, but the consensus accepted the tenth. On the other hand, they spurned all attempts to reduce the tax-in-kind or to limit the number of articles to which it applied. The House Ways and Means Committee was primarily interested in making the existing tax laws more equitable, and on March 3, 1865, reported a catch-all bill for injustices in the system which were remediable. After a few small changes it became law on March 13.

The new law sifted through the procedure of assessment and saw that the producer paid no more than a tenth of his average grade goods assessed at their market prices. When collection was impractical the tithe could be commuted into the corresponding money value. In areas suffering crop failure or destruction the local quartermaster could sell provisions to the public from his supply depots.[106] These concessions were justified in view of the fact that any deficit in supplies could be made up by impressment, and the deferment of impressment claims for future settlement made monetary considerations by this time of small consequence to the army.

The history of other taxes during the last session of Congress followed closely that of the tithe. While the Senate's objection to higher taxation was public gossip, it was equally disinclined to reductions. The House Ways and Means Committee received sundry bills to raise or lower one or more taxes, but in January, 1865, reported unfavorably on batches of bills at a time. This action was as wise as courageous, for most of the bills would relieve from taxation areas hard-pressed but not lost, an example being H. P. Bell's measure to suspend taxes in Georgia for 1865. On January 18 the Committee reported a bill levying a 20% tax on gross incomes, repealing most tax abatements, and doubling all other tax rates. Three of the more conservative committeemen submitted an alternative plan offering only two significant changes: a $3\frac{1}{4}\%$ tax on all property, goods, and credits at their market value, and a 10% tax on all gross incomes.[107]

After discussing these bills until February 11 the House, hopelessly divided, referred the entire matter to a select committee of one from each state. At this point President Davis, chafing at the delay, sharply told Congress that matters were "so critical that objections which . . . would be regarded as insurmountable may well be waived in favor of any scheme . . . that will enable the Treasury promptly to meet our most pressing wants. . . ."[108] With this prompting, the select committee, composed largely of higher tax men, quickly formulated quite a different plan. A major objection to the Ways and Means bills of January 18 was that they assessed taxes at existing currency rates, which not only made them higher but which perpetuated inflation by basing all public transactions on a rising price level. The new plan was to restore the old specie rate of valuation. It proposed to buy or impress all cotton and tobacco in the Confederacy and to pay for the goods in bonds bearing interest payable in specie. It also provided $200,000,000 of "revenue bills," to be issued at specie value and redeemable at any time in government cotton at 50¢ a pound. The purpose was to grant the government immediate use of cotton and tobacco as a basis for credit and to devise a type of currency which would circulate at specie value. The committee bill also proposed to double the income tax and the tithe and to continue all property taxes at their 1865 rates.[109]

Since debate on this measure was usually in Committee of the Whole and in secrecy, there is no clue as to the nature of the discussion. On the last day of debate Gilmer of North Carolina offered a substitute simply doubling all taxes and removing the abatement of the tithe from the property tax. Apparently the select committee's plan had gained few adherents and the final issue was merely whether Gilmer's more moderate proposals asked too much. On February 23 Gilmer's substitute was adopted unamended by a vote of 44-30. By this time finances were so hopeless that no voting alignment materialized; to most representatives taxation was now academic.[110]

The Senate Committee on Finance summarily rejected the House bill, and substituted one that doubled the existing property tax but required the entire increase to be assessed at the small 1860 valuation. It boosted most other taxes by from 50% to 100% and doubled the tithe with the increase payable in currency.[111] When these features proved unpopular the Senate took up a plan by Oldham of Texas, which levied small increases in taxes ranging from ½% to 2%. The innovation was that the new taxes were assessed at their specie value but were made payable in Treasury notes or certificates of indebtedness. This meant, explained Oldham, that a 1% tax on an item worth $1 in specie and $10 in currency would amount to a 10% tax on its market value and would net the government $1 in taxes. These rates actually amounted to about the same as the Finance Committee's plan; the supposed improvement was that specie valuation would equalize the value of all taxes and prevent further inflation.[112]

...... *Financing the War* *217*

The House found this bill unacceptable, considering it virtually an experiment in taxation and suspecting that it would raise much less than the House's own bill. The conference committee that resulted quickly wrote a compromise measure much akin to the original Senate Finance Committee's plan, and this became law on March 11. It levied no new taxes and simply increased the existing rates. To the existing 5% property tax it added an 8% tax assessed on 1860 valuations. It increased by 5% the taxes on all money except Confederate currency and on all solvent credits except Confederate and state bonds. It added a 10% increase to taxes on gold, silverware, and jewelry, and to all profits in business; there was a 25%-more tax on business profits of over 25%. The tax on gold and silver coin and bullion was increased by 20%. Half the taxes paid must be made in Treasury notes.[113] The Confederacy ended before any of these changes could be put into effect.

XV

THE LOYAL OPPOSITION

ANYONE OBSERVING THE PREVALENCE OF EXPERIENCED POLITICIANS flocking to Montgomery in February, 1861, might have foretold one part of the Confederacy's future: that not even a war for survival would bring political harmony to the South. Certainly, conditions in the early days of the Confederacy were favorable to such harmony. Grievances against the North had been temporarily resolved by secession and could no longer serve as political vehicles; many people had questioned the advisability of secession, but, once faced with its accomplished fact, Southerners were in essential agreement on matters of government; the threat of possible coercion by the United States accentuated the need for political unity. Nevertheless, when Robert Toombs wrote from Montgomery that there was no difference of opinion in Congress,[1] he was correct only in reference to devotion to the Cause. Considering the total picture of the South at the time, the continuation of practical politics in the Confederacy was inevitable.

Undoubtedly, however, the leaders in the Provisional Congress at first attempted to bury the political hatchet for the duration;[2] in one respect their efforts were rewarded, for the expected rivalries within Congress of secessionist versus conservative and Democrat versus Whig never fully materialized. Past politics never influenced law-making and was significant in Congress only regarding patronage. Although in the Provisional Congress the former Democrats and secessionists outnumbered their old rivals only by about a three-to-two ratio, during the first session the former cliques could not conceal their hope for political preferment nor their pique at not receiving it. For instance, Thomas R. R. Cobb, the Georgia radical, deplored the fact that *"Hunter* (milk and water), *Rives* (submissionist) and *Brockenbrough* and

The Loyal Opposition 219

such like are placed in the front rank for honor and emolument."[3] On the other hand, Whigs and unionists originally felt that President Davis could not be intimate and confidential with anyone whom he had always looked upon as a political opponent.[4] Within six months Davis's political impartiality annoyed only a bitter little group which had expected the plums of office. The only significant manifestation in Congress of past politics was the unsuccessful effort of Florida to block the nomination of Mallory as Secretary of the Navy because his soundness on the Secession question was doubted.[5] After the first few weeks, therefore, past politics became important only as name-calling devices during election campaigns.

The main bases of politics in the Confederate Congress were the wartime policies of President Davis and his administration. John Beauchamp Jones, the gossipy clerk in the Confederate War Department, wrote, somewhat inaccurately to be sure, that originally "no Executive had ever such cordial and unanimous support"; as early as June, however, he began to report "murmurs" against the President.[6] Jones, at least on this occasion, was tardy in his gossiping, for some secessionists had opposed Davis's election to the presidency for fear that he was a reconstructionist. Shortly before the First Battle of Manassas on July 21, 1861, the Richmond newspapers reported discord in the government; after the battle some congressmen blamed Davis for not ordering the enemy pursued. In August Secretary Mallory reported that a spirit of opposition to the President and administration was growing up in Congress;[7] a month later he wrote that the Florida delegation was undoubtedly hatching an opposition to the administration in the belief that Florida defenses were being neglected.[8] Some congressmen began to express their opposition openly. In June Lawrence M. Keitt pronounced Jeff Davis a failure.[9] Later, the ambitious Robert M. T. Hunter resigned his office of Secretary of State lest his association with the Davis administration handicap his plans for the presidency. By the spring of 1862 rumors of discord had reached across the Mississippi River and had been so magnified by their journey that Governor Reynolds of Missouri feared a "counter-revolution."[10] In these and many other instances the Confederate sources reveal at least some early opposition to Davis and his administration.

During the Provisional Government most of this opposition stemmed from personal and doctrinal differences between some members and the Executive. Though these differences continued throughout the Confederacy, they dominated congressional politics only for the first year.

While Davis spoke in state rights terms, he acted with increasing nationalism, as previous chapters have indicated; individual congressmen who could not accept this contradiction soon found themselves in opposition to the administration. In February, 1861, when Davis first vetoed a bill, Thomas R. R. Cobb wrote viciously that he would "strive hard to pass it over his head, it will do my very soul good to *rebuke* him at the outset of his *vetoeing.*"[11] Four years later Senator Graham, implacably opposed to the whole administration program, declared that the frequency of the President's vetoes led to the suspicion that he did not understand his powers.[12] The charges of "dictator," "military despotism," "bayonet rule," and many others became common terms used by some congressmen to describe Davis's conduct of the war.

A few congressmen simply did not like President Davis personally. W. W. Boyce considered him puffed up with his own conceit, and as one who considered an independent opinion as an attack upon him.[13] Thomas J. Withers thought that Davis had been rude to him when Davis was Secretary of War, and in March, 1861, Mrs. Chesnut wrote that Withers's old grudge had returned with increased venomousness. She regretted that men were willing to risk an injury to the Confederate cause only to hurt Jeff Davis.[14] The *Charleston Mercury* wrote that the South Carolina secessionists objected to Davis's being "treated as 'our Moses.' "[15] They in turn were accused of disliking Davis because he occupied what they considered Barnwell Rhett's rightful place.[16] Mallory felt that most of the early administration opposition was based on envy and ambition.[17] Many congressmen found Davis aloof and ill-humored. His bitterest personal and political enemy was Foote of Tennessee. In 1847 the two men had exchanged blows in the United States Congress and had never become reconciled. For the last three and a half years of the Confederacy Foote kept up a running fire against the administration and "never spoke without indulging in denunciatory invective" against Davis and his Cabinet.[18]

The accusations against Davis personally ranged from nepotism to the charge that he made arrangements with the enemy to spare his own cotton or else to buy it. Some congressmen disliked his preference for West Point-trained officers. Initially a close friend of the President, Louis T. Wigfall became enraged on learning that Davis had listened attentively to his advice about a Cabinet appointment without saying that the post had just been filled. For two years Wigfall corresponded with friends seeking confirmation of his contempt for Davis, once expressing the belief that Davis's mind was becoming unsettled.[19] In December, 1863, he confessed that he would like to hang Jeff Davis.[20] William L. Yancey disagreed with Davis mainly on principle, but picked quarrels with him over patronage matters. When Davis refused to increase the number of brigadier-generals from Alabama, Yancey considered the refusal discourteous and even hostile;[21] when he could not secure for a friend the office of postmaster general at Montgomery, he haughtily withdrew his application for his son Dalton's army commission and accused Davis of personal enmity toward him. Davis gently replied that, though he was aware that Yancey's political opposition was not of that measured kind resulting from occasional differences of opinion, Yancey was misinformed as to any enmity.[22]

Even Davis's friends disliked the way in which he kept Congress in comparative ignorance on executive matters. Burgess S. Gaither, one of the few North Carolina representatives who consistently supported the President, confessed that the latter did things pretty much in his own way, without consulting anyone and that it was difficult to find out any contemplated move.[23] Curry of Alabama claimed that Davis gave Congress very little information and apparently expected Congress to do what he deemed best for the interests of the Confederacy.[24]

A master politician or a consummate fraud might have overcome this personal type of opposition, but Davis was neither. Always distant to mere acquaintances, he became more so as President. He could never muster the careless informality that most congressmen relished, nor would he curry their favor otherwise. Mallory noted that Davis openly displayed his personal opinions toward certain congressmen, never making any attempt to cultivate their good will by little polite acts of attention or deference, not even sacrificing a smile for any man who did not stand well in his esteem.[25]

Davis disliked informal visits from congressmen and usually dealt personally with them through calls by state delegations. Even here he was not at his best, and Mallory admitted that every delegation left Davis unsatisfied because of an indescribable something in his manner which offended their self esteem.[26] Editor Edward A. Pollard said that no man "could receive a delegation of Congressmen . . . with such a well-bred grace, with a politeness so studied as to be almost sarcastic, with a manner that so plainly gave the idea that his company talked to a post."[27]

On one occasion a Tennessee delegation abruptly left the executive offices, believing, so Henry S. Foote charged, that Davis had posted spies outside to overhear the conversation.[28] When the same delegation later asked that General Beauregard be restored to the command of the Army of Tennessee, Davis replied that if the whole world should ask him to restore General Beauregard to the command already given to General Bragg, he would refuse.[29] In March, 1863, the Arkansas delegation charged that Davis had trifled with their request for a change in the military command in their state.[30] Senator Edwin G. Reade, who considered Davis "as bitter as gall," described an interview between the President and the North Carolina congressmen. He said that toward the end of a two-hour session Davis flared up when Reade called him dictatorial and soon both had to be calmed by easy-going William N. H. Smith. After this display of temper "we all formed a sort of long circle with Mr. Davis at one end of it. I extended my hand & walked up toward him & said . . . 'Mr. President, trust North Carolina & *let her alone.*' He grasped my hand cordially & said 'I earnestly hope that your strong faith in your state may be realized.' "[31]

Davis, it can be assumed, offended no one deliberately. He entertained congressmen frequently and impartially at his receptions. His correspondence with them, written under more relaxed circumstances, pictured him favorably. He patiently answered their letters on patronage and promotion. He also wrote long letters to arm-chair generals in Congress, discussing military strategy, supply movement, and in general how to win the war. Occasionally he even chatted in the streets with congressmen, though War Clerk Jones observed that such behavior was not common with him.[32] Unfortunately such negative manifestations of camaraderie reconciled none of Davis's opponents, nor were they intended to do so. These men knew that Davis wanted their subservience, that he would not play favorites, that he scorned politics, and that he considered everything subordinate to winning the war. Those holding personal or doctrinal differences with him saw little of compromise in his actions and consequently had no compulsion to abandon their opinions.

The administration's legislative program was a comparatively minor influence in congressional politics for the first year and a half of the Confederacy. Victory seemed imminent and sacrificial

...... *The Loyal Opposition* 223

legislation unnecessary. The President's messages were encouraging, and the laws of Congress, which generally passed easily, were seldom vigorous enough to offend those to whom they applied. Opposing congressmen either sublimated their convictions and voted yea, or voted nay quietly and bowed to the majority will for the sake of harmony. Most debates were secret and received little publicity. Since much of the Confederacy was unoccupied by the enemy and the laws were being executed over the nation with fair uniformity, few districts felt discriminated against.

The elections of November, 1861, gave every indication that this political pattern would continue indefinitely. No major disaster had occurred, while First Manassas and Stonewall Jackson's victories in the Shenandoah Valley had stimulated added confidence in the government. Despite the scattered opposition that had arisen against them, Davis and Stephens were unanimously re-elected. Congressional elections went off quietly, and during the first session of the First Congress the political alignments of the Provisional Congress continued.

During the spring of 1862, however, the pace of war quickened. The Confederate government began to need more money, more supplies, more men, more aggressive action in the field—all of which required emergency measures from Congress. The results were conscription laws, impressment laws, heavier taxation, currency inflation, staple crop limitation, and the occasional suspension of the writ of *habeas corpus*. But it became increasingly evident that these laws could not be uniformly applied. States and districts which were being invaded or which had been seized by the enemy were effectively removed from Confederate jurisdiction. This situation not only exempted people of these areas from the laws but placed additional burdens upon remaining Confederates. Thus a diminishing number of people were asked for ever greater sacrifices. To cap these troubles the military situation worsened. The disturbing reversals in the West and in various coastal sections, the failure of the Confederacy to launch a successful counter-attack, the war of attrition and its accompanying discouragements—all persuaded an increasing number of people that the government was not conducting the war properly.

Inevitably the people voiced their discomfort through their congressmen, and for the last three years of the Confederacy the administration's total war program dominated congressional politics. Some congressmen claimed that the laws were badly executed, some believed that they were too severe, others considered them discriminatory, while still others objected to the entire course of legislation. They criticized the administration on these grounds alone or used them in combination with the old state rights arguments that had dominated the opposition voice in the Provisional Congress. For instance, Senator Reade, representing the extreme anti-administration sentiment in North Carolina, said that his state's dissatisfaction with the war program indicated "an excess of loyalty to the State, without any abatement towards the Confederacy."[33]

As the major basis of administration opposition shifted from President Davis to his war measures, the opposition became bolder and more open. For the first year of the war Davis's prestige had been so great that attacks upon him or his ideas had simply not been good politics. But honest differences on how to run the war needed no concealment, and those who opposed the administration on this basis made little effort to hide their feelings. The unfortunate corollary was that Davis's personal enemies now had a perfect shield behind which to attack him. John B. Jones's prediction that the last session of the First Congress would see a conflict between Congress and the President was borne out when soon they were "at loggerheads," with "the dispute . . . becoming angry."[34] A little later the *Richmond Enquirer* reported that some members were trying to postpone matters until the Second Congress, which anti-administration forces were expected to dominate.[35] During the last year of the Confederacy newspapers continually deplored the lack of political harmony in Richmond, while a few congressmen even talked unofficially of deposing Davis. In January, 1865, Mrs. Chesnut wrote that Davis no longer had any reliable friends in Congress who would sustain him upon principle.[36]

According to the *Journal of Congress,* there were 113 members of the Provisional Congress active enough to establish a legislative record;[37] an examination of the record of each congressman showed that twenty-four were administration opponents.[38] The fact that this opposition was quite scattered, with only Georgia having a threatening concentration, indicated that it stemmed from conflicts of personalities and ideas of government, which knew no territorial limits, rather than from sectional opposition to abusive legislation. Its size indicated why this opposition had little effect on the work of the Provisional Congress.

Administration support was at its strongest during the early months of the First Congress, but soon the districts within Con-

The Loyal Opposition   225

federate lines began to feel the burden of the demands being made upon them. People from these districts expressed their discontent through their congressmen, and one congressman after another gradually swung into opposition to the administration's war program. Senator Hunter was one of several who changed loyalties. Originally an administration bulwark, for the last three years he tried desperately, though in vain, to divide his loyalty between Virginia and the administration. Toward the last his opposition was so strong that after Appomattox Lincoln advised his officers not to arrest Hunter, because his final hostility to Davis did much to make the Confederate President unpopular in Virginia.[39] On the other hand, members representing districts imminently threatened or already lost quite naturally sanctioned all the more aggressive measures. By the middle of the war the Davis program found its most consistent support in the border and occupied states. In the First Congress there were 28 senators and 122 representatives, with 11 and 27 of them respectively being administration opponents.

Congressional division on the administration's war program reached its greatest height in the Second Congress. The election of 1863 had been based primarily on this program, and men elected out of opposition to it had no compunctions about bold-faced opposition to the program. Congressmen representing states outside the Confederate lines naturally advocated even sterner measures. At the beginning of the Second Congress, Arkansas, Louisiana, Mississippi, Missouri, Kentucky, and Tennessee were largely in enemy hands; these states with 47 districts had only five administration opponents representing them. The remaining states with 59 districts had 36 opponents. It is not remarkable that Josiah Turner of North Carolina wrote that he "would rather plough and feed hogs than legislate . . . with Missouri and Kentucky to help me."[40]

While during the last half of the Confederacy the administration received its main support from the occupied states, it was abetted for the entire war by two other factors. First, there was a universal desire in Congress to win the war. Had the relatively small early administration opposition wished to do so, it could have created far greater political discord than it actually did. However, its members deferred to Davis's suggestions when they could; when this was impossible, they demurred unobtrusively. Herschel V. Johnson later wrote that he "acquiesced in what I could not approve and sought to eliminate the best results from it . . .;"[41] other congressmen expressed similar views. Even in the Second Congress the opposition strategy was primarily to modify rather than to reject the administration measures. For instance, the North Carolinians, ten of whom opposed every administration measure, had as their objective the reform, not the wreckage, of the government. Second, the opposition lacked consistency. There were no political organizations seeking undivided loyalty nor was there consistent pressure from the electorate. Conditions changed, opinions changed, consequently administration sympathies changed. Most administration opponents supported at least part of the government's war measures, and their shifting support was sometimes decisive.

Despite predictions at the time to the contrary, this administration opposition never evolved into an actual party in the sense of an organized group working together. It is true that the records of the Confederacy abound in such terms as "the coalition against Jeff Davis," "anti-administration man," "Faction," "Boyce party," "class of obstructionists," and others. Such words and phrases, however, applied to an anticipated party or to a group generally hostile to Davis and his administration. None of them referred to the existence of a specific and organized anti-administration party. In 1878 Jefferson Davis tried to whitewash his administration by asking several friends to recall the congressional "Cabal" that had worked against him. Letters came true to form, picking up his use of the word "Cabal" and describing its activities.[42] Even these letters, however, did not refer to an actual political organization, for there was none. All three congresses contained men opposed to a majority of the administration's measures, but the constantly shifting voting alignments of these men indicated that their opposition fluctuated according to their individual approval or dislike of these measures. However much Davis's personal enemies scourged him publicly, they also generally voted against his measures rather than against him.

This opposition never seriously threatened Davis's executive position. Yancey, who considered Davis a "conceited, wrongheaded, wranglesome, obstinate" traitor, admitted that a "crew may not like their captain, but if they are mad enough to mutiny while a storm is raging, all hands are bound to go to the bottom."[43] The strongest revolutionary talk naturally came from Henry S. Foote. On December 29, 1863, while debating Davis's usurpations, he stated that, if the Confederacy must have a dictator, he favored Lee for the position.[44] For the rest of the war the idea of Lee's dictatorship was bandied about by disgruntled congressmen, who had no intention of activating it. There is even the tradition that Representative William C. Rives of Virginia, speaking for a congressional cabal, offered Lee the dictatorship and that Lee refused it. No record, however, substantiates this tale and anyone knowing Lee would never have expected him to join such a conspiracy. President Davis once said that he himself would resign if Stephens would, but that he would never surrender the government to one who would immediately turn it over to the enemy.[45]

The only significant frontal assault on Davis's position came early in 1865. On January 9 Senator Sparrow from the Committee on Military Affairs introduced a bill providing for a general-in-chief to command all the military forces. It was debated for five days and finally tabled. Thereupon Henry of Tennessee proposed to "advise" Davis to appoint Lee as general-in-chief, Beauregard to command South Carolina, Georgia, and Florida, and Joseph E. Johnston to head the Army of Tennessee.[46] This resolution passed by a vote of 14 to 2 and implied that Congress wished to assert itself on war policy. Acting swiftly, the administration worked out a compromise with the Senate. On January 16 the general-in-chief bill was resurrected and passed with only two negative votes. Congress then passed an unassuming resolution stating that Johnston's reassignment would promote "joy" and "confidence" in the nation.[47]

Davis emerged from the fracas unscathed; Congress had had no wish to impair his effectiveness and optimistically awaited the results of its action. Everyone assumed that Lee would be made general-in-chief and on February 6 he was so honored. Davis, however, considered Johnston unfit for command and actually prepared a message to that effect. Upon consideration he realized that he would also have to rebuke Congress for interfering in executive matters and, showing more restraint than usual, merely ignored the resolution regarding Johnston. On February 24 Davis permitted Lee to restore Johnston to the Army of Tennessee.

Davis had no qualms about being able to handle Lee. The law of January 23 was open to wide interpretation, for it simply stated that the general-in-chief should have command of the military forces of the Confederate States of America. During the law's passage Representative Warren Akin of Georgia had proposed that the rights of the President should not be interfered with by the appointment of Lee;[48] the fact that Akin's amendment failed implied that Congress expected much of Lee. Lee, however, acted according to Davis's calculations. In thanking the President for his "high and arduous office," Lee said, "As I have received no instructions as to my duties, I do not know what [the President] desires me to undertake."[49] In a reply to a request by sixteen senators for Johnston's reinstatement, Lee wrote, "I do not consider that my appt. as Gen. in chief . . . confers the rights which you assume belongs to it, nor is it proper that it should. I can only employ such troops & officers as may be placed at my disposal by the War Dept."[50] Surely Lee's interpretation of this law had been foreseen by Davis, who accordingly accepted with relief the compromise with Congress.

Whereas Davis was well-nigh invulnerable to criticism, his official family was not, and Congress focused its criticism of executive affairs upon the Cabinet. Some congressmen hoped to counteract executive influence by carefully maintaining the separation of the powers of government; others attacked certain Cabinet members for personal reasons; a few congressmen struck at the Cabinet in general merely to hurt President Davis; after the tide of battle had noticeably turned, some were merely seeking scapegoats. Most criticism of Cabinet members, however, was due to genuine concern for policy in and management of the executive departments.

For two years Congress, in the opinion of many, came dangerously close to the British cabinet form of government. Under the Provisional Constitution, which was silent on the matter, Hunter, Memminger, Reagan, and Toombs served in the dual capacity of congressman and Cabinet member. The system worked well and the Committee on the Permanent Constitution secured the provision that "Congress may, by law, grant to the principal officer in each of the Executive Departments a seat upon the floor of either House, with the privilege of discussing any measure appertaining to his Department."[51] On February 26, 1862, the House Judiciary Committee reported such a bill, but it was dropped before a final vote was taken.[52] A little later the Senate Judiciary Committee reported that it would not be proper to pass such a bill at that time.[53] When Wigfall raised the issue the following year, the Senate removed any real value of the bill by prohibiting discussion by Cabinet members, and the idea was permanently laid to rest.[54]

Both friend and foe of the administration had been dubious about such close contact with the Executive. Almost everyone respected the traditional separation of the powers of government. Some congressmen believed that, if an administration measure should be defeated, the Cabinet might feel compelled to resign. Others said that department heads would be too embarrassed to use their executive influence in Congress. Davis's supporters felt that they could handle his program without Cabinet assistance. Many disliked the thought of having Secretary Judah P. Benjamin, the brilliant Jew, in their midst.

Since most congressmen did not oppose Cabinet members *per se,* Davis's nominations were generally confirmed routinely. He maneuvered cleverly on the only one likely to fail. Under the Permanent Constitution he wanted Benjamin as his secretary of war, and, in hope of persuading the Senate to confirm Benjamin, waited almost a month before submitting a slate of department heads. He finally had to compromise and appointed Benjamin as secretary of state; even this appointment was confirmed by only a small majority.[55] Aside from those of Benjamin and Mallory, no other nomination had difficulty.

Congress directed its closest scrutiny toward Secretary of the Treasury Memminger. Conservative, industrious, and commonplace, Memminger did not foresee a long war and based his early recommendations on time-honored credit expedients. Without any better advice from Congress the administration wound its cautious way through two years of unimaginative finance and increasing inflation; by mid-1863 financial matters were hopelessly snarled. Compulsory funding and heavier taxation were then tried, but without much success. Congress and Memminger then began blaming each other for the currency debacle. Congress had usually accepted the framework of the Secretary's recommendations, but had added costly modifications to his tax and currency suggestions. Memminger in turn exaggerated the effects of these alterations and by 1864 wished to resign. He refrained only because Davis doubted that a new secretary could set up the funding plan within the 40-day limit set by the law of February 17, 1864. Congressmen from the lower South nursed a special grudge, for they believed that Memminger's influence had defeated the proposed government purchase of the entire cotton crop.

When Congress met in May, 1864, it ignored Memminger's proposals and began proceedings to oust him. Soon Foote's resolution asking for Memminger's removal was on the verge of passing, and was dropped only when assurances reached the House that the Secretary would resign at the end of the session.[56] On June 15 Memminger wrote Davis that the differences between his policies and those of Congress made cooperation impossible and only drew criticism upon the administration. Davis accepted Memminger's resignation, complimented him for excellent service, and blamed the Confederacy's financial troubles on a "deficiency of resources and the want of legislation best adapted to the existing circumstances."[57]

Memminger was no more responsible for the financial muddle than was Congress, for not until 1864 did the two begin to differ fundamentally. He possessed certain advanced financial ideas, but lacked the courage to voice them until too late. A pleasant demeanor would have been to his advantage in dealing with Congress, but personally he was headstrong and overbearing. His piteous bleatings against Congress made him the opposition's favorite target. Congress considered Memminger's successor, George A. Trenholm, a "high-toned gentleman" who was "exceedingly easy of access either in official or private intercourse."[58] It generally ignored Trenholm's financial suggestions, but the friendship of the two suppressed most of the political attacks upon the Treasury Department.

No other Cabinet member received such abuse. The critics of Secretary Mallory, while harsh, were relatively few, and were more interested in getting a navy than in ousting Mallory. After a year and a half without seeing a navy appear magically, Congress gave the Navy Department a thorough investigation. In a report which the Florida congressmen considered a whitewashing, the committee praised highly Mallory's management.[59]

After Walker and Benjamin, the succeeding secretaries of war got along remarkably well with most congressmen. In fact, James A. Seddon, who succeeded George W. Randolph on November 22, 1862, did more than any other Cabinet member to relieve Congress's worries about the conduct of the war. Seddon was an able and energetic administrator and soon became an intimate and influential friend of the President. For two years Henry S. Foote was his only severe critic in Congress. Even Wigfall, who had fallen out with Davis over Seddon's appointment, credited Seddon with developing and executing a real Western policy. His best recommendation was that, during 1863 and 1864, when he was willing to resign to help Davis politically, the opposition leaders in Congress urged him to sit tight. Wigfall asked Seddon to stay in the Cabinet to keep Davis from provoking issues with Congress; it was not until Seddon loyally refused to reply that Wigfall disgustedly wrote, "The Truth is Seddon is subjugated and has lost his manhood. . . ."[60]

Seddon's eventual resignation came from a desire of the people for a change of men and measures.[61] On January 16, 1865, the Virginia representatives met to consider means of bolstering Confederate morale. Deciding that Cabinet reconstruction was a prerequisite, they assigned Thomas S. Bocock, Speaker of the House for its entire life, so to advise the President. Bocock had a pleasant interview with Davis and on January 20 clarified Virginia's actions by letter. He wrote that Congress was on the verge of declaring want of confidence in the Cabinet and the administration. Such a resolution, he predicted, would win three-fourths of the House. Virginia merely wished "to prevent so distinct an issue between the executive and the legislative branches of the Government, and to save you from a position so unpleasant. . . ."[62] Davis, however, interpreted Virginia's action as a warning, if not an actual threat,[63] and decided on a showdown. Seddon had resigned on January 18 and on February 1 Davis by letter questioned whether the Secretary should be controlled by an expression of opinion on the part of the Virginia delegation. Davis accepted the resignation, but added,[64]

> I cannot however recognize the propriety of your decision because I cannot admit the existence of a power or right in the legislative branch of the Government or in any part or branch of it to control the continuance in office of those "principal officers in each of the executive departments" whose choice the Constitution has vested in the Chief Magistrate; whose advice in writing he is empowered to require, and whose tenure of office is exceptional, being made to depend expressly on the "pleasure of the President. . . ."

To let Congress know his position, Davis allowed both letters to be published in the Richmond newspapers.

Bocock replied immediately. In a published statement he condemned Davis both for publishing a confidential correspondence and for distorting Virginia's position. The Virginia delegation had not implied Congress's authority to compel a Cabinet resignation, but others contemplated just this and Virginia had wished Davis to forestall them. Virginia had not requested dismissal of the entire Cabinet, for her delegation could neither "indicate the details" of the President's functions nor imply dissatisfaction with a fellow Virginian.[65]

Both parties had acted badly. Probably to make his point better, Bocock had exaggerated the size and intent of the opposition to the Cabinet. Davis's actions were more calculated. Seddon, never robust and now worn ragged, had been longing to resign. Instead of trying to dissuade him, which probably would have been impossible, Davis seized this opportunity to chastise Congress. By interpreting the Virginians' request in a fashion which even they admitted was an invasion of his realm, he put Congress on the defensive and gained respite for the remainder of his Cabinet.

The only wholesale assault on the Cabinet came from Senator Waldo P. Johnson of Arkansas. On December 10, 1863, he proposed to limit the term of a department head to two years, with the expiration date to be the end of each Congress. There was to be no restriction on the number of terms one could serve, though Senate approval was required for each re-nomination. Johnson maintained that public confidence in the Cabinet was lost, but that his bill would restore this confidence by preventing an oligarchy of executive officers.[66] The bill was debated for two months and John B. Jones considered it a declaration of war between the Senate and the President. The Judiciary Committee favored it, arguing that incoming presidents, by successively adopting the Cabinets of retiring presidents, could retain secretaries for twenty years or more without further Senate approval. The term of office of department heads, therefore, should be a matter of legislative discretion, just as creation or establishment of the departments themselves. Admittedly the right of removal was conferred on the President, but Congress had the constitutional right to establish the executive departments and to regulate them and their heads in every other respect. "The power to fix the tenure of office, is as distinct and different from the power of removal, as is the power to remove from the power of impeachment." When a secretary was responsible to the people as well as to the President he would discharge his duties far better.[67] Despite the Committee recommendation, Johnson's bill never came to a vote; and this is but one of many instances of a clear administration victory when only basic ideas of government were involved.

Two other officials kept Davis in political hot water, perhaps unnecessarily so, because criticism against them was largely personal. Davis had appointed Lucius B. Northrop, a sickly cavalry colonel, as his Commissary General, and Congress confirmed the appointment reluctantly. Northrop was eccentric, stubborn, and belligerent, and had once brazenly asserted that impressment was intended to secure all necessary army supplies, not to please the people. Investigations never attributed fraud or supply failures to Northrop, but this fact seldom deterred Congress from scourging and belittling him and, through him, the President. Davis probably should have dismissed him and let the people see that the emergency and not the man was to blame. More out of stubbornness than anything else, however, he retained Northrop against all opposition.

Abraham C. Myers originally occupied the post of quartermaster general, but, though popular with Congress, was disliked by the President if for no other reason than having called Mrs. Davis "an old squaw."[68] In March, 1863, Congress tried to promote Myers by making the rank and pay of brigadier general attach to the office of quartermaster general. Davis had no intention of sharing his right of nomination and seized the opportunity to dismiss Myers. In December Davis explained to the irate Senate that "Colonel" Myers had been only an "acting" quartermaster general; that when Congress specified that the position be filled with a brigadier general he had no alternative but to give the post to a qualified officer. Consequently he had appointed Alexander R. Lawton, who had been a brigadier general since 1861.[69] The Senate Military Committee retorted that Myers had legally been the quartermaster general rather than an "acting functionary." Since Lawton's name had never been submitted to the Senate for the position, the Committee concluded that Myers still served with the advanced rank.[70] The Senate adopted the report by a vote of 15 to 6, and 76 congressmen petitioned for retention of Myers.[71] The Senate's constitutional position was weak and Davis offered it an easy retreat. On January 27 he explained that, according to his understanding, Congress had intended the position to go to a brigadier general whose nomination need not be re-confirmed. He then cited a law of March 6, 1861, letting the President assign brigadier generals to any duties he might specially direct. Refraining from commenting on the Senate's resolutions except for maintaining his conviction that they were not sustained by the Constitution or the law, Davis politely submitted Lawton's nomination.[72] The Senate accepted the reprieve and immediately confirmed the nomination.

The failure of the anti-administration congressmen to establish much control over the executive branch of government was only a little greater than their failure, for three years, to dominate legislation. During the Provisional and the First Congresses, most parts of the administration program encountered some opposition at certain stages of their development, but generally this opposition was an impediment instead of a block. The only major executive proposal that Congress flatly rejected during these three years was that of a third suspension of the writ of habeas corpus. As late as February, 1864, War Clerk Jones thought that Davis could pass whatever bills he pleased,[73] and opposition newspapers begged Congress to cease being a "register of royal proclamations."

Nevertheless, during the First Congress the opposition won converts, and in the Second Congress it numbered slightly over 40% of the total membership. The opposition now represented a stronger degree of protest, was far more vocal, and was less inclined to succumb to Executive pressure. The result was that in the Second Congress the administration was defeated on four major counts. (1) Davis wanted complete control of determining who should work and who should fight; Congress continued the system of class exemptions begun in 1862. (2) Congress pretty much disregarded the financial proposals of the Treasury Department. (3) Congress refused to suspend the writ of habeas corpus during 1865. (4) Congress waited until March 16, 1865, before authorizing the President to arm the slaves for military duty. It might be added that on January 31, 1865, Congress, for its first and only time, overrode a veto, one condemning the franking of newspapers to soldiers.[74]

Considering everything, however, the Confederate government ran more smoothly than did that of the United States and Lincoln was far more bothered with politics than was Davis. Nevertheless, Davis would have taken small comfort from this. He despaired of Congress's amendments, delays, and occasional rejections. Only subservience satisfied him, and, as his influence with Congress was based primarily on an agreement of ideas, not on party discipline, he ultimately lost some of this influence. On the other hand Senator Oldham of Texas expressed the opposition viewpoint on the role of Congress during the war as follows:[75]

The Loyal Opposition 235

Others have attributed the failure of our cause, to the Confederate Congress in not passing promptly the necessary laws demanded for the safety of the country. If by this is meant, and which is true as to most of those who make the charge, that Congress failed to do its duty, in not passing promptly every measure recommended by the Executive and military authorities as necessary for the public safety, the acts of Congress will prove the charge to be unfounded—but if it is meant that in many instances Congress lost sight of the fact that it was the representative law making and governing power of the country, and instead of acting upon its own judgment, in the passage of laws deemed necessary for the good of the country, subordinated that judgment to that of the President and military authorities, in the passage of such laws as they recommended, without regard to their adaptation to the sentiments, mode of thought, and habits of the people upon whom they were to operate, then the charge is unfortunately and calamitously true.

APPENDIX

BIOGRAPHICAL NOTES ON CONFEDERATE CONGRESSMEN

THE FOLLOWING ARE BIOGRAPHICAL NOTES ON THE CONFEDERATE CONgressmen mentioned in the preceding text. Whenever possible I have included the subject's full name, his state, the place and year of his birth, his education, his livelihood, his public service, his politics, his military experience, and his Confederate congressional record.

Anderson, James Patton, Florida. B. in Tenn., 1822; Jefferson College, Penn.; lawyer, planter; Miss. legislature; Democrat; secessionist; lt. col. in Mexican War; (P).[1]

Arrington, Archibald Hunter, North Carolina. B. in N.C., 1809; academic education; lawyer, planter; U.S. Cong.; Democrat; secessionist; (1); (0).[2]

Ashe, Thomas Samuel, North Carolina. B. in N.C., 1812; U. of N.C.; lawyer; Whig; unionist;[3] (1); (0).

Atkins, John De Witt Clinton, Tennessee. B. in Tenn., 1825; East Tenn. U.; planter, politician; Tenn. legislature, U.S. Cong.; Democrat; unionist; CSA lt. col., 1861; (P, 1, 2); (+, +, +).

Avery, William Waigstill, North Carolina. B. in N.C., 1816; U.

---

1. The first set of parentheses used indicates whether the subject was in the Provisional, the First, or the Second Congress, or a combination of them.

2. The second set of parentheses used indicates the subject's voting record on President Davis's program. The "+" indicates that in a particular congress the subject approved a majority of the administration's measures; the "0" indicates that he opposed a majority of these measures. These symbols are to be correlated to the information in the preceding set of parentheses. The omission of any such symbol indicates that the subject did not remain in Congress long enough to establish a voting record for that Congress.

3. For brevity, the term "unionist" is here used to include anyone who opposed immediate secession after Lincoln's election.

of N.C.; lawyer, planter; N.C. legislature; Democrat; secessionist; (P); (+).

Ayer, Lewis Malone, South Carolina. B. in S.C., 1821; S.C. College, U. of Va., Harvard Law School; lawyer, planter; S.C. legislature; Democrat; secessionist; (1, 2); (0, 0).

Baker, James McNair, Florida. B. in S.C., 1821; Davidson College; lawyer; judge; Whig, Const. U.; unionist; (1, 2); (+, 0).

Baldwin, John Brown, Virginia. B. in Va., 1820; U. of Va.; lawyer; Va. legislature; Whig, Const. U.; unionist; col. in Va. infantry, 1861; (1, 2); (+, 0).

Barksdale, Ethelbert, Mississippi. B. in Tenn., 1824; editor of the *Mississippian;* Democrat; unionist; CSA major, 1861; (1, 2); (+, +).

Barnwell, Robert Woodward, South Carolina. B. in S.C., 1801; Harvard; lawyer, president S.C. College, planter; S.C. legislature, U.S. Cong.; Democrat; opposed secession until eve of S.C. convention; (P, 1, 2); (+, +, +).

Bartow, Francis Stebbins, Georgia. B. in Ga., 1816; U. of Ga., Yale Law School; lawyer; Whig, American, Breckinridge Democrat; secessionist; (P); (0).

Bell, Hiram Parks, Georgia. B. in Ga., 1827; academic education; lawyer; Ga. legislature; Const. U.; unionist; CSA colonel; (2); (0).

Blandford, Mark Hardin, Georgia. B. in Ga., 1826; Mercer U.; businessman, lawyer; CSA officer, judge of CSA army military court; (2); (0).

Bocock, Thomas Stanley, Virginia. B. in Va., 1815; Hampden-Sydney; lawyer; Va. legislature, U.S. Cong.; Democrat; secessionist by Jan., 1861; (P, 1, 2); (+, +, +).

Bonham, Milledge Luke, South Carolina. B. in S.C., 1813; S.C. College; lawyer; S.C. legislature, U.S. Cong.; Democrat; secessionist; lt. col. in Mexican War, CSA brig. gen.; (1); (0).

Boteler, Alexander Robinson, Virginia. B. in Md., 1815; Princeton; planter, mill owner; U.S. Cong.; Whig; unionist; (P, 1); (+, +).

Boyce, William Waters, South Carolina. B. in S.C., 1818; S.C. College, U. of Va., Columbia U.; lawyer, planter; U.S. Cong.; Democrat; secessionist; (P, 1, 2); (+, 0, 0).

Bridgers, Robert Rufus, North Carolina. B. in N.C., 1819; U. of N.C.; lawyer, planter, banker, president Wilmington & Weldon R.R., businessman; N.C. legislature; Democrat; secessionist; (1, 2); (+, 0).

Brockenbrough, John White, Virginia. B. in Va., 1815; William & Mary; lawyer; Va. legislature, U.S. dist. judge in Va.; Democrat; secessionist; (P); (+).

Brown, Albert Gallatin, Mississippi. B. in S.C., 1813; Jefferson College (Miss.); lawyer; Miss. legislature, U.S. Cong.; Democrat; secessionist; (1, 2); (+, 0).

Bruce, Eli Metcalfe, Kentucky. Lived in Nicholas Co. in 1861; commission merchant; Democrat; (1, 2); (0, +).

Bruce, Horatio Washington, Kentucky. B. in Ky., 1830; academic education; store clerk, postmaster, lawyer; judge, Ky. legislature; Whig, American, Const. U.; secessionist; (1, 2); (+, +).

Burnett, Henry Cornelius, Kentucky. B. in Va., 1825; academic education; lawyer; U.S. Cong.; Democrat; opposed secession until Ft. Sumter; (P, 1, 2); (+, +, +).

Campbell, Josiah A. Patterson, Mississippi. B. in S.C., 1830; Davidson College; lawyer; Miss. legislature; Democrat; (P); (+).

Caperton, Allen Taylor, Virginia. B. in Va., 1810; Yale; lawyer; Va. legislature, U.S. Cong.; Whig; unionist; (1, 2); (0, 0).

Chambers, Henry Cousins, Mississippi. B. in Ala., 1823; Princeton; planter; Miss. legislature; Democrat; (1, 2); (+, +).

Chesnut, James, South Carolina. B. in S.C., 1815; Princeton; planter, lawyer; S.C. legislature; Democrat; secessionist; (P); (+).

Chilton, William Parish, Alabama. B. in Ky., 1810; sketchy academic education; lawyer; Ala. legislature, Ala. Supreme Court; Whig; unionist; (P, 1, 2); (+, +, +).

Clark, John Bullock, Missouri. B. in Ky., 1812; little education; lawyer; Mo. legislature, U.S. Cong.; Democrat; Black Hawk War, CSA brig. gen.; (P, 1, 2); (+, +, +).

Clark, William W., Georgia. B. in 1822; attended college; lawyer, planter; (1); (+).

Clay, Clement Claiborne, Alabama. B. in Ala., 1816; U. of Ala., U. of Va. Law School; editor *Huntsville Democrat*, lawyer; Ala. legislature, U.S. Cong., gov. of Ala.; Democrat; secessionist; (1); (+).

Clayton, Alexander M., Mississippi. B. in Va., 1801; academic education; lawyer, planter; consul at Havana, U.S. judge for Ark. Terr., judge Miss. high court of appeals; Whig; secessionist; (P); (+).

Cobb, Howell, Georgia. B. in Ga., 1815; U. of Ga.; lawyer, planter; gov. of Ga., U.S. Cong., Sec. of Treasury under Buchanan; Democrat; secessionist; (P); (0).

Cobb, Thomas Reade Rootes, Georgia. B. in Ga., 1823; U. of Ga.; lawyer, law professor; U.S. Cong.; Democrat; secessionist; (P); (0).

Colyar, Arthur St. Clair, Tennessee. B. in Tenn., 1818; academic education; lawyer; Whig, Const. U.; unionist; (2); (+).

Conrad, Charles Magill, Louisiana. B. in Va., 1804; lawyer, planter; La. legislature, U.S. Cong., Sec. of War under Fillmore; Whig, Const. U.; unionist; (P, 1, 2); (+, +, +).

Crawford, Martin Jenkins, Georgia. B. in Ga., 1820; Mercer U.; lawyer, planter; Ga. legislature, U.S. Cong.; Democrat; secessionist; (P); (0).

Cruikshank, Marcus Henderson, Alabama. B. in Ala., 1826; academic education; lawyer, mayor of Talladega, editor of *Reporter;* Whig, Const. U.; unionist; ran salt works in early part of Confederacy; (2); (0).

Curry, Jabez Lamar Monroe, Alabama. B. in Ga., 1825; U. of Ga.,

Harvard Law School; lawyer; Ala. legislature, U.S. Cong.; Democrat; secessionist; served in Mexican War; (P, 1); (+, +).

Dargan, Edmund Strother, Alabama. B. in N.C., 1805; self-educated; lawyer; Ala. legislature, Ala. Supreme Court, U.S. Cong.; Democrat; secessionist; (1); (+).

Davidson, Allen Turner, North Carolina. B. in N.C., 1819; academic education; lawyer, bank president; Whig; unionist; (P, 1); (+, 0).

Davis, George, North Carolina. B. in N.C., 1820; U. of N.C.; lawyer; Whig; became secessionist with failure of Washington Peace Conference; (P, 1); (+, +).

Davis, Reuben, Mississippi. B. in Tenn., 1819; little schooling; studied medicine and practiced some, then became lawyer; Miss. legislature, U.S. Cong.; Whig, then Democrat; secessionist; colonel in Mexican War, maj. gen. in Miss. troops, 1861; (1); (0).

Dortch, William Theophilus, North Carolina. B. in N.C., 1824; academic education; lawyer, planter; N.C. legislature; Democrat; secessionist; (1, 2); (+, +).

Dupré, Lucien Jacques, Louisiana. B. in La., 1822; U. of Va., U. of La. Law School; lawyer; judge; Whig; secessionist; enlisted as CSA private, 1861; (1, 2); (+, +).

Echols, Joseph Hubbard, Georgia. Planter, at one time president Madison Female Academy; Ga. legislature; (2); (0).

Fearn, Thomas, Alabama. B. in Va., 1789 or 1790; Washington College, Va., Philadelphia Medical College; physician; Ala. legislature; Democrat; unionist; (P).

Foote, Henry S., Tennessee. B. in Va., 1804; Washington College, Va.; lawyer; Miss. legislature, U.S. Cong., gov. of Miss.; Democrat; unionist; (1, 2); (0, 0).

Foster, Thomas Jefferson, Alabama. B. in Tenn., 1809; planter, manufacturer; not in politics; (1, 2); (+, 0).

Gaither, Burgess Sidney, North Carolina. B. in N.C., 1807; U. of Ga.; lawyer, supt. of mint at Charlotte; N.C. legislature, superior court judge; Whig; unionist; (1, 2); (0, 0).

Garland, Augustus Hill, Arkansas. B. in Tenn., 1832; St. Joseph's College, Ky.; lawyer; Whig, Const. U.; opposed secession until after Ft. Sumter; (P, 1, 2); (+, +, +).

Garland, Rufus K., Arkansas. B. in 1830; lawyer, planter, occasional Methodist preacher; unionist; CSA captain; (2); (0).

Gartrell, Lucius Jeremiah, Georgia. B. in Ga., 1821; U. of Ga.; lawyer; Ga. legislature, U.S. Cong.; Whig, then Democrat; secessionist; CSA colonel; (1); (+).

Gilmer, John Adams, North Carolina. B. in N.C., 1805; academic education; lawyer; N.C. legislature, U.S. Cong.; Whig; unionist — considered secession unconstitutional; Lincoln offered him Cabinet post; (2); (0).

Goode, John, Virginia. B. in Va., 1829; Emory & Henry, Lexington Law School; lawyer; Democrat; secessionist; enlisted as CSA private; (1, 2); (+, +).

Graham, Malcolm D., Texas. B. in Ala., 1827; lawyer; Tex. legislature, Tex. att. gen.; Democrat; secessionist; (1); (+).

Graham, William Alexander, North Carolina. B. in N.C., 1804; U. of N.C.; lawyer; N.C. legislature, U.S. Cong., gov. of N.C.; Sec. of Navy under Fillmore; Whig; unionist; (2); (0).

Hanly, Thomas Burton, Arkansas. B. in Ky., 1812; lawyer; Ark. legislature, Ark. Supreme Court; Democrat; secessionist; (1, 2); (0, +).

Harris, Thomas A., Missouri. B. in 1826; editor of *Missouri Courier*; Mo. legislature; Democrat, then American; unionist; CSA major, 1861; (1, 2); (0, +).

Harris, Wiley Pope, Mississippi. B. in Miss., 1818; U. of Va., U. of Ky.; lawyer; circuit judge, U.S. Cong.; Democrat; secessionist; (P); (+).

Harrison, James Thomas, Mississippi. B. in S.C., 1811; U. of S.C.; lawyer, planter; Democrat; (P); (+).

Hartridge, Julian, Georgia. B. in Ga., 1829; Brown U., Harvard Law School; lawyer; Ga. legislature; Democrat; CSA lt., 1861; (1, 2); (+, 0).

Haynes, Landon Carter, Tennessee. B. in Tenn., 1816; Washington College, Tenn.; lawyer; Tenn. legislature; Democrat; (1, 2); (0, 0).

Heiskell, Joseph Brown, Tennessee. B. in Tenn., 1823; U. of East Tenn.; lawyer; Tenn. legislature; Whig; secessionist; (1, 2); (+, +).

Henry, Gustavus Adolphus, Tennessee. B. in Ky., 1804; Transylvania U.; lawyer, planter; Whig; unionist; (1, 2); (+, +).

Herbert, Caleb Claiborne, Texas. Tex. legislature; Democrat; secessionist; (1, 2); (0, 0).

Hill, Benjamin Harvey, Georgia. B. in Ga., 1823; U. of Ga.; lawyer; Whig, Const. U.; unionist; (P, 1, 2); (+, 0, +).

Hilton, Robert B., Florida. Editor of the *Tallahassee Floridian*; Democrat; secessionist; enlisted as CSA private; (1, 2); (+, +).

Hodge, Benjamin Louis, Louisiana. Lawyer; secessionist; CSA colonel until 1862, resigned; (2); (+).

Holt, Hines, Georgia. B. in Ga., 1805; U. of Ga.; lawyer; Ga. legislature, U.S. Cong.; Whig, Know-Nothing; unionist; (1); (+).

Hunter, Robert Mercer Taliaferro, Virginia. B. in Va., 1809; U. of Va.; lawyer, planter; U.S. Cong.; Whig, then Democrat; secessionist by Feb., 1861; (P, 1, 2); (+, 0, 0).

Jemison, Robert, Alabama. B. in Ga.; planter; Ala. legislature; Whig; unionist; (1, 2); (0, 0).

Johnson, Herschel Vespasian, Georgia. B. in Ga., 1812; U. of Ga.; lawyer; Ga. circuit judge, gov. of Ga., U.S. Cong.; Democrat; unionist; (1, 2); (0, 0).

Johnson, Robert Ward, Arkansas. B. in Ky., 1814; St. Joseph's College, Mo., Yale Law School; lawyer, editor of *True Democrat*;

...... *Appendix* *241*

att. gen. of Ark., U.S. Cong.; Democrat; secessionist; (P, 1, 2); (+, +, +).

Johnson, Waldo Porter, Missouri. B. in Va., 1817; Rector College, Va.; lawyer, planter; Mo. legislature, U.S. Cong.; Democrat; unionist; CSA officer; (1, 2); (+, +).

Jones, Thomas McKissick, Tennessee. B. in N.C., 1816; U. of Ala., U. of Va.; lawyer; Tenn. legislature; Democrat; (P); (+).

Keitt, Lawrence Massillon, South Carolina. B. in S.C., 1824; S.C. College; lawyer; S.C. legislature, U.S. Cong.; Democrat; secessionist; CSA colonel; (P); (0).

Kenan, Augustus Holmes, Georgia. B. in Ga., 1805; academic education; lawyer; Ga. legislature; Whig, Const. U.; unionist; (P, 1); (0, +).

Lander, William, North Carolina. B. in Ireland, 1817; academic education; lawyer; N.C. legislature; Democrat; secessionist; (1); (+).

Leach, James Thomas, North Carolina. B. in N.C., 1803; planter, physician; N.C. legislature; Whig; unionist; (2); (0).

Lewis, David W., Georgia. B. in Ga., 1815; U. of N.C., U. of Ga.; planter, lawyer; Ga. legislature; (1); (+).

Lewis, John W., Georgia. B. in S.C., 1801; physician, then supt. of Western & Atlantic R.R.; Ga. and S.C. legislatures; (1); (0).

Lyon, Francis Strother, Alabama. B. in N.C., 1800; lawyer; Ala. legislature, U.S. Cong., Ala. State Commissioner of Banks; Whig; secessionist; (1, 2); (+, +).

Lyons, James, Virginia. B. in Va., 1801; William & Mary College; lawyer; Va. legislature; Whig; secessionist; (1); (+).

McDowell, Thomas David Smith, North Carolina. B. in N.C., 1823; U. of N.C.; lawyer, planter; N.C. legislature; Whig; secessionist; (P, 1); (+, 0).

MacFarland, William H., Virginia. B. in Va., 1799; William & Mary College; lawyer, owned coal mining interests, bank president; Whig; unionist; (P); (0).

Machen, Willis Benson, Kentucky. B. in Ky., 1810; Cumberland College; lawyer, iron manufacturer, planter; Ky. legislature; Democrat; secessionist by March, 1861; (1, 2); (+, +).

McMullen, Fayette, Virginia. B. in Va., 1805; academic education; state driver and teamster, gov. of Washington Terr.; Va. legislature, U.S. Cong.; Democrat; (2); (0).

McRae, Colin John, Alabama. B. in N.C., 1812; Catholic U.; financier and commission merchant; Whig; (P); (+).

McRae, John Jones, Mississippi. B. in N.C., 1815; Miami U., Ohio; lawyer; Miss. legislature, U.S. Cong., gov. of Miss.; Democrat; secessionist; (1); (+).

Marshall, Henry, Louisiana. Lived in Black Jack in 1861; secessionist; (P, 1); (0, 0).

Marshall, Humphrey, Kentucky. B. in Ky., 1812; West Point

Academy; resigned U.S. Army, became lawyer; U.S. Cong., minister to China; Whig, Know-Nothing, Breckinridge Democrat; secessionist by early 1861; Mexican War, CSA general; (2); (0).

Maxwell, Augustus Emmett, Florida. B. in Ga., 1820; U. of Va.; lawyer; U.S. Cong., U.S. Navy agent at Pensacola; Democrat; (1, 2); (+, +).

Memminger, Christopher Gustavus, South Carolina. B. in Württemberg, Ger., 1803; S.C. College; lawyer; S.C. legislature; Democrat; secessionist; (P); (+).

Miles, William Porcher, South Carolina. B. in S.C., 1822; Charleston College; lawyer, then math prof.; U.S. Cong.; Democrat; secessionist; (P, 1, 2); (+, +, 0).

Mitchel, Charles Burton, Arkansas. B. in Tenn., 1815; U. of Nashville, Jefferson Med. School in Phila.; physician; Ark. legislature, U.S. Cong.; Democrat; unionist; (1, 2); (+, +).

Moore, James William, Kentucky. B. in Ky., 1818; lawyer, judge; Democrat; "among the first to renounce Lincoln"; (1, 2); (+, +).

Morton, Jackson, Florida. B. in Va., 1794; William & Mary; lumber business and manufacturing, then became planter; Fla. legislature, U.S. Cong., Navy agent at Pensacola; Whig, Const. U.; (P); (0).

Oldham, Williamson Simpson, Texas. B. in Tenn., 1813; academic education; lawyer, editor; Tex. legislature; Democrat; secessionist; (P, 1, 2); (0, 0, 0).

Orr, Jehu Amaziah, Mississippi. B. in S.C., 1828; Erskine, Princeton; lawyer, editor; Miss. legislature; Democrat; unionist; CSA colonel between terms of Cong.; (P, 2); (+, 0).

Orr, James Lawrence, South Carolina. B. in S.C., 1822; U. of Va.; edited *Anderson Gazette* for 2 years, lawyer; S.C. legislature, U.S. Cong.; Democrat; cooperationist; (P, 1, 2); (+, 0, 0).

Owen, James B., Florida. Baptist preacher; Democrat; secessionist; (P); (0).

Perkins, John, Louisiana. B. in Miss., 1819; Yale; lawyer, planter, banker; U.S. Cong., U.S. dist. judge; Democrat; secessionist; (P, 1, 2); (0, +, +).

Peyton, Robert Ludwell Yates, Missouri. B. in Va., 1825; Miami U., U. of Va. Law School; planter, lawyer; Mo. legislature; Democrat; (P, 1); (+, +).

Phelan, James, Mississippi. B. in Ala., 1820; editor of *Flag of the Union*, then lawyer; Miss. legislature; Democrat; secessionist; (1); (+).

Preston, Walter, Virginia. B. in Va., 1818; U. of Va., Yale; lawyer, planter; Ark. legislature; Whig; (P, 1); (+, 0).

Preston, William Ballard, Virginia. B. in Va., 1805; Hampden-Sydney, U. of Va.; lawyer; Va. legislature, U.S. Cong., Sec. of Navy under Taylor; Whig; unionist; (P, 1); (0, 0).

Pugh, James Lawrence, Alabama. B. in Ga., 1820; academic education; lawyer, planter; U.S. Cong.; Democrat; secessionist; enlisted as CSA private, 1861; (1, 2); (+, +).

Ralls, John Perkins, Alabama. B. in Ga., 1822; Augusta Medical School; physician; cooperationist; (1); (+).

Reade, Edwin Godwin, North Carolina. B. in N.C., 1812; academic education; lawyer; U.S. Cong.; Whig, American; unionist; (1); (0).

Reagan, John Henninger, Texas. B. in Tenn., 1809; academic education; overseer, then lawyer; dist. judge, Tex. legislature, U.S. Cong.; Democrat; unionist; (P); (+).

Rhett, Robert Barnwell, South Carolina. B. in S.C., 1820; academic education; planter, lawyer; S.C. legislature, U.S. Cong.; Democrat; secessionist; (P); (0).

Rives, William Cabell, Virginia. B. in Va., 1793; William & Mary; lawyer; Va. legislature, U.S. Cong., minister to France; Whig; unionist; (P, 2); (0, +).

Royston, Grandison D., Arkansas. B. in Tenn., 1809; academic education; lawyer; Ark. legislature; unionist; (1); (+).

Russell, Charles Welles, Virginia. B. in Va., 1818; Jefferson College (Pa.); lawyer; Va. legislature; Democrat; secessionist; (P, 1, 2); (+, +, +).

Seddon, James Alexander, Virginia. B. in Va., 1815; U. of Va.; planter, lawyer; Va. legislature; Democrat; secessionist; (P); (+).

Semmes, Thomas Jenkins, Louisiana. B. in Washington, D.C., 1824; Georgetown College, Harvard Law School; lawyer; La. legislature, La. att. gen.; Democrat; secessionist; (1, 2); (+, +).

Sexton, Francis Barlow, Texas. B. in Indiana, 1828; Wesleyan College, Tex.; printer, then lawyer; Tex. legislature; Democrat; CSA Army, 1861; (1, 2); (+, +).

Simms, William Elliott, Kentucky. B. in Ky., 1822; country school education, Transylvania U. Law School; lawyer, editor of *Kentucky State Flag;* Ky. legislature, U.S. Cong.; Democrat; secessionist; Mexican War, CSA colonel; (1, 2); (+, +).

Simpson, William Dunlap, South Carolina. B. in S.C., 1823; S.C. College; lawyer; S.C. legislature, judge; Democrat; secessionist; (1, 2); (+, 0).

Singleton, Otho Robards, Mississippi. B. in Ky., 1814; St. Joseph's College, Ky., U. of Lexington Law School; lawyer; Miss. legislature, U.S. Cong.; Democrat; secessionist; (1, 2); (+, +).

Smith, William, Virginia. B. in Va., 1797; academic education; ran mail coach service, then became lawyer; Va. legislature, U.S. Cong., gov. of Va.; Democrat; CSA colonel; (1); (+).

Smith, William Nathan Harrell, North Carolina. B. in N.C., 1812; Yale; lawyer; N.C. legislature, U.S. Cong.; Whig; unionist; (P, 1, 2); (0, 0, 0).

Smith, William Russell, Alabama. B. in Ky., 1815; U. of Ala.; editor, then lawyer; Ala. legislature, U.S. Cong.; Whig; cooperationist; CSA colonel, 1861; (1, 2); (0, 0).

Snead, Thomas Lowndes, Missouri. B. in Va., 1828; U. of Va.; lawyer; Democrat; unionist; colonel in Mo. state guard; (2); (+).

Sparrow, Edward, Louisiana. Kenyon College; planter; La. legislature; Whig; secessionist; (P, 1, 2); (+, +, +).

Staples, Waller Redd, Virginia. B. in Va., 1826; William & Mary; lawyer; Va. legislature; Whig; unionist; (P, 1, 2); (+, +, 0).

Stephens, Alexander Hamilton, Georgia. B. in Ga., 1812; U. of Ga.; lawyer; Ga. legislature, U.S. Cong.; Whig, then Const. U.; unionist; (P); (0).

Swan, William Graham, Tennessee. Lawyer; judge, att. gen. of Tenn.; Whig; secessionist; enlisted as CSA private, 1861; (1, 2); (+, +).

Toombs, Robert Augustus, Georgia. B. in Ga., 1810; Union College, N.Y.; lawyer, planter; Ga. legislature, U.S. Cong.; Whig, Const. U., then Breckinridge Democrat; secessionist on failure of Crittenden Compromise; (P); (+).

Turner, Josiah, North Carolina. B. in N.C., 1821; U. of N.C.; editor of *Hillsboro Recorder;* N.C. legislature; Whig; unionist; (2); (0).

Tyler, John, Virginia. B. in Va., 1790; William & Mary; lawyer; U.S. Cong., ex-president of U.S.; Whig; unionist; (P); (+).

Vest, George Graham, Missouri. B. in Ky., 1830; Centre College, Translyvania Law School; lawyer; Mo. legislature; Democrat; secessionist; CSA Army, 1861; (P, 1, 2); (0, +, +).

Walker, Richard Wilde, Alabama. B. in Ala., 1823; U. of Va., Princeton; lawyer, planter; Ala. legislature; Whig; (P, 2); (+, 0).

Watson, John William Clark, Mississippi. B. in Va., 1808; Va. Law School; lawyer; Whig; unionist: (2); (0).

Wigfall, Louis Trezevant, Texas. B. in S.C., 1816; S.C. College; lawyer; Tex. legislature, U.S. Cong.; Democrat; secessionist; CSA brig. gen.; (P, 1, 2); (+, +, 0).

Withers, Thomas J., South Carolina. B. in S.C., 1804; planter, lawyer, editor of *Columbia Telescope;* S.C. Supreme Court; Democrat; secessionist; (P); (+).

Wright, Augustus Romaldus, Georgia. B. in Ga., 1813; lawyer; U.S. Cong.; Democrat, Const. U.; unionist; CSA maj. gen.; (P, 1); (+, 0).

Yancey, William Lowndes, Alabama. B. in Ga., 1814; Williams College; editor of *Greenville Mountaineer,* lawyer, planter; Ala. legislature, U.S. Cong.; Democrat; secessionist; (1); (0).

NOTES

CHAPTER I

1. Laurence T. Lowrey, *Northern Opinion of Approaching Secession* (Northampton, Mass., 1918), 213.
2. Quoted in Percy S. Flippin, *Herschel V. Johnson of Georgia, State Rights Unionist* (Richmond, 1931), 171.
3. Quoted in Percy L. Rainwater, *Mississippi, Storm Center of Secession* (Baton Rouge, 1938), 151.
4. Keitt to Mrs. Federick Brown, March 4, 1861, Lawrence M. Keitt Papers, Duke University.
5. Quoted in Louis Pendleton, *Alexander H. Stephens* (Philadelphia, 1908), 158.
6. Quoted in Flippin, *Herschel V. Johnson*, 176.
7. Edward McPherson (comp.), *The Political History of the United States of America, During the Great Rebellion* . . . (Washington, 1865), 37.
8. "From the Autobiography of Herschel V. Johnson, 1856-1867," *American Historical Review*, XXX (1924-1925), 323.
9. McPherson, *Political History of the United States*, 37.
10. *Journal of the Convention of the People of South Carolina, Held in 1860, 1861 and 1862* . . . (Columbia, 1862), 480-83.
11. William R. Smith, *The History and Debates of the Convention of the People of Alabama . . . 1861* (Montgomery, 1861), 131.
12. *Ibid.*, 360.
13. D. L. Yulee to Joseph Finegan, January 7, 1861, *The War of the Rebellion: A Compilation of the Official Records of the Union and Confederate Armies* (128 vols., Washington, 1880-1901), Ser. I, Vol. I, 443, 444. Hereafter cited as *Official Records*.
14. Rhett protested this abdication of leadership and argued that if South Carolina stood firm the other states would fall into line. He preferred Montgomery because it was Yancey's home and he hoped to have Yancey's aid in establishing a Confederacy that would never seek reconstruction. Charles E. Cauthen, *South Carolina Goes to War* (Chapel Hill, 1950), 84, 85.
15. *Ordinances and Constitution of the State of Alabama, with the Constitution of the Provisional Government and of the Confederate States of America*, 32.
16. *Journal of the Proceedings of the Convention of the People of Florida, Begun . . . January 3 . . . 1861* (Tallahassee, 1861), 75, 77.
17. Smith, *Debates of the Convention of Alabama*, 132.
18. *Ibid.*, 149, 150.
19. Quoted in Richard M. Johnston and William M. Browne, *Life of Alex-*

ander H. Stephens (Philadelphia, 1878), 387.
20. William E. Dodd, *Jefferson Davis* (Philadelphia, 1907), 216.
21. John R. Horsey to William Porcher Miles, December 10, 1860, William P. Miles Papers, University of North Carolina.
22. Thomas R. R. Cobb to his wife, February 9, 1861, A. L. Hull (ed.), "Correspondence of Thomas Reade Rootes Cobb, 1860-1862," Southern History Association, *Publications*, XI (1907), 169.
23. *Ibid.*, 168.
24. Quoted in Alexander H. Stephens, *A Comprehensive and Popular History of the United States* (Raleigh, 1884), 588.
25. Howell Cobb to his wife, February 6, 1861, Ulrich B. Phillips (ed.), *The Correspondence of Robert Toombs, Alexander H. Stephens, and Howell Cobb*, American Historical Association, *Annual Report*, 1911, Vol. II (Washington, 1913), 537.
26. Howell Cobb to his wife, February 3, 1861, *ibid.*
27. Harrison to his wife, February 17, 1861, James T. Harrison Papers, University of North Carolina.
28. Thomas R. R. Cobb to his wife, February 4, 1861, Hull, "Correspondence of Thomas Reade Rootes Cobb, 1860-1862," *loc. cit.*, 161, 167.
29. Howell Cobb to Augustus R. Wright, February 18, 1861, Alexander H. Stephens Papers, Manuscripts Division, Library of Congress.
30. The term "Whig" was still used in 1860 even though the party had disintegrated. It, or "Old Whig," was usually used to include those who had previously been Whigs, Constitutional Unionists, or Americans.

CHAPTER II

1. Thomas R. R. Cobb to his wife, February 4, 1861, Hull, "Correspondence of Thomas Reade Rootes Cobb, 1860-1862," *loc. cit.*, 162.
2. T. O. Chestney to Clement C. Clay, May 11, 1861, Clement C. Clay Papers, Duke University.
3. Thomas R. R. Cobb to his wife, February 22, 1861, Hull, "Correspondence of Thomas Reade Rootes Cobb, 1860-1862," *loc. cit.*, 237.
4. Quoted in Ann Easby-Smith, *William Russell Smith of Alabama, His Life and Works* (Philadelphia, 1931), 124.
5. *Ordinances and Constitution of Alabama*, 53, 54.
6. May 3, 1861.
7. James M. Matthews (ed.), *The Statutes at Large of the Provisional Government of the Confederate States of America* (Richmond, 1864), 161, 165. Hereafter cited as Matthews, *Statutes*.
8. Charles W. Ramsdell (ed.), *Laws and Joint Resolutions of the Last Session of the Confederate Congress . . .* (Durham, 1941), 172, 173. Hereafter cited as Ramsdell, *Laws*.
9. Edward A. Pollard, "The Confederate Congress," *The Galaxy*, VI (1868-1869), 754-755.
10. "Proceedings of the Confederate Congress," Southern Historical Society, *Papers*, XLVII, 143, hereafter cited as "Proceedings of Congress"; *Richmond Daily Enquirer*, February 3, 1863.
11. *Journal of the Congress of the Confederate States of America, 1861-1865* (Washington, 1904-1905), VI, 6, 27, 28. Hereafter cited as *Journal of Congress*.
12. *Richmond Daily Enquirer*, September 3, 1861.
13. Mary Boykin Chesnut, *A Diary from Dixie*, ed. Ben Ames Williams (Boston, 1949), 6. Hereafter cited as Chesnut, *Diary*.
14. Josiah Turner to his wife, December 5, 1864, Josiah Turner Papers, University of North Carolina.
15. Pollard, "The Confederate Congress," *loc. cit.*, 755, 756; *Montgomery Daily Mail*, December 20, 1864.
16. Thomas C. De Leon, *Four Years in Rebel Capitals* (Mobile, 1892), 32.

17. Mary S. Estill (ed.), "Diary of a Confederate Congressman, 1862-1863," *Southwestern Historical Quarterly*, XXXIX (1935-1936), 38.
18. Chesnut, *Diary*, 9.
19. Francis B. Sexton to James H. Starr, March 1, 1862, James H. Starr Papers, University of Texas.
20. Estill, "Diary of a Confederate Congressman, 1862-1863," *loc. cit.*, XXXVIII, 276.
21. *Richmond Daily Enquirer*, February 14, 1863.
22. Pollard, "The Confederate Congress," *loc. cit.*, 755, 756.
23. Matthews, *Statutes*, 100.
24. James M. Matthews (ed.), *Public Laws of the Confederate States of America* . . . (Richmond, 1862-1864), 53. Hereafter cited as Matthews, *Public Laws*.
25. *Official Records*, Ser. IV., Vol. II, 126-31.
26. James H. Echols to President Davis, October 8, 1864, Box 108, Domestic Letters, 1861-1864, Col. John T. Pickett Papers, Manuscripts Division, Library of Congress.
27. Estill, "Diary of a Confederate Congressman, 1862-1863," *loc. cit.*, XXXVIII, 283.
28. Harrison to his wife, December 16, 1861, Harrison Papers.
29. B. N. Clements to J. M. Martin, January 12, 1864, Post Office Department Letter Book, 1863-1865, Pickett Papers.
30. *Acts of Louisiana* (1865), 11.
31. *Richmond Daily Examiner*, April 30, 1863.
32. Estill, "Diary of a Confederate Congressman, 1862-1863," *loc. cit.*, XXXIX, 33.
33. *Ibid*, XXXVIII, 275, 276.
34. Louis T. Wigfall to Clement C. Clay, December 11, 1863, Clay Papers.
35. "Hon. Thomas J. Semmes," *Southern Historical Society, Papers*, XXV (1897), 326.
36. Chesnut, *Diary*, 368.
37. Clay to his wife, December 9, 1863, and March 12, 1864, Clay Papers.
38. *Richmond Daily Enquirer*, April 17, 1863.
39. Thomas R. R. Cobb to his wife, February 9, 1861, Hull, "Correspondence of Thomas Reade Rootes Cobb, 1860-1862," *loc. cit.*, 169.
40. Chesnut, *Diary*, 366.
41. The Letter Books of Governor Thomas C. Reynolds of Missouri, Pickett Papers, are full of such escapades.
42. Chesnut, *Diary*, 384.
43. *Richmond Daily Examiner*, November 23, 1864.
44. *Richmond Daily Enquirer*, January 8, 1864.
45. *Journal of Congress*, III, 157.
46. *Richmond Daily Enquirer*, March 14, 1863.

CHAPTER III

1. Lawrence M. Keitt to James H. Hammond, February 13, 1861, James H. Hammond Papers, Manuscripts Division, Library of Congress.
2. Robert H. Smith to Helen ――――, January 31, 1861, Charles C. Jones (collector), *Autograph Letters and Portraits of Signers of the Constitution of the Confederate States* (Augusta, 1884). Hereafter cited as Jones, *Autograph Letters*.
3. *Journal of Congress*, I, 20.
4. *Ibid.*, 20, 21, 26.
5. *Constitution and Ordinances of Florida, 1861* (Tallahassee, 1861), 112.
6. Florida Delegation to the President of the State Convention of Florida, February 23, 1861, *Official Records*, Ser. IV, Vol. I, 109.
7. Manuscript speech of Clayton, J. H. F. Claibourne Papers, University of North Carolina.
8. Quoted in Johnston and Browne, *Life of Stephens*, 385. For a good discussion of the Provisional Constitution see William M. Robinson, "A New Deal in Constitutions,"

Journal of Southern History, IV (1938), 449-61.
9. James T. Harrison to _____, February 9, 1861, Jones, *Autograph Letters*.
10. Matthews, *Statutes*, 9.
11. Robert H. Smith to Helen _____, January 31, 1861, Jones, *Autograph Letters*.
12. Quoted in Johnston and Browne, *Life of Stephens*, 393.
13. *Journal of Congress*, I, 864, 865.
14. A. L. Hull (ed.), "The Making of the Confederate Constitution," Southern History Association, *Publications*, IX (1905), 289. Robert H. Smith later wrote that most of those present realized the "necessity of keeping the Presidential election away from the people," but "because of the inherent difficulty of adopting a plan," they "hurried over the subject." Smith to William C. Rives, January 1, 1864, William C. Rives Papers, Manuscripts Division, Library of Congress.
15. *Journal of Congress*, I, 878-81.
16. William M. Robinson, "Legal System of the Confederate States," *Journal of Southern History*, II (1936), 460, 461.
17. *Journal of the Called Session of the Convention of Florida* . . . 1861, 15, 16.
18. Easby-Smith, *William Russell Smith*, 121.
19. John Manning to his wife, April 21, 1861, Williams-Chesnut-Manning Papers, University of North Carolina.
20. *Journal of the South Carolina Convention of 1860, 1861 and 1862*, 39.
21. William H. Trescott to William P. Miles, February 6, 1861, Miles Papers.
22. "Memoir concerning organization of Confederate Government . . . F. M. Gilmer," Dunbar Rowland (ed.), *Jefferson Davis, Constitutionalist* . . . (Jackson, 1923), VIII, 462.
23. The *Charleston Mercury*, with other papers, believed that the Mississippi state convention had sent its delegation to Montgomery with but one instruction: "Get Davis elected President." February 6, 1861.
24. Howell Cobb to his wife, February 6, 1861, Phillips, *Correspondence of Toombs, Stephens, and Cobb*, 537. Cobb was of course only partly correct.
25. "Memoir concerning organization of Confederate Government . . . F. M. Gilmer," Rowland, *Jefferson Davis*, VIII, 463.
26. Alexander H. Stephens, *A Constitutional View of the Late War Between the States* (Philadelphia, 1868), II, 329, 330; Thomas R. R. Cobb to his wife, February 11, 1861, Hull, "Correspondence of Thomas Reade Rootes Cobb, 1860-1862," *loc. cit.*, 171.
27. Thomas R. R. Cobb to his wife, *ibid.*
28. Robert U. Johnson and Clarence C. Buel (eds.), *Battles and Leaders of the Civil War* (New York, 1884-1887), I, 101-03; Jefferson Davis, *The Rise and Fall of the Confederate Government* (New York, 1881), I, 240, 241.
29. Thomas R. R. Cobb to his wife, February 11, 1861, Hull, "Correspondence of Thomas Reade Rootes Cobb, 1860-1862," *loc. cit.*, 171; Johnston and Browne, *Life of Stephens*, 390.
30. Stephens wrote that Toombs "never lets Cobb pass without giving him a lick." Quoted in Johnston and Browne, *ibid.*, 386.
31. *Ibid.*, 390; Thomas R. R. Cobb to his wife, February 11, 1861, Hull, "Correspondence of Thomas Reade Rootes Cobb, 1860-1862," *loc. cit.*, 171.
32. Thomas R. R. Cobb to his wife, *ibid.*
33. Thomas R. R. Cobb to his wife, February 9, 1861, *ibid.*, 169.
34. John H. Reagan, *Memoirs, with Special Reference to Secession and the Civil War*, ed. Walter F. McCaleb (New York, 1906), 109.
35. Matthews, *Statutes*, 27.

36. Ibid., 94.
37. *Journal of Congress*, I, 252, 253.
38. Matthews, *Statutes*, 39, 40, 111.
39. Ibid., 39; *Richmond Daily Enquirer*, May 30, 1864; Ramsdell, *Laws*, 8.
40. Matthews, *Statutes*, 277.
41. Ibid., 149; Matthews, *Public Laws*, 109, 110.
42. Matthews, *Statutes*, 149, 277.
43. Ibid., 39, 40, 277.
44. *Richmond Daily Enquirer*, August 21, 1862.
45. For the whole story see Dallas D. Irvine, "The Fate of Confederate Archives," *American Historical Review*, XLIV (1938-1939), 823-41.
46. *Journal of Congress*, III, 282, 283, 520, 521, 592.
47. *Richmond Daily Enquirer*, June 15 and October 5, 1861; *Richmond Daily Examiner*, November 21, 1864.
48. Quoted in Johnston and Browne, *Life of Stephens*, 385.
49. *Journal of Congress*, I, 17-19.
50. Ibid., II, 18; ibid., V, 40.
51. *Richmond Daily Examiner*, May 18, 1861.
52. August 9, 1861.
53. *Journal of Congress*, V, 301. Unfortunately in both houses a member often refused to state his reasons for desiring privacy, but after taking his body into secret session he might offer material deserving no secrecy at all; after this, the easier procedure would be to remain in secret session.
54. Charles H. Smith, *Bill Arp, So Called* . . . (New York, 1866), 53.
55. Thomas R. R. Cobb to his wife, March 4, 1861, Hull, "Correspondence of Thomas Reade Rootes Cobb," *loc. cit.*, 252. Yancey was one who did this.
56. Matthews, *Statutes*, 58.
57. *Richmond Daily Enquirer*, March 7, 1862; Matthews, *Public Laws*, 4, 5.
58. Ramsdell, *Laws*, 11, 92.
59. Reagan, *Memoirs*, 109.
60. Congress granted the above-mentioned monopoly when Reagan reported that the Southern Express Company had perpetrated "numerous frauds" against the Post Office Department. *Report of the Postmaster General, February 28, 1862.*
61. Matthews, *Public Laws*, 77-79.
62. *Report of the Postmaster General, December 7, 1864.*
63. *Report of the Postmaster General, November 27, 1861.*
64. Art. III, Sec. 1, Cl. 3.
65. Matthews, *Statutes*, 168.
66. *Journal of Congress*, V, 26.
67. "Proceedings of Congress," XLIV, 137, 138; ibid., XLVI, 246.
68. The Alabama delegation was afraid that Alabama unionist J. A. P. Campbell would be appointed to the Supreme Court.
69. Enemies of the Davis administration feared that Davis would pack the Supreme Court with his "pets" and particularly that Judah P. Benjamin would become Chief Justice.
70. *Journal of Congress*, III, 38.
71. *Richmond Daily Enquirer*, January 28, 1863.
72. "Proceedings of Congress," XLVII, 200.
73. See the key vote on Clay's amendment, *Journal of Congress*, III, 176, 177. The four referred to were Albert G. Brown, Horatio C. Burnett, John B. Clark, and Edward Sparrow.
74. Matthews, *Statutes*, 82.
75. For a masterly treatment of the Confederate judicial system see William M. Robinson, *Justice in Grey. A History of the Judicial System of the Confederate States of America* (Cambridge, Mass., 1941).
76. Thomas C. Reynolds to Waldo P. Johnson, August 28, 1863, Reynolds Private Letter Book, II, 1863-1864, Pickett Papers.
77. *Report of the Secretary of War, November 26, 1863.*
78. *Richmond Daily Enquirer*, November 9, 1861.
79. James W. Fertig, *The Secession and Reconstruction of Tennessee* (Chi-

cago, 1898), 31; James W. Patton, *Unionism and Reconstruction in Tennessee, 1860-1869* (Chapel Hill, 1934), 28, 29.

80. *Journal of Congress*, I, 159, 160.

81. *Journal of Congress*, I, 585, 701; Matthews, *Statutes*, 242-47.

82. The text of these treaties make up a large portion of the official acts of Congress in Matthews, *Statutes*.

CHAPTER IV

1. Matthews, *Statutes*, 122.
2. Pollard, "The Confederate Congress," loc. cit., 750.
3. Matthews, *Public Acts*, 157, 158, 173, 174. When there was no legislative sanction for soldiers to vote the governors ordered this privilege extended to them as part of their rights as citizens. The reason Congress made no specific provisions for Texans and Kentuckians in the army to vote was that their state governors had already done so.
4. A. J. Galloway to Thomas D. McDowell, September 30, 1861, Thomas D. McDowell Papers, University of North Carolina.
5. Duncan S. Cage to Andrew McCollam, October 9, 1861, Andrew McCollam Papers, University of North Carolina.
6. "I must request the favor of you to make two or three appointments for me to address the people in different parts of the country." A. H. Arrington to William A. Graham, William A. Graham Papers, University of North Carolina. Candidates usually published their itineraries in local papers not more than a week before their speaking engagements.
7. John Goode, *Recollections of a Lifetime* (New York, 1906), 76.
8. *Richmond Daily Examiner*, October 28, 1861.
9. *Raleigh Standard*, October 5, 1861.
10. *Paulding Eastern Clarion*, August 16, 1861.
11. *Ibid.*, October 19 and 25, 1861.
12. David Y. Thomas, *Arkansas in War and Reconstruction, 1861-1874* (Little Rock, 1926), 332.
13. R. T. Scott to Clement C. Clay, October 11, 1861, Clay Papers.
14. *Savannah Republican*, September 30, 1861.
15. *Richmond Daily Enquirer*, October 3, 1861.
16. *Marietta Family Friend*, August 17, 1861.
17. *Knoxville Register*, October 17, 1861.
18. *Jackson Weekly Mississippian*, September 18, 1861; *Raleigh Standard*, October 26, 1861.
19. *Charleston Mercury*, October 7, 1861.
20. Edwin G. Reade to William A. Graham, July 2, 1861, William A. Graham Papers, Department of Archives and History, Raleigh, North Carolina.
21. January 3, 1862.
22. *Wilmington Daily Journal*, June 17, 1861; *Raleigh Standard*, October 23, 1861.
23. Thomas R. R. Cobb to his wife, February 25, 1861, Hull, "Correspondence of Thomas Reade Rootes Cobb, 1860-1862," loc. cit., 241.
24. Clay to Virginia Clay, November 1, 1861, Clay Papers.
25. October 24, 1861.
26. Martin J. Crawford to Alexander H. Stephens, September 26, 1861, Stephens Papers.
27. *Savannah Republican*, October 31, 1861.
28. These states were Alabama, Arkansas, Mississippi, Missouri, and South Carolina.
29. The *Richmond Daily Examiner* condemned Hunter on the grounds that he could best serve Virginia in the Cabinet and that his resignation intimated dissatisfaction with the Davis administration. December 9, 1861.

30. Quoted in Isaac W. Avery, *The History of the State of Georgia from 1850 to 1881* (New York, 1881), 222. The legislature's reluctance to return Toombs was partly due to the desire to avoid embarrassing the administration and partly to a dislike of heavy taxation, which Toombs had favored. Ulrich B. Phillips, *The Life of Robert Toombs* (New York, 1913), 241.
31. There was a disputed election in the third district of Arkansas, but the House Committee on Elections decided that unless Jilson P. Johnson "could produce overwhelming proof" of his claim that he had received a majority over Augustus H. Garland, the original ballot count must prevail and Garland would retain his seat. "Proceedings of Congress," XLVI, 210; *Journal of Congress*, V, 112-14.
32. May 28, 1863.
33. Thomas C. Reynolds to Waldo P. Johnson, August 27, 1863, Reynolds Letter Book, II, 1862-1864, Pickett Papers.
34. *Hillsboro Recorder*, September 22, 1863.
35. The opponents of William P. Chilton accused him of refusing to take his salary in Confederate money and of insisting on specie. *Montgomery Weekly Mail*, August 5, 1863.
36. Memoirs of Williamson Simpson Oldham, Confederate Senator, 1861-1865, 62. Typed copy, University of Texas.
37. *Savannah Republican*, August 19, 1863.
38. "Dr. Leach is for peace, but fails to tell us how that inestimable jewel is to be obtained." *Wilmington Daily Journal*, October 15, 1863.
39. James D. Armstrong to Stuart, December 3, 1862, Alexander H. H. Stuart Papers, Manuscripts Division, Library of Congress.
40. W. L. Love to Zebulon B. Vance, April 3, 1863, Zebulon B. Vance Papers, Department of Archives and History, Raleigh, North Carolina.
41. September 2, 1863.
42. *Raleigh Weekly Standard*, November 23, 1863.
43. *Richmond Daily Examiner*, May 28, 1863.
44. *Charleston Mercury*, July 3, 1863.
45. William A. Graham to Edward J. Hale, September 21, 1863, Edward J. Hale Papers, Department of Archives and History, Raleigh, North Carolina.
46. Reynolds to Robert A. Hatcher, June 6, 1864, Reynolds Private Letter Book, II, 1863-1864, Pickett Papers.
47. Vance to William A. Graham, January 1, 1864, Graham Papers, Raleigh. James T. Leach, a thoroughgoing Holdenite, said that at the least sign of peace prospects, "the last battle will have been fought, and ... this terrible war will soon be ended." *Broadside to the Soldiers of the 7th Congressional District*, Vance Papers.
48. *Raleigh Standard*, August 29, 1863.
49. Edward J. Hale to Zebulon B. Vance, November 29, 1864, Vance Papers.
50. *Charleston Mercury*, September 8, 1863.
51. Quoted in *Richmond Daily Enquirer*, August 10, 1863.
52. The investigating committee found that Cobb had the reputation of being "a disloyal man," that "of his own free will" he joined the enemy when they penetrated his district, and that he was "unfit to be the Representative of a Southern Constituency. . . ." *Richmond Daily Examiner*, November 16, 1864.
53. W. Y. Walthall to Lt. Col. G. W. Lay, August 6, 1863, *Official Records*, Ser. IV, Vol. II, 726.
54. Francis B. Sexton to James H. Starr, August 30, 1863, Starr Papers.
55. Thomas C. Reynolds to the Missouri Delegation, December 12, 1863, Reynolds Letter Book, Pickett Papers.
56. Thomas C. Reynolds to Jefferson Davis, May 10, 1864, Private Letter Book, II, 1863-1864, Pickett Papers.

CHAPTER V

1. *Journal of Congress*, I, 65.
2. Matthews, *Statutes*, 43, 44.
3. Davis, *Rise and Fall of the Confederate Government*, II, 304. Davis also wished more than 100,000 three-year volunteers, but the Committee felt that the war would last only a short time and that one Southerner could outfight two Yankees. Davis believed that the Committee should "recognize the necessity of man for man," but after being unable to extend the enlistment term for more than one year he accepted the figure of 100,000. Reagan, *Memoirs*, 117.
4. *Journal of Congress*, I, 167.
5. *Charleston Mercury*, May 7, 1861.
6. Matthews, *Statutes*, 104, 105.
7. *Ibid.*, 115.
8. *Journal of Congress*, I, 273.
9. Matthews, *Statutes*, 176.
10. For good analyses of Confederate army problems see the following: Frank L. Owsley, *State Rights in the Confederacy* (Chicago, 1925); Charles W. Ramsdell, *Behind the Lines in the Southern Confederacy* (Baton Rouge, 1944); Albert B. Moore, *Conscription and Conflict in the Confederacy* (New York, 1924).
11. Matthews, *Statutes*, 174, 196, 197.
12. *Ibid.*, 186.
13. A disadvantage of this law was that troops could enter the Confederate service for local defense and thus appear very patriotic; but they would still be a part of the state militia and without their governor's consent could not be moved outside the state.
14. Judah P. Benjamin to the President, November 30, 1861, *Official Records*, Ser. IV, Vol. I, 763. General James Longstreet advised the chairman of the Military Committee that the furlough would also give officers time to "fill up their ranks" from their home districts. Longstreet to W. P. Miles, December 19, 1861, *ibid.*, Ser. I, Vol. V, 1001, 1002.
15. Matthews, *Statutes*, 223, 224. Congress later gave the same bounty to the Navy and the Marine Corps. *Ibid.*, 241; Matthews, *Public Laws*, 26. The Secretary of War estimated that all the bounties would cost about $11,000,000. Judah P. Benjamin to Robert W. Barnwell, February 11, 1862, *Official Records*, Ser. IV, Vol. I, 917.
16. Pollard, "The Confederate Congress," *loc. cit.*, 751.
17. Matthews, *Statutes*, 226, 254.
18. *Ibid.*, 248, 252.
19. *Journal of Congress*, V, 25, 26.
20. *Ibid.*, 26; *Charleston Mercury*, March 25, 1862.
21. *Journal of Congress*, II, 106.
22. "Proceedings of Congress," XLV, 26-28.
23. Oldham, *Memoirs*, 198.
24. *Journal of Congress*, II, 154; *ibid.*, V, 228.
25. Matthews, *Public Laws*, 29-32. The Secretary of War ruled that the law did not relieve from the service all those over thirty-five who had reenlisted for the war. *Savannah Republican*, May 23, 1862.
26. April 11, 1862.
27. *Texas Republican*, April 26, 1862.
28. *Tallahassee Florida Sentinel*, April 22, 1862.
29. *Texas Republican*, April 26, 1862.
30. June 20, 1862.
31. *Savannah Republican*, March 18, 1862.
32. February 13, 1862.
33. April 9, 1862.
34. *Houston Tri-Weekly Telegraph*, April 16, 1862.
35. *Journal of Congress*, V, 280.
36. Matthews, *Public Laws*, 51, 52.
37. *Journal of Congress*, V, 299.
38. *Richmond Daily Enquirer*, August 23, 1862.
39. "Proceedings of Congress," XLV, 204-07.
40. *Richmond Daily Enquirer*, August 25, 1862.

Notes 253

41. For the debate on extending conscription see "Proceedings of Congress," XLVI, 27-166.
42. *Journal of Congress,* V, 336, 337, 344.
43. *Richmond Daily Examiner,* September 4, 1862. The *Examiner* added that the Committee seemed "to have had the fear of Governor Brown before their eyes. . . ."
44. *Journal of Congress,* V, 344, 345, 400, 401. The delegations of Virginia, North Carolina, South Carolina, Alabama, Mississippi, Louisiana, and Arkansas had half or more of their members opposing the Committee bill and favoring additional rights of raising troops being left to the states.
45. Estill, "Diary of a Confederate Congressman, 1862-1863," *loc. cit.,* XXXVIII, 281.
46. *Richmond Daily Examiner,* September 4, 1862; *Richmond Daily Enquirer,* September 2, 1862; *Journal of Congress,* II, 260, 261. The short Senate debate was mainly constitutional. Hill argued that the "national life was at stake." Yancey denied that there was a "national life," and said that conscription was entirely a state matter. "Proceedings of Congress," XLVI, 32-35. Oldham said that not only was it unconstitutional but "the manner in which it is attempted to be exercised, is in conflict with the whole theory . . . of our federative system of government." *Speech upon the Bill to amend the conscript Laws, Made in the Senate, September 4, 1862.*
47. *Journal of Congress,* V, 443. The Secretary of War estimated that extending the draft to 40 would add 145,000 men to the army and recommended that only these be called at first. Davis complied. G. W. Randolph to Jefferson Davis, August 20, 1862, *Official Records,* Ser. IV, Vol. I, 132.
48. Matthews, *Public Laws,* 61, 62. Governor Joseph E. Brown of Georgia immediately began insisting that the President use the latter device. Louise B. Hill, *Joseph E. Brown and the Confederacy* (Chapel Hill, 1939), 84.
49. Senator Brown avowed that every man "who could put a squirrel skin in a sardine box and cover it with a piece of bark" claimed to be a tanner. *Richmond Daily Enquirer,* September 4, 1862.
50. Postmaster General Reagan advised a congressman that "men above middle age cannot be learned to be experts in the rapid manipulation of letters, & passing through their hands. . . ." Reagan to William P. Chilton, September 25, 1862, Post Office Letter Book, 1861-1862, Pickett Papers.
51. "Proceedings of Congress," XLVI, 31.
52. *Richmond Daily Enquirer,* September 15, 1862.
53. "Proceedings of Congress," XLVI, 64.
54. *Journal of Congress,* II, 294, 310, 311.
55. Matthews, *Public Laws,* 77-79.

CHAPTER VI

1. George W. Randolph to Jefferson Davis, March 12, 1862, *Official Records,* Ser. IV, Vol. II, 45.
2. Matthews, *Public Laws,* 70.
3. *Ibid.,* 74, 75, 90.
4. "Proceedings of Congress," XLV, 153.
5. Matthews, *Public Laws,* 48.
6. *Report of the Secretary of War, November 26, 1863.*
7. Brigadier-General Thomas D. Rosser to R. E. Lee, January 11, 1864, *Official Records,* Ser. I, Vol. XXXIII, 1082.
8. Matthews, *Public Laws,* 302.
9. Thomas H. Watts to George W. Randolph, May 3, 1862, Opinion Book of the Confederate Attorneys-General, 1861-1865, New York Public Library.
10. Judah P. Benjamin to Robert Bunch, May 24, 1862, Department of State Extracts from Letter Books,

March, 1861-January 15, 1864, Pickett Papers.
11. "Proceedings of Congress," XLVII, 121, 122; *Journal of Congress*, III, 321; *ibid.*, VI, 258.
12. "Proceedings of Congress," XLVII, 120.
13. *Richmond Daily Enquirer*, January 14, 1863.
14. January 6, 1863.
15. For the various legal problems resulting from conscription and exemption see the following: Edward Felgar, "The Civil War in Texas" (unpublished dissertation in the University of Texas Library, 1938); Sidney D. Brumer, "The Judicial Interpretation of the Confederate Constitution," *Studies in Southern History and Politics* (New York, 1914); Moore, *Conscription and Conflict;* Owsley, *State Rights in the Confederacy;* Frank L. Owsley, "Local Defense and the Overthrow of the Confederacy: A Study in State Rights," *Mississippi Valley Historical Review*, XI (1924-1925), 490-525.
16. *Richmond Daily Enquirer*, August 23, 1862.
17. "Proceedings of Congress," XLVIII, 188, 189.
18. In the House, Virginia, North Carolina, South Carolina, Texas, and Tennessee were overwhelmingly for retaining substitution, with enough states divided to enable them to defeat the Senate bills.
19. *Report of the Secretary of War, November 26, 1863.* He stated that repealing substitution would add 50,000 men to the army.
20. *Laws of Mississippi* (1863), 229; John B. Jones, *A Rebel War Clerk's Diary at the Confederate States Capital,* ed. Howard Swiggett (New York, 1935), II, 123. Hereafter cited as Jones, *Rebel War Clerk's Diary.*
21. Matthews, *Public Laws*, 172. Questions raised during debate were whether to allow substitutes for farmers and skilled workers and whether the government was obligated to return to the principal the price of his substitute. Both were brushed aside.
22. *Communication from the Secretary of War, December 17, 1863, relative to Exemptions.*
23. *A Bill to be entitled "An Act to amend the law in relation to substitution." December 21, 1863.* Robert B. Hilton of the Committee explained that the evil was in abuses, not the practice of substitution, and that the War Department was to blame for these abuses. Under the Committee bill these abuses would be remedied while those principals necessary to the home front would be exempt. *Richmond Daily Enquirer*, December 23, 1863.
24. Matthews, *Public Laws*, 172. Senators Johnson and Orr opposed it only on constitutional grounds. For the final vote see *Journal of Congress*, III, 561, and VI, 499.
25. Orr to James H. Hammond, January 3, 1864, Hammond Papers.
26. Evan G. Richards to Clement C. Clay, February 19, 1863, Clay Papers.
27. *Journal of Congress*, VI, 19.
28. Reuben Davis, *Recollections of Mississippi and Mississippians* (Boston, 1889), 434.
29. *Richmond Daily Examiner*, February 18, 1863.
30. "Proceedings of Congress," XLVII, 160; *Richmond Daily Enquirer*, February 3, 1863.
31. "Proceedings of Congress," XLVII, 174.
32. For the report of the conference committee, see *Journal of Congress*, III, 299, 300.
33. Matthews, *Public Laws*, 158.
34. Reagan to the President, March 11, 1863, Post Office Letter Book, 1861-1863, Pickett Papers.
35. Matthews, *Public Laws*, 105.
36. Jones, *Rebel War Clerk's Diary*, I, 243.
37. James A. Seddon to W. P. Miles, February 9, 1863, *Official Records,* Ser. IV, Vol. II, 44.
38. The Alabama Legislature complained of Pillow's activities, but

the Senate Military Committee was "deeply impressed" with his "vigor and usefulness" and asked to be discharged of the matter. *Richmond Daily Examiner*, January 15, 1864.
39. Graham to George W. Randolph, November 17, 1862, War Department Letters Received, Confederate Archives.
40. Davidson to Zebulon B. Vance, May 5, 1863, Vance Papers.
41. May 5, 1863.
42. Matthews, *Public Laws*, 75, 76.
43. Brown refused to let the act be enforced until the Georgia Supreme Court and Legislature had decided its legality; he then did all possible to hamper it by means of exemptions, interference, and direct disobedience. Hill, *Joseph E. Brown*, 88.
44. Matthews, *Public Laws*, 77.
45. *Ibid.*, 158.
46. *Acts of Georgia* (1863), 104.
47. As early as January 3, 1863, Seddon wished Congress to abolish class exemptions and let the President maintain production entirely through details. Seddon to the President, January 31, 1863, *Official Records*, Ser. IV, Vol. II, 997.

CHAPTER VII

1. *Montgomery Weekly Advertiser*, January 6, 1864.
2. *Journal of Congress*, III, 446. At this time Virginia, North Carolina, South Carolina, and Georgia contained 64,830 exempt men. Communication from the Secretary of War. December 17, 1863.
3. *Report of the Secretary of War, November 26, 1863.*
4. *Richmond Daily Examiner*, December 12, 1863.
5. *State of the Country. Speech delivered in the Confederate Senate, December 24, 1863.*
6. *A Bill to Organize Forces to Serve during the War. December 14, 1863.*
7. *Journal of Congress*, VI, 594.
8. *Richmond Daily Enquirer*, January 7, 1864.
9. *Journal of Congress*, III, 554, 572, 573. The number of overseers exempt by this law was slightly over 4,000. John C. Schwab, *The Confederate States of America, 1861-1865* (New York, 1901), 198.
10. *Journal of Congress*, VI, 712-14, 728, 729. Barksdale had placed Davis's program before the House in an amendment to give the President complete powers of details, but it was decisively defeated. *Ibid.*, 728, 729.
11. Sparrow to Davis, February 12, 1864, Jones, *Autograph Letters*.
12. *Journal of Congress*, III, 739.
13. Matthews, *Public Laws*, 211-15.
14. Preston to James A. Seddon, November 23, 1863, *Official Records*, Ser. IV, Vol. III, 850.
15. *Laws of North Carolina* (1864), 24.
16. *Journal of Congress*, VII, 188.
17. Moore, *Conscription and Conflict*, 90.
18. Lee to Davis, September 2, 1864, Rowland, *Jefferson Davis*, VI, 327.
19. *Official Records*, Ser. IV, Vol. III, 735, 736, 683, 685.
20. *Report of the Secretary of War, November 3, 1864;* Preston to W. P. Miles, November 5, 1864, Rowland, *Jefferson Davis*, VI, 379-83.
21. *Journal of Congress*, IV, 256, 257.
22. Oldham, *Memoirs*, 43.
23. *Journal of Congress*, VII, 289.
24. *Richmond Daily Examiner*, November 16 and 26, 1864.
25. *Journal of Congress*, IV, 689.
26. *Ibid.*, VII, 253.
27. Jefferson Davis to the House of Representatives, February 21, 1865, *Official Records*, Ser. IV, Vol. III, 1099-1110.
28. Report of the Committee on Military Affairs, March 16, 1865, *Official Records*, Ser. IV, Vol. III, 1145.
29. For the votes of Clark's and Henry's bills see *Journal of Congress*, IV, 720, and VII, 776.
30. Ramsdell, *Laws*, 4, 23, 24.

31. November 11, 1864.
32. Graham to David L. Swain, November 26, 1864, Graham Papers, Raleigh.
33. They insisted that the nation's production was their only concern. *Richmond Daily Examiner*, January 14, 1865; *Richmond Daily Enquirer*, January 16, 1865.
34. *Journal of Congress*, VII, 460, 487. The four states referred to were North Carolina, South Carolina, Georgia, and Alabama.
35. Ramsdell, *Laws*, 140, 141.
36. *Journal of Congress*, VII, 749, 750.
37. Ramsdell, *Laws*, 146.
38. *Ibid.*, 86-88.
39. A. T. Bledsoe to W. S. Turner, August 2, 1861, *Official Records*, Ser. IV, Vol. I, 529.
40. Jefferson Davis to General W. H. Y. Walker, January 13, 1864, *ibid.*, Ser. I, Vol. LII, pt. 2, 596. For a thorough discussion see Thomas R. Hay, "The South and the Arming of the Slaves," *Mississippi Valley Historical Review*, VI (1919-1920), 34-73.
41. *Yorkville Enquirer*, September 9, 1863.
42. *Houston Tri-Weekly Telegraph*, February 11, 1864.
43. *Richmond Daily Enquirer*, October 6 and 18, November 1, 1864; *Montgomery Daily Mail*, November 9, 1864.
44. In Mississippi Historical Society, *Publications*, I, 556.
45. *Report of the Secretary of War, November 1, 1864.*
46. *Journal of Congress*, VII, 255.
47. *Ibid.*, IV, 407.
48. Thomas L. Snead to General Sterling Price, January 10, 1865, *Official Records*, Ser. I, Vol. XLVIII, pt. 1, 1321.
49. *Ibid.*
50. Thomas S. Gholson of Virginia maintained that the "Confederate government has not a foot of land upon which to bury a slave, much less to settle him, after he is liberated." *Speech on the Policy of Employing Negro Troops.* . . .
51. *Richmond Daily Examiner*, February 7, 1865.
52. *Hillsboro Recorder*, February 8, 1865. The North Carolina Legislature had just passed a resolution against arming the slaves. *Laws of North Carolina* (1864-1865), 33.
53. Oldham, Memoirs, 44; *Richmond Daily Examiner*, February 11, 1865; *A Bill to increase the military forces of the Confederacy. February 10, 1865.*
54. Turner to his wife, February 11, 1865, Turner Papers, University of North Carolina.
55. Five members submitted a minority report opposing the arming of slaves under any circumstances. *Minority Report on the bill to increase the military forces of the Confederacy.* Rogers of Florida wrote a second minority report agreeing to their being armed when all other resources were exhausted. *Mr. Rogers' Minority Report. February 15, 1865.*
56. *Richmond Daily Enquirer*, February 25, 1865.
57. *Journal of Congress*, VII, 612, 613. South Carolina and Florida were divided. It won Georgia and Virginia by a majority of one each.
58. William A. Graham to David L. Swain, February 22, 1865, Graham Papers, Raleigh.
59. *Richmond Daily Enquirer*, March 7, 1865; Oldham, Memoirs, 44, 45; *Journal of Congress*, IV, 585, 670, 671.
60. *A Bill to increase the military forces of the Confederacy, February 10, 1865.*
61. *Richmond Daily Enquirer*, February 25, 1865. For Lee's role here see Nathaniel W. Stephenson, "The Question of Arming the Slaves," *American Historical Review*, XVIII (1912-1913), 295-308.
62. Ramsdell, *Laws*, 118, 119.
63. *Journal of Congress*, IV, 704.
64. *Ibid.*, 726, 727.
65. Matthews, *Statutes*, 223, 241.
66. *Report of the Secretary of the Navy, November 5, 1864; Richmond Daily*

Notes

Enquirer, January 26, 1865; Ramsdell, *Laws*, 19.
67. Matthews, *Statutes*, 100-02, 150.
68. *Wilmington Daily Journal*, September 1, 1862.
69. *Official Records of the Union and Confederate Navies in the War of the Rebellion* (30 vols., Washington, 1894-1922), Ser. II, Vol. II, 124, 125. Hereafter cited as *Naval Records*.
70. *An Act to establish a volunteer navy. February 12, 1862.*
71. Matthews, *Public Laws*, 111-13.
72. *Ibid.*, 185.

CHAPTER VIII

1. For a more detailed account see John T. Scharf, *History of the Confederate States Navy from Its Organization to the Surrender of Its Last Vessel* (Albany, 1894), 27.
2. General Beauregard, a personal friend of Chairman of the Military Committee W. P. Miles, had the most influence.
3. For a thorough treatment of Confederate-state military controversies see Owsley, *State Rights in the Confederacy*, passim.
4. Matthews, *Public Acts*, 32, 52.
5. Randolph to Jefferson Davis, August 12, 1862, *Official Records*, Ser. IV, Vol. II, 45, 46.
6. *Journal of Congress*, II, 228.
7. "Proceedings of Congress," XLVI, 249.
8. Matthews, *Public Laws*, 85-87.
9. Seddon to Jefferson Davis, January 3, 1863, *Official Records*, Ser. IV, Vol. II, 1001.
10. Matthews, *Public Laws*, 232, 260.
11. *Richmond Daily Examiner*, January 6, 1863.
12. Ramsdell, *Laws*, 92, 93.
13. Dodd, *Jefferson Davis*, 282. See Robinson, *Justice in Grey* for a thorough discussion of the question of Confederate courts-martial.
14. Matthews, *Public Laws*, 71, 72.
15. Matthews, *Public Laws*, 157, 193, 229, 230.
16. *Richmond Daily Examiner*, September 3, 1862.
17. Randolph to Jefferson Davis, August 12, 1863, *Official Records*, Ser. IV, Vol. II, 44, 45.
18. Matthews, *Public Laws*, 62.
19. *Report of the Secretary of War, November 26, 1863.*
20. *Journal of Congress*, III, 447.
21. Matthews, *Public Laws*, 203, 232.
22. Ramsdell, *Laws*, 49-52.
23. *Journal of Congress*, II, 263; "Proceedings of Congress," XLVI, 202-04.
24. *Journal of Congress*, V, 107, 108.
25. A. L. Hull (ed.), "Thomas Reade Rootes Cobb, Extracts from Letters to His Wife, February 3, 1861-December 10, 1862," Southern Historical Society, *Papers*, XXVIII (1900), 291.
26. Ramsdell, *Laws*, 22, 23.
27. *Journal of Congress*, IV, 105-09.
28. Matthews, *Public Laws*, 281, 282.
29. *Ibid.*, 58.
30. *Ibid.*, 211.
31. *Ibid.*, 30, 221; Matthews, *Statutes*, 223.
32. Ramsdell, *Laws*, 146, 147.
33. *Journal of Congress*, I, 569.
34. *Ibid.*, 744, 745.
35. John B. Downing to Thomas D. McDowell, September 27, 1862, McDowell Papers. For a thorough history of Confederate medical problems see Horace H. Cunningham, *Doctors in Gray* (Baton Rouge, 1958).
36. *Official Records*, Ser. IV, Vol. I, 884.
37. *Journal of Congress*, V, 557, 558.
38. Matthews, *Public Laws*, 63, 64, 153, 154.
39. Harrison Trexler, "The Opposition of Planters to the Employment of Slaves as Laborers by the Confederacy," *Mississippi Valley Historical Review*, XXVII (1940-1941), 213, 216, 217.
40. Matthews, *Public Laws*, 48, 49, 89, 90, 104.

41. *Journal of Congress*, VI, 507.
42. *Report of the Secretary of War, November 26, 1863.*
43. Matthews, *Public Laws*, 235, 236. The House Military Committee estimated that 40,000 free Negroes could be raised under this law without diminishing the nation's production. *Richmond Daily Examiner*, January 25, 1864.
44. *Journal of Congress*, VII, 254, 255.
45. The Virginia delegation repeatedly requested that impressment of slaves be suspended in their state until a later date, or at least in Virginia districts raising provisions. The War Department insisted that the state could easily sacrifice 20% of its slaves.
46. Ramsdell, *Laws*, 61-64.
47. January 31, 1862.
48. Cooper to W. P. Miles, November 28, 1861, *Official Records*, Ser. IV, Vol. I, 757, 758.
49. "Proceedings of Congress," XLIX, 249.
50. Matthews, *Public Laws*, 262.
51. Matthews, *Public Laws*, 69, 193.
52. *Ibid.*, 230; Matthews, *Statutes*, 154.
53. Quoted in Douglas S. Freeman, *R. E. Lee* (New York, 1934-1936), III, 538.
54. Matthews, *Statutes*, 154; Matthews, *Public Laws*, 54.
55. *Official Records*, Ser. II, Vol. V, 919-24.
56. *Ibid.*, Ser. II, Vol. VIII, 337-42.
57. Matthews, *Public Laws*, 106, 109, 174.
58. *Communication from the Secretary of War, February 2, 1863,* relating to flogging and branding; Matthews, *Public Laws*, 106.
59. Matthews, *Public Laws*, 47, 48.
60. Thomas J. Foster of Alabama disliked this tolerance. He thought that the "great victory" of Shiloh was "mainly attributable to the movement made by our President in suppressing ardent spirits." "Proceedings of Congress," XLV, 97.
61. *Journal of Congress*, I, 496, 497.
62. Matthews, *Statutes*, 99, 210, 229; Matthews, *Public Laws*, 42, 45.

CHAPTER IX
Part I

1. Clement C. Clay to Virginia Clay, March 12, 1863, Clay Papers.
2. *Merchants and Millers of Petersburg, Va. to the Senate and the House of Representatives, March 3, 1863.*
3. Edward C. Betts to Clement C. Clay, January 23, 1863, Clay Papers.
4. "Proceedings of Congress," XLVII, 127.
5. *Journal of Congress*, II, 441, 442, 482.
6. James A. Seddon to Jefferson Davis, January 3, 1863, *Official Records*, Ser. IV, Vol. II, 292.
7. "Proceedings of Congress," XLVIII, 245.
8. *Ibid.*, 204.
9. *Acts of Virginia, Adjourned Session* (1863), 123, 124; *Richmond Daily Enquirer*, February 28, 1863.
10. "Proceedings of Congress," XLVIII, 259.
11. *Journal of Congress*, III, 147, 148.
12. Matthews, *Public Laws*, 102-04.
13. Robert Toombs to Alexander H. Stephens, May 17, 1862, Phillips, *Correspondence of Toombs, Stephens, and Cobb*, 595.
14. *Richmond Daily Enquirer*, March 26, 1863; *Houston Tri-Weekly Telegraph*, July 20, 1863.
15. Matthews, *Public Laws*, 127.
16. *Richmond Daily Enquirer*, August 2, 1864.
17. *Acts of Georgia* (1863), 102.
18. *Richmond Daily Enquirer*, December 16, 1863.
19. Lucius B. Northrop to the Office of Chief Commissary of Subsistence, January 16, 1864, *Official Records*, Ser. I, Vol. XXXV, pt. 1, 522.

20. The Texas Legislature asked its congressmen to prevent the illegal impressment of beef for export to Mexico. *Laws of Texas* (1865), 23.
21. *Correspondence Between the President, War Department and Governor T. O. Moore, Relating to the Defenses of New Orleans*, 99.
22. Jones, *Rebel War Clerk's Diary*, II, 10.
23. *Richmond Daily Examiner*, December 16, 1863. For significant House action, see *Journal of Congress*, VI, 534, 552, 553.
24. The Senate Judiciary Committee had the audacity to claim that the producers had always been willing to accept schedule prices. *Richmond Daily Examiner*, January 19, 1864.
25. Matthews, *Public Laws*, 192, 193.
26. *Ibid.*, 196, 197.
27. *Journal of Congress*, VII, 56, 57.
28. Report of the Secretary of War, March 28, 1864, *Official Records*, Ser. IV, Vol. III, 338.
29. *Communication from the Secretary of the Treasury recommending certain changes in the impressment laws. May 20, 1864.*
30. *A Bill providing supplies for the army and prescribing methods of impressment.*
31. *Journal of Congress*, VII, 205.
32. Matthews, *Public Laws*, 271, 272.
33. *A Bill to provide supplies for the army and to prescribe a mode of making impressments.*
34. Ramsdell, *Laws*, 151, 152. The commissioners retained the right to fix schedules for goods impressed from men exempt from army duty for the purpose of raising provisions.
35. *Richmond Daily Enquirer*, January 28, 1865.
36. Ramsdell, *Laws*, 153. Senator Hill said that the "miserable executive officers of this government could not take in one idea." They failed to see that the impressment law must be protective, not oppressive. The fault lay in the agents, not in the law. *Richmond Daily Enquirer*, January 28, 1865.

PART 2

WAR MATERIEL

37. Matthews, *Statutes*, 43.
38. *Ibid.*, 45.
39. *Ibid.*, 282.
40. *Ibid.*, 26.
41. Ramsdell, *Laws*, 46-48.
42. Matthews, *Statutes*, 28, 173.
43. Judah P. Benjamin to Jefferson Davis, March 12, 1862, *Official Records*, Ser. IV, Vol. I, 987, 988.
44. Matthews, *Public Laws*, 27, 28, 33, 114.
45. *Report of the Secretary of War, November 26, 1863.*
46. For a good discussion see Charles W. Ramsdell, "The Control of Manufacturing by the Confederate Government," *Mississippi Valley Historical Review*, VIII (1921-1922), 239ff.
47. Ramsdell, *Laws*, 165, 167.
48. Stephen R. Mallory to Charles M. Conrad, May 10, 1861, *Naval Records*, Ser. II, Vol. II, 69.
49. Ramsdell, *Laws*, 162, 163.
50. Matthews, *Statutes*, 105-07.
51. *Journal of Congress*, I, 305.
52. *Ibid.*, 470; Matthews, *Statutes*, 258, 259.
53. *Journal of Congress*, I, 782. Senator Oldham maintained that lobbyists had swung the majority narrowly in support of the bill. "Proceedings of Congress," XLV, 159.
54. Ramsdell, *Laws*, 101.
55. *Journal of Congress*, I, 379; *Report of the Committee on Military Affairs on the bill authorizing the President to regulate and take control of railroads in certain cases. January 15, 1862.*
56. A. C. Myers to William P. Chilton, October 3, 1862, *Official Records*, Ser. IV, Vol. II, 108.

57. "Proceedings of Congress," XLVII, 72.
58. *A Bill to provide for the safe and expeditious transportation of troops and munitions of war by railroad.* January 27, 1863.
59. "Proceedings of Congress," XLIX, 174-77.
60. Ramsdell, *Laws*, 60, 61.
61. E. Merton Coulter, "The Movement for Agricultural Reorganization in the Cotton South During the Civil War," *North Carolina Historical Review*, IV (1927), 27, 28.
62. "Proceedings of Congress," XLIV, 147-49, 163-71.
63. Matthews, *Public Laws*, 166, 167.
64. For this debate see "Proceedings of Congress," XLIV, 99-103.
65. Matthews, *Public Laws*, 2.
66. August 22, 1862.
67. *Richmond Daily Examiner*, December 30, 1863.
68. Ramsdell, *Laws*, 80, 81.
69. Smith, *Bill Arp*, 33.
70. Letter to the Senators and Representatives from Florida, August 18, 1862, Milton Letter Book, Milton Papers.
71. *Journal of Congress*, VII, 320, 321.
72. Matthews, *Public Laws*, 78.
73. *Report of the Committee on Claims.* n.d.
74. Matthews, *Statutes*, 197, 199.
75. *A Bill to be entitled An Act to establish the court for the investigation of claims against the Government of the Confederate States of America. January 20, 1863.* See Robinson, *Justice in Grey*, 501, 502, for an analysis of the claims problem.
76. *Richmond Daily Enquirer*, March 11, 1863.
77. *Letter of the Secretary of the Treasury submitting the report of the Auditor, September 5, 1863.*
78. *Report of the Committee on Claims, February 9, 1864.*
79. Matthews, *Statutes*, 152, 153, 180; Matthews, *Public Laws*, 46.
80. Matthews, *Public Laws*, 181, 182.
81. *Laws of Texas* (1863), 37.
82. Oldham, Memoirs, 357.
83. Felgar, "The Civil War in Texas," 257, 258, 273.
84. Matthews, *Public Laws*, 50, 105, 154.
85. For this controversy with the States see Owsley, *State Rights in the Confederacy*, 110-39.
86. Matthews, *Public Laws*, 179-83.
87. *A Bill to be entitled An Act to establish a Bureau of Foreign Supplies. January 28, 1864; Journal of Congress*, III, 799, 800; *ibid.*, IV, 231.
88. Frank Moore (comp.), *The Rebellion Record: A Diary of American Events....* (New York, 1861-1863), VIII, 596, 597.
89. *Journal of Congress*, VII, 13.
90. James D. Richardson (ed.), *A Compilation of the Messages and Papers of the Confederacy ...* (Nashville, 1906), I, 467, 468. For the house vote see *Journal of Congress*, VII, 206.
91. *Official Records*, Ser. I, Vol. XLII, pt. 3, 1149, 1150.
92. *Journal of Congress*, VII, 368-71.
93. *Ibid.*, 738.

CHAPTER X

1. *Journal of Congress*, VII, 444.
2. *Charleston Mercury*, September 28, 1861.
3. Davis, *Recollections*, 245.
4. Rembert W. Patrick, *Jefferson Davis and His Cabinet* (Baton Rouge, 1944), 38.
5. *Journal of Congress*, V, 15.
6. *Richmond Daily Enquirer*, February 21, 1862.
7. *Journal of Congress*, V, 367, 371.
8. Johnston to Wigfall, February 14, 1863, Wigfall Papers.
9. *Report of the Roanoke Island Investigating Committee.* For the Secretary of War's role see Robert D. Meade, *Judah P. Benjamin, Confederate Statesman* (New York, 1943), 220-22.
10. *Report of the Special Committee on*

the Recent Military Disasters at Forts Henry and Donelson, and the Evacuation of Nashville; Richmond Daily Enquirer, April 18, 1862.
11. Richmond Daily Enquirer, February 3, 1863.
12. Proceedings of the Court of Inquiry upon the fall of New Orleans, Official Records, Ser. I, Vol. VI, 554.
13. Richmond Daily Enquirer, April 9, 1864.
14. Richmond Daily Examiner, November 26, 1864.
15. Thomas C. Reynolds to Waldo P. Johnson, August 27, 1863, Reynolds Private Letter Book II, 1863-1864, Pickett Papers.
16. Richmond Daily Examiner, June 12, 1864.
17. Jefferson Davis to Governor John J. Pettus and others, June 20, 1863, Official Records, Ser. I, Vol. LII, pt. 2, 498.
18. Miles to Seddon, May 11, 1863, ibid., Ser. I, Vol. XIV, 933.
19. Jones, Rebel War Clerk's Diary, II, 151.
20. Journal of Congress, V, 303, 322; Richmond Daily Examiner, August 29, 1862.
21. Richmond Daily Examiner, February 18, 1864.
22. Patrick, Jefferson Davis and His Cabinet, 104, 105.
23. Cobb to his wife, May 3, 1861, Hull, "Correspondence of Thomas Reade Rootes Cobb, 1860-1862," loc. cit., 318.
24. Henry S. Foote, War of the Rebellion: or Scylla and Charybdis (New York, 1866), 365.
25. Official Records, Ser. IV, Vol. I, 883-87.
26. Report of the Committee on the Quartermaster and Commissary Departments on the case of Major Frank Ruffin; Matthews, Public Laws, 159, 160.
27. Journal of Congress, IV, 689, 690.
28. Richmond Daily Examiner, January 17, 1862; Rowland, Jefferson Davis, V, 120, 121. For the best information on Beauregard see T. Harry Williams, P. G. T. Beauregard (Baton Rouge, 1954), 81-99.
29. Quoted in Alfred Roman, The Military Operations of General Beauregard . . . (New York, 1884), 173.
30. Review of Certain Remarks made by the President when requested to restore General Beauregard to the Command of Department No. 2, by C. J. Villere.
31. Richmond Daily Examiner, December 10, 1863; Foote, War of the Rebellion, 363, 364.
32. Davis, Rise and Fall of the Confederate Government, II, 38.
33. Edmund S. Dargan to the War Department, August 14, 1863, War Department Letter Books, IX, 29, Confederate Archives.
34. Richmond Daily Enquirer, January 10, 1865.
35. Boteler to James A. Seddon, February 6, 1863, Official Records, Ser. I, Vol. LI, pt. 2, 677.
36. Jefferson Davis to W. P. Harris, December 13, 1861, Rowland, Jefferson Davis, V, 179.
37. Missouri Delegation to General Sterling Price, December 13, 1861, Official Records, Ser. I, Vol. LIII, 761, 762.
38. Ibid; Charleston Mercury, December 4, 1861.

CHAPTER XI

1. Matthews, Public Laws, 1.
2. Jones, Rebel War Clerk's Diary, I, 120.
3. Matthews, Public Laws, 40.
4. July 14, 1863.
5. April 17, 1863.
6. "Proceedings of Congress," XLV, 19.
7. Henry S. Foote, Casket of Reminiscences (Washington, 1874), 147.
8. Journal of Congress, V, 318.
9. Ibid., II, 237, 271, 272.
10. "Proceedings of Congress," XLVII, 82.
11. Ibid., XLV, 244.

12. *Richmond Daily Enquirer,* August 26, 1862.
13. "Proceedings of Congress," XLVII, 82, 83.
14. *Journal of Congress,* V, 373-77. The Senate asked Davis the status of suspension; on October 8 he admitted that sometimes it had been interpreted as martial law, but now the time limitation of suspension had expired and nowhere in the Confederacy did either exist. *Ibid.,* II, 397, 445.
15. For this resolution see *Ibid.,* II, 393, 394, 444.
16. *Richmond Daily Enquirer,* September 18, 1862.
17. "Proceedings of Congress," XLVI, 187, 188; Matthews, *Public Laws,* 84.
18. Vance to the North Carolina General Assembly, November 17, 1862, *Official Records,* Ser. IV, Vol. II, 188.
19. April 20, 1863.
20. For background information see the following: Owsley, *State Rights in the Confederacy;* Moore, *Conscription and Conflict;* Brumer, "The Judicial Interpretation of the Confederate Constitution," *loc. cit.;* Robinson, *Justice in Grey.*
21. "Proceedings of Congress," XLIX, 141.
22. *Journal of Congress,* VI, 516. David Funsten of Virginia favored suspension.
23. *Ibid.,* III, 669-71.
24. Diary of Robert B. Hilton, February 3, 1863, University of Florida.
25. *Journal of Congress,* III, 712; *ibid.,* VI, 764.
26. Matthews, *Public Laws,* 187-89.
27. February 19, 1864.
28. May 6, 1864.
29. *Laws of Mississippi* (1864), 98.
30. *Acts of Georgia* (1864), 154.
31. *Official Records,* Ser. IV, Vol. III, 736.
32. "Gartrell . . . boasts of his authorship of the bill and puts its necessity on the state of things in N. Carolina." Joseph E. Brown to Alexander H. Stephens, March 4, 1864, Phillips, *Correspondence of Toombs, Stephens, and Cobb,* 634.
33. *Richmond Daily Enquirer,* May 13, 1864.
34. *Journal of Congress,* VII, 54, 58, 81.
35. *Minority Report of the Committee on the Judiciary on the Suspension of the writ of Habeas Corpus by the act of February 15, 1864.* May 28, 1864.
36. Resolution by James T. Leach. May 27, 1864.
37. *Journal of Congress,* VII, 266, 267; *Charleston Mercury,* November 16, 1864.
38. Stephens said that the Committee at first was divided, but that after some indecision Chairman Rives shifted his vote in favor of suspension. Johnston and Browne, *Life of Stephens,* 483.
39. *Journal of Congress,* VII, 329-50, *passim.*
40. *Ibid.,* IV, 364.
41. *Ibid.,* 705.
42. *Ibid.,* 719-21; *Richmond Daily Examiner,* March 18, 1865.

CHAPTER XII

1. Matthews, *Statutes,* 91, 92.
2. *Ibid.,* 100.
3. *Ibid.,* 174, 175.
4. *Journal of Congress,* I, 758, 759.
5. Matthews, *Statutes,* 28, 36-38.
6. See the particulars in E. Merton Coulter, "Effects of Secession upon the Commerce of the Mississippi Valley," *Mississippi Valley Historical Review,* III (1916-1917), 280.
7. *Journal of Congress,* V, 404-07.
8. Several members from the Valley worked for a political alliance with any state outside New England that would secede. Jones, *Rebel War Clerk's Diary,* I, 247, 248; *Knoxville Daily Register,* February 3, 1863.
9. *Richmond Daily Enquirer,* February 11, 1863.
10. *Journal of Congress,* VI, 450.

11. Chesnut, *Diary*, 218.
12. Matthews, *Statutes*, 281. See pp. 75, 76 for more on this subject.
13. *Journal of Congress*, I, 273; Matthews, *Statutes*, 198.
14. *Richmond Daily Examiner*, July 25, 1862.
15. Beauregard to William P. Miles, October 13, 1862, *Official Records*, Ser. II, Vol. IV, 916.
16. "Proceedings of Congress," XLVII, 31.
17. *Journal of Congress*, V, 546, 547, 551, 565.
18. *Ibid.*, VI, 17.
19. *Richmond Daily Enquirer*, May 16, 1863; Matthews, *Public Laws*, 167, 168.
20. Ramsdell, *Laws*, 36.
21. *Journal of Congress*, I, 49.
22. Quoted in John W. DuBose, *The Life and Times of William Lowndes Yancey* (New York, 1942), II, 600.
23. *Journal of Congress*, I, 252, 253; Laura A. White, *Robert Barnwell Rhett*, 253.
24. *Atlanta Southern Confederacy*, July 18, 1861.
25. For a thorough study of Confederate diplomacy see Frank L. Owsley, *King Cotton Diplomacy* (Chicago, 1931).
26. Matthews, *Statutes*, 98, 99.
27. *Ibid.*, 152, 153. In August it extended this to tobacco, sugar, rice, molasses, syrup, and naval stores. *Ibid.*, 170.
28. *Ibid.*, 213.
29. William C. Rives wrote that they had been confirmed "unanimously, though they do not seem altogether to satisfy the judgments of the members of Congress. But they are the logical result of the program." Rives to his wife, August 29, 1861, Rives Papers.
30. *Journal of Congress*, II, 192, 193.
31. *Richmond Daily Examiner*, August 8, 1862.
32. *Richmond Daily Enquirer*, March 31, 1862.
33. *Richmond Daily Examiner*, January 20, 1863.
34. *Richmond Daily Enquirer*, February 7, 1863.
35. Judah P. Benjamin to Jefferson Davis, April 16, 1863, Report Book Vol. I, State Department Book no. 105, Pickett Papers.
36. *Journal of Congress*, III, 348.
37. Milledge L. Bonham, *The British Consuls in the Confederacy* (New York, 1911), 18.
38. *Journal of Congress*, V, 424. A minority report said that the President was handling the matter properly and should not be bothered. *Miority Report of the Committee on Foreign Affairs*. n.d.
39. Benjamin to A. Fullarton, October 8, 1863, Domestic Letters, State Department Book no. 106, Pickett Papers.
40. Benjamin to Davis, October 8, 1863, *ibid.*
41. To one such communication Congress hastened to deny that "they had no intention of trenching upon the President's powers...," *Journal of Congress*, V, 493.

CHAPTER XIII

1. *Montgomery Advertiser*, August 12, 1862.
2. *Journal of Congress*, V, 385, 386. Foote admitted that the "weak and vacillating" Lincoln would probably refuse the offer, but said that the South would have exonerated itself before the world. "Proceedings of Congress," XLVI, 161.
3. *Raleigh Weekly Standard*, October 12, 1864.
4. James Phelan to Jefferson Davis, December 9, 1862, *Official Records*, Ser. I, Vol. XVI, pt. 2, 789.
5. Reminiscences of Jehu A. Orr. Typed copy in the Department of Archives and History, Jackson, Mississippi.

6. *Richmond Daily Enquirer*, February 18, 1863.
7. *Raleigh Weekly Standard*, July 22, 1863.
8. *Ibid.*, December 30, 1863. Holden wrote that the "only power that can close the war is the power that made it, that of the sovereign States."
9. Zebulon B. Vance to William A. Graham, January 1, 1864, Graham Papers, Raleigh.
10. Zebulon B. Vance to Edward J. Hale, December 30, 1863, Hale Papers.
11. Jefferson Davis to Zebulon B. Vance, January 8, 1864, *Official Records*, Ser. I, Vol. LI, pt. 2, 808.
12. North Carolina Representatives to Zebulon B. Vance, January 25, 1864, Vance's Letter Book, IX, 2, Confederate Archives.
13. Matthews, *Public Laws*, 238, 239.
14. Hiram P. Bell, *Men and Things* (Atlanta, 1907), 100.
15. *Richmond Daily Enquirer*, May 24, 1864.
16. *Ibid.* Leach had intended to offer this resolution the first day of the session, but Josiah Turner persuaded him to delay until after the campaign from the Wilderness to Cold Harbor, the latter of which was a Confederate victory. Turner to his wife, May 7, 1864, Turner Papers, University of North Carolina.
17. *Journal of Congress*, VII, 84, 85.
18. Reminiscences of Orr, 5. Orr's account of the action within Congress differs at times from the account in the *Journal of Congress*, but only in detail.
19. Matthews, *Public Laws*, 286-88.
20. *Raleigh Weekly Standard*, October 12, 1864.
21. October 20, 1864.
22. Quoted in *Richmond Daily Enquirer*, October 16, 1864.
23. *Journal of Congress*, VII, 526.
24. Jones, *Rebel War Clerk's Diary*, II, 287.
25. Chesnut, *Diary*, 448.
26. Foote of Tennessee proposed a convention of the Southern states to advise the Confederate government. *Journal of Congress*, VII, 312, 313; Turner of North Carolina would ask the President to appoint 13 commissioners to request a peace conference with the United States. *Ibid.*, 360; McMullen of Virginia attempted to avoid embarrassing the Lincoln administration by proposing to hold this conference on neutral territory. *Ibid.*, 363; McMullen said that he had information that Grant had signified that any persons appointed by the Confederate government would be received into the United States wherever they might designate. *Richmond Daily Examiner*, December 19, 1864.
27. *Journal of Congress*, VII, 360.
28. Orr of Mississippi stated that originally the Committee majority disliked the resolutions, but that its mind was changed by the fall of Savannah and by the fact that Lee had informed a secret session of Congress that he needed 50,000 more men for the coming spring campaigns. Reminiscences of Orr, 7.
29. Josiah Turner to his wife, January 25, 1865, Josiah Turner Papers, Duke University. For a detailed story of the Blair visit to Richmond and of the subsequent peace negotiations at Hampton Roads, Virginia, see the following: Edward C. Kirkland, *The Peacemakers of 1864* (New York, 1927); Robert M. T. Hunter, "The Peace Commission of 1865," *Southern Historical Society, Papers*, III (1877), 168-76.
30. Bell, *Men and Things*, 100.
31. *Journal of Congress*, VII, 451.
32. Foote, *War of the Rebellion*, 375.
33. *Journal of Congress*, VII, 452.
34. Quoted in Johnston and Browne, *Life of Stephens*, 486.
35. Turner to his wife, January 20, 1865, Turner Papers, University of North Carolina.
36. Graham to his wife, January 24, 1865, Graham Papers, Raleigh.

37. Samuel F. Phillips to David L. Swain, January 31, 1865, David L. Swain Papers, Department of Archives and History, Raleigh, North Carolina.
38. The action of the Senate was not invoked in appointing this commission because the appointment of formal ministers might have been considered inadvisable until the question of recognition was settled in favor of the Confederacy. William A. Graham to David L. Swain, January 28, 1865, Swain Papers.
39. *Journal of Congress*, VII, 545.
40. John Goode, "The Confederate Congress," *The Conservative Review*, IV (1900), 112.
41. *Journal of Congress*, IV, 526.
42. Diary of Stephen R. Mallory, 209. Typed copy in the University of North Carolina. Mallory obviously misjudged Lincoln's steadfastness.
43. *Journal of Congress*, VII, 606, 607.
44. Ramsdell, *Laws*, 134, 135.
45. *Journal of Congress*, VII, 458, 465, 466, 490-92.
46. Josiah Turner to his wife, February 19, 1865, Turner Papers, University of North Carolina.
47. "Letter of Jefferson Davis to J. W. Jones, March 27, 1865," Southern Historical Society, *Papers*, V (1878), 223.

CHAPTER XIV

1. Memminger to John Boston, March 23, 1861, Stephens Papers.
2. Matthews, *Statutes*, 27, 28, 91, 92.
3. Lawrence M. Keitt to James H. Hammond, February 13, 1861, Hammond Papers.
4. Matthews, *Statutes*, 42, 43.
5. From July 20 to November 16, 1861, only $1,311.65 was collected.
6. Matthews, *Statutes*, 54-56.
7. Henry D. Capers, *The Life and Times of C. G. Memminger* (Richmond, 1893), 417-21.
8. *Journal of Congress*, I, 65.
9. James D. B. DeBow to William P. Miles, February 15, 1861, Miles Papers.
10. Matthews, *Statutes*, 28, 69, 164.
11. *Journal of Congress*, I, 120, 121, 242. Mississippi and Georgia wanted higher tariff rates, not free trade.
12. Matthews, *Statutes*, 127-35.
13. February 4, 1862.
14. *Wilmington Daily Journal*, October 25, 1861.
15. *Acts of Georgia* (1861), 138; *Laws of Texas* (1861), 146.
16. *Journal of Congress*, I, 820, 821.
17. "Proceedings of Congress," XLV, 60.
18. *Journal of Congress*, II, 134; *ibid.*, V, 171.
19. Matthews, *Public Laws*, 69, 130, 254, 255.
20. Edward A. Pollard, *Life of Jefferson Davis* . . . (Atlanta, 1869), 173.
21. *Journal of Congress*, I, 186.
22. *Journal of the South Carolina Convention of 1860, 1861 and 1862*, 540.
23. Matthews, *Statutes*, 117, 118. The high rate of interest caused much embarrassment later by establishing 8% as a fair return on investments. Any attempt thereafter to reduce rates provoked howls of anguish from patriotic investors.
24. Capers, *Memminger*, 420, 421.
25. Matthews, *Statutes*, 118.
26. Report of the Secretary of the Treasury, July 24, 1861, Christopher G. Memminger Papers, University of North Carolina.
27. *Richmond Daily Examiner*, August 21, 1861; *Journal of Congress*, I, 334-36, 359.
28. Matthews, *Statutes*, 177-83.
29. *Ibid.*, 151.
30. *Ibid.*, 201-05.
31. Richard C. Todd, *Confederate Finance* (Athens, 1954), 133.
32. Capers, *Memminger*, 434-36. Between the first war tax and 1863, Memminger only referred to new taxes in two of his numerous reports.

These were on March 14 and October 6, 1862. In neither did he specifically ask for new taxes.

33. *Journal of Congress*, V, 82, 367; *A Bill to be entitled An Act to Raise Revenue. September 11, 1862.*

34. On the final vote the border and lower South states were evenly divided; the almost unanimous opposition of the ten Trans-Mississippi members was the deciding factor. *Journal of Congress*, V, 497.

35. See the report in *Official Records*, Ser. IV, Vol. II, 60, 61.

36. James D. B. DeBow to John Perkins, September 16, 1861, John Perkins Papers, University of North Carolina; C. G. Memminger to Howell Cobb, January 20, 1862. *Report of the Secretary of the Treasury.*

37. Martin J. Crawford to Alexander H. Stephens, November 3, 1861, Stephens Papers.

38. Johnson and Buel, *Battles and Leaders of the Civil War*, I, 110.

39. Meade, *Judah P. Benjamin*, 166; Todd, *Confederate Finance*, 37, 38; "From the Autobiography of Herschel V. Johnson, 1856-1867," *loc. cit.*, 332.

40. Matthews, *Statutes*, 177-83. This was extended to $150,000,000 on December 24. *Ibid.*, 231.

41. *Journal of Congress*, II, 123; *Richmond Daily Examiner*, April 2, 1862. Holt's bill in particular was criticized because it offered the planter only 4¢ a pound at the time, the balance being paid when the proceeds were sold by the government.

42. "Proceedings of Congress," XLVII, 219, 220.

43. Matthews, *Statutes*, 231.

44. Capers, *Memminger*, 429-37.

45. Matthews, *Public Laws*, 28, 29, 34, 47.

46. Ramsdell, *Laws*, 164, 165.

47. Matthews, *Statutes*, 260-64.

48. Matthews, *Public Laws*, 104.

49. Ramsdell, *Laws*, 34, 35.

50. *Report of the Secretary of the Treasury, October 1, 1862.*

51. *Report of the Secretary of the Treasury, October 6, 1862.*

52. Matthews, *Public Laws*, 87.

53. *Report of the Secretary of the Treasury, January 10, 1863.*

54. *Journal of Congress*, VI, 18.

55. "Proceedings of Congress," XLVIII, 248-50.

56. Davidson to Zebulon B. Vance, March 23, 1863, Vance Papers.

57. *Journal of Congress*, VI, 234, 235.

58. *Report of the Committee on Finance on the Bill to lay taxes for the common defense and to carry on the government of the Confederate States of America. April 6, 1863.*

59. Johnson to Alexander H. Stephens, April 8, 1863, Stephens Papers.

60. Estill, "Diary of a Confederate Congressman, 1862-1863," *loc. cit.*, XXXIX, 58.

61. Matthews, *Public Laws*, 115-26.

62. April 6, 1863.

63. April 29, 1863.

64. Matthews, *Public Laws*, 171, 177, 186.

65. Todd, *Confederate Finance*, 144, 145.

66. Matthews, *Public Laws*, 99-101.

67. Lancaster & Co. to Thomas Ruffin, March 23, 1863, Joseph G. de Roulhac Hamilton (ed.), *The Papers of Thomas Ruffin* (Raleigh, 1920), III, 306.

68. Hill, *Joseph E. Brown*, 141-43; Earnest A. Smith, "The History of the Confederate Treasury," Southern History Association, *Publications*, V (1901), 110.

69. Ramsdell, *Laws*, 166.

70. Capers, *Memminger*, 457-75. The President gave him 100% support the next day. *Journal of Congress*, VI, 503-07.

71. *A Bill to levy additional taxes for the common defense and support of the government. December 31, 1863.*

72. *Journal of Congress*, VI, 674.

73. Matthews, *Public Laws*, 208-11. The exemptions cited in the last sentence

Notes 267

were in another tax law of the same day which repeated without much change the tax law of 1863.
74. Sexton to James H. Starr, December 16, 1863, Starr Papers.
75. Louis M. Ayer to James H. Hammond, December 29, 1863, Hammond Papers.
76. *Journal of Congress*, VI, 591, 592; Minority Report on the Currency, December 31, 1863.
77. Louis M. Ayer to James H. Hammond, December 29, 1863, Hammond Papers.
78. *Journal of Congress*, VI, 644.
79. *Report of the Committee on Finance on the Bill (H. R. 92) to tax, fund and limit the currency. January 25, 1864.* The Senate substitute is in *Journal of Congress*, III, 625-26.
80. *A Bill to provide for Exchequer notes, February 4, 1864.* Senate.
81. *Journal of Congress*, III, 763, 764; ibid., VI, 843.
82. Matthews, *Public Laws*, 205-08.
83. Memminger's supporters seem to consider this Congress's main crime.
84. *Report of the Secretary of the Treasury, May 2, 1864.*
85. Waldo P. Johnson to Thomas C. Reynolds, March 1, 1864, Reynolds Letter Books, 1863-1864, Pickett Papers.
86. Todd, *Confederate Finance*, says that it was rejected; Schwab, *The Confederate States of America*, said that it was not.
87. Thomas C. Reynolds to Waldo P. Johnson, March 30, 1864, Reynolds Letter Books, Pickett Papers.
88. *Report of the Secretary of the Treasury, May 2, 1864.*
89. *Communication from the Secretary of the Treasury recommending certain changes in the impressment laws. May 20, 1864; A Bill to authorize certificates of indebtedness to be given for property purchased or impressed. . . . May 24, 1864.*
90. Richardson, *Messages and Papers of the Confederacy*, 470-72.
91. Matthews, *Public Laws*, 272, 277.
92. *Report of the Secretary of the Treasury, November 7, 1864.*
93. *A Bill to provide more effectively for the reduction and redemption of the currency, November 25, 1864.*
94. *Richmond Daily Examiner*, January 26, 1865.
95. Ramsdell, *Laws*, 12, 13.
96. *Journal of Congress*, VII, 789, 790.
97. George A. Trenholm to the President, December 15, 1864, George A. Trenholm Papers, Manuscripts Division, Library of Congress; Ramsdell, *Laws*, 13.
98. Ramsdell, *Laws*, 121, 122, 129, 130, 147-50.
99. *Report of the Secretary of the Treasury, May 2, 1864.* Todd estimated that the repeal of these rates would have trebled the total tax receipts. *Confederate Finance*, 153.
100. *A Bill to amend the tax laws. May 23, 1864.*
101. *Minority Report of the Ways and Means Committee. June 1, 1864.*
102. *Journal of Congress*, IV, 192; ibid., 140, 142.
103. Matthews, *Public Laws*, 273-75.
104. *Ibid.*, 264, 265.
105. *Report of the Secretary of the Treasury. January 9, 1865.*
106. Ramsdell, *Laws*, 113, 114.
107. *A Bill to levy additional taxes for 1865. January 18, 1865; A Bill to levy taxes for the support of the government during 1865. January 20, 1865.*
108. Richardson, *Messages and Papers of the Confederacy*, 533.
109. *A Bill to provide means for the support of the government. February 17, 1865.*
110. *Journal of Congress*, VII, 640-42.
111. *A Bill to levy additional taxes for 1865 and the amendment proposed by the Committee on Finance. February 28, 1865.*
112. *Minority Report of the Committee on Finance. February 28, 1865.*
113. Ramsdell, *Laws*, 101-07.

CHAPTER XV

1. F. M. Robertson to S. J. Anderson, February 15, 1861, *Official Records*, Ser. II, Vol. II, 612.
2. See pages 7-9.
3. Thomas R. R. Cobb to his wife, April 30, 1861, Hull, "Correspondence of Thomas Reade Rootes Cobb, 1860-1862," *loc. cit.*, 313.
4. Charles M. Conrad to Charles Gayarré, February 20, 1861, Jones, *Autograph Letters*.
5. Thomas R. R. Cobb to his wife, March 21, 1861, Hull, "Correspondence of Thomas Reade Rootes Cobb, 1860-1862," *loc. cit.*, 252, 253.
6. Jones, *Rebel War Clerk's Diary*, I, 52.
7. Diary of Mallory, August 11, 1861.
8. *Ibid.*, September 1, 1861.
9. Chesnut, *Diary*, 65.
10. "Memorandum relative to the appointment of Confederate Senators from Missouri," Reynolds Letter Books, Pickett Papers.
11. Thomas R. R. Cobb to his wife, February 28, 1861, Hull, "Correspondence of Thomas Reade Rootes Cobb, 1860-1862," *loc. cit.*, 243.
12. *Richmond Daily Examiner*, January 30, 1865.
13. W. W. Boyce to James H. Hammond, March 17, 1862, Rosser H. Taylor, "Boyce-Hammond Correspondence," *Journal of Southern History*, III (1937), 350.
14. Chesnut, *Diary*, 9.
15. May 23, 1862.
16. Chesnut, *Diary*, 108.
17. Diary of Mallory, August 11, 1861.
18. Bell, *Men and Things*, 103.
19. Louis T. Wigfall to Clement C. Clay, August 13, 1863, Clay Papers.
20. Chesnut, *Diary*, 329.
21. Quoted in DuBose, *Life of Yancey*, II, 748.
22. *Ibid.*
23. Burgess S. Gaither to Thomas Ruffin, April 1, 1862, Hamilton, *Papers of Thomas Ruffin*, III, 227.
24. Quoted in Edwin A. Alderman and Armistead C. Gordon, *J. L. M. Curry* (New York, 1911), 164.
25. Diary of Mallory, September 27, 1865.
26. *Ibid.*
27. Edward A. Pollard, *The Lost Cause. . . .* (New York, 1866), 656.
28. Pollard, "The Confederate Congress," *loc. cit.*, 749.
29. *Ibid.*
30. Jefferson Davis to Augustus H. Garland, March 28, 1863, *Official Records*, Ser. I, Vol. LIII, Supplement, 861-63.
31. Edwin G. Reade to Zebulon B. Vance, February 10, 1864, Vance Papers.
32. Jones, *Rebel War Clerk's Diary*, II, 330.
33. William W. Holden, *Memoirs* (Durham, 1911), 39.
34. Lawrence M. Keitt to his wife, January 27, 1864, Keitt Papers.
35. January 25, 1864.
36. Chesnut, *Diary*, 467.
37. Debates within Congress and talk outside, while they stimulated gossip and controversy, are unsatisfactory criteria for deciding a man's loyalty to the administration. The quiet but consistent opposition of Ashe of North Carolina and Ayer of South Carolina was far more dangerous to administration measures than that of some noisier critics. For instance, Wigfall, who gained an evil reputation as Davis's enemy, did not join the legislative opposition until the Second Congress.
38. Anyone opposing the administration on at least half of its major measures during a term of Congress has been considered an opponent for that term.
39. H. W. Halleck to U. S. Grant, May 5, 1865, *Official Records*, Ser. II, Vol. VIII, 534.
40. Josiah Turner to his wife, May 2,

1864, Turner Papers, Duke University.
41. "From the Autobiography of Herschel V. Johnson, 1856-1867," loc. cit., 333.
42. There are several such letters in Rowland, *Jefferson Davis*, VIII, passim.
43. Chesnut, *Diary*, 207.
44. *Richmond Daily Examiner*, December 30, 1863.
45. James Lyons to W. T. Walthall, June 10, 1878, Rowland, *Jefferson Davis*, VIII, 213.
46. *Journal of Congress*, IV, 432, 453, 454.
47. *Ibid.*, 457, 458.
48. *Ibid.*, VII, 462.
49. Robert E. Lee to Gen. Samuel Cooper, February 4, 1865, quoted in J. William Jones, *Life and Letters of Robert Edward Lee* (New York, 1906), 351.
50. Robert E. Lee to Sixteen Senators, February 13, 1865, Wigfall Papers.
51. *Journal of Congress*, I, 853.
52. *Ibid.*, V, 23, 31, 123.
53. *Richmond Daily Enquirer*, April 1, 1862.
54. *Journal of Congress*, III, 24, 44, 146, 153.
55. Foote, *War of the Rebellion*, 357. For the full story of Davis's Cabinet appointments see Patrick, *Jefferson Davis and His Cabinet*, passim.
56. *Journal of Congress*, VII, 110; *Richmond Daily Examiner*, June 15, 1864; Foote, *War of the Rebellion*, 357, 358.
57. Christopher G. Memminger to Jefferson Davis, June 15, 1864, printed in *Daily Richmond Enquirer*, July 19, 1864; Jefferson Davis to Christopher G. Memminger, June 21, 1864, Memminger Papers.
58. Francis B. Sexton to James H. Starr, December 18, 1864, Starr Papers.
59. *Richmond Daily Enquirer*, August 21, 1862.
60. Louis T. Wigfall to Clement C. Clay, August 13, 1863, Clay Papers.
61. *Richmond Daily Enquirer*, February 9, 1865.
62. Thomas S. Bocock to Jefferson Davis, January 21, 1865, *Official Records*, Ser. I, Vol. XLVI, pt. 2, 118.
63. *Ibid.*, endorsement by President Davis.
64. Jefferson Davis to James H. Seddon, January 1, 1865, Rowland, *Jefferson Davis*, VI, 459.
65. *Richmond Daily Enquirer*, February 15, 1865.
66. *A Bill to limit and define the term of office of the Secretary or principal officer of each of the Executive Departments . . . December 10, 1863; Speech of Mr. Johnson . . . on the Bill to Limit and Define the Tenure of Office of the Principal officers or Heads of Departments.*
67. *Richmond Daily Enquirer*, January 20, 1864.
68. Louis T. Wigfall to Clement C. Clay, August 13, 1863, Clay Papers.
69. *Message of the President Transmitting a communication from the Secretary of War, relative to the Quartermaster General. December 21, 1863.*
70. *Report of the Committee on Military Affairs on the Message of the President transmitting a communication from the Secretary of War . . . January 21, 1864.*
71. *Journal of Congress*, III, 622; *Richmond Daily Examiner*, December 24, January 25 and 27, 1864.
72. *Journal of Congress*, III, 627, 628.
73. Jones, *Rebel War Clerk's Diary*, II, 153.
74. *Journal of Congress*, IV, 502, 508.
75. Oldham, Memoirs, 138, 139.

BIBLIOGRAPHY

PRIMARY SOURCES

I. Manuscripts

Alexander, Edward P., Papers, University of North Carolina.
Claibourne, J. H. F., Papers, University of North Carolina.
Clay, Clement C., Papers, Duke University.
Confederate Archives, in the National Archives, Washington, D.C.
Davis, Jefferson, Papers, Duke University.
Graham, William A., Papers, Department of Archives and History, Raleigh, North Carolina.
Graham, William A., Papers, University of North Carolina.
Hale, Edward J., Papers, Department of Archives and History, Raleigh, North Carolina.
Hammond, James H., Papers, Manuscripts Division, Library of Congress.
Harrison, James T., Papers, University of North Carolina.
Hilton, Robert B., Diary, University of Florida.
Johnson, Waldo P., Papers, Manuscripts Division, Library of Congress.
Keitt, Lawrence M., Papers, Duke University.
Letter Book, Confederate Attorneys-General, 1861-1865, New York Public Library.
McCollam, Andrew, Papers, University of North Carolina.
McDowell, Thomas D., Papers, University of North Carolina.
MaGrath, Andrew G., Papers, University of North Carolina.
Mallory, Stephen R., Diary, typed copy, University of North Carolina.
Mason, James M., Papers, Duke University.
Memminger, Christopher G., Papers, University of North Carolina.
Miles, William P., Papers, University of North Carolina.
Milton, John, Papers, Florida Historical Society, St. Augustine, Florida.
Oldham, Williamson S., Memoirs of a Confederate Senator, 1861-1865, typed copy, University of Texas.

Opinion Book, Confederate Attorneys-General, 1861-1865, New York Public Library.
Orr, Jehu A., Reminiscences of, typed copy, Department of Archives and History, Jackson, Mississippi.
Perkins, John, Papers, University of North Carolina.
Pickett, Col. John T., Papers, Manuscripts Division, Library of Congress.
Rives, William C., Papers, Manuscripts Division, Library of Congress.
Starr, James H., Papers, University of Texas.
Stephens, Alexander H., Papers, Manuscripts Division, Library of Congress.
Stuart, Alexander H. H., Papers, Manuscripts Division, Library of Congress.
Swain, David L., Papers, Department of Archives and History, Raleigh, North Carolina.
Trenholm, George A., Papers, Manuscripts Division, Library of Congress.
Turner, Josiah, Papers, Duke University.
Turner, Josiah, Papers, University of North Carolina.
Vance, Zebulon B., Papers, Department of Archives and History, Raleigh, North Carolina.
Walser Papers, University of North Carolina.
Wigfall, Louis T., Papers, University of Texas.
Williams-Chesnut-Manning Papers, University of North Carolina.
Yancey, William L., Papers, Department of Archives and History, Montgomery, Alabama.

II. OFFICIAL PUBLICATIONS

ALABAMA

Acts of the Alabama Assembly, 1861-1864.
Journal of the House of Representatives, 1861-1864.
Journal of the Senate, 1861-1864.
Ordinances and Constitution of the State of Alabama, with the Constitution of the Provisional Government and of the Confederate States of America.

ARKANSAS

Acts of Arkansas, 1861, 1862.
Journal of the House of Representatives, 1861, 1862.
Journal of the Senate, 1861, 1862.

CONFEDERATE STATES

Congress ordered printed a large number of resolutions, bills, amendments, reports, communications, correspondences, petitions, and the like. These are cited in the footnotes according to their published titles. The largest depositories of these are the Library of Congress, the Virginia State Library, and the Confederate Museum in Richmond.

Matthews, James M. (ed.), *Statutes at Large of the Provisional Government of the Confederate States of America* (Richmond, 1864).

―――――, *Public Laws of the Confederate States of America. First Congress, Sessions 1-4; Second Congress, First Session* (Richmond, 1862-1864).

FLORIDA

Acts of Florida, 1861-1864.
Journal of the Proceedings of the House of Representatives, 1860-1864.
Journal of the Proceedings of the Senate, 1860-1864.
Journal of the Proceedings of the Convention of the People of Florida, Begun . . . January 3 . . . 1861 (Tallahassee, 1861).
Constitution . . . as Revised and Amended at a Convention of the People Begun . . . on the Third Day of January . . . 1861, Together with the Ordinances Adopted by Said Convention (Tallahassee, 1861).

GEORGIA

Acts of Georgia, 1861-1864.
Journal of the House of Representatives, 1861-1865.
Journal of the Senate, 1861-1865.

LOUISIANA

Acts of Louisiana, 1861-1865.
Official Journal of the Proceedings of the Convention of the State of Louisiana, 1861 (New Orleans, 1861).

MISSISSIPPI

Laws of Mississippi, 1861-1865.
Journal of the House of Representatives, 1861-1865.
Journal of the Senate, 1861-1865.
Proceedings of the Mississippi State Convention, Held January 7th to 26th A.D., 1861 (Jackson, 1861).

NORTH CAROLINA

Laws of North Carolina, 1861-1865.
Journal of the House of Commons, 1861-1865.
Journal of the Senate, 1861-1865.

..... *Bibliography* *273*

SOUTH CAROLINA

Statutes at Large of South Carolina, 1861-1865.
Journal of the Convention of the People of South Carolina, Held in 1860, 1861 and 1862, Together with the Ordinances, Reports, Resolutions, Etc. (Columbia, 1862).

TENNESSEE

Public Acts of Tennessee, 1861, 1862.

TEXAS

Laws of Texas, 1861-1865.
Journal of the House of Representatives, 1861-1864.
Journal of the Senate, 1861-1864.
Journal of the Secession Convention of Texas, 1861 (Austin, 1912).

UNITED STATES OF AMERICA

Journal of the Congress of the Confederate States of America, 1861-1865 (7 vols., Washington, 1904-1905).
Official Records of the Union and Confederate Navies in the War of the Rebellion (30 vols., Washington, 1894-1922).
The War of the Rebellion: A Compilation of the Official Records of the Union and Confederate Armies (128 vols., Washington, 1880-1901).

VIRGINIA

Acts of Virginia, 1861-1865.
Journal of the House of Delegates, 1861-1864.
Journal of the Senate, 1861-1864.

III. COLLECTED SOURCES

Candler, Allen D. (ed.), *The Confederate Records of the State of Georgia* (6 vols., Atlanta, 1909-1911).
Davenport, F. Garvin (ed.), "The Essay on *Habeas Corpus* in the Judge Sharkey Papers," *Mississippi Valley Historical Review,* XXIII (1936-1937), 243-46.
Hamilton, Joseph G. de Roulhac (ed.), *The Papers of Thomas Ruffin* (4 vols., Raleigh, 1920).
Hull, A. L. (ed.), "Correspondence of Thomas Reade Rootes Cobb, 1860-1862," Southern History Association, *Publications,* XI (1907), 147-85, 233-60, 312-28.
————, "The Making of the Confederate Constitution," Southern History Association, *Publications,* IX (1905), 272-92.
————, "Thomas Reade Rootes Cobb, Extracts from Letters to his wife, February 3, 1861-December 10, 1862," Southern Historical Society, *Papers,* XXVIII (1900), 280-301.

Jones, Charles C. (collector), *Autograph Letters and Portraits of Signers of the Constitution of the Confederate States* (August, 1884). The copy used is in the Manuscript Division of the Duke University Library.
"Letter of Jefferson Davis to Rev. J. W. Jones, March 27, 1878," Southern Historical Society, *Papers*, V (1878), 222-24.
"Letter of Stephen R. Mallory, 1861," *American Historical Review*, XII (1906-1907), 103-08.
McPherson, Edward (compiler), *The Political History of the United States of America, During the Great Rebellion from November 6, 1860, to July 4, 1864* (Washington, 1865).
Moore, Frank (compiler), *The Rebellion Record: A Diary of the American Events, with Documents, Narratives, Illustrative Incidents, Poetry, etc.* (11 vols., New York, 1861-1863).
Phillips, Ulrich B. (ed.), *The Correspondence of Robert Toombs, Alexander H. Stephens, and Howell Cobb*, American Historical Association, *Annual Report*, 1911, Vol. II (Washington, 1913).
"Proceedings of the Confederate Congress," Southern Historical Society, *Papers*, XLIV-L (1923-1953).
Ramsdell, Charles W. (ed.), *Laws and Joint Resolutions of the Last Session of the Confederate Congress (November 7, 1864-March 18, 1865) Together with the Secret Acts of Previous Congresses* (Durham, 1941).
Richardson, James D. (ed.), *A Compilation of the Messages and Papers of the Confederacy, Including the Diplomatic Correspondence, 1861-1865* (2 vols., Nashville, 1906).
Rowland, Dunbar (ed.), *Jefferson Davis, Constitutionalist. His Letters, Papers, and Speeches* (10 vols., Jackson, 1923).
Smith, C. C., "Some Unpublished History of the Southwest," *Arizona Historical Quarterly*, IV-VI (1933-1935) *passim*.
Taylor, Rosser H., "Boyce-Hammond Correspondence," *Journal of Southern History*, III (1937), 348-54.

IV. PAMPHLETS

Brown, Albert Gallatin, *State of the Country. Speech Delivered in the Confederate Senate. December 24, 1863*.
Gholson, Thomas S., *Speech on the Policy of Employing Negro Troops*. . . .
Johnson, Waldo P., *Speech in the Confederate Senate . . . on the Bill to Limit and Define the Tenure of Office of the Principal Officers or Heads of Departments*.
Oldham, Williamson S., *Speech upon the Bill to Amend the Conscript Laws, Made in the Senate, September 4, 1862*.
Villere, C. J., *Review of Certain Remarks Made by the President when Requested to Restore General Beauregard to the Command of Department No. 2*.

V. Personal Accounts

Bell, Hiram P., *Men and Things* (Atlanta, 1907).
Chesnut, Mary Boykin, *A Diary from Dixie*, ed. Ben Ames Williams (Boston, 1949).
Clay-Clopton, Mrs. Virginia, *A Belle of the Fifties* (New York, 1905).
Davis, Reuben, *Recollections of Mississippi and Mississippians* (Boston, 1889).
Davis, Varina Howell, *Jefferson Davis, Ex-President of the Confederate States of America. A Memoir by His Wife* (2 vols., New York, 1890).
De Leon, Thomas C., *Belles, Beaux and Brains of the 60's* (New York, 1909).
————, *Four Years in Rebel Capitals* (Mobile, 1892).
Estill, Mary S. (ed.), "Diary of a Confederate Congressman, 1862-1863," *Southwestern Historical Quarterly*, XXXVIII (1934-1935), 270-301, and XXXIX (1935-1936), 33-65.
Foote, Henry S., *Casket of Reminiscences* (Washington, 1874).
————, *War of the Rebellion: or Scylla and Charybdis* (New York, 1866).
"From the Autobiography of Herschel V. Johnson, 1856-1867," *American Historical Review*, XXX (1924-1925), 311-36.
Goode, John, *Recollections of a Lifetime* (New York, 1906).
Holden, William W., *Memoirs* (Durham, 1911).
Jones, John Beauchamp, *A Rebel War Clerk's Diary at the Confederate States Capital*, ed. Howard Swiggett (2 vols., New York, 1935).
Reagan, John H., *Memoirs with Special Reference to Secession and the Civil War*, ed. Walter F. McCaleb (New York, 1906).
Russell, William H., *Pictures of Southern Life* (New York, 1861).
Smith, Charles H., *Bill Arp, So Called. A Side Show of the Southern Side of the War* (New York, 1866).
Smith, William R., *The History and Debates of the Convention of the People of Alabama, Begun and Held in the City of Montgomery, on the Seventh Day of January, 1861* (Montgomery, 1861).

VI. Newspapers

Arkansas State Gazette, 1861-1864.
Atlanta Southern Confederacy, 1861-1863.
Augusta Tri-Weekly Constitutionalist, 1861-1864.
Austin Gazette, 1861-1865.
Baton Rouge Gazette and Comet, 1861-1862.
Charleston Mercury, 1861-1865.
Clarksville (Texas) *Standard*, 1861-1865.
Hillsboro (North Carolina) *Recorder*, 1861-1865.
Houston Tri-Weekly Telegraph, 1861-1865.
Jackson Weekly Mississippian, 1861-1865.
Knoxville Register, 1861-1865.

Marietta (Florida) *Family Friend*, 1861-1862.
Montgomery Daily Advertiser and Weekly Advertiser, 1861-1865.
Montgomery Daily Mail and Weekly Mail, 1861-1865.
New Orleans Crescent, 1861-1862.
Paulding (Mississippi) *Eastern Clarion*, 1861-1862.
Raleigh Daily Standard and Weekly Standard, 1861-1865.
Savannah Republican, 1861-1865.
Shreveport Semi-Weekly News, 1861-1865.
Richmond Daily Enquirer, 1861-1865.
Richmond Daily Examiner, 1861-1865.
Tallahassee Florida Sentinel, 1861-1862.
Texas Republican, 1861-1862.
Wilmington Journal, 1861-1865.
Yorkville (South Carolina) *Enquirer*, 1861-1865.

SECONDARY SOURCES

Abel, Annie H., "The Indians in the Civil War," *American Historical Review*, XV (1909-1910), 281-96.
Adams, George W., "Confederate Medicine," *Journal of Southern History*, VI (1940), 151-66.
Alderman, Edwin, and Armistead C. Gordon, *J. L. M. Curry* (New York, 1911).
Avery, Isaac W., *The History of the State of Georgia from 1850 to 1881* (New York, 1881).
Bettersworth, John K., *Confederate Mississippi* (Baton Rouge, 1946).
Bonham, Milledge L., *The British Consuls in the Confederacy* (New York, 1911).
Bragg, Jefferson Davis, *Louisiana in the Confederacy* (Baton Rouge, 1941).
Brumer, Sidney, "The Judicial Interpretation of the Confederate Constitution," *Studies in Southern History and Politics* (New York, 1914).
Capers, Henry D., *The Life and Times of C. G. Memminger* (Richmond, 1893).
Cauthen, Charles E., *South Carolina Goes to War* (Chapel Hill, 1950).
Christian, Rebecca, "Georgia and the Confederate Policy of Impressing Supplies," *Georgia Historical Quarterly*, XXVIII (1944), 1-33.
Cleveland, Henry, *Alexander H. Stephens, in Public and Private. With Letters and Speeches, Before, During and Since the War* (Philadelphia, 1866).
Constitution of the United States . . . the Rules of the House of Representatives of the Fifty-seventh Congress of the United States (Washington, 1902).
Coulter, E. Merton, *The Confederate States of America, 1861-1865* (Baton Rouge, 1950).

———, "Effects of Secession upon the Commerce of the Mississippi Valley," *Mississippi Valley Historical Review*, III (1916-1917), 275-300.

———, "The Movement for Agricultural Reorganization in the Cotton South During the Civil War," *North Carolina Historical Review*, IV (1927), 22-36.

Craven, John J., *Prison Life of Jefferson Davis* (New York, 1866).

Cunningham, Horace H., *Doctors in Gray* (Baton Rouge, 1958).

Curry, Jabez L. M., *Civil History of the Government of the Confederate States with Some Personal Reminiscences* (Richmond, 1901).

Davis, Jefferson, *The Rise and Fall of the Confederate Government* (2 vols., New York, 1881).

Dodd, William E., *Jefferson Davis* (Philadelphia, 1907).

Douglas, Henry K., *I Rode with Stonewall* (Chapel Hill, 1940).

DuBose, John W., *The Life and Times of William Lowndes Yancey* (2 vols., New York, 1942).

Dumond, Dwight L., *The Secession Movement, 1860-1861* (New York, 1931).

Easby-Smith, Ann, *William Russell Smith of Alabama, His Life and Works* (Philadelphia, 1931).

Farish, Thomas E., *History of Arizona* (8 vols., Phoenix, 1915-1916).

Felgar, Edward, The Civil War in Texas (unpublished dissertation in the University of Texas Library, 1938).

Fertig, James W., *The Secession and Reconstruction of Tennessee* (Chicago, 1898).

Fleming, Walter L., *Civil War and Reconstruction in Alabama* (New York, 1905).

Flippin, Percy S., *Herschel V. Johnson of Georgia, State Rights Unionist* (Richmond, 1931).

Freeman, Douglas S., *A Calendar of Confederate Papers, with a Bibliography of Some Confederate Publications* (Richmond, 1908).

———, *R. E. Lee* (4 vols., New York, 1934-1936).

Goode, John, "The Confederate Congress," *The Conservative Review*, IV (1900), 97-112.

Govan, Gilbert E., and James W. Livingood, *A Different Valor: The Story of Joseph E. Johnston, C.S.A.* (New York, 1956).

Hamer, Phillip M. (ed.), *Tennessee, A History, 1673-1932* (4 vols., New York, 1933).

Hay, Thomas R., "The South and the Arming of the Slaves," *Mississippi Valley Historical Review*, VI (1919-1920), 34-73.

Hill, Louise B., *Joseph E. Brown and the Confederacy* (Chapel Hill, 1939).

"Hon. Thomas J. Semmes," Southern Historical Society, *Papers*, XXV (1897), 317-33.

Hunter, Robert M. T., "The Peace Commission of 1865," Southern Historical Society, *Papers*, III (1877), 168-76.

Irvine, Dallas D., "The Fate of Confederate Archives," *American Historical Review*, XLIV (1938-1939), 823-41.
Johnson, Robert U., and Clarence C. Buel (eds.), *Battles and Leaders of the Civil War* (4 vols., New York, 1884-1887).
Johnston, Richard M., and William M. Browne, *Life of Alexander H. Stephens* (Philadelphia, 1878).
Jones, John William, *Life and Letters of Robert E. Lee* (New York, 1906).
Kirkland, Edward C., *The Peacemakers of 1864* (New York, 1927).
Lonn, Ella, *Desertion During the Civil War* (New York, 1928).
Lowrey, Laurence T., *Northern Opinion of Approaching Secession* (Northampton, Mass., 1918).
McCaleb, Walter F., "The Organization of the Post-Office Department of the Confederacy," *American Historical Review*, XII (1906-1907), 66-74.
Meade, Robert D., *Judah P. Benjamin, Confederate Statesman* (New York, 1943).
Moore, Albert B., *Conscription and Conflict in the Confederacy* (New York, 1924).
Owsley, Frank L., *King Cotton Diplomacy* (Chicago, 1931).
————, "Local Defense and the Overthrow of the Confederacy: A Study in State Rights," *Mississippi Valley Historical Review*, XI (1924-1925), 490-525.
————, *State Rights in the Confederacy* (Chicago, 1925).
Patrick, Rembert W., *Jefferson Davis and His Cabinet* (Baton Rouge, 1944).
Patton, James W., *Unionism and Reconstruction in Tennessee, 1860-1869* (Chapel Hill, 1934).
Pendleton, Louis, *Alexander H. Stephens* (Philadelphia, 1908).
Phillips, Ulrich B., *The Life of Robert Toombs* (New York, 1913).
Pollard, Edward A., *Life of Jefferson Davis with a Secret History of the Southern Confederacy* (Atlanta, 1869).
————, "The Confederate Congress," *The Galaxy*, VI (1868-1869), 749-58.
————, *The Lost Cause* (New York, 1866).
Rainwater, Percy L., *Mississippi, Storm Center of Secession* (Baton Rouge, 1938).
Ramsdell, Charles W., *Behind the Lines in the Southern Confederacy* (Baton Rouge, 1944).
————, "The Confederate Government and the Railroads," *American Historical Review*, XXII (1916-1917), 794-810.
————, "The Control of Manufacturing by the Confederate Government," *Mississippi Valley Historical Review*, VIII (1921-1922), 231-49.
Robinson, William M., *The Confederate Privateers* (New Haven, 1928).

———, *Justice in Grey. A History of the Judicial System of the Confederate States of America* (Cambridge, Mass., 1941).
———, "Legal System of the Confederate States," *Journal of Southern History*, II (1936), 453-67.
———, "A New Deal in Constitutions," *Journal of Southern History*, IV (1938), 449-61.
Roman, Alfred, *The Military Operations of General Beauregard in the War Between the States, 1861 to 1865* (New York, 1884).
Scharf, John T., *History of the Confederate States Navy from Its Organization to the Surrender of Its Last Vessel* (Albany, 1894).
Schwab, John C., *The Confederate States of America, 1861-1865* (New York, 1901).
Smith, Earnest A., "The History of the Confederate Treasury," Southern History Association, *Publications*, V (1901), 1-34, 99-150, 188-227.
Stephens, Alexander H., *A Comprehensive and Popular History of the United States* (Raleigh, 1884).
———, *A Constitutional View of the Late War Between the States* (2 vols., Philadelphia, 1868).
Stephenson, Nathaniel W., "The Question of Arming the Slaves," *American Historical Review*, XVIII (1912-1913), 295-308.
Tatum, Georgia Lee, *Disloyalty in the Confederacy* (Chapel Hill, 1934).
Thomas, David Y., *Arkansas in War and Reconstruction, 1861-1874* (Little Rock, 1926).
Todd, Richard C., *Confederate Finance* (Athens, 1954).
Trexler, Harrison, "The Opposition of Planters to the Employment of Slaves as Laborers by the Confederacy," *Mississippi Valley Historical Review*, XXVII (1940-1941), 211-24.
White, Laura A., *Robert Barnwell Rhett, Father of Secession* (New York, 1931).
Williams, T. Harry, *P. G. T. Beauregard* (Baton Rouge, 1954).

INDEX

Absentee voting, 42, 43, 48

Address, in relation to the war, 175

Administration opposition, in elections, 46-59; early existence of, 219; clauses of, 219-25; strength of, 224, 225; distribution of, 224, 225; moderation of, 225, 226; lack of unity of, 226; against Davis, 226, 227; against the Cabinet, 228, 229, 232; against department heads, 229-34; effect of, on legislation, 234, 235

Akin, Warren, proposes amendment to general-in-chief bill, 227, 228, 236

Alabama, 108, 145, 185, 221; secession of, 4; calls Southern convention, 7; political activity in, 7-9; wants capital at Montgomery, 13; constitutional ideas in, 20; supports Davis for president, 31; elections in, 42, 45-47, 50, 52, 55, 56; peace sentiment in, 174, 178; makes loan to the Confederacy, 184; the Produce Loan in, 193; opposes forced funding, 206, 207; opposes taxation-in-kind, 212

Alexander, G. W., commandant of Castle Thunder, 114

Allen, Henry W., Governor of Louisiana, 56, 96

Anderson, James P., 42, 236

Appomattox, 225

Arizona Territory, secedes, 40; elections in, 43

Arkansas, 171, 187, 225; secedes, 40; elections in, 43, 45, 47, 56, 57; opposes Negro conscription, 97; local defense problems of, 142; dislikes Theophilus Holmes, 149; attacks Davis, 222

Army, Confederate, pay, allowances, and rations, 56, 112-14; terms of enlistment, 60-64, 103; bounties and furloughs, 61, 63, 109, 110; recruiting, 63; camps of instruction, 66; transportation for soldiers, 110; labor, 111, 112; discipline, 114, 115; chaplains, 115; *see also* Army organization, Conscription, Exemption, Militia, Special service, Substitutes

Army of Northern Virginia, 121

Army of Tennessee, 141, 222, 227

Army organization, for the Provisional Army, 60; officer appointments and elections, 60-66, 103-109; based on United States laws, 102; for the Regular Army, 103; vacancies and promotions, 103-105; courts martial and discharges of officers, 105-107; assignment and transfer of troops, 106, 109; invalid corps, 107; commanding general, 108; staff legislation, 108, 109; consolidation and reorganization, 103-107; *see also* Militia, Special service, Skeleton regiments, Volunteers

Arrington, Archibald, congressional candidate, 44, 236

Ashe, Thomas S., congressional candidate, 54, 236

Atkins, John D. C., proposes impressment bill, 123, 236

Attorney General's Office, 134; opinion on impressment, 119; asks for settlement of claims, 134

Augusta Tri-Weekly Constitutionalist, opposes peace convention, 171

Avery, William W., congressional candidate, 48, 236-37

Ayer, Louis M., congressional candidate, 55; opposes forced funding, 206, 237

Index   281

Baker, James M., 237
Baldwin, John, opposes habeas corpus suspension, 156, 237
Ballard House, peace meeting at, 179
Barksdale, Ethelbert, 98, 237; congressional candidate, 44; opposes exemption of overseers, 79; proposes to arm the Negroes, 97, 98; proposes habeas corpus suspension, 152, 155; proposes retaliation bill, 164; opposes peace negotiations, 179; resolution to expel Foote, 182; proposes funding bill, 210
Barnwell, Robert W., 161, 237; advocates Davis for president, 32; financial scheme of, 209
Bartow, Francis S., 42, 237
Beauregard, Pierre G. T., 109, 143, 227; controversy with Davis, 147; requests for transfer of, 147, 148, 222; favors retaliation for enemy outrages, 124
Bell, Hiram P., 175, 237; proposes to suspend taxes in Georgia, 215
Bell, John, 47; presidential candidate, 2, 3
Benjamin, Judah P., 178; favors long enlistments, 63; urges conscription, 64, 65, 76, 98; rules on officer appointments, 103; sanctions illegal impressment, 121, 122; responsible for loss of Roanoke Island, 141, 142, 145; appointment of, 145, 229; proposes treaties with France, 167, 168; refuses to release state secrets, 169; expels foreign consuls, 169
Blair, Francis P., peace mission of, 179-81
Blandford, Mark H., 237; proposes to abolish class exemptions, 92
Blockade, 128, 135, 185, 188; discourages privateering, 100; and cotton diplomacy, 166-68; limits cotton exports, 195
Blockade-running, 188; regulation of, 137-39
Board of Sequestration Commissioners, 39
Bocock, Thomas S., 237; requests Cabinet reform, 231, 232
Bonds, 184; issues of, 185, 189, 193-95, 202, 203, 208; sale of, 185, 190, 192, 193, 195, 197, 198, 202, 209, 212; debates upon, 186, 189, 194, 197, 203, 206, 216; exempt from taxation, 190, 203, 208; interest rates on, 192, 195, 197, 201, 202, 205; *see also* Funding

Bonham, Milledge L., 237; prefers volunteering to conscription, 69, 70
Border states, 6, 25, 28; secession of, 4, 8, 31, 39-41; admission of, 39-41
Boteler, Alexander R., 18, 106, 237; criticizes defense of Shenandoah Valley, 149
Bounties, 61, 63, 110
Boyce, William W., 181, 226, 237; advocates peace, 55, 176-78; opposes conscription, 69; favors destruction of property, 132; criticizes Davis, 172, 173, 220; proposes currency plan, 206
Bragg, Braxton, 104, 147-49, 222; enforces conscription law, 82
Breckinridge, John C., 149; presidential candidate, 2, 3; appointed Secretary of War, 146
Bridgers, R. R., 237
Brockenbrough, John W., 218, 237
Brown, Albert G., 237; proposes to extend conscription, 86; proposes crop limitation, 131; criticizes General D. R. Jones, 149
Brown, John, 1
Brown, Joseph E., 44, 174, 178; appoints Georgia senator, 48; opposes conscription, 83, 85; retains guns of Georgia militia, 125, 126; denounces habeas corpus suspension, 155; refuses to guarantee bond issue, 203
Bruce, Eli M., 17, 18, 237; proposes privateering bill, 100
Bruce, Horatio W., 142, 238
Buchanan, James, 1, 23, 30; refuses to block secession, 6
Bunch, _____, British consul at Charleston, 166.
Bureau of Conscription, 74, 81, 89; operation of, 82; abolished, 94
Bureau of foreign supplies, vetoed by Davis, 137, 138
Bureau of Indian Affairs, established, 40
Bureau of polytechnics, considered by Congress, 128, 129
Burnett, Henry C., 238; criticizes Bragg, 148

"Cabal," against the administration, 179, 226
Cabinet, 39, 48, 144, 146, 193, 220, 230; members of, in Congress, 228, 229; appointment of, 229; opposition to, 228, 231, 232

Call Certificates, issued, 194, 195, 207; circulation of, 195; funding of, 202
Campbell, John A., Hampton Roads commissioner, 181, 182
Campbell, Josiah A. P., 10, 106, 238
Camps of instruction, 66
Caperton, Allen T., 238; congressional candidate, 54
Castle Thunder, management investigated, 114
Census of 1860, 134; basis of direct taxation, 204
Chambers, Henry C., 238; congressional candidate, 44, 45; presents impressment scheme, 123
Charleston, S. C., 2, 76, 147; defense of, 143, 149
Charleston Democratic Convention, 2, 46
Charleston Mercury, favors moving capital, 13; dislikes secret sessions, 35; opposes habeas corpus suspension, 152, 155; financial ideas of, 203; criticizes Davis, 230
Chesnut, James, 20, 42, 238; advocates Davis for president, 32
Chesnut, Mrs. James B., 19, 20; comments on peace agitation, 178; comments on congressional politics, 220, 224
Chilton, William P., 238; proposes committee on the conduct of the war, 140
Claims against the Confederacy, 133-35
Clark, John B., 238; conduct in Richmond, 20; congressional candidate, 53, 57; proposes Confederate control of militia, 92; opposes state impressment commissioners, 119; defends martial law, 153; favors retaliation, 164
Clark, William W., 238; opposes conscription, 69; reports on hospital conditions, 110
Clay, Clement C., 19, 145, 167, 238; attacks Supreme Court bill, 37, 38; congressional candidate, 45, 56; proposes to draft foreigners, 76; reports abuses in impressments, 117
Clay, Hugh Lawson, comments on elections, 46
Clayton, Alexander M., warns of United States attack, 23
Cleburne, Patrick, plan to draft Negroes, 95
Clingman, Thomas L., 238; congressional candidate, 48

Cobb, Howell, 29, 42, 238; opinion of Montgomery convention, 8, 9; considered for the presidency, 30-32; custodian of journals of Congress, 33, 34
Cobb, Thomas R. R., 26, 32, 42, 218, 219, 238; urges secession, 3; fears reconstruction, 9; joins army, 9; visits wounded soldiers, 17; proposes committee on the constitution, 23; opposes pay for congressmen, 36; criticizes Secretary Walker, 145; proposes naturalization law, 162; criticizes Davis, 220
Cobb, Williamson R. R., expelled from Congress, 55
Colyar, Arthur St. C., 238; favors extending tax-in-kind, 210, 211; tax proposal of, 213
Commercial and Planters Convention, 188
Commissary Department, 16, 91, 114; corruption in, 121, 146; impressment policies of the, 121; investigated, 146; proposals to reform, 146, 147
Commissary General, reports adequate provisions in Virginia, 89; Lucius B. Northrop appointed, 233.
Confederate Judiciary, in Provisional Constitution, 25
Confederate navy, 99-101; see also Privateering
Confiscation, see Sequestration and confiscation
Confiscation, United States, 132, 191
Congress, Permanent, working conditions, 13-15; addresses to the people, 16; proclaims day of fasting and prayer, 16; serves guard duty, 17; declines vaccination, 17; controversy with the press, 20, 21; considers digest of laws, 32, 33; rules of order of, 34-36; pay of members in, 36
Congress, Provisional, 113, 234; personnel of, 7-10; meeting place in Montgomery, 11; working conditions of, 13-15; created from Montgomery convention, 22-24; continues United States laws, 32; establishes library, 32; publication of laws and journals, 33, 34; rules of order for, 34-36; pay of members in, 36; establishes executive departments, 36, 37, 184; political rivalry in, 218, 219
Congress, United States, 1, 140, 179, 229

Index 283

Conrad, Charles M., 10, 167, 238; opposes destruction of property, 132; proposes to abolish Navy Department, 144

Conscription, 28, 99, 103, 105, 107, 133, 144, 149, 158, 159, 196, 223; in elections, 48, 50, 52, 55; original need for, 64; age limits of, 64-66, 68-71, 77, 86-88; debated, 65, 68-70, 76-79, 86-88, 90-92; constitutionality of, 65, 67, 69, 77, 78, 83, 98; opinion on, 66-70, 89; abuses in, 69, 80, 81, 83; of refugees, 74; of foreigners, 75, 76, 163; how applied, 82, 83, 85, 94, 95; of department workers, 147; and habeas corpus, 155; *see also* Local defense, Militia, Negro soldiers, Principles of substitutes, *and* Substitutes

Conservatives, 4-6; favor Davis for president, 31; strength of, in Montgomery convention, 7, 8, 218, 219; in elections, 46, 48, 49, 53, 54, 58

Constitution, Confederate, 87, 131, 152-54, 179, 204, 233; based on United States Constitution, 6, 22, 24; provisions for Cabinet in, 228

Constitution, Permanent, 26, 47, 78, 119, 145, 229; forbids plural office-holding, 9, 42; writing of, 22, 25, 26; features, 26-29; ratification, 29, 30; Supreme Court provision, 37, 38; census requirements, 198

Constitution, Provisional, written in haste, 22, 23; features, 24, 25; Supreme Court provision, 37; permits plural office-holding, 42

Constitution, United States, 1, 24-26, 29; basis for Confederate constitutions, 2, 22, 24

Constitutional Union party, 2,3

Consuls, interest in conscription of, 76; expulsion of, 168, 169

Cooper, Samuel, 113

Cooperationists, 174; oppose secession, 5, 7; role in Montgomery convention, 8, 9

Cotton, proposed government purchase of, 46, 51, 193, 194, 216, 229; falling into enemy hands, 120, 132, 189; crop limitation of, 131; regulation of trade in, 135-39; speculation in, 136; impressment of, 136, 197; in foreign diplomacy, 161, 165-68, 187-89; export duty on, 185, 186; as basis for credit, 189, 193, 195, 196, 202, 203, 211, 212, 216

Cotton, F. R., congressional candidate, 45

Cotton Bureau, 136-38

Cotton certificates, 195, 196

Courts of Claims, constitutional provision for, 27; action of Congress on, 38, 39, 134, 135

Crawford, Martin J., 32, 238

Crop control, state limitations on, 131, 223; considered by Congress, 131

Cruikshank, Marcus H., 238; congressional candidate, 56; proposes to repeal habeas corpus suspension, 157

Curry, Jabez L. M., 238-39; congressional candidate, 56; favors destruction of property, 132; opinion on Davis, 221

Dahlgren, Ulric, 17

Daniel, John, editor of *Richmond Examiner*, 21

Dargan, Edmund S., fight with Foote, 15, 16; defends martial law, 143

Davidson, Allen T., 199, 239; congressional candidate, 52; criticizes conscription, 82

Davis, George, 239; Confederate senator, 47, 54; appointed Attorney General, 54

Davis, Jefferson, President, 18-20, 74, 87, 98, 100, 103, 117, 122, 125, 128, 140, 141, 144, 154, 169, 174, 225, 228; opposition to, 9, 97, 172, 173; elected President, 31, 32, 223; requests Supreme Court, 37; favors autonomous Trans-Mississippi Department, 39; as a factor in elections, 46-48, 52, 54-59; attitude toward peace negotiations, 50, 175, 177-83; seeks control of state militia, 60-62, 91, 92; and officer appointments and promotions, 60-63, 104, 105; conscription proposals, 64, 65, 68, 77, 78, 86, 90, 99; exemption proposals, 71, 77-81, 85, 86, 89, 90, 94; habeas corpus policies of, 83, 150-52, 155-59; and Negro conscription, 95, 96, 111, 112; suggestions of army organization, 106-109, 126; opposes permanent navy, 101; and Medical Department problems, 110, 111; reports on prisoners of war, 114; impressment proposals of, 118, 124; asks appropriation for railroad construction, 129; requests crop limitation, 131; refuses to aid border states, 142, 143; controversy with Beauregard, 147; calls special session, 161; commercial ideas of, 162, 163, 186; ideas on retaliation, 163, 164; role in foreign affairs, 165-68; patronage policies of, 219; controversy over general officers, 147-49; attributes Produce Loan ideas to Congress, 189; sequestration policies of, 196; requests taxes, 198, 215; *see also* Administration opposition *and* Cabinet

Davis, Reuben, 79, 239; urges secession, 3; urges offensive war, 140; opposes habeas corpus suspension, 152

Debates of Congress, reporting and printing of, 33, 34; secrecy in, 35, 36

De Bow, James D. B., Chief Commissioner of the Produce Loans, 189, 193

Declaration of Paris, 100, 167

Democratic party, 1, 2, 31, 177; in election of 1864, 173

Democrats, 4; in elections, 4, 44-49, 52, 54-58; strength at Montgomery convention, 19, 218, 219

Deserters, apprehension of, 86; punishment of, 114, 115; influenced by peace agitation, 175

Destruction of property, 131, 132, 134, 135; tax exemption of such property, 201

Details from the army, 80, 111, 127; used for recruiting, 63; favored by Davis, 79, 81, 85, 86, 89, 90; debated, 86-88, 90, 91, 93, 94

Digest of laws, 32, 33

Dodd, William E., quoted, 8

Donations to the Treasury, 211, 212

Dortch, William T., 239; in elections, 48, 54; proposes to exempt justices of the peace, 72; desires peace negotiations, 175

Douglas, Stephen A., 31; presidential candidate, 2, 3

Dred Scott decision, 1, 2

Dupré, Lucien J., 239; opposes conscription, 69

Early, Jubal A., 149

Echols, Joseph H., 239; favors sale of government cotton, 211

Economic control and organization, of telegraphic facilities 129; of railroads, 129-31; of agriculture, 131; destruction of property, 131, 132; of speculation, 72, 132, 133; of claims against the government, 133-35; *see also* Foreign trade

Election of officers, 61, 63, 65

Elections, to the secession conventions, 4, 5; of 1860, 2, 3, 47; to Montgomery convention, 6, 7, 40; of the chief executives, 30-32; for the First Congress, 43-49, 223; for the Second Congress, 49-59, 174, 175, 225; the soldier vote in, 48, 53, 57, 58

Emancipation Proclamation, 164

Embargo, on cotton, 165, 166, 168

England, 47, 131, 153, 186, 188; proposal of commercial treaty with, 165, 166, 168; commissioners to, 167

Erlanger Loan, 18, 196

Europe, 128, 131, 169, 182, 196

Everett, Edward, 3

Exchequer notes, proposed, 207

Executive departments, established, 36, 37

Exemptions from the army, 127, 133, 159, 234; of railroad employees, 36, 37; in elections, 50; of overseers, 50, 71, 72, 79-81, 87, 88, 93, 94; of militia, 65, 89; of state officers, 67, 71, 72, 81, 85, 87, 89, 91; debates upon, 71, 72, 76-81, 86-88, 90-94; requests for, 71, 84, 89; of postal employees, 81; abuses of, 81, 82, 89, 94, 95; of editors, 90

Fearn, Thomas, 9, 10, 239

First Manassas, Battle of, 17, 61, 140, 147, 171, 219, 223

Florida, 144, 171, 185, 227; elections in, 7, 42, 45, 55; opposes Montgomery convention becoming a congress, 23; influences on Confederate constitutions, 26-28; supports Davis for president, 31; complains of neglect, 143, 219; dislikes Mallory, 219

Florida Sentinel, criticizes enforcement of conscription, 82

Floyd, John B., congressional candidate, 54

Foote, Henry S., 58, 142, 163, 239; his fisticuffs, 15, 16; opposes habeas corpus suspension, 52, 159; criticizes conscription, 68, 70; proposes to draft foreigners, 76; opposes executive details, 80; favors destruction of property, 132; urges curbs on speculation, 133; favors aggressive war, 140, 141; criticizes the administration, 144, 146, 220, 222, 226, 227, 229, 230; condemns martial law, 153, 154; peace efforts of, 171, 172, 176, 182; proposes government purchase of cotton crop, 194

Foreign affairs, commissioners to Europe, 165, 167, 168; recall of Confederate ministers, 168; *see also* Cotton, Consuls, Peace negotiations, United States

Foreign trade, regulation of, 136-39; *see also* Cotton

Fort Donelson, 142

Fort Henry, 142

Fort Sumter, 23, 61, 161

Fortress Monroe, 142

Foster, Thomas J., 239; advocates conscription, 69

France, 18, 180, 186, 188; commercial treaty with proposed, 165, 166, 168; commissioners to, 167

Franking of newspapers, 234

Free trade, 51, 167, 168, 186-88

Fugitive slaves, in the Provisional Constitution, 25

Funding, forced, 229; debated, 192, 201, 202, 205-207, 210; proposed, 197, 198, 203; provisions for, 197, 202, 207, 208, 210, 211; reaction to, 208, 209; *see also* Bonds *and* Treasury notes

Funding, voluntary, 158, 193, 195; provisions for, 194; failure of, 197, 198, 202; *see also* Bonds *and* Treasury notes

Furloughs, 63, 109-11, 126

Gaither, Burgess S., 239; opposes extending conscription, 68, 70, 158; opinion of Davis, 221

Garland, Augustus H., 19, 239; congressional candidate, 45, 57; condemns martial law, 155; opinion on habeas corpus suspension, 157, 158

Garland, Rufus K., 239; congressional candidate, 57

Garnett, Muscoe R. H., proposes investigation of martial law, 153

Gartrell, Lucius J., 239; urges price ceiling, 133; proposes to suspend habeas corpus, 155, 156

General-in-chief, authorized, 108, 227; Lee as, 227, 228

Georgia, 90, 122, 131, 148, 159, 178, 187, 193, 203, 227; elections in, 9, 32, 42-44, 48, 50, 52, 55; influences on Confederate constitutions, 22, 26, 27; exemption practices in, 85, 89; opposes conscription, 89, 92; protests illegal impressment, 121; requests Johnston's removal, 148; requests end of habeas corpus suspension, 157; peace sentiment in, 174, 176, 180; tariff policy of, 188; Produce Loan in, 193; opposes tax-in-kind, 212; administration opposition in, 224

"Georgia Project," 23

Georgia State Railroad, 45

Gettysburg, 174

Gilmer, John A., 239; protests impressment practices, 121; introduces tax bill, 216

Gist, Christopher, 5

Goode, John, 240; congressional candidate, 44; protests impressment practices, 121

Gorgas, Josiah, 126

Graham, Malcolm D., 106, 239; criticizes conscription practices, 82

Graham, William A., 239; congressional candidate, 54; fears executive despotism, 92, 220; works for peace, 176, 178, 180, 182

Grant, Ulysses S., 158, 178

Greeley, Horace, 1

Guaranteeing bonds by the states, 197, 198, 202, 203

Habeas corpus suspension, 149, 223, 234; an election issue, 51; and conscription, 83; occasions for, 150, 154-57; dislike of, 151, 152, 155; debated, 152-60

Hampton Roads Conference, 181, 182

Hanly, Thomas B., 239; congressional candidate, 57; fight with Foote, 16

Hardee, William J., proposes levy en masse, 86

Harpers Ferry, Va., 1

Harris, Isham, Governor of Tennessee, 58

Harris, Thomas A., 240

Harris, Wiley P., favors offensive war, 140

Harrison, James T., 8, 16, 240

Hartridge, Julian, 240; proposes to amend impressment laws, 122; opposes Confederate control of shipping, 138

Haynes, Landon C., 240; criticizes Davis, 97; condemns martial law, 153
Heath, Henry, 149
Heiskell, Joseph B., 240; votes to override veto, 108; impressment scheme, 123
Henry, Gustavus A., 240; proposes Confederate control of militia, 92; proposes sequestration bill, 196; attempts to instruct the President, 227
Herbert, Caleb C., 240; opposes conscription, 69; investigates Castle Thunder, 114
Herbert, Peter O., 151
Hexall, Crenshaw & Co., 146
Hill, Benjamin H., 240; fight with Yancey, 16; proposes Supreme Court bill, 37; congressional candidate, 48; favors overseer exemption, 79; protests illegal impressment, 121; criticizes railroad management, 130; proposes court of claims, 134; proposes to investigate Quartermaster and Commissary Departments, 146; expresses confidence in cotton diplomacy, 166; peace sentiments of, 174, 181
Hilton, Robert B., 240; opinion on overseer exemption, 79; proposes resolution thanking Lee, 141
Hindman, Thomas C., 149, 151
Hodge, Benjamin L., 240; congressional candidate, 56
Holcombe, James B., proposes to regulate impressments, 118
Holden, William W., favors peace negotiations, 50, 54, 174, 175
Holmes, Theophilus, 149
Holt, Hines, 240; proposes peace commission, 171, 172; proposes government purchase of cotton crop, 194
Hood, John B., 148
Houston Tri-Weekly Telegraph, opposes impressment, 120
Huger, Benjamin, 141
Hunter, Robert M. T., 12, 18, 47, 119, 218, 225, 228, 240; proposes bill to regulate impressment, 118; Hampton Roads commissioner, 181; proposes reconstruction, 182; advocates tax-in-kind, 199; advocates forced funding, 201; leaves Cabinet, 219

Illinois, 163
Impressment, 28, 88, 133, 144, 146, 209, 215, 223; in elections, 5, 52, 55; need for, 116; abuses in practice of, 116, 117, 121-25; ascertaining prices for impressed goods, 117-20, 122-25; demands for regulation of, 117, 118; difficulties of regulating, 120, 122, 124, 125; claims for illegal seizures, 134, 135; of cotton, 136, 216
Indiana, 163
Indians, treaties with, 33, 41, 142; admitted into Confederacy, 40, 41; elections by, 43, 45, 51; trouble with, 142, 151
Inflation, 113, 116, 120, 121, 126, 133, 191-94, 202, 205, 206, 209, 210, 212, 223, 228; in elections, 50, 51; debated, 186
Investigations by Congress, of Castle Thunder, 114; of the Texas Cotton Bureau, 137; of military defeats, 141, 142; of executive departments, 144-47

Jackson, Andrew, 153
Jackson, Claibourne, 39
Jackson, Thomas J., 18, 223; favors conscription, 64; urges laws against deserters, 114
Jemison, Robert, 12, 56, 240
Johnson, Herschel V., 240; vice-presidential candidate, 2; congressional candidate, 48; opposes drafting principals, 78; works for peace, 176-78; cooperates with the administration, 225, 226
Johnson, Robert W., 199, 240; congressional candidate, 47, 57
Johnson, Waldo P., 241; congressional candidate, 50, 57; comments on fiscal matters, 208; proposes funding bill, 210; proposes Cabinet reform, 232
Johnston, Albert Sidney, 148, 149
Johnston, Joseph E., 95, 114; urges impressment of Negroes, 111; requests thanks for his army, 141; commander of Army of Tennessee, 148, 227, 228
Jones, David R., 149
Jones, John B., observations and comments of, 78, 82, 151, 219, 222, 224, 232, 234
Jones, Thomas M., 241; condemns martial law, 153

Kansas, 1, 142
Keitt, Lawrence M., 9, 241; urges secession, 3; denounces Davis, 219
Kenan, Augustus H., 15, 241

Kentucky, 109, 148, 163, 225; secedes, 39; elections in, 47, 48, 58; admiration for Breckinridge, 149; favors peace negotiations, 180
Know-Nothing party, 2-3

Lake, W. A., congressional candidate, 44
Lamar, Lucius Q. C., 168
Lander, William, 241; congressional candidate, 46
Lane, Joseph, vice-presidential candidate in 1860, 2
Lawton, Alexander R., Quartermaster General, 233, 234
Leach, James T., 241; hostility to reporters, 20; denies right of secession, 52; defends state exemption laws, 91; advocates peace, 176, 182
Lee, Fitzhugh, 149
Lee, Robert E., 18, 20, 66, 88, 141, 176, 181; advocates conscription, 64, 65; dislikes partisan rangers, 75; proposes army reform, 86; asks tighter manpower control, 90; proposes Negro conscription, 96-98; dislikes officer elections, 104; requests permanent court martial system, 105; as general-in-chief, 108, 227, 228; urges laws against deserters, 114; urges habeas corpus suspension, 159; reassigns Johnston, 227
Letcher, John, 14
Lewis, David W., 241
Lewis, John W., 241; congressional candidate, 45; appointed senator, 48
Lewis, L. M., congressional candidate, 57, 58
Lincoln, Abraham, 22, 140, 142, 151, 152, 164, 180, 182, 184, 234; elected president, 2, 3, 173, 176, 178; effect of election on South, 3, 4; calls for volunteers, 39; refuses to recognize Confederacy, 161; threatens to outlaw privateers, 163; and peace negotiations, 177, 179-82; orders non-arrest of Hunter, 225
Loans, from Alabama, 184; provisions for, 185, 186, 189, 190, 194-97, 202, 203, 208; administration of loans, 185, 186; debated, 186, 188, 189, 192, 196, 203, 206; foreign, 211; specie, 212; see also Erlanger Loan and Funding
Local defense, in elections, 50; and the militia, 61, 91; special service for, 62

74, 75; endangered by conscription, 83, 84; reserve corps for, 87, 88, 92, 94; problems of, 142-44
Louisiana, 28, 131, 153, 186, 225; secession of, 9; interest in soldier relief, 17; influences on the Confederate constitutions, 26, 27; elections in, 31, 43, 56; opposes overseer exemption, 79
Lowell, Mansfield, 142
Lyon, Francis S., 241; proposes martial law bill, 151
Lyons, James, 14, 20, 241; congressional candidate, 46, 50; favors extending tax-in-kind, 211

McClellan, George B., 176
McDowell, Thomas David Smith, 241
McFarland, William H., 241; congressional candidate, 44
Machen, Willis B., 241; proposal of transfer of army units, 109
McMullen, Fayette, 241; urges curbs on speculation, 133; opposes tax-in-kind, 211
McRae, Colin J., 9, 241; proposes volunteer navy, 101
McRae, John J., 241; congressional candidate, 44
Magrath, Andrew G., urges stricter detail practices, 9
Mallory, Stephen R., desires permanent navy, 99, 100; approves volunteer navy, 100, 101; proposes iron-clads, 128; investigated, 144, 145; opinion on Hampton Roads Conference, 181, 182; opposition to, 219, 229, 230; reports administration opposition, 219-21
Mann, A. Dudley, commissioner to Europe, 165, 167
Marshall, Charles, writes conscription bill, 65
Marshall, Henry, 241; congressional candidate, 56
Marshall, Humphrey, 241; congressional candidate, 58
Marshall, John, 38
Martial law, 150, 151, 155; debated, 152-55
Mason, James M., commissioner to Europe, 167
Maryland, and Confederate conscription laws, 76, 163; efforts to secure secession of, 163; proposed conscription of citizens of, 163

Maximilian of Mexico, 180
Maxwell, Augustus E., 242; urges curb on speculation, 133; advocates peace, 178
Medical Department, 110, 111
Memminger, Christopher G., 9, 137, 161, 185, 189, 191, 214, 242; chairman of the Committee on the Constitution, 24; impressment scheme of, 123, 124; financial ideas of, 166, 192, 193, 202, 208, 212; requests economy in government, 184; avoids heavy taxation, 185, 192; financial proposals of, 186, 188, 190, 192-99, 203, 204, 209, 213; urges more export taxes, 188; accusation against Governor Brown, 203; controversies with Congress, 208, 210, 212, 229, 230
Mercier, Robert, encourages cotton diplomacy, 167
Mexican War, 31, 102
Mexico, and the Monroe Doctrine, 180, 181; trade with, 135, 136, 167
Miles, William P., 9, 141, 242; proposes Supreme Court bill, 37; advocates conscription, 69, 87; proposes to end class exemptions, 80; favors army reorganization, 105, 107; concerned for Charleston's defenses, 143
Military strategy, congressmen's concern with, 140, 141, 144
Militia, in the Confederate army, 60, 61, 63, 64, 70, 103; proposed exemption of, 65; conscription of, 83, 84, 87-89, 91, 92; further control of, sought, 90-92, 103; guns of, 125, 126; see also Volunteers and Army organization
Milton, John, appoints delegates to Montgomery convention, 7; urges curbs on speculation, 133
Mississippi, 187, 225; constitutional ideas in, 22, 23, 26; supports Davis for president, 31; elections in, 43-45, 49, 56; proposes to draft substitutes, 78; enforcement of conscription in, 82; seeks aid for Vicksburg, 143; urges repeal of habeas corpus suspension, 157; Produce Loan in, 193
Mississippi River, 82, 143, 186, 210; diplomacy relating to, 162, 163
Missouri, 109, 142, 149, 225; secedes, 39; elections in, 43, 48, 57, 58; opposes Negro conscription; dislikes Henry Heath, 149

Mitchel, Charles B., 242; congressional candidate, 47; died, 57
Monroe Doctrine, 180, 181
Montgomery, Ala., 162, 218, 221; site of Southern convention, 6, 7; description of, 11; life of congressmen in, 12; removal of capital from, 13, 46
Montgomery Advertiser, 55; opposes peace convention, 177
Montgomery convention, impetus to, 5, 6; personnel of, 7-10; political sentiments in, 8, 9; becomes the Provisional Congress, 22-24
Montgomery Mail, regrets party feelings, 52; supports class exemptions, 92; favors Negro conscription, 95; favors peace convention, 177
Moore, Andrew B., 12
Moore, James W., 242; urges price limits, 133
Moore, Thomas O., disobeys impressment laws, 121, 122
Morrill Tariff, 187
Morton, Jackson, 9, 242
Mosby's Rangers, 75
Murrah, Pendleton, 136
Myers, Abraham C., opposes clothing commutation, 113; opposes government ownership of railroads, 130; controversy over appointment of, 233, 234

Napoleon III, 167, 168, 180
Naturalization and citizenship, 162
Navy, vessels for, 128; see also Privateering
Navy Department, 100, 128, 141, 144; seeks war materiel, 125, 128; investigated by Congress, 144, 230
Negro labor, 111, 112
Negro soldiers, considered outside Congress, 95, 96; rewarded by freedom, 95, 96, 98; debated, 96-99; United States use of, 164
New Orleans, 69, 142, 144
Norfolk, Va., 150
North Carolina, 141, 158, 159, 187, 224; secedes, 39; elections in, 42, 44-47, 50, 52-54; opposes overseer exemption, 79; opposes conscription, 89; criticizes exemption laws, 89; abuses exemption privileges, 89, 92; opposes Negro conscription, 97; opposes impressment laws, 120, 121, 124; opposes habeas

corpus suspension, 157; feels abused by central government, 173; peace sentiments in, 174-76, 178, 180, 182; opposes high taxes, 190, 200, 212; administration opposition in, 226

Northrop, Lucius B., defends impressment, 121; disliked by Congress, 122, 233

Oldham, Williamson S., 124, 242; proposes Negro conscription, 97; opposes impressment of cotton, 136; complains of West's defenses, 142, 143; opposes habeas corpus suspension, 156; proposes tax bill, 216; criticizes Congress, 234, 235

Ordnance Bureau, 126

Orr, James L., 167, 242; opposes conscription, 65; opposes drafting principals, 77, 78; favors overseer exemption, 79; opposes executive details, 91; favors more class exemptions, 93; attacks Bragg, 104; opposes state control of railroads, 130; works for peace, 176, 182

Orr, Jehu Amaziah, 242

Oury, Granville H., elected congressman, 40

Overseers, see Exemption

Owen, James B., 9, 242

Partisan rangers, 75

Patronage, 16, 17; in Congress, 218, 219, 221

Peace negotiations, 163; in elections, 50, 52, 54-56; causes of, 171-73; demands for, 171, 174, 175, 177; debated, 171, 172, 176, 178-80; by separate state action, 174, 175; discussed at Hampton Roads Conference, 180-82; for reconstruction, 182, 183

Pearson, Richmond M., grants writs of habeas corpus, 51, 83, 157

Pemberton, John C., 149

Pennsylvania, invasion of, 141, 173

Perkins, John, 34, 242; congressional candidate, 56; works for soldier relief, 17; proposes free trade, 188; favors extending taxation in kind, 211

Permanent government, proposed by South Carolina, 6; judiciary of, relies on state courts, 38, 39

Peyton, Robert L. Y., 242; death of, 57

Phelan, James, 106, 242; lectures Lee, 20; congressional candidate, 56; favors conscription, 70; opinion on exemption, 72; criticizes enforcement of conscription, 82; opposes destruction of property, 132; defends martial law, 153; proposes habeas corpus suspension, 156; proposes government purchase of the cotton crop, 194; advocates forced funding, 201

Philadelphia constitutional convention, 24

Pierce, Franklin, 31

Pike, Albert, 20; Commissioner of Indian Affairs, 40, 41

Pillow, Gideon J., 82

Pollard, Edward S., 16; attributes Produce Loan idea to Davis, 188, 189; criticizes Davis, 221, 222

Ports of entry, designated, 184

Portsmouth, Va., 150

Post Office Department, requirement of self-sufficiency of, 27, 36, 115; difficulties of, 36, 37; opposes franking of mail, 37, 115; mail service of, 38, 81; rates of, 129

Postmaster General, 17, 129

Preston, John S., reports on state exemption practices, 89, 92; opposes class exemptions, 90, 92

Preston, Walter, 242

Preston, William B., 242; death of, 53, 54

Price, Sterling, 149

Principles of substitutes, exemption of, 76-79; obtain writs of habeas corpus, 157

Printing and publication, 33, 34

Prisoners of war, 114; see Retaliation

Privateering, provisions for, 100, 101

Produce Loans, 192; origin of ideas, 188, 189; laws authorizing, 189, 194, 195, 203; administration of, 189, 190, 203; proceeds from, 193, 195; criticized by planters, 193

Provisional Government, proposed by South Carolina, 6; why used, 22

Provost guards, 88, 151

Prussian General Staff, 108

Pryor, Roger A., favors destruction of property, 132

Pugh, James L., 242-43

Quartermaster Department, 16, 88, 91, 114; investigated by Congress, 146, 147; criticized by Beauregard, 147; collection of tax-in-kind by, 212

Railroads, 63, 110, 188; mail contracts for, 36, 37; Confederate control of, 129-31; appropriations for construction of, 129
Raleigh Standard, advocates peace negotiations, 50, 174, 177; opposes conscription, 67; opposes substitution, 76, 77; opposes high taxes, 201; financial ideas of, 203
Ralls, John P., 243; congressional candidate, 45, 55
Randolph, George W., 20, 230; requests law enrolling refugees, 74; dislikes promotion by seniority, 104; opposes skeleton regiments, 106; appointed Secretary of War, 145
Reade, Edwin G., appointed senator, 54; administration foe, 54, 222; defends North Carolina's loyalty, 173, 224
Reagan, John H., 9, 10, 228, 243; problems of, as Postmaster General, 36, 37; requests exemption of postal employees, 81
Recognition, foreign, 165-69
Reconstruction, feared by Montgomery convention, 8, 9, 165; in elections, 53-56, 174; as a means of peace, 175, 176, 178-82
Rector, Henry, 57
Reid and Shorter, printers for Congress, 33
Republican Party, 1-3, 175
Retaliation, to enemy outrages, 163, 164
Revenue bills, proposed issue of, 216
Reynolds, Thomas C., 20, 53; claims West's defenses ignored, 39; in elections, 57, 58; complains of currency repudiation, 209; fears counterrevolution, 209
Rhett, Robert Barnwell, 8, 243; fears reconstruction, 8, 9; wants to expel non-slaveholding states, 29; political ambitions of, 30-32, 55, 161, 220; foreign policies of, 165, 166
Richmond, Va., 40, 129, 150, 151, 156-58, 167, 178, 182, 188, 224, 231; as Confederate capital, 13, 14; conditions in, 17-20; defense of, emphasized, 144; suspension of the habeas corpus in, 150, 154, 155
Richmond Enquirer, reports inflation, 19; barred from sessions of Congress, 21; supports James Lyons' candidacy, 46; opinion on peace negotiations, 50, 177; approves conscription, 66; favors Negro conscription, 95; approves of impressments, 120; comments on destruction of property, 132; demands Roanoke Island investigation, 141; approves of habeas corpus suspension, 155, 157; criticizes tax program, 200; opposes more Treasury notes, 203; reports opposition to Davis, 224
Rives, William C., 218, 243; advocates peace, 178; offers Lee dictatorship, 227
Roanoke Island, 141, 142, 145
Rost, Pierre A., commissioner to Europe, 165, 167
Royston, Grandison, 243; congressional candidate, 57
Ruffin, Frank, 146
Rules of order, 34-36
Russell, Charles B., congressional candidate, 54
Russell, Charles W., 243; proposes exemption bill, 93; seeks to regain West Virginia, 144; proposes a congressman for Maryland, 163
Russia, 168

Sage, B. J., proposes volunteer navy, 100, 101
Savannah, Ga., 179
Savannah, 163
Savannah Republican, opposes habeas corpus suspension, 157
Scott, Winfield, 13
Secession, 17, 175, 184, 218, 219; of the states, 1-7, 39-41; debated in constitutional convention, 29; of part of the United States, 162, 163
Secessionists, begin agitation, 3; in convention elections, 4; cooperate with conservatives, 7, 8; fear reconstruction, 8; strength of, at Montgomery, 9, 218, 219; in executive elections, 31, 32, 219, 220; in congressional elections, 43-49, 52-56, 58
Seddon, James A., 143, 149, 243; favors autonomous Trans-Mississippi Department, 39; opposes partisan rangers, 75; opposes substitution, 78; opposes class exemptions, 79; attempts to control militia, 84; requests wider conscription, 86; opinion of Negro soldiers, 96; opposes promotion by seniority, 105; compliments court martial

Index 291

system, 106; proposes army reorganization, 106, 107; desires Negro laborers, 111; requests impressment regulation, 118, 123; appointed Secretary of War, 145; in congressional politics, 230-32
Selective Draft Law Cases, 66
Semmes, Thomas J., 18, 19, 243; proposes Supreme Court, 37; opinion on overseer exemption, 72; requests Beauregard's transfer, 147; proposes to investigate habeas corpus suspension, 153; proposes to prohibit material law, 154; opposes peace convention, 177
Semmes, Mrs. Thomas J., 20
Sequestration and confiscation, 132, 135; laws upon, 191; administration of, 196; proposal of, 196
Seven Days' Battles, 66
Seward, William H., 181
Sexton, Francis B., 15, 16, 18, 19, 243; fears inflation, 205
Shenandoah Valley, 142, 149, 223
Sherman, William T., 148, 158, 178
Shiloh, battle of, 147
Simms, William E., 17, 243; opposes state impressment commissioners, 119
Simpson, William D., 114, 243
Singleton, Otho R., 68
Skeleton regiments, 62, 69, 70, 106; accepted by War Department, 103
Slavery, 177, 180, 182; as a secession issue, 1, 2; in the Confederate constitutions, 25, 28
Slaves, arming of, 95-99, 234; impressment of, 97, 118, 119, 122; as army laborers, 111, 112; emancipation of, 180; taxation of, 198, 199
Slave trade, constitutional provisions of, 25, 28, 30
Slidell, John, commissioner to Europe, 167; negotiates Erlanger Loan, 196
Smith, Charles H., 35, 36
Smith, E. Kirby, 149; impresses cotton, 136
Smith, Richard M., 33
Smith, William, 243; proposes partisan rangers, 75
Smith, William N. H., 222, 243; proposes reserve state armies, 69; favors more exemptions, 90, 91
Smith, William R., 7, 12, 243-44; wants Constitution ratified by people, 29

Snead, Thomas L., 96, 149, 244
South Carolina, 90, 148, 159, 161, 187, 227; secession convention of, 4-7; proposes Southern Confederacy, 6; constitutional ideas of, 22, 26, 28-30; in presidential election, 31, 32; congressional elections in, 42, 43, 49, 54, 55; criticizes John C. Pemberton, 149; promises to support Produce Loans, 189
Southern Address, 3, 5, 6
Spain, 168
Sparrow, Edward, 19, 146, 244; urges emergency reserve crops, 87, 88; impressment scheme of, 124; urges curbs on speculation, 133; requests Bragg's transfer, 147; requests habeas corpus suspension, 158; opposes tax law, 214; proposes general-in-chief, 227
Specie, 184, 188; payment of interest in, 185; tax-in-kind on, 204, 205; value of compared with Treasury notes, 210; donations of, 211, 212; loans of, 212
Speculation, 18, 130, 151, 208, 213; practice of, 116, 117, 123, 132, 133; curbs on, 72, 133, 200; in cotton, 136
Spotsylvania, 176
Stanard, Mrs. Robert G., 20
Stanton, Edwin G., 182
Staples, Waller R., 244; proposes to investigate state exemption laws, 91
State, Department of, 145, 161, 169
Stephens, Alexander H., 19, 108, 157, 180, 227, 244; opposes secession, 4; compliments personnel of Montgomery convention, 7; approves of the Provisional Constitution, 24; constitutional ideas of, 25, 26; desires presidency, 30; nominates Toombs for president, 32; elected vice-president, 32, 223; writes rules of order, 34; promises Virginia a Cabinet post, 39; opposes martial law, 153; opposes habeas corpus suspension, 155; advocates peace, 177, 181; favors government purchase of cotton, 193
Stephens, Linton, 26
Stuart, Alexander H. H., congressional candidate, 52
Stuart, J. E. B., dislikes partisan rangers, 75
"Submissionists," 5
Substitutes, 133; authorized, 66; conscription of, 76-79

Supreme Court, Confederate, provisions for, 25, 27, 37; controversy over establishment of, 37, 38
Supreme Court, United States, 1, 38
Swan, William G., 97, 244; fight with Foote, 16; congressional candidate, 45; opposes Negro conscription, 96

Tariff, export, constitutional provision for, 25, 27; on cotton, 185, 186, 188; debated, 185, 188
Tariff, import, constitutional provisions for, 25, 27, 30; provisions of, 127, 130, 184-87; exemptions of certain Northern states from, 162, 163, 187; protection, 165, 186, 187; debated, 186, 187; exemptions from, 187, 188
Tariff of 1857, 187
Tattnall, Josiah, 142
Taxation, 144, 203, 223, 229; in elections, 51; early dislike of, 185, 187; administration of, 185, 190-92, 201; debated, 186, 190, 192, 198-201, 204, 205, 210, 211, 213-17; provisions for, 190, 200, 205, 212, 214, 215, 217; exemptions from, 190, 200, 205, 210, 214; proposals of, 186, 197, 198, 204, 210, 211; census obstacles to, 198, 199; opinion on, 200, 201, 204, 212, 213
Tax-in-kind, 123; in elections, 51; debated, 199, 200, 204, 205, 210, 211, 213-16; provisions for, 200, 201, 205, 213-15; opinion on, 200, 201, 212, 213; collection of, 201, 212, 214, 215; on specie, 204, 205, 212
Telegraph operations, 129
Tennessee, 158, 181, 187, 225; secedes, 39; elections in, 40, 42, 43, 45, 47, 58; defense of, 144; requests Bragg's removal, 148; criticizes Albert S. Johnston, 148, 149; favors peace negotiations, 180, 182; has interview with Davis, 222
Texas, 28, 131; elections in, 43-45, 47, 49, 56; opposes overseer exemption, 79; criticizes conscription, 84; opposes Negro conscription, 97; opposes impressment of cotton, 136; local defense problems of, 142; favors free trade, 188
Texas State Gazette, opposes habeas corpus suspension, 152
Tobacco, state limitations on, 13; prevention of seizure of by enemy, 132; as a basis for credit, 216

Toombs, Robert, 9, 17, 25, 39, 161, 228, 244; presidential candidate, 30-32; declines senatorship, 48; favors high tariff, 165; reports harmony at Montgomery, 218
Trading with the enemy, 132; attempts to prevent, 135, 136, 166, 167; permitted, 136, 137
Trans-Mississippi Department, 19, 148, 185; becomes autonomous, 39; power of commanding general in, 39; cotton trade in, 136; defense of, 142, 143; dissatisfaction with Bragg in, 147; peace sentiment in, 174
Treasury Department, 136, 190, 230, 234; as auditor of claims, 134; establishment of, 184, 185; issues cotton certificates, 195
Treasury notes, debated, 186, 201-203, 205-207, 210, 211; issues of, 186, 189, 193-95, 202, 207, 208; redundancy of, 192-95, 197, 198, 202-203, 205-207, 209-12; interest rate of, 194, 195; funding of, 193-95, 197, 198, 202, 203, 205-11; repudiation of, 198, 203-209, 211; *see also* Funding *and* Taxation
Treaties, with Indians, 33, 41, 142; offered to the Northwest United States, 162, 163; offered to European countries, 165-68
Tredegar iron works, 125
Trenholm, George A., appointed Secretary of the Treasury, 210; financial proposals of, 210, 211, 214; relations with Congress, 230
Turner, Josiah, 244; congressional candidate, 44, 45; criticizes Davis, 97; opposes Negro conscription, 97; works for peace, 180; opposes tax-in-kind, 211; quoted, 225
Tyler, John, 10, 39, 244; congressional candidate, 44

Unionists, 172; in secession movement, 3-5; strength at Montgomery convention, 8, 9; in elections, 45, 46, 52, 54-57; hurt by conscription, 66; share in patronage, 219
United States, 22, 27, 28, 32, 35, 40, 48, 67, 75, 76, 83, 102, 105, 107, 128, 134, 135, 140, 156, 166-68, 171, 175, 178, 188, 218, 234; publishes *Journal of the Confederate Congress*, 34; postal service of, 36; Judiciary Act of 1789 of, 38; electoral practices of, 42, 47;

prepares for war, 61; recognition from, sought, 161; naturalization laws of, 162; enforces blockade, 167; *see also* Trading with the enemy *and* Peace negotiations

Vance, Zebulon B., 54; desires peace negotiations, 64; opposes habeas corpus suspension, 83, 155, 157; opposes separate state action on peace, 175
Van Dorn, Earl, 15
Vest, George G., 15, 244; congressional candidate, 58; proposes to draft United States citizens, 76
Vicksburg, Miss., 143, 149
Virginia, 108, 158, 159, 186, 187, 225; fears radicalism, 31; secedes, 39; elections in, 42, 43, 45, 47, 52, 54; requests suspension of exemption, 89; instructs her senators, 98, 118, 119; opposes impressment of Negroes, 112; demands impressment regulations, 117, 118; criticizes impressment system, 120, 121, 124; pledges support to war effort, 181; opposes high taxes, 190, 200, 204; requests Cabinet reform, 231, 232
Virginia, 128, 142
Volunteers, from border states, 62; permitted under conscription laws, 65, 66; preferred to conscription, 67-70; equipment of, 125; *see also* Militia, Army organization, Furloughs, Bounties

Walker, Leroy Pope, relations with Congress, 145, 230
Walker, Richard W., 145, 244; congressional candidate, 56
War Department, 18, 75, 76, 83, 97, 102, 106, 109, 141, 142-44, 148, 149, 201, 219, 228; and state militia, 62, 84, 91, 103; exemption policies of, 71, 77, 81; enrolling practices of, 85; opposes Negro conscription, 95; labor problems of, 111; seeks war materiel, 125-29; trades with United States, 135, 136; abolishes Cotton Bureau, 136; investigated, 145-47; uses martial law, 154
War materiel, 125-29
War Tax Bureau, 191

Washington, D. C., 40, 147, 169, 171, 176, 180
Watson, John W. C., 244; congressional candidate, 56; works for peace, 176
Watts, Thomas H., 75, 76
West Point, 141, 220
West Virginia, 144
Whig party, 1, 2, 9
Whigs, 172; in elections, 45-47, 49, 52, 54-58; strength at Montgomery convention, 218, 219; share in patronage, 219
Whitner, John C., 34
Wigfall, Louis T., 18, 19, 39, 56, 141, 144, 145, 163, 167, 244; congressional candidate, 47; proposes conscription bills, 65, 86; argues for conscription, 70; exemption ideas of, 72; impressment ideas of, 118; criticizes railroad management, 130; urges offensive war, 140; criticizes Bragg, 148; advocates habeas corpus suspension, 150, 158; advocates tax-in-kind, 200; administration opposition of, 220, 221, 230, 231; bill to allow Cabinet members on floor of Congress, 228
Wilderness, Battle of, 176
Wilmington Journal, 112; favors secessionist candidates, 46; approves conscription, 67
Winder, John H., provost marshal of Richmond, 150
Wise, Henry A., 141, 142
Withers, Thomas J., 19, 32, 244; enmity with Davis, 220
Wright, Augustus R., 244; favors large army, 61

Yancey, William L., 8, 15, 17, 244; fight with Hill, 16; desires presidency, 30, 31; opposes Supreme Court bill, 38; congressional candidate, 47; death of, 56; proposes exemption law, 67; opposes extending conscription, 70; favors overseer exemption, 79; defends promotion by seniority, 104; proposes apportionment of general officers, 108; commissioner to Europe, 165, 167; opposition to Davis, 221, 226
Yancey platform, 2
Yorkville Enquirer, opposes conscription, 67